The *Teacher's* *Book* of *Lists*

Second Edition

Sheila Madsen
Bette Gould

Illustrated by Kimble Mead

GoodYearBooks

An Imprint of ScottForesman

A Division of HarperCollinsPublishers

GoodYearBooks

are available for most basic curriculum subjects plus many enrichment areas. For more GoodYearBooks, contact your local bookseller or educational dealer. For a complete catalog with information about other GoodYearBooks, please write:

GoodYearBooks
ScottForesman
1900 East Lake Avenue
Glenview, IL 60025

Cover Illustration by Slug Signorino.
Cover design by Christine Ronan.
Text design by Monotype Composition Corporation.
Illustrations on p. 208–211 by Rebecca Hershey.

ISBN 0-673-36074-1

5 6 7 8 9 – ER – 01 00 99 98 97

Table of Contents

Introduction

Reassuring things, lists. They affirm that the buzzing, blooming confusion of the universe can be reduced to a tidy vertical column. But wait, there's a better way to do this: Herewith the Top Four Reasons Why People Love Lists:

1. Lists are fun.
2. Lists are quick.
3. Lists help us remember things.
4. Lists give us something to argue about.

Lists have been around forever.

Richard Stengel, "Best of the '90s," *Time*, Dec. 31, 1990, p. 40.

This brief quote neatly sums up our sentiments and echoes the thoughts that originally led us to writing *The Teacher's Book of Lists* ten years ago. The stimulus for writing this book was to revise that book. We realized that many of the lists were now dated and that others were not quite as interesting as they had once seemed. Once we got into the process of revising, we realized that we wanted to do a lot more than just revise a small percentage of the material. Therefore, we undertook a substantially new book, keeping some of the original lists that we felt worked best for teachers and children.

But why lists in the first place? The answer is that we like lists, make lists, and use them as a basic organizational activity. In planning for the classroom, we often started with a list. In encouraging students to get organized or to figure out a way to present some learning or information, we often started them working on a preliminary list. In planning for back-to-school night we jotted down a list of items to talk about, hand-outs to copy, and notes to be written on the board.

We also remembered when we wanted to find a bit of information and ended up plowing through several books or encyclopedias before finding it, or, worse, gave up finding it at all because it was too much trouble. The lists in *The Teacher's Book of Lists* are intended as a reference for you, your students, and parents. Sometimes we wanted to find out more information once we had a few facts on a subject. For example, if we found unicorns and chimeras to be fascinating characters to our class, we would want to know what other such creatures there were. We might use a list such as **Literary Monsters and Creatures**, p. 150, to give us ideas for other characters to learn about. So the lists in this book are also meant to provide a bridge from what has been learned to related topics.

Our belief is that kids are natural learners and that school is a place to find out things, perhaps many things that the teacher may not know. We believe a rich environment, full of all kinds of raw materials, such as a variety of paper, pens, pencils, crayons, chalk, mini-chalkboards, and markers along with enticing and appealing books, videos, film-strips, charts, booklets, and other information-giving items is one of the keys to a vital and successful classroom. We have found that students who are encouraged to make decisions about how they spend their time in school, and what they will study, and how they will share learning with others are students who are empowered to express their natural ability to learn. We see the lists and activities in this book as being appealing to the natural curiosity of children and to lend themselves to creative and thought-provoking experiences.

We want to hear from you about your successes or problems using items from this book. And, if you have some great lists of your own, please send them to us to include in the next book.

THE TEACHER'S BOOK OF LISTS AND THE VARIOUS METHODS AND STYLES OF TEACHING

We recognize that teachers employ different methods and styles of teaching. Although there are many additional methods we could have included here, we will briefly mention a few current educational strategies to indicate how the lists and activities in *The Teacher's Book of Lists* fit comfortably into each.

Cooperative learning

Many activities in this book invite the student to "work with a friend or a group" to research, learn about, or complete a product. We mean by this a group of varied abilities and talents—not the traditional everybody's-at-the-same-reading-level kind of group—so that students are able to learn from each other and develop some of each other's skills. Cooperative group projects also develop social skills by providing a need for a leader and several other roles such as motivators, recorders, and workers, and by demanding responsibility of each member. Small groups, perhaps just two to three children of varying talents or skill levels, are able to tackle a problem or project that any one of them would not be able to do in quite the same way alone.

Because many of the book's activities are open-ended, they can be easily adapted to a cooperative learning situation. We have often enjoyed seeing a whole-class project develop out of something that began with a small group and then caught on with everyone. We can't think of one of the lists or related activities that couldn't be pursued cooperatively. (See the following examples.)

Space Talk—Space Terms Used in Air-To-Ground Communication
This list is ready-made for cooperative learning activities. As they use the vocabulary, some children will want to make such things as instrument panels, or models of the interior of the Space Shuttle. Two or three students might work on each part to be developed, referring to books or literature from NASA for ideas.

U.S. History Events
Within a unit on Conflict, groups can be organized to study each of the wars in U.S. history. Students either self-select or are assigned to a group. The groups can act out the main events of the war they are studying, chart a timeline of their war, or do any other appropriate sharing project.

Theme-based curriculum

A theme-based curriculum is one that recognizes that learning is not an accumulation of un-associated facts. Curriculum is developed around what might be called "big ideas" or "overarching concepts" so that students begin to see the interrelatedness of what is learned at school.

The following list of broad-based themes is one donated by Sandra Kaplan, a specialist in gifted and talented education and teacher training. It should be said that there are other lists and other themes, but this gives the gist of what kinds of topics constitute "themes."

courage	power	order
traditions	rights	communication
patterns	change	truth
systems	forces	origins
symbols	discoveries	justice
conflict	relationships	progress
freedom	adaptation	beginnings
revolution	survival	influences
structure		

The California Science Framework (May 1989 draft edition), while saying that many other themes could be identified, developed the framework based on these themes:

energy	evolution	patterns of change
stability	systems & interaction	scale & structure

The point is that activities organized around a theme cut across specific content matter, and help ensure that learning of isolated facts is not the goal of any discipline.

We have not related any of our lists to specific themes or usual units of study, believing that teachers will easily see connections for themselves. The lists are loosely grouped in the traditional subject areas but many overlap with lists in other parts of the book. Here's one example of how material from lists and related activities might be integrated into a theme-based unit:

THEME—Communication
    Related lists: **Abbreviations**—Tell-a-Phone worksheet (How do abbreviated forms aid us in communicating?)

                    Short Forms—Activity #1, Advertising Slogans (How does language change as words and phrases are shortened, or "casualized"?)

                    250 Things to Write (How do the ways we communicate in writing affect ourselves and others?)

                    Codes and Ciphers—Secret Writing—Decode It worksheet (When and why does communication sometimes need to be secret?)

                    Communication—Tools and Methods (What need preceded the development of these items? What might we need in the future?)

                    Foreign Words and **Foreign Phrases**—(Where do words in our language come from? How can we trace the origins of some of our words? What do the words in our language say about us?)

                    Additional activities and projects

Experiential/discovery learning

Seeing and handling real things, participating in real-life activities, and learning functional skills are important parts of any vital classroom. Many of our activities are built upon this knowledge. Children are asked to:

- interview people
- design business cards
- write stories, poetry, and ads
- help edit each other's writing
- read to each other
- play with cans and containers to learn geometry
- learn the hand alphabet
- survey and graph results
- consult the telephone book
- develop a campaign to save an animal
- write letters to their favorite author and sports team

Many lists with no accompanying activities, such as **Inventions and Inventors**, can be adapted to an experiential activity. For example, the class can develop a classroom display by bringing in items from home, such as various types of light bulbs, ballpoint pens, items utilizing Velcro,® and x-rays. An ambitious group may go to garage sales or develop a scavenger hunt to find old cameras, mason jars, phonographs, etc.

Whole language

We support any whole language approaches and believe that classrooms function best when oral and written language are integrated and the development of skills grows out of the needs felt during the reading and writing process. In the construction of the activities attached to lists in this book, we have taken care to include ones that ask students to do, write, listen, read, and share so that a growth in literacy is a natural outcome. Although there are many additional alternatives, we have often cited children's books for teachers to read aloud or for students to read alone or with each other. We "hear" classrooms as exciting places, with various tasks going on simultaneously, a nearly constant murmur of children's voices discussing with each other or reading with each other. We see all kinds of writing, such as posters, charts, journals, diaries, letters, stories, poems, etc. We have indicated with our activities that whole language practices apply across the curriculum; therefore our social studies and science lists' activities include reading and writing of fiction, creating plays and dialogs and other products, as well as focusing on the usual skills of the subject area.

The writing process

Although there are many versions of the writing process, there seem to be major strands that are found in most of these. These strands are briefly outlined below. Alongside each step is an example of how one activity in *The Teacher's Book of Lists* provides for teaching or student participation in the area.

List: **Planet Table**, p. 228
Activity: #4, Design a travel brochure or poster for one of the planets. Use your imagination. It's okay to be unscientific.

Prewriting	In a group, read all or parts of the planet table; look at travel brochures or imagine what travel brochures look like. Brainstorm ideas that might be included. Prioritize (number) the brainstormed ideas to focus on the most interesting.
Draft stage	Write or type and sketch art for a travel brochure, using ideas from the brainstorming session. At some other time, do the same thing again, if desired (not all of a draft must be done at one sitting); select ideas and elements you like best for brochure draft.
Revision of draft	Working with someone else—another student, a group, or the teacher or other adult—decide if the brochure tells what it needs to say, whether the artwork captures the reader, and whether any other revisions will be made. Dictionaries, a thesaurus, or an astronomy book might be used at this time.
Editing	Work with an editing partner or read-around group to check for spelling, consistency, verb usage, etc. You may work through some of the revision techniques again. Check planet table for use of facts, if any are used (even though some of the idea is to get imaginative).
Final work/ sharing/ publishing	A finished copy of the brochure is made. Some method of sharing is necessary. A travel kiosk, cut out of a box, or even a manila folder that has been stapled to form a pocket can become the display place for travel brochures students have made. Or a group of students could get together to hold a "trip day" during which they use their brochures to "sell" potential travelers on going to the planet they wrote about.

The writing process is intended for certain written products—those that have an amount of importance to the writer or that will be presented for others to read, such as stories, essays, news articles, or independent study projects. Many creative, enjoyable, and casual products of student writing may be done just for the pleasure of self-expression and may involve little or no formal preplanning, editing, or sharing.

How the Book Is Organized

The book is organized into subject area chapters that contain lists with the following components:

- notes
- list entries
- activities
- worksheets or task cards

Notes

Notes provide background information about the list, suggestions for uses, cross references to other lists, and frequently, reference books and literature that relate to the list.

List entries

The lists cover a wide range of subject matter and skills. There are lists related to basic skills and functional literacy, such as antonyms, measurement abbreviations, similes and metaphors. Other lists—endangered species, author's addresses, and women—are related to themes, units of study, and children's interests. And then there are lists that are seemingly just for fun like flip-flop words and syllabic showoffs, but in fact contain inherent learning value.

Lists are presented in a variety of formats—as pictures, definitions, addresses, tables, diagrams, and annotated. Some are short, some are long, and others, which are mainly for reference, are very long.

Environmental Recipes

Concern for the environment has led many families back to old-fashioned chemical-free cleaning and pest control methods. Here are just a few that are not only safe, but economical as well. Two references that contain many other "recipes" are: Heloise, Hints for a Healthy Planet, Perigree Books, and Making the Switch: Alternatives to Using Toxic Chemicals in the Home, send $6 to Publication Dept., Local Government Commission, 909 12th St., Suite 205, Sacramento, CA 95814.

BUG OFF

Soap Spray

2 tbsp. liquid soap   1 gal. water
spray bottle

Mix liquid soap in water. Pour into sprayer. Mist leaves of plants to kill whiteflies, spider mites, mealybugs, cinch bugs, and aphids. Label properly.

BUG OFF

Flea Trap

Place a shallow aluminum pan of soapy water on the floor next to a lamp with the bulb one or two feet above the pan. Leave the lamp on overnight with no other lights on in the room. Fleas are attracted to light, and will jump toward the heat, then fall into the pan where the soapy water finishes them off.

BUG OFF

Vegetable Spray

1 garlic bulb   1 small onion
1 tbsp. cayenne pepper   1 tbsp. liquid
                                          soap
1 qt. boiling water

Chop garlic and onion into small pieces. Mix with cayenne pepper and water. Let mixture stand for one hour, then add soap. Effective for one week as an all-purpose insect spray. Label properly.

BUG OFF

Aphid Trap

Paint a 10" x 10" piece of wood with bright yellow paint. When it is thoroughly dry, coat it with petroleum jelly. Place the wood on a stake next to the infested plants.

Clara Barton (1821–1912)

Simone de Beauvoir (1908–1986)

Sarah Bernhardt (1844–1923)

Mary McLeod Bethune (1875–1955)

Nellie Bly (Elizabeth Cochrane Seaman) (1867–1922)

Evangeline Booth (1865–1950)

Margaret Bourke-White (1906–1971)

Belle Boyd (1843–1900)

...S. (1971–1974); businesswoman, ...of Sri Lanka) ...Angeles

Founded Pan American National Bank of East Los Angeles

Founded the American Red Cross; began relief work during Civil War

French author; leading proponent of women in politics and intellectual life

French actress; greatest actress of her day

American educator who worked to improve educational opportunities for blacks

American journalist; famous for her attempt to beat the record of Phineas Fogg (Around the World in Eighty Days)

First woman to become international leader and general of the Salvation Army

U.S. photographer and war correspondent; covered World War II and the Korean War for Time-Life

Confederate spy; caught in 1862, she was released for lack of evidence

Worksheets and task cards

Student worksheets are included for many lists. Many of the worksheets are designed to be used with a copy of the related list. For example, to complete the worksheet, **U.S. Space Missions Debriefing Questions**, p. 240, students must use the **U.S. Space Missions** list, p. 235, to answer the questions. Other worksheets can be used with a copy of the entire list, a portion of the list, or without any list.

Open-ended and closed worksheets

Some of the worksheets are open-ended and can be used over and over with the same list as the answers can vary. Other open-ended worksheets can be used with many lists. Closed worksheets such as **Tell-A-Phone Answering Service**, p. 6, have definite correct answers.

Types of worksheets

The various format and activities of the worksheets and task cards serve as models for developing your own worksheets and task cards. Some worksheet formats that are included are:

- crossword
- cut and paste
- diagrams
- fill in the blanks
- graphs and grids
- table interpretation
- puzzles
- labeling pictures
- matching
- categorizing and classifying

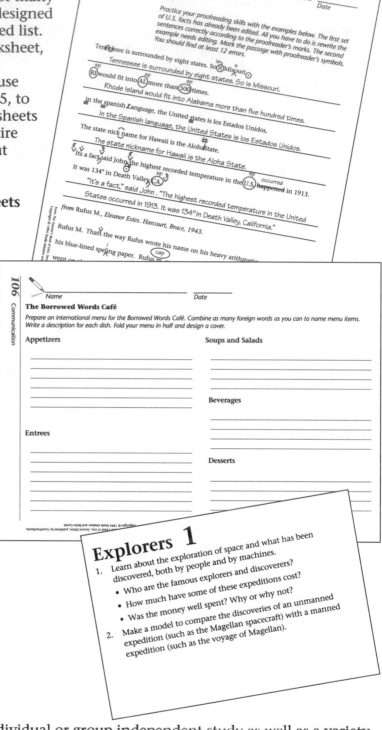

Task cards

Task cards provide activities for individual or group independent study as well as a variety of suggestions for unique end products. Duplicate the task cards onto card stock and laminate them. Make them accessible to students by placing them in a box or by displaying them in an area of the room.

Activities

Activities follow many of the lists. In addition to reinforcing and using basic skills such as following directions, categorizing, and research, the activities also provide for a variety of learning processes and teaching styles. There are activities that encourage creative thinking and cooperative learning, and emphasize creation of unique end products.

Worksheet and task card reference

Whenever a worksheet or task card is included, its title and page number is referenced. If needed, direction to the teacher regarding the preparation or use of the materials are also included.

Worksheet answer keys

Answer keys for worksheets requiring definite answers and sample answers for worksheets that may have varied responses are provided at the back of the book.

Activities: **Careers**

1. Write verbs to describe what each worker does.

2. Use the workers listed in one category for the characters in a story. Some examples of titles might be: "The Butler Did It," using the workers in the B list, and "The Plumber's Helpers," using the workers in the P list as characters.

3. List the workers within general categories, such as Office, Entertainment, Industry, or Workers Who Come to Your Home.

4. Choose some of the following "planned communities" and list all the workers who might live there: Beauty Burg, Fix-it Ville, Healthy Hamlet, Food Farm, Sports Spa, Number Town.

5. Use the list and another source, such as the newspaper want ads, to find all the different kinds of mechanics, computer workers, engineers, doctors, designers, artists, inspectors, managers, reporters, clerks, supervisors, technicians, writers, and so on.

6. On your own, or with several friends, set up a display titled Tools of the Trade. Display actual tools, or pictures and drawings of tools used in several of the careers from the list.

7. Many surnames (last names) originally came from people's work. For example, the name Smith comes from the work of the blacksmith, or smith. Select several names you believe are last names (carpenter? painter? tailor?) and check a telephone book to see if you are correct. Make a chart of the career names you find in the phone book as people's last names. Do research on your last name to find out what it originally meant or was related to.

8. Create fancy names to make some of the careers sound more exciting or desirable.

stylist de bouffant for hairdresser

excellence expert for quality control manager

From The Teacher's Book of Lists, Second Edition, published by GoodYearBooks. Copyright © 1994 Sheila Madsen and Bette Gould.

Worksheet

Business Card Design Service worksheet, p. 267.
Job Application worksheet, p. 268.

266 Social Studies

When Greek Meets Latin

Choose a Greek and Latin stem. Write each stem on the appropriate column. Create and draw a symbol for each stem on top of each column. Complete the columns. Use several of the words in a story about a Greek god meeting a Latin god.

(symbol)

meter
(stem)

measure
(meaning of stem)

List words that contain the stem:

speedometer
odometer
diameter
perimeter
metronome
metrology
geometry

GREEK

(symbol)

octo
(stem)

eight
(meaning of stem)

List words that contain the stem:

octopus
octagon
October
octogenarian
octane
octarchy
octosyllabic

LATIN

(answers will vary)

Latin and Greek Stems *21*

How to Use the Book

The Teacher's Book of Lists isn't a book to read cover to cover. Unlike most books, it is a book that you might want to tear apart and file away by subject, topic, or skill. What you really need are two copies of *The Teacher's Book of Lists*—one that is intact to keep on your desk as a reference and one to dismantle to become part of your files. You will find your own unique ways to use the lists and activities in the book, depending on the nature of your class and the topics and skills your class will study. Here are some general use suggestions to get you started:

Information Resource
You'll notice that *The Teacher's Book of Lists* is not tied to a given age or grade level. It deliberately encompasses a wide variety and range of subject and skill areas, and topics that appeal to children so that you can quickly locate information that might not be on the "tip of your tongue." If you are asked a question like, "How, when, and who invented the zipper?" you can turn to the list of **Inventors and Inventions** to find a quick answer that might lead not only to an independent study of Otto Zipper, but perhaps also develop into a broader study of fasteners.

Class Handouts
Duplicate entire lists for students to use to complete a worksheet, to keep in their notebooks for reference, or to motivate for independent or group study. If an entire list is not appropriate for students, duplicate only part of it, or select appropriate items from the list to use in making up your own list.

Home Handouts
Every list has a potential for home use. A list accompanied by a cover letter is an ideal way to involve and inform parents of what their child is doing in school. Some of the lists are specifically intended for home use. For example, the **Home References** list, p. 359–364, provides tips and items for a basic home library and makes a good handout during parent conferences and back-to-school orientation meetings.

Resource for Creating Learning Materials
Use the lists and activities to make teaching and learning aids such as charts, games, puzzles, task cards, and worksheets. We developed the following examples of various learning materials using information from the **A–Z List of Things to Eat**, p. xix.

Charts and Task Cards

Teaching Chart

Activity Chart

Task Card

Games and Puzzles

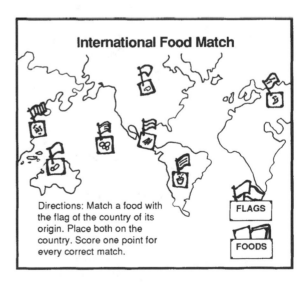

Game

Worksheets

A variety of worksheet types and formats have been included in this book to give you ideas for developing new ones, especially if you're a new teacher and don't yet have a big repertoire in your files. Worksheets can be either open-ended (answers may vary) or closed (specific answers are required).

FOOD COMPOUNDS

Match		Write new word	Draw
water	nut	watermelon	
pea	apple	peanut	
pine	cress		
sea	plant		
water	nut		
dough	melon		
egg	weed		

Closed

$$ MARKET SURVEY

Choose ten foods you know least about. Go to the market with your parents or a friend. Write a brief description of each food and its price.

kumquats _____ $1.98/lb.

bok choy _____ $.70/bunch

daikon _____ $.89/lb.

Open-ended

Another way to develop worksheets is to consider recycling your most successful ones by replacing the original content with new content. The new worksheet below on the topic of foods could easily have become a worksheet on compound words, vowel sounds, or abbreviations. The lists in this book provide many content options to choose from.

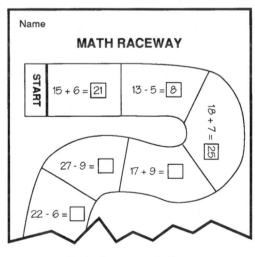

Existing worksheet

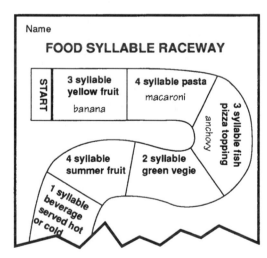

New worksheet

Bulletin Boards

Some teachers groan at the thought of putting up a bulletin board; some teachers can't get enough of them. Since a bulletin board is really another teaching tool, a big teaching tool with plenty of exposure, it should be useful and worth the time spent in creating it.

Bulletin boards can be used as motivators to pique interest in a new theme or unit of study, as interactive teaching and learning areas where children can add to and manipulate items, and as places for students to share information with others. The material in lists can be adapted for all those purposes.

Interactive

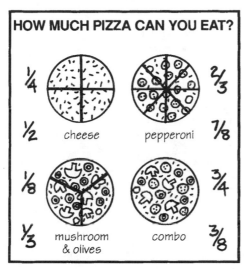

Motivator/Teaching

Sharing

Learning Centers

Charts, games, puzzles, worksheets, task cards, a bulletin board—once you've constructed and gathered these items, you have the basics for a learning center. If it's a center that's right for your class, not only will skills be learned and reinforced, but students' interests will veer off in many directions that you wouldn't have predicted. Some additional essentials for a well-rounded learning center are:

- Learning tasks designed to cover a range of abilities and interests
- Books, lots of books
- Videos and tapes (if you're lucky enough to have a VCR and tape recorder) and other audio visual ads
- Supplies, such as all kinds of paper, pens, pencils, glue, scissors. A supply center works best—that way you don't have to have these materials at every center. And don't forget junk. Children love to put things together, take things apart, and use junk in project making. And as a bonus you and your class will be participating in recycling (see **Environmental Checklist**, p. 252–253).

A comprehensive reference on developing and using learning centers is *Change for Children*, GoodYearBooks, 1980.

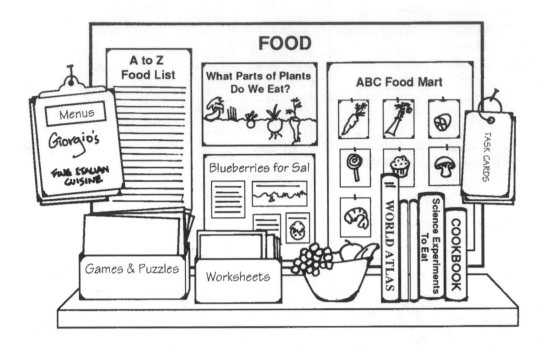

Independent Study, Themes, and Units of Study

Many of the subject-oriented lists can be used to initiate an independent study program or to continue one that already exists in your classroom. Charts or booklets of lists will provide students with many topics to select from. Other lists can be used with skill units, such as the several lists of addresses which can be employed during a letter-writing unit. If you focus on themes, you may combine some of the lists. For example, the theme of discovery may involve study of **Explorers and Discoveres** , p. 271–272, and **Inventions and Inventors**, p. 223. Here are some other suggestions:

- Use the research projects in the activities section of the lists as independent study starters.
- If your entire class is about to embark on a theme or unit of study, make a copy of a list for each student. Most lists have enough entries so that each child or group of students can choose a different subtopic.
- Tear out lists and activities that are related to each of your units of study and file with your existing materials. When preparing for a new topic, you'll be ready to integrate the lists with your other activities or display them for students to use.

Independent Study lists and worksheets are included in Chapter 11, Teacher and Home References.

Eat Your Way Through the Alphabet—An A to Z List of Things to Eat

Ā	apricot
Ă	anchovy, apple, asparagus, aspic
B	bacon, bagels, bamboo shoots, bananas, beans, berries, blintzes, bologna, bok choy, bouillon, bread, broccoli, burritos
hard C	cabbage, cake, canapes, cantaloupe, carrots, cauliflower, caviar, cclams, cocoa, cookies, corn, crab, crackers, cranberries, crepes, curry
soft C	celery, cereal, ceviche, cilantro, cinnamon
D	daikon, dates, dill, doughnuts, duck
Ē	ear of corn, Easter eggs, eel
Ĕ	egg flower soup, eggplant, escargot, escarole
F	felafel, figs, filets, fish, fondue, frankfurters, french fries, fudge
hard G	garbanzo beans, gobo, goose, gooseberries, grapefruit, grapes, gravy
soft G	ginger, gingerbread
H	hamburgers, hazelnuts, herring, hickory nuts, hominy, honey, horseradish, hot dogs, Hungarian goulash
Ī	ice cream, iced tea
Ĭ	Indian curry, Indian corn
J	jam, jello, jelly, jicama (pronounced hee-kah-ma, could be used under *H* words)
K	kale, ketchup, kreplach, kugel, kumquats
L	lasagna, lemonade, lemons, lentils, lichee nuts, lima beans, limes, chopped liver, liverwurst, lobster, lollipops
M	macaroni, mango, marshmallows, marzipan, mayonnaise, matzah, muffins, mushrooms, mustard
N	noodles, nuts
Ō	oatmeal, okra, oranges
Ŏ	octopus, olives, omelette
P	papaya, parsley, peanut butter, peanuts, peas, pepper, pickles, pineapples, pita bread, pizza, potatoes, prunes, pudding, pumpkin
Q	quail, quince, quinine water
R	radishes, raisins, rhubarb, rice, rutabagas
S	salami, salmon, salt, seaweed, sesame seeds, shrimp, soup, spaghetti, spinach, squash, squid, steak, stew, strudel, succotash
T	tea, toast, tofu, tomatoes, tortillas, trout, turkey, tuna, turnips, TV dinner
Ŭ	upset stomach, upside down cake
V	vanilla, venison, vichyssoise, vinegar
W	waffles, walnuts, water chestnuts, watercress, watermelon, wild rice, won ton
X	extra helping
Y	yam, yeast, yogurt
Z	zucchini

Developing Your Own Lists

Once you have used several of the lists in this book, you'll want to start generating some lists specific to your needs. Some you will want to do on your own, but your students will enjoy helping you on others. Try as many of the formats as possible and soon your class will be list-making experts. We've provided the **A-Z Topics** list, p. xxi, for starter ideas.

List formats you may want to consider:

A–Z
numerical
annotated: single items defined or accompanied by a brief note
picture lists
comparative lists: most to least, shortest to tallest, etc.
chronological
items separated into various topics or headings (categorized lists)
checklists
illustrated lists
random order lists
list information shown as tables

Ways to generate lists in your classroom (or with fellow teachers):

brainstorm

look through textbooks (use several different ones on the same subject)

flip through encyclopedias, with each person getting one or two volumes

look through almanacs

post several "list strips" around the classroom with titles such as "streets in our town" or "favorite fictional mice"; anyone may add an item to any list

bring in lists from various resources and get students to do the same (there are many lists in magazines, on T.V., in newspapers, on billboards)

start a list, to be added to over the next few days, whenever a point of interest comes up in read-aloud stories or in other activities (for example, terms for animals: hen, rooster, chick; goose, gander, gosling, etc.)

tape record several items to begin a list and have students in turn listen to the tape and add items to the list

begin a picture list by cutting and pasting items from magazines on a chart, in a booklet, etc.

A–Z Topics List

A   actors/actresses, adjectives, airports, announcers (news, sports, etc.)

B   bad movies, birds, bones, buildings

C   cars, cheese, chemicals, cities, countries

D   dances, dangerous things, dinosaurs, disasters, dogs

E   Easter things, egg dishes, energy sources

F   fads, foods, football players, furniture pieces

G   garden flowers, gargantuan things, gems, German things

H   hats, heroes, high places, hobbies, holidays, horses

I   ice cream flavors, illnesses, Indian tribes, insects, instruments, inventions

J   jams and jellies, jingles, jobs, juices, junk foods

K   kids, kings

L   lakes, landforms, languages, long and lean things

M   Mexican foods, monetary units, monsters, mountains, movies

N   names, numbers, nuts

O   Olympic events, things you turn on, onomatopoeic names, outfielders

P   parks, parties, pets, places, politicians

Q   famous quips, T.V. quiz shows

R   railroads, things to read, rivers, rocks, roses

S   seas, sci-fi words, sculptures, spooky places, sports

T   teams, television shows, trees, towers, towns, toys

U   undersea dwellers, ungulates, unsafe things, things that go up and down

V   Van Gogh's paintings, vegetables, vehicles, verbs

W   bodies of water, weather words, worries, writers

X   Xmas words, things that are X-rayed

Y   things that make you yawn, yellow things

Z   zany people, things that zig-zag, things that have a zipper, zoo inhabitants

The Teacher's Book of Lists

Second Edition

CHAPTER

1

Words

Abbreviations—Abbr.

These often-used abbreviations are listed with their most common meanings. Many abbreviations have more than one meaning, such as cont. *for continued, contents,* and *continent. In many abbreviations periods are optional.*

acct.	account	E.S.T.	Eastern Standard Time
aka	also known as	etc.	and so forth (et cetera)
A.M.	before noon (ante meridiem)	F	fahrenheit
anon.	anonymous	fig.	figure
approx.	approximate	ft.	foot
appt.	appointment	fwy., frwy.	freeway
apt.	apartment	g, gr	gram
arr.	arrival	gal.	gallon
ASAP	as soon as possible	Gov.	Governor
assn., assoc.	association	govt.	government
asst.	assistant	hosp.	hospital
attn.	attention	hr.	hour
atty.	attorney	hwy.	highway
Ave.	Avenue	ibid.	in the same place (ibidem)
avg.	average	id.	the same (idem)
bet.	between	i.e.	that is, for example (id est)
bldg.	building	illus.	illustration, illustrated
Blvd.	Boulevard	in.	inch
C	centigrade, Celsius	inc.	incorporated
cc	carbon copy	init.	initial
ch., chap.	chapter	intro.	introduction
clsd.	closed	I.O.U.	I owe you
Co.	Company	I.Q.	intelligence quotient
c/o	in care of	Jr.	Junior
C.O.D.	cash on delivery	Kb	kilobyte
cont.	continues, contents, continent	kg	kilogram
Corp.	Corporation	km	kilometer
C.S.T.	Central Standard Time	l	liter
ctr.	center	lat.	latitude
dbl.	double	lb.	pound
dep.	departure	lit.	literature
dept.	department	long.	longitude
doz.	dozen	Ltd.	Limited
Dr.	Doctor	m	meter
D.S.T.	Daylight Saving Time	Mb	megabyte
e., E.	east	mdse.	merchandise
ea.	each	mfg.	manufacturing
ed.	edition, education	mgr.	manager
e.g.	for example (exempli gratis)	mi.	mile
elem.	elementary	min.	minute
encl.	enclosure	misc.	miscellaneous
ency.	encyclopedia	mm	millimeter
env.	envelope	mo.	month
est.	established, estimate	mpg	miles per gallon

From *The Teacher's Book of Lists, Second Edition,* published by GoodYearBooks. Copyright © 1994 Sheila Madsen and Bette Gould.

mph	miles per hour	secy.	secretary
Mr.	Mister	sing.	singular
Mrs.	Missus	sp.	spelling
Ms.	form of address suitable for any female	sq.	square
ms, MS	millisecond, manuscript	Sr.	Senior
M.S.T.	Mountain Standard Time	St.	Saint, Street
mt.	mount, mountain	sta.	station
mtg.	meeting	stmt.	statement
n., no., N., No.	north	subj.	subject
natl.	national	tbsp.	tablespoon
no.	number	tel. no.	telephone number
obj.	object, objective	tpk.	turnpike
org.	organization	tsp.	teaspoon
orig.	original	v., vs.	versus
oz.	ounce	vocab.	vocabulary
p., pp.	page, pages	vol.	volume
par.	paragraph	w., W.	west
pd.	paid	wk.	week
pk.	park	w/	with
pkg.	package	w/o	without
pkwy.	parkway	wt.	weight
pl.	plural	yd.	yard
P.M.	after noon (post meridiem)	yr.	year, your
P.O.	Post Office		
pop.	population		
ppd.	prepaid		
pr.	pair		
pred.	predicate		
pres.	president		
P.S.	post script, written after (post scriptum)		
P.S.T.	Pacific Standard Time		
pt.	pint		
qt.	quart		
rd.	road		
recd.	received		
rpm	revolutions per minute		
rpt.	repeat, report		
RR	railroad, rural route		
RSVP	please reply (répondez s'il vous plaît)		
rte.	route		
s., so., S., So.	south		
SASE	self-addressed stamped envelope		
sci.	science		

Days of the Week

Sun.	Sunday
Mon.	Monday
Tue., Tues.	Tuesday
Wed.	Wednesday
Thu., Thurs.	Thursday
Fri.	Friday
Sat.	Saturday

Months of the Year

Jan.	January
Feb.	February
Mar.	March
Apr.	April
Jul.	July
Aug.	August
Sept.	September
Oct.	October
Nov.	November
Dec.	December

From *The Teacher's Book of Lists, Second Edition,* published by GoodYearBooks. Copyright © 1994 Sheila Madsen and Bette Gould.

Tell-A-Phone Answering Service

Rewrite the telephone messages, using complete words in place of each abbreviation.

MESSAGE
To: Sam

Call your apt. mgr. ASAP
about the pkg. he recd.

_____
_____
_____
_____
_____

MESSAGE
To: Asst. Coach Brown

The ctr. is ill. His dbl. w/ a
shooting avg. of 60% will
replace him for the
E. vs. S. Game.

_____
_____
_____
_____

MESSAGE
To: Paul

Your ency. will be sent C.O.D.
in c/o your atty.

_____
_____
_____
_____
_____
_____

MESSAGE
To: Sally

Your assignment is to read
ch. 5, pp. 114–130, and do
problem nos. 2–6.

_____
_____
_____
_____
_____

MESSAGE
To: Dr. Jones

Fwy. clsd. Take alternate rte.
Best bet would be So. Blvd.

_____
_____
_____
_____
_____

MESSAGE
To: Jane

Your acct. at Smith Corp. was
pd. on Wed., Feb. 9.

_____
_____
_____
_____
_____

From *The Teacher's Book of Lists, Second Edition,* published by GoodYearBooks. Copyright © 1994 Sheila Madsen and Bette Gould.

Antonyms

An excellent companion book to a study of antonyms is Push Pull, Empty Full: A Book of Opposites, *Tana Hoban, Macmillan, 1972. The small amount of text makes it accessible to primary-age children, while the black and white photographs illustrating fifteen pairs of opposites are appealing to all ages. Older students may even decide to develop a photo album of their own to illustrate other opposites.*

abet—hinder
above—below
accept—decline
addition—subtraction
advance—retreat
against—for
agree—refuse
allow—forbid
answer—question
arrive—depart
artificial—real
asleep—awake

back—front
beautiful—ugly
beginning—end
big—little
bold—timid
boring—interesting
bottom—top
boy—girl
brave—craven
busy—idle

capture—release
cheap—expensive
clean—dirty
close—distant
closed—open
cold—hot
come—go
complex—simple
contract—expand
cooked—raw
cool—warm
crooked—straight

dangerous—safe
dark—light
dawdle—hurry

day—night
death—life
deposit—withdrawal
division—multiplication
down—up
dry—wet
dull—shiny

eager—reluctant
early—late
east—west
easy—difficult
empty—full
entrance—exit
evening—morning

failure—success
false—true
far—near
fast—slow
fat—thin
female—male
few—many
fierce—gentle
finish—start
first—last
flexible—rigid
follow—lead
foolish—wise
forget—remember
found—lost
fragile—tough
freeze—melt
fresh—stale

guilty—innocent

halt—proceed
happy—sad
hard—soft

hate—love
heavy—light
high—low
hit—miss
horizontal—vertical

in—out

left—right
less—more
long—short
loser—winner
loss—gain
loud—soft

most—least

new—old
no—yes
noisy—quiet

off—on
ordinary—strange
over—under

polite—rude
poor—rich
pull—push

rough—smooth

short—tall
shout—whisper
sick—well
sit—stand
start—stop
strong—weak

tame—wild
thick—thin

Activities: Antonyms

1. Select an antonym pair. Create a list of words that could be described by either antonym. Write a haiku or cinquain featuring some words from the list.

> wet—dry
> hair
> weather
> sand

> Beaches of <u>wet</u> sand.
> Glowing weather brings the sun.
> Now <u>dry</u> sand appears.

2. Select a pair of antonyms. Make a list of synonyms for each word in the pair of antonyms.

> BEGINNING—start, origin, preface
>
> END—finish, terminal, terminate, complete

3. Use a pair of antonyms in the same sentence.

> I arrived <u>early</u> at school, but was <u>late</u> coming home.
>
> The <u>crooked</u> path led to a <u>straight</u> road.

4. Make antonym steps by starting a new pair of antonyms with the last word of the preceding pair.

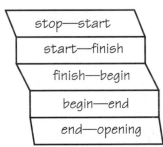

> stop—start
> start—finish
> finish—begin
> begin—end
> end—opening

5. Design and put up a bulletin board of magazine pictures or other items that illustrate antonyms. Or, work with a small group to fill an antonym scrapbook with pictures and drawings.

Worksheet

Antonym Album worksheet, p. 9

From *The Teacher's Book of Lists, Second Edition*, published by GoodYearBooks. Copyright © 1994 Sheila Madsen and Bette Gould.

Antonym Album

Look at the pictures on this album page. Label each picture with a pair of antonyms.

From *The Teacher's Book of Lists, Second Edition,* published by GoodYearBooks.
Copyright © 1994 Sheila Madsen and Bette Gould.

Compound Words

Here is an easy-to-read collection of compounds found in many word lists and beginning readers.

afternoon
airmail
airplane
another
anything

baseball
birthday
blackboard
bluebird
breakfast
busboy

campfire
catfish
chalkboard
classroom
countdown

daytime
dollhouse
doorbell
doorway
downstairs
downtown
driveway

everyone
everywhere

faraway
fireman
fireplace
fisherman
football
footstep

getaway
goldfish
greenhouse

headlight
homework

houseboat
housework

icebox
inside
into

lighthouse

mailbag
mailbox
mailman
maybe
meatballs
moonlight

newspaper
nighttime
nobody

outside

pancake
playground
popcorn

sandbox
sandpaper
schoolhouse
snowball
snowman
somebody
someday
someone
something
sometimes
somewhere
spaceman
starfish
sunflower
sunlight

treehouse

upstairs
uptown

wallpaper
workman

. . . and some more

airport
armchair
ashtray

basketball
bathrobe
bathroom
bedspread
beeswax
bellhop
billboard
blackberry
blueberry
bookcase
bookshelf
breakwater
bridegroom
bridesmaid
butterfly

candlelight
chairperson
checkmate
checkout
chestnut

dashboard
doughnut
driftwood
drugstore

earmuff
earphone
earring

From *The Teacher's Book of Lists, Second Edition,* published by GoodYearBooks. Copyright © 1994 Sheila Madsen and Bette Gould.

earthquake
eyebrow

fingernail
flashlight
footprint
forehead
freeway

gentleman
grapefruit
grasshopper
Greenland
grownup

hairpin
handcuffs
handkerchief
headache
headquarters
hereinafter
heretofore
highway
homesick
honeymoon
hopscotch
hourglass
housekeeper
hubcap

iceberg
Iceland

kettledrum
keyboard
keyhole
kindergarten

landlady
landlord
landmark
landslide

lifeguard
lipstick

masterpiece
mushroom

necklace
necktie
nickname
nightclub
nightgown
nightmare
notebook

oatmeal
offshore
offspring
outdoors
overcast

passport
password
pawnshop
peanut
pineapple
pocketbook
postcard

racetrack
railroad
rainbow
roadrunner
roommate

sailboat
salesperson
seashell
seaway
seaweed
skateboard
slowpoke
snapdragon

snowstorm
steamboat
stepladder
strawberry
suitcase
sunburn
sunglasses
supermarket
surfboard
swordfish

tattletale
teakettle
teapot
teaspoon
tenderfoot
textbook
thunderbolt
thundercloud
thunderstorm
thunderstruck
timepiece
tiptoe
toothpaste
turnpike

underpants
undershirt
undertaker
upset

wastebasket
waterfall
weekend
wheelchair
whirlpool
wildcat
woodpecker

yourself

From *The Teacher's Book of Lists, Second Edition*, published by GoodYearBooks. Copyright © 1994 Sheila Madsen and Bette Gould.

Activities: Compound Words

1. Illustrate the words.

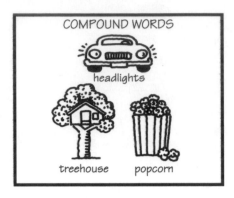

COMPOUND WORDS

headlights

treehouse   popcorn

2. Invent definitions based on the words that make up the compound.

> bridesmaid—a woman who washes, cooks, and cleans for a bride

3. Make new compounds by dividing words and recombining parts to form new words.

> busboy + doorbell = doorboy + busbell

4. Select one compound word that can be an adjective for another compound word. Use as story titles or subjects of sentences.

> The Sunburned Lifeguard

5. Invent some meaningful three-part compound words and use them in sentences.

> breakfasttime, airportlane, earphonewire

Worksheet (teacher directions)

*Copy the entire list of compound words, or make up your own list with words that are appropriate for your group. Provide the list to the students along with the **Categorize the Compounds** worksheet, p. 13.*

From *The Teacher's Book of Lists, Second Edition,* published by GoodYearBooks. Copyright © 1994 Sheila Madsen and Bette Gould.

Categorize the Compounds

Read the list of compounds words. Write the words on the pictures below.

FOOD

PEOPLE

PLACES

ANIMALS

Eponyms—Words from People's Names

Sylvester Graham (1794–1851) advocated a vegetarian diet and other natural foods. His followers ate unleavened biscuits made of whole grain flour that were called graham crackers. The history of the development of any one of the eponyms can be fascinating; see the **Independent Study** *section, p. 365–372, for ways to get students involved. Many other words we use have come from people's names. Here are 80 more.*

ampere

babbitt
beef stroganoff
begonia
bloomers
boycott
boysenberry
braille
bunsen burner

caesarean
camellia
cardigan
Celsius
cereal
chauvinist
chicken tetrazzini

dahlia
decibel
diesel engine
doily
dunce

fahrenheit
ferris wheel
forsythia
fuchsia

gaillardia
galvanize
gardenia

geiger counter
gerrymandering
guillotine

hooligan

kaiser
klieg light

leotard
loganberry
lothario
lynch

macadam
mach
machiavellian
macintosh
magnolia
malthusian
marcel
marconigram
mason jar
maverick
melba toast
mercerize

nicotine

ohm

pasteurize
poinsettia

Pollyanna
pompadour
praline
pullman

quisling
quixotic

raglan
ritzy

salmonella
sandwich
saxophone
sequoia
shrapnel
silhouette
sousaphone
spoonerism
St. Bernard dog

teddy bear
timothy
titian
tommy-gun

victorian
volt

watt
wisteria

zeppelin

Generic Words

Over the years some brand names have become generic names for similar products manufactured by other companies. Most of us ask for a Kleenex instead of a tissue, and our shopping list is more likely to include Jell-O® instead of fruit-flavored gelatin. In fact, each of these product names are trademarks or registered trademarks, indicated by the ™ symbol or ® symbol (a hunt through stores by your students will yield hundreds of such names). The stories behind these names and how the products evolved make fascinating and fun topics for research.

Ace (bandage)

Baggies
Band-aid
Brillo

Chapstick
Clorox
Coca Cola
Con-Tact (paper)
Crayola

Frisbee

Hi-Lighter

Jacuzzi
Jeep
Jell-O

Kitty Litter
Kleenex

Levis
Life Savers

Magic Marker
MIG
Moog
Muzak

Ping-Pong
Plexiglas
Popsicle
Post-it
Pyrex

Q-tip

Raid

Sanka
Saran (wrap)
Scotch (tape)
Styrofoam

Teflon

Vaseline
Velcro

Windex

X-Acto (knife)
Xerox

From *The Teacher's Book of Lists, Second Edition*, published by GoodYearBooks. Copyright © 1994 Sheila Madsen and Bette Gould.

Homonyms—Write It Right

acclamation, acclimation
adds, ads, adz
aerie, airy
ail, ale
air, ere, err, heir
aisle, I'll, isle
allowed, aloud
altar, alter
ate, eight
auger, augur
auricle, oracle

bail, bale
baize, bays
bald, balled, bawled
balm, bomb
band, banned
bare, bear
based, baste
beat, beet
beer, bier
bell, belle
better, bettor
blew, blue
bloc, block
boar, bore
boarder, border
bough, bow
bouillon, bullion
braise, brays, braze
brake, break
bridal, bridle

cache, cash
capital, capitol
carat (karat), caret, carrot
cedar, ceder, seeder
cell, sell
cense, cents, scents, sense
cent, scent, sent
cereal, serial
cetaceous, setaceous

cheap, cheep
chews, choose
choler, collar
choral, coral
chorale, corral
chord, cord, cored
chute, shoot
cite, sight, site
clause, claws
coarse, course
coax, Cokes
colonel, kernel
core, corps
cue, queue
cymbal, symbol

dear, deer
dense, dents
descent, dissent
desert, dessert
dew, do, due
die, dye
doe, dough
ducked, duct

ewe, yew, you

faint, feint
fair, fare
faze, phase
feat, feet
fisher, fissure
flair, flare
flea, flee
flew, flu, flue
flocks, phlox
flour, flower
foaled, fold
for, fore, four
foul, fowl
frays, phrase
frees, freeze, frieze

gait, gate
gamble, gambol
genes, jeans
gilt, guilt
gneiss, nice
gnu, knew, new
gored, gourd
grate, great
grease, Greece
groan, grown
grocer, grosser
guessed, guest
guise, guys

hair, hare
hall, haul
handsome, hansom
hart, heart
hay, hey
heal, heel, he'll
hear, here
heard, herd
higher, hire
him, hymn
hoard, horde
hoarse, horse
hoes, hose
hole, whole
hour, our
humerus, humorous

idle, idol, idyll
in, inn
invade, inveighed

jam, jamb
jinks, jinx

kill, kiln
knave, nave
knead, need

From *The Teacher's Book of Lists, Second Edition*, published by GoodYearBooks.
Copyright © 1994 Sheila Madsen and Bette Gould.

knight, night
knit, nit
knows, noes, nose

lacks, lax
laps, lapse
leak, leek
lessen, lesson
levee, levy
links, lynx
load, lode, lowed
loan, lone
locks, lox

made, maid
magnate, magnet
mail, male
main, Maine, mane
marshall, martial
mean, mien
meat, meet, mete
might, mite
moose, mousse
muscle, mussel

oar, or, ore
one, won

paced, paste
packed, pact
pail, pale
pair, pare, pear
palate, palette, pallet
patience, patients
pause, paws
peace, piece
peal, peel
pearl, purl

pedal, peddle
peer, pier
plait, plate
pore, pour
praise, prays, preys
presence, presents
prince, prints
principal, principle
profit, prophet

quarts, quartz

rain, reign, rein
raise, raze
rapped, rapt, wrapped
read, red
read, reed
real, reel
right, rite, write
ring, wring
road, rode, rowed
roes, rose, rows
rote, wrote
rye, wry

sail, sale
scene, seen
seam, seem
seas, sees, seize
serf, surf
sew, so, sow
shear, sheer
side, sighed
sighs, size
sleight, slight
soar, sore
sole, soul
some, sum

staid, stayed
stair, stare
stake, steak
stationary, stationery
step, steppe
straight, strait
suede, swayed
suite, sweet
sundae, Sunday

tail, tale
taught, taut
team, teem
tear, tier
teas, tease, tees
their, there, they're
threw, through
throes, throws
thyme, time
tic, tick
to, too, two
toad, toed, towed
toe, tow
tracked, tract

undo, undue

vain, vane, vein

wade, weighed
waist, waste
waits, weights
war, wore
ware, wear
weak, week
wood, would

yoke, yolk

A Homonym Gift List

*Write in a homonym for the underlined word
and the name or kind of person who might get the gift.*

1. a new boat _____sail_____ on *sale* for _____Captain Hornblower_____

2. a _____ donut with a *hole* for _____

3. a pretty _____ and a bag of *flour* for _____

4. *hoes* and a _____ for _____

5. a night at the _____ *in* Washington, D.C. for _____

6. every *Sunday*, an ice cream _____ for _____

7. a new *red* book that can be easily _____ for _____

8. a _____ of music would bring *peace* to _____

9. a _____ of paint in a *pale* color for _____

10. *wood* _____ be good for _____

11. a fishing *reel* made of _____ steel for _____

12. a _____ about the monkey's *tail* for _____

13. the *right* kind of pen to _____ with for _____

14. a sweet-smelling _____ to be *sent* to _____

15. a _____ of knives to *pare* a *pear* for _____

16. a *scene* from a play to be _____ by _____

17. a pink *rose* and three _____ of sunflowers for _____

18. the bus _____ to get to the county *fair* for _____

19. _____ giving a party in *your* castle for _____

20. _____ tickets *to* Disneyland for _____

From *The Teacher's Book of Lists, Second Edition,* published by GoodYearBooks.
Copyright © 1994 Sheila Madsen and Bette Gould.

Latin and Greek Stems

Latin Stems

Act (do, drive)
actor, deactivate, reaction

Aqua (water)
aquarium, aquanaut, aqueduct

Audi (hear)
audio, audition, audience

Cent (hundred)
centipede, cent, century

Creat (make)
creation, creative, recreation

Dic, Dict (say, speak, declare)
diction, dictator, indictment, prediction

Duc, Duct (lead, draw, bring, take)
produce, productive, aqueduct, deduct

Equ (same, even)
equity, equation, equator, unequal, equilateral

Fer (carry, bring)
transfer, ferry

Flex (bend)
flexible, reflection

Fract (break)
fragile, fragment, fraction, fracture

Fuse (pour)
transfusion, refuse, confused

Gress (step, go)
progress, aggressive, digress

Ject (throw)
project, inject, subject, eject

Liber (free)
liberation, liberal, liberty

Loc (place)
location, local, locate

Mal (bad)
malice, malign, malediction

Manu (hand)
manipulate, manuscript, manual, manufacture

Mare (sea)
marine, submarine, maritime, aquamarine

Mem (keep in mind)
memory, memorize, remember

Mit (go, send)
remit, transmitter, admit, emit

Mob, Mot, Mov (move, movable)
mobile, motor, promoted, automobile

Octo (eight)
octave, octet, octagon, octopus, octogenarian

Ped (foot)
pedal, pedestal

Pel (push, drive)
propel, expel, repelled

Pend (hang)
append, pendant, dependent, suspend

Pli (fold)
pliable, duplicate, complicate

Port (carry)
portable, export, report, import

Scrib, Script (write)
prescription, postscript, describe

Uni (one, single)
uniform, reunite, unicycle, unity

Vac (empty)
vacate, vacuum, evacuate

Vis (see)
vision, vista, revise, invisible

Greek Stems

Astro (star)
astrology, astronomy, astrologer

Auto (self)
autograph, autobiography, automobile

Bio (life, living things)
biography, biology, biopsy

Geo (earth, land)
geography, geometry, geology

Gram (something written down, drawn, or recorded)
telegram, electrocardiogram

Graph (something that writes or is written)
autograph, photograph, telegraph

Gyro, Gyr (circle, spiral)
gyroscope, gyrate

Hemi (half)
hemisphere

Hydro (water)
hydrofoil, hydrogen, hydrophone

Meter (measure)
speedometer, odometer

Micro (small)
microscope, microphone, microfilm

Mono (single, one)
monotone, monograph, monogram

Ology, Logy (study of, science of)
biology, geology, psychology

Phone (sound, voice)
microphone, telephone, phonograph

Photo (light)
photograph, phototype

Poly (many, much)
polyhedron

Scope (instrument for seeing or observing)
telescope, microscope

Sphere (ball, globe)
atmosphere, hydrosphere

Tele (far away, distant)
teletype, television, telegram

Therm, Thermo (heat)
thermometer, thermostat

Zoo (animal)
zoo, zoology, zoography

From *The Teacher's Book of Lists, Second Edition*, published by GoodYearBooks. Copyright © 1994 Sheila Madsen and Bette Gould.

Ωηεν Γρεεκ Μεετσ Λατιν
When Greek Meets Latin

Choose a Greek and Latin stem. Write each stem on the appropriate column. Create and draw a symbol for each stem on top of each column. Complete the columns. Use several of the words in a story about a Greek god meeting a Latin god.

(symbol)   (symbol)

(stem)   (stem)

(meaning of stem)   (meaning of stem)

List words that contain the stem: List words that contain the stem:

GREEK   LATIN

Activities: Phonics Lists

Use the lists to prepare charts, worksheets, and other teaching aids. Using the lists in a whole language classroom depends on the students' needs at any given time. Words from any of the lists may be introduced from read-aloud stories, songs, or poems. Children should use words in class stories, oral stories, and other activities that use them in context, before beginning to study them in list form.

Some books that are useful as a starting place for beginning blends are *Happy Birthday, Moon*, Frank Asch, Prentice Hall, 1982, and *Mooncake*, Frank Asch, Prentice Hall, 1983. Both contain many words with TH and WH. Another natural for beginning sounds are tongue twisters, which can be constructed with beginning blends as well as with beginning single consonants.

Some suggested uses for the phonics lists:

- After a list is mastered (such as "cr" words), duplicate the list and send it home to parents with the reminder that words should be read and related to meaning, as in a sentence or phrase.

- Students can make up an alliterative story with several words from one list. The story is then shared orally with the class.

- Make a "word ring" for each child, using a chart rack ring and note cards. Children add words and pictures, one per note card, as they study the lists. A ring makes it easy to add new words and to store words and pictures in alphbetical order. Some uses:

—A child arranges several cards in a sequence. Another child orally makes up a sentence that contains each of the pictured words.

—In a small group, one child holds up a card for all to see. Other members of the group say rhyming words and use them in sentences.

—On the backs of the cards, children can write new words they learn that begin with the same sound.

Worksheet (teacher directions)

Word Book worksheet, p. 35

*The Word Book is for use with all of the phonics lists in this section. Students need to cut out and assemble their books. You can select a list for a child or group to study, or students can self-select. Word Books can also be used with your own lists, other lists in this book, such as **Abbreviations**, p. 4, vocabulary from a class story, or words from a unit of study.*

Beginning Consonant Blends

These words have been arranged so that short vowel words are listed first, then long vowel words, and finally, words containing other vowel sounds.

BL

blanket
blast
blender
bless
blink
block
blotter
blunt
blame
bleed
blind
blow
blue

BR

branch
brat
bread
breath
bridge
brig
brought
brunt
brush
brave
breed
bright
broken
brook
brown
broom

CL

clap
claw
clef
clip
clock
clod
closet
club
clay
clean
climb
cloak
clout
cloud
clue

CR

crab
crack
crest
crib
crop
cross
crumb
crane
cradle
crate
crayon
crazy
cream
creep
crime
cry
croak
crawl
crew
crowd

DR

drab
dress
dread
drift
drip
drop
dropper
drug
drum
drake
dream
drive
drone
drawl
droop
drew
drought

FL

flag
flat
flesh
fling
flop
flutter
flake
flame
flea
flier
fly
float
fluke
flour
flower

FR

fraction
fresh
fret
friend
frill
frog
frost
from
frustrate
freight
freeze
fry
frozen
frugal
fruit
frown

GL

glad
glen
glitter
glob
gloves
glutton
glade
glee
glide
globe
glow
glare
gloom
glue

From *The Teacher's Book of Lists, Second Edition,* published by GoodYearBooks. Copyright © 1994 Sheila Madsen and Bette Gould.

GR

grab
grand
grasshopper
Greg
grid
grin
grip
grovel
grain
grapes
grate
gray
green
greet
grind
groan
grow
group
groom
growl

PL

plan
plank
plant
plastic
plaid
pledge
plenty
plod
pluck
plug
plum
place
plate
play
plead
please
ply
plot
Pluto
ploy
plow

PR

practice
press
present
prince
print
principal
prod
promise
pray
preen
pride
prize
probe
prose
prune
proof
prowl

SC, SK

scamp
scat
scarf
scum
scale
scold
scope
scare
score
scout

skeleton
skeptical
sketch
skim
skin
skip
skull
skunk
skate
ski

SL

slam
slap
sled
slept
slip
slippers
slit
slot
slug
slumber
slump
slate
sleep
slice
slide
slope
slow
sloop

SM

smash
smack
smell
Smith
small
smog
smug
smear
smile
smoke
smooth

SN

snack
snag
snap
sniff
snip
snob
snore
snuff
snuggle
snail
sneak
snide
snare
snoop
snout

SP

spank
spatter
sped
spill
spot
spunk
space
speak
spear
spy
spew
spider
spore
spoil
spool
spoon
spout

ST

stab
staff
standard
star
steps
stick
sting
stock
stop sign
stumble
steel
steak
style
stole
stove
stare
student
stoop
stool
stout

SW

swam
swan
swell
sweater
swept
swift
swim
swing
swab
sway
sweet
swipe
swollen
swoon
swoop

TR

track
traffic
trap
trend
tread
trinket
trip
trod
tropical
truck
trump
trust
trouble
trail
train
treat
tree
tribe
tricycle
troll
true
trout

TW

twelve
twenty
twig
twins
twist
twinkle
twitch
twill
twain
tweed
tweak
tweet
tweezers
twice
twine

QU

quack
question
quickly
quit
quake
quail
queen
quite
quote
quarrel
quart

SPL

splash
splendid
splint
splinter
split
splotch
spleen
splice
splurge

SCR

scramble
scrap
scrimmage
script
scrub
scrape
screen
scream
scribe
scroll
screw

SPR

spread
spring
sprinkle
sprocket
sprung
sprain
spray
spree
spritely
spry

From *The Teacher's Book of Lists, Second Edition*, published by GoodYearBooks. Copyright © 1994 Sheila Madsen and Bette Gould.

SQU	CH	SH	TH (voiced)
squid	chat	shadow	that
squiggle	chap	shamrock	them
squint	check	shed	then
squish	checkers	shell	they
squander	children	ship	there
squash	chip	shock	
square	chipmunk	shut	
squeeze	chocolate	shade	**WH**
squirrel	chop	sheen	
squirt	chuckle	sheep	when

	CH	SH	WH
	chain	shine	whether
	chase	shone	which
STR	cheap	show	whip
	chime	shoot	whiskers
strap	choke	shawl	whistle
strength	choose	shelf	whale
strip	chew	shower	wheel
string	chow	shark	whine
strong	cherries		white
straw	church		where

strawberry
struggle
strum
stray
stream
street
strike
stripe
stroll
strew

TH (unvoiced)

TH (unvoiced)	SHR
thatch	
thimble	
thin	shrank
think	shred
thought	shrill
thumb	shrimp
thunder	shrink
thief	shrub
thermometer	shriek
	shrine

Consonant Blend Endings

These words have been arranged so that short vowel words are listed first, then long vowel words, and finally, words containing other vowel sounds.

-FT

craft
draft
raft
cleft
left
drift
sift
soft
tuft

-MP

champ
clamp
cramp
lamp
ramp
hemp
chimp
limp
shrimp
romp
dump
hump

-ND

band
hand
land
sand
stand
wind
wand
bond
fond
pond
fund
blind
kind
mind
pound
round

-NG

bang
clang
hang
sang
king
ring
sting
string
wing
gong
long
wrong
hung
lung

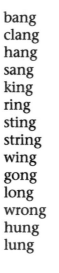

-NK

bank
spank
tank
thank
link
pink
shrink
sink
honk
chunk
junk
skunk
trunk

-NT

pant
plant
slant
bent
present
tent
hint
tint
front
hunt
punt
runt
faint
paint
quaint
pint
count
point

-SK

bask
flask
mask
task
desk
brisk
risk
whisk
husk
tusk
kiosk

-SP

asp
rasp
clasp
grasp
crisp
lisp
cusp

From *The Teacher's Book of Lists, Second Edition,* published by GoodYearBooks. Copyright © 1994 Sheila Madsen and Bette Gould.

-ST	-CH	-SH	-TH
blast	bench	crash	bath
fast	which	mash	path
last	crunch	trash	breath
best	lunch	flesh	tenth
nest	bleach	fresh	month
quest	peach	mesh	faith
test	reach	dish	teeth
fist	teach	fish	tooth
mist	coach	wish	truth
wrist	porch	gosh	mouth
cost	couch	squash	uncouth
lost	ouch	blush	
rust	staunch	crush	
trust	church	gush	
waist		rush	
beast		wash	
least			
coast			
most			
roost			

Short Vowel/Silent e Pairs

Selected words may be made into word cards or games such as Lotto. *Activities should stress reading the words aloud. This list may also be sent home for at-home reading reinforcement.*

Al—ale
at—ate
ban—bane
bar—bare
cam—came
can—cane
cap—cape
car—care
dam—dame
Dan—Dane
fad—fade
fat—fate
flak—flake
gag—gage
gal—gale
gam—game
gap—gape
hat—hate
Jan—Jane
lam—lame
mad—made
man—mane
mar—mare
mat—mate
nap—nape
pal—pale
pan—pane
par—pare
past—paste
pat—pate
plan—plane
rag—rage
rat—rate

sag—sage
Sam—same
sat—sate
slat—slate
spat—spate
stag—stage
tam—tame
tap—tape
van—vane
wag—wage
wan—wane

met—mete
pet—Pete

bid—bide
bit—bite
dim—dime
din—dine
fin—fine
fir—fire
grim—grime
grip—gripe
jib—jibe
kit—kite
mit—mite
pin—pine
pip—pipe
quit—quite
rid—ride
rip—ripe
shin—shine

sin—sine
sir—sire
sit—site
slid—slide
slim—slime
spit—spite
strip—stripe
Tim—time
tin—tine
trip—tripe
twin—twine
win—wine

con—cone
cop—cope
cot—cote
dot—dote
glob—globe
hop—hope
lop—lope
mop—mope
not—note
pop—pope
rod—rode
rot—rote
ton—tone
tot—tote

cut—cute
hug—huge
jut—jute
us—use

From *The Teacher's Book of Lists, Second Edition*, published by GoodYearBooks. Copyright © 1994 Sheila Madsen and Bette Gould.

SHHHH!

Silents, Please— Common Silent Letters

Silent letters present one of the most difficult situations for children who are intent on correct spelling. It is best to encourage students to first spell by sound as they are writing, and then to begin gradually to learn about these tricky combinations. It is surprising to see how many of the following words have homonyms. An activity related to this oddity may help draw attention to the spellings that follow. Any student especially interested might benefit by learning about the derivations of the various spelling patterns.

silent gh	gh, silent h	gn, silent g	kn, silent k	wr, silent w
bought	ghastly	align	knack	wrap
caught	ghetto	arraign	knapsack	wreath
dough	ghost	feign	knave	wreck
eight	ghoul	gnarl	knead	wren
flight		gnash	knee	wrench
high		gnat	knew	wrestle
right		gnaw	knife	wring
sleigh		gneiss	knight	wrinkle
sigh		gnome	knit	wrist
taught		gnu	knob	write
thought		reign	knock	wrong
		sign	knot	wrote
			know	
			knowledge	
			knuckle	

mb, silent b

bomb
climb
comb
crumb
jamb
lamb
limb
numb
thumb
tomb

From *The Teacher's Book of Lists, Second Edition,* published by GoodYearBooks. Copyright © 1994 Sheila Madsen and Bette Gould.

Vowel Digraphs and Diphthongs

Digraphs

ai as in sail	ay as in day	ea as in team	ea as in head	ea as in break
afraid	clay	cream	bread	steak
aim	crayon	deal	feather	
chain	gray	easy	heather	
fail	lay	flea	lead	
jail	may	gleam	measure	
maize	play	grease	read	
paid	prayer	leak	tread	
paint	slay	mean	treasure	
praise	stay	peak	weather	
proclaim	sway	plead		
rain	tray	preach		
snail		repeal		
stain		seam		
straight		squeal		
train		teach		

ee as in week	ei as in eight	ey as in key	ie as in piece	oa as in boat
flee	freight	donkey	belief	coat
free	neigh	honey	chief	float
glee	neighbor	monkey	relief	load
green	rein	trolley		moat
heed	skein	volley		poach
need	sleigh			road
queen	vein			roam
seed				soak
sheen				toad
sheet				
sneeze				
steed				
sweet				
three				
tree				

From *The Teacher's Book of Lists, Second Edition,* published by GoodYearBooks. Copyright © 1994 Sheila Madsen and Bette Gould.

oo as in foot	oo as in moon	ow as in crow	ue as in blue
book	balloon	blow	due
cook	bassoon	flow	glue
crook	croon	low	gruesome
good	fool	mow	sue
hood	hoot	row	true
look	room	slow	
shook	school	throw	
stood	shoot	tow	
took	spoon		
wood	stool		
	swoon		
	too		
	tool		
	toot		
	zoo		

Digraphs followed by r

air as in pair	ear as in year	ear as in earth	ear as in bear	eer as in deer
eclair	appear	Earl	pear	beer
fair	beard	early	swear	cheer
flair	clear	earn	tear	leer
hair	dear	heard	wear	peer
lair	dreary	hearse		queer
stair	ear	learn		seer
	fear	pearl		sheer
	gear	search		steer
	hear			
	near			
	rear			
	spear			
	tear			

ier as in pier	oar as in oar	our as in four	our as in hour
fierce	boar	court	flour
pierce	roar	pour	our
tier	soar	your	sour

Diphthongs

au as in taught	aw as in saw	ew as in grew	oi as in oil	ou as in out
caught	crawl	blew	avoid	blouse
flaunt	draw	crew	coil	cloud
haul	drawl	dew	coin	couch
haunt	fawn	drew	foil	foul
maul	gawk	flew	hoist	house
pauper	hawk	new	join	loud
sausage	law	slew	loin	mouse
taut	lawn	stew	loiter	mouth
	raw	threw	noise	ouch
	shawl		point	pouch
	straw		poison	pound
	tawny		soil	round
	yawn		spoil	shout
			toil	south
			voice	trout

ow as in cow	oy as in boy
down	coy
drown	destroy
flower	employ
fowl	enjoy
frown	joy
gown	ploy
how	Roy
plow	toy
renown	voyage
shower	
town	
trowel	

From *The Teacher's Book of Lists, Second Edition*, published by GoodYearBooks.
Copyright © 1994 Sheila Madsen and Bette Gould.

Word Book

Cut out each page of the Word Book. Stack the pages with the cover on top. Staple your book together. Write your name on the cover. Now, follow the directions on page 2 of your word book.

_____'s

(your name)

WORD BOOK

2

1. Write the name of a list you are studying at the top of a page.

2. Learn to read the list.

3. Read the words to each person listed on the page.

4. Ask each person to check their box to show you can read the words.

5. Color in your award when all boxes are checked.

6. Now, repeat with 5 other word lists.

3

_____
(name of list)

❑ to yourself

❑ to a friend

❑ to a relative

❑ to the teacher

4

_____
(name of list)

❑ to yourself

❑ to a friend

❑ to a relative

❑ to the teacher

5

_____
(name of list)

❑ to yourself

❑ to a friend

❑ to a relative

❑ to the teacher

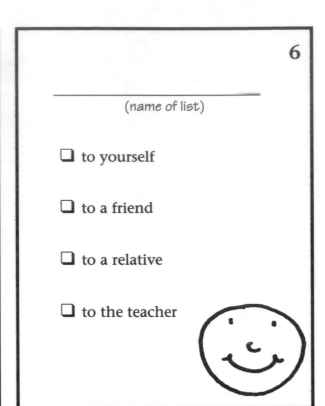

6

_____
(name of list)

❑ to yourself

❑ to a friend

❑ to a relative

❑ to the teacher

7

_____
(name of list)

❑ to yourself

❑ to a friend

❑ to a relative

❑ to the teacher

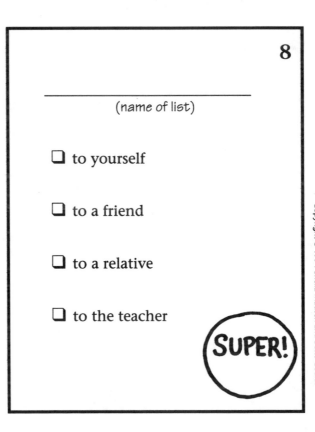

8

_____
(name of list)

❑ to yourself

❑ to a friend

❑ to a relative

❑ to the teacher

SUPER!

From *The Teacher's Book of Lists, Second Edition*, published by GoodYearBooks.
Copyright © 1994 Sheila Madsen and Bette Gould.

Portmanteaus

*A portmanteau is a word formed by the arbitrary combination of two words. Lewis Carroll invented the portmanteaus snark, from snake and shark, and slithy, from slimy and lithe. Children can create their own portmanteaus from words on the **Twins and Triplets** list, p. 44–45, or from familiar word pairs such as blue jeans, cottage cheese, and jump rope.*

beefalo = beef + buffalo

bishaw = bicycle + rickshaw

bit = binary + digit

botel = boat + hotel

broasted = broiled + roasted

brunch = breakfast + lunch

chortle = chuckle + snort

clash = clap + crash

dumbfound = dumb + confound

eggler = egg + dealer

Eurasia = Europe + Asia

fantabulous = fantastic + fabulous

fishwich = fish + sandwich

flurry = flutter + hurry

galumphing = gallop + triumphing

guesstimate = guess + estimate

heliport = helicopter + airport

meld = melt + weld

mingy = mean + stingy

motel = motor + hotel

motorcade = motor car + cavalcade

pixel = picture + element

slosh = slop + slush

smog = smoke + fog

splatter = splash + spatter

splotch = spot + blotch

splurge = splash + surge

telex = teleprinter + exchange

transistor = transfer + resistor

vegeburger = vegetable + hamburger

Prefixes and Suffixes

Definitions for these common prefixes and suffixes have been simplified. Only the most frequently used meanings of the prefixes and suffixes have been selected for the list. The words given as examples generally contain a root word that children can easily identify. Teachers may wish to duplicate the entire list for students to keep in their notebooks as reference during learning activities. Or, teachers can select only those prefixes and suffixes most appropriate for their classes and prepare their own lists and worksheets.

Prefixes

AD-, AC-
1. to, toward: *ad*verb, *ad*equate, *ac*credit, *ac*custom
2. near: *ad*renal

ANTE-
1. before, prior: *ante*date
2. in front of: *ante*chamber, *ante*room

ANTI-
1. against, opposite of, in opposition to: *anti*slavery, *anti*freeze, *anti*climax, *anti*aircraft

BI-
1. two: *bi*cycle, *bi*annual
2. twice during every or once in every two: *bi*weekly, *bi*monthly

CIRCUM-
1. around: *circum*navigate, *circum*lunar

CO-, COM-, CON-
1. with, together: *co*exist, *com*patriot, *con*form

CONTRA-, COUNTER-
1. against, opposite: *contra*diction, *counter*balance, *counter*clockwise

DE-
1. opposite of: *de*code
2. remove from: *de*horn, *de*throne
3. reduce or lower: *de*flate, *de*grade

DEC-, DECA-, DEKA-
1. ten: *dec*ade, *deca*liter

DIS-
1. not, opposite of, reverse: *dis*belief, *dis*orderly, *dis*approve
2. apart, away from: *dis*lodge

EN-
1. put on or into: *en*throne, *en*danger, *en*act
2. cover or surround: *en*close, *en*wrap, *en*fold, *en*circle, *en*compass, *en*gulf
3. make: *en*able, *en*large

EX-
1. former, before: *ex*president
2. from, out of, beyond: *ex*change, *ex*hale, *ex*port

EXTRA-, EXTRO-
1. beyond, outside the scope or region of, besides: *extra*sensory, *extra*ordinary, *extro*vert

HYPER-
1. more than usual, in excess: *hyper*active, *hyper*critical, *hyper*sensitive

From *The Teacher's Book of Lists, Second Edition*, published by GoodYearBooks. Copyright © 1994 Sheila Madsen and Bette Gould.

HYPO-
1. under, beneath: *hypo*dermic

IM-, IN-
1. not, without: *im*possible, *in*active,

IN-, INTRA-
1. in, into, within: *in*born, *intra*spinal

INTER-
1. jointly, together: *inter*lace, *inter*twine
2. between or among: *inter*island, *inter*continental

MID-
1. middle: *mid*way, *mid*town, *mid*term, *mid*summer, *mid*brain, *mid*day

MIS-
1. wrong, wrongly: *mis*quote, *mis*advise, *mis*copy, *mis*inform, *mis*judge, *mis*read, *mis*pronounce
2. bad, badly: *mis*fortune, *mis*treat, *mis*adventure, *mis*shapen, *mis*conduct

MONO-
1. one, single: *mono*rail, *mono*tone

NON-
1. not: *non*fiction, *non*-American, *non*conformity, *non*breakable

OUT-
1. greater, better: *out*distance, *out*dance, *out*run, *out*fight, *out*do, *out*live
2. outer place: *out*doors, *out*side, *out*field, *out*post

OVER-
1. beyond, too much: *over*eat, *over*act, *over*heat, *over*ripe, *over*sleep

POST-
1. after, later: *post*war
2. positioned behind: *post*dental

PRE-
1. before or at an earlier time: *pre*school, *pre*historic, *pre*mature
2. in front of: *pre*fix

PRO-
1. for, in favor of: *pro*-American *pro*-labor

RE-
1. again: *re*do, *re*finish
2. back: *re*turn, *re*bound, *re*call

RETRO-
1. backward: *retro*gress, *retro*active, *retro*rocket

SUB-
1. under: *sub*soil, *sub*way
2. not up to, inadequate, less than: *sub*standard, *sub*normal
3. part of a whole: *sub*station, *sub*culture, *sub*district, *sub*committee

TRANS-
1. move from one place to another: *trans*plant
2. across: *trans*continental, *trans*atlantic, *trans*oceanic
3. change: *trans*form, *trans*figuration

TRI-
1. three: *tri*colored, *tri*lingual, *tri*angle, *tri*motor
2. once in every three: *tri*monthly
3. three times during every: *tri*weekly, *tri*annual

UN-
1. not, opposite of: *un*clean, *un*clear
2. reverse or opposite of an action: *un*button, *un*pack
3. lack of: *un*easy, *un*rest

From *The Teacher's Book of Lists, Second Edition*, published by GoodYearBooks. Copyright © 1994 Sheila Madsen and Bette Gould.

Suffixes

-ABLE, -BLE, -IBLE
1. able to, capable of, possible to: erase*able*, reproduc*ible*
2. tending or likely to: peace*able*, perish*able*

-AL
1. belonging to, having the characteristics of: music*al*, norm*al*, industri*al*, trib*al*
2. process of action: refus*al*, arriv*al*

-ANCE, -ANCY, -ENCE, -ENCY
1. quality, act, or condition: resist*ance*, assist*ance*, depend*ence*, emerg*ency*

-ANT, -ENT
1. be in or perform a certain act: serv*ant*, deodor*ant*, solv*ent*

-ATE
1. result or act of, provide with: refriger*ate*, hyphen*ate*

-DOM
1. area ruled by: king*dom*
2. condition or state of being: free*dom*, martyr*dom*

-ESS
1. female: godd*ess*, host*ess*, lion*ess*

-EST
1. superlative of adjectives: bigg*est*, slow*est*, small*est*, healthi*est*

-FUL
1. full of: joy*ful*, beauti*ful*
2. character of: shame*ful*, grace*ful*, man*ful*
3. quantity that would fill: cup*ful*

-FY
1. to form into or become: beauti*fy*, classi*fy*, lique*fy*, nulli*fy*, sissi*fy*, solidi*fy*

-HOOD
1. state of being: child*hood*, man*hood*
2. membership in a group: brother*hood*, priest*hood*

-IC
1. pertaining to, of, part of: angel*ic*, alcohol*ic*, volcan*ic*

-ICS
1. art, science, study of: ceram*ics*, systemat*ics*, tact*ics*
2. act or practice of: athlet*ics*, gymnast*ics*

-ISH
1. nationality: Turk*ish*, Scott*ish*
2. likeness to: mann*ish*, clown*ish*, child*ish*
3. somewhat: brown*ish*, warm*ish*, tall*ish*

-IVE
1. having the quality of: mass*ive*
2. tending to: disrupt*ive*, instruct*ive*

-LESS
1. lack of, without: penni*less*, head*less*, shoe*less*, shirt*less*, meat*less*

-LET
1. smallness in size or importance: play*let*, leaf*let*
2. worn on the body: ank*let*

-LIKE
1. similar to: child*like*, life*like*

-LY
1. in a certain manner: sad*ly*, quick*ly*, efficient*ly*
2. like, having a resemblance to: man*ly*, queen*ly*
3. occurring every: year*ly*, month*ly*
4. in a certain place: third*ly*

From *The Teacher's Book of Lists, Second Edition*, published by GoodYearBooks. Copyright © 1994 Sheila Madsen and Bette Gould.

-MENT
1. result of, thing produced by: engage*ment*, entangle*ment*
2. process or act of: develop*ment*, detach*ment*
3. state, quality, or condition of: amaze*ment*, enjoy*ment*

-NESS
1. manner or state of being: dark*ness*, unhappi*ness*

-OR
1. person or thing that performs: audit*or*, creat*or*, escalat*or*, govern*or*, investigat*or*
2. state, manner, or act: err*or*, pall*or*

-SHIP
1. state of: kin*ship*, friend*ship*
2. office, rank, level: intern*ship*, lord*ship*
3. art or skill: author*ship*, horseman*ship*, marksman*ship*

-SION, -TION
1. action or process of: pronuncia*tion*, rejec*tion*
2. condition: comple*tion*, starva*tion*, confu*sion*
3. result of: discus*sion*, transla*tion*

-TY, -ITY
1. state, quality, or amount: fals*ity*, humid*ity*, safe*ty*, mediocr*ity*, obes*ity*, inferior*ity*
2. ten times: six*ty*

-WARD, -WARDS
1. toward, in the direction of: back*wards*, north*ward*

-WISE
1. way, direction, or manner: counterclock*wise*, length*wise*
2. in respect to: time*wise*, money*wise*

-Y
1. characterized by, resembling, having: rain*y*, storm*y*, slim*y*, thirst*y*
2. quality or state of: jealous*y*, victor*y*
3. act, place, or business: baker*y*
4. little or small: bunn*y*, pant*y*

Short Forms

Through time and usage, many words and phrases become shortened. We often use the shortened form in our everyday communications. Students should notice short forms used in advertising, the media, and various businesses. These words will be useful to children in role playing, play writing, and dialogue writing in their stories. Many bilingual or ESL children will benefit from familiarity with this category of words, as they are often not in school books but are often used in everyday speech and writing.

ASAP	as soon as possible	math	mathematics
awol	absent without leave	mayo	mayonnaise
bems	bug-eyed monsters (sci-fi jargon)	max	maximum
bits	binary integers	memo	memorandum
biz	business	morn	morning
BLT	bacon, lettuce, and tomato sandwich	mums	chrysanthemums
		OJ	orange juice
caps	capital letters	PC	personal computer
CD	compact disk	PE	physical education
celebs	celebrities	peke	Pekinese dog
chimp	chimpanzee	perm	permanent wave
co-op	a cooperative	photo	photograph
copter	helicopter	pix	pictures
croc	crocodile	pixel	picture elements
cuke	cucumber	p.j.s	pajamas
D.J., deejay	disk jockey	prez	president
deli	delicatessen	ref	referee
doc	doctor	reps	representatives
M.C., emcee	master or mistress of ceremonies	revs	revolutions
exam	examination	rhino	rhinoceros
flu	influenza	RV	recreational vehicle
gator	alligator	sarge	sergeant
gym	gymnasium	sax	saxophone
hi fi	high fidelity	sci fi	science fiction
hippo	hippopotamus	sitcom	situation comedy
home ec	home economics	stats	statistics, photostats
hood	hoodlum	temp	temperature, temporary
hose	hosiery	thru	through
ID	identification	tux	tuxedo
info	information	TV	television
intro	introduction	ump	umpire
KO	knock out	veep	vice president
lab	laboratory	vet	veteran, veterinarian
limo	limousine	VIP	very important person
lube	lubricate, lubrication	wiz	wizard

Activities: Short Forms

1. Write advertising slogans containing short forms for products or jobs.

   Hire a <u>limo</u> from Mr. Nimo.
   End each of your days in Smith's <u>P.J.s</u>.
   For the answers to a quiz, go to see your local <u>wiz</u>.

2. Write sentences that contain several short forms.

   The <u>croc</u> and the <u>chimp</u> had <u>cukes</u> from the <u>deli</u>.

3. Fill in phrase patterns with a short-form word and a word that rhymes with it. Here are some blank phrase patterns.

   _____ of _____

   a _____ _____

   the _____ by a _____

Examples of completed phrase patterns:

	rows	of	hose
a	large		sarge
the	ump	by a	dump
the	chimp	in a	blimp
a	cuke	for a	Duke
a	cab	with a	lab

The completed phrases can be used:

- as story titles
- as lines of poetry
- to make up silly questions
- to make silly stories by linking several phrases together

From *The Teacher's Book of Lists, Second Edition*, published by GoodYearBooks.
Copyright © 1994 Sheila Madsen and Bette Gould.

Word Twins, Triplets, and Quadruplets

Twins

aches and pains
Aunt and Uncle

back and forth
black and blue
black and white
blood and guts
bread and butter
bright and shiny
bright-eyed and
    bushy-tailed

cake and ice cream
cat and mouse
cats and dogs
cease and desist
chips and dip
cloak and dagger
coat and tie
cold and clammy
cops and robbers
cowboys and Indians
cup and saucer
cut and dried
cut and paste

dogs and cats
dos and don'ts

ebb and flow

fish and chips
foot-loose and fancy-free

hearts and flowers
hide and seek
high and dry
high and mighty

hill and dale
hither and yon
huff and puff
hugs and kisses

in and out

jump and shout

knife and fork

lathe and plaster
life and death
light and fluffy
long and short
lost and found
loud and clear

Mom and Dad
Mother and Father

nickel and dime
night and day
now or never
nuts and bolts

old and gray
on and off
open and closed
open and shut

paper and pencil
peace and quiet
pen and ink
pins and needles
potatoes and gravy
pots and pans
ps and qs

read and write
rest and relaxation
rise and fall
rise and shine
rough and ready

safe and sound
salt and pepper
shoes and socks
short but sweet
show and tell
sister and brother
slip and slide
soap and water
sound and fury
soup to nuts
spic and span
sticks and stones
stop and go
strange but true
strong and silent
sugar and spice

table and chairs
the tortoise and the hare
toss and turn

up and down

vinegar and oil

wash and dry
whether or not
wild and woolly

From *The Teacher's Book of Lists, Second Edition,* published by GoodYearBooks. Copyright © 1994 Sheila Madsen and Bette Gould.

Triplets

animal, vegetable, or
   mineral

bacon, lettuce, and tomato
bell, book, and candle

coffee, tea, or milk

hop, skip, and a jump

men, women, and children

reading, writing, and
   arithmetic
red, white, and blue

snap, crackle, and pop

tall, dark, and handsome

up, up, and away

Quadruplets

ear, eyes, nose, and throat
eeny, meeny, miney, moe

rain, hail, sleet, or snow
rich man, poor man,
   beggarman, thief

Activities: Word Twins, Triplets, and Quadruplets

1. List word pairs that are opposites, such as *long and short* or *rise and fall.*

2. Find word pairs that repeat the same word, such as *over and over, coast to coast,* and *higher and higher.* Make a chart of them and use some of them in a piece of poetry or in a song.

3. Write sentences that use word twins as similes. See how many you can illustrate.

The pillow was as light and fluffy as a freshly baked doughnut.

4. Make up a gallery of people who are often thought of in two-somes or threesomes, such as Laurel and Hardy, Mutt and Jeff, and Larry, Moe, and Curly. Tell about the likenesses and differences of the partners.

5. Make a chart that shows word pairs grouped into categories such as foods, people, directions, and actions.

FOODS	PEOPLE
• fish & chips	• cops & robbers
• coffee, tea, or milk	• Mom & Dad
• peanut butter & jelly	• Jack & Jill

ACTIONS	DIRECTIONS
• hugs & kisses	• up & down
• cut & paste	• in & out
• open & shut	• hither & yon

From *The Teacher's Book of Lists, Second Edition,* published by GoodYearBooks. Copyright © 1994 Sheila Madsen and Bette Gould.

Worksheet

Word Twins Crossword worksheet, p. 47

Word Twins Crossword

Work the crosswood puzzle by filling in the word that completes each twin or triplet.

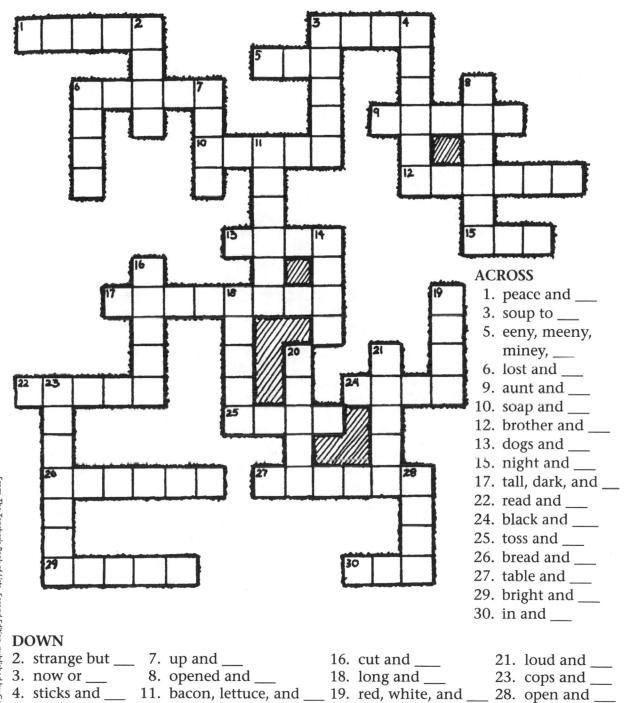

ACROSS

1. peace and ___
3. soup to ___
5. eeny, meeny, miney, ___
6. lost and ___
9. aunt and ___
10. soap and ___
12. brother and ___
13. dogs and ___
15. night and ___
17. tall, dark, and ___
22. read and ___
24. black and ___
25. toss and ___
26. bread and ___
27. table and ___
29. bright and ___
30. in and ___

DOWN

2. strange but ___
3. now or ___
4. sticks and ___
6. knife and ___
7. up and ___
8. opened and ___
11. bacon, lettuce, and ___
14. hide and ___
16. cut and ___
18. long and ___
19. red, white, and ___
20. back and ___
21. loud and ___
23. cops and ___
28. open and ___

CHAPTER

2

Spelling

Spelling Odds and Ends

These ten words appear in more than a quarter of all that we write:

the	a
and	in
of	that
to	you
I	for

Some words from a grade-school spelling book published in 1845:

cornucopiae	amanuensis
bacchanalian	circumambient
pusillanimity	

A 1950 article by Leslie W. Johnson cited these 5 words, from a list of 100, as most frequently misspelled by 14,643 children in the elementary grades.

their	they
too	then
there	

These 5 were the least often misspelled of the 100:

jumped
around
dropped
babies
money

The longest word in *Webster's New Collegiate Dictionary, 8th edition:*

pneumonoultramicroscopicsilicovolcanoconiosis

The longest word in the *Oxford English Dictionary:*

floccinaucinihilipilification

The first spelling book was printed in 1643 by Stephen Day in Cambridge, Massachusetts.

From *The Teacher's Book of Lists, Second Edition,* published by GoodYearBooks. Copyright © 1994 Sheila Madsen and Bette Gould.

100 Spelling Demons

ache
again
always
among
answer
any

been
beginning
believe
blue
break
built
business
busy
buy

can't
choose
color
coming
cough
could
country

dear
doctor
does
done
don't

early
easy
enough
every

February
forty
friend

grammar
guess

half
having
hear
heard
here
hoarse
hour

instead

just

knew

laid
loose
lose

making
many
meant
minute
much

often
once

piece

quiet

raise
read
ready

said
says
seems
separate
shoes
since
some
straight
sugar
sure

tear
their
there
they
though
through
tired
tonight
too
trouble
truly
Tuesday
two

used

very

wear
Wednesday
week
where
whether
which
whole
women
won't
would
write
writing
wrote

From *The Teacher's Book of Lists, Second Edition*, published by GoodYearBooks. Copyright © 1994 Sheila Madsen and Bette Gould.

From W. F. Jones, *A Concrete Investigation of the Materials of English Spelling*, University Press: University of South Dakota, 1913.

243 Additional Spelling Demons

abrupt
absence
accommodate
accumulate
accurate
acquire
across
address
adequate
adjourn
advice
amateur
analysis
analyze
angle
apologize
apparently
appearance
appreciate
arctic
argument
arrangement
athletic
audience

before
benefited
bicycle
breathe
brilliant
bulletin

calendar
campaign
canceled
career
cemetery
certain
chief
colonel
column
committee
conscience

continuous
correspondence
courteous
criticism
curiosity
cylinder

decision
definitely
difference
different
difficulty
dining
disappear
disappoint
discipline
disease
dissatisfied
division

eighth
embarrass
environment
equipped
especially
etc.
exaggerate
excellent
existence
experience
extremely

familiar
fascinate
finally
foreign
formally
formerly
fulfill
fundamental

glimpse
gorgeous

government
governor
groceries
guarantee
guard
guidance

handsome
height
heroes
hoping
humorous
hurriedly

illegible
illustrate
imaginary
immediately
incidentally
independence
indispensable
intelligence
interesting
interpreted
interrupt
irrelevant
its
it's

jealous
jewelry
journey
judgment

khaki
kindergarten
knead
knowledge

laboratory
leisure

library
license
licorice
lightning
likely
listen
livelihood
loneliness

maintenance
maneuver
manufacture
marriage
mathematics
medicine
mileage
miniature
miscellaneous
mischievous
misspell
mortgage
muscle

naturally
necessary
nickel
niece
ninety
ninth
noticeable
nuisance

occasion
occur
occurred
o'clock
omission
omitted
opinion
opportunity
opposite
original

From *The Teacher's Book of Lists, Second Edition*, published by GoodYearBooks. Copyright © 1994 Sheila Madsen and Bette Gould.

pamphlet	realize	strength	vacancy
parallel	receive	studying	vacuum
particular	recognize	succeed	vegetable
pastime	recommend	sufficient	vinegar
peaceable	rehearse	surprise	visible
performance	relevant		volume
permanent	relief		
personal	relieve	temperature	
personnel	religious	temporary	
persuade	repetition	tendency	weather
pleasant	restaurant	therefore	wholly
possession	rheumatism	thorough	who's
precede	rhubarb	together	whose
privilege	rhythm	tomorrow	
probably	ridiculous	tongue	
procedure		transferred	
proceed		typical	yacht
professor	safety		yield
pronunciation	schedule		yolk
psychology	scissors	unanimous	your
pumpkin	seize	undoubtedly	you're
pursue	sergeant	unique	youth
	severely	unnecessary	
quantity	similar	until	
quarrel	sizable	usually	
quite	souvenir	utensil	zealous

Spelling Plurals

Add *es* to words that end in *o* to make plurals.

buffalo*	motto*	torpedo
cargo*	potato	veto
domino*	tomato	volcano*
echo	tornado*	
embargo		
hero*		
mango*		

*These words add either *s* or *es*.

Add *es* to words that end in *s, ch, z, x,* or *sh* to make plurals.

ax	speech
buzz	splash
crush	tax
glass	topaz
guess	waltz
mash	watch
sandwich	wish

Change the *f* or *fe* to *v* before adding *es* to words that end in *f* or *fe* to make plurals.

calf	life	thief
half	loaf	wharf
knife	self	wife
leaf	shelf	wolf

Change the *y* to *i* before adding *es* to words that end in a consonant and *y* to make plurals.

ally	city	history	sky
apply	copy	lady	spy
army	cry	lily	story
baby	fairy	marry	worry
berry	fancy	mystery	
body	fly	reply	

From *The Teacher's Book of Lists, Second Edition,* published by GoodYearBooks.
Copyright © 1994 Sheila Madsen and Bette Gould.

Irregular Plurals

Singular	Plural
analysis	analyses
antenna	antennae
axis	axes
bacterium	bacteria
basis	bases
cactus	cactuses, cacti
child	children
crisis	crises
curriculum	curricula, curriculums
datum	data
die	dice
foot	feet
goose	geese
hippopotamus	hippopotamuses, hippopotami
man	men
medium	media
mouse	mice
nebula	nebulae
oasis	oases
ox	oxen
parenthesis	parentheses
phenomenon	phenomena
radius	radii
stratum	strata
tooth	teeth
woman	women

From *The Teacher's Book of Lists, Second Edition*, published by GoodYearBooks. Copyright © 1994 Sheila Madsen and Bette Gould.

For Syllabic Showoffs

Most children love to impress family and friends by spelling long words or words with repetitive spelling patterns. Here's a list to show off with. Many of the words are known to children, but others such as tintinnabulation, would make good starting places for searching out meaning and origin.

3 syllables

Chihuahua
committee
cucumber
cumulus

discotheque

Frankenstein

labyrinth

millionaire

4 syllables

Chattanooga

eucalyptus

gargantuan
gobbledegook
graduation

harum-scarum
hocus-pocus

independent

kookaburra

Minnehaha
Mississippi

Tallahassee
Transylvania

5 syllables

abracadabra
auditorium

bibliography

dieffenbachia

hippopotamus

thingamadoodle
tonsillectomy

whatchamacallit

6 syllables

autobiography

encyclopedia

octogenarian
onomatopoeia

paleontology

tintinnabulation
Tyrannosaurus Rex

12 syllables

humuhumunukunukuapuaa (the state fish of Hawaii)

antidisestablishmentarianism

13 syllables

supercalifragilisticexpialidocious

A Spelling List For Teachers

accept	compulsory	field	lounge	recognize
achievement	conference	foreign	luncheon	reference
address	coordinator		Lutheran	repetition
adequate	correspondence	genius		reprimand
adjust	corridor	grammar	mathematics	requirements
administrator	counselor	government	mischievous	responsible
adolescents	courteous	group	motivated	
affect	criticism	guidance	municipal	salary
aggressive	curriculum	guilty		secondary
algebra		gymnasium	necessary	secretary
alternative	decision		negative	segregation
anonymous	deficient	handicapped	Negroes	sensitive
anxiety	delinquency	hectic		significant
applies	democratic	height	observant	sincerely
argument	despite	heterogeneous	opportunities	smoking
arithmetic	destructive	history	orchestra	sophomore
assignment	detention	homogeneous		status
assistant	different	honorary	parental	strength
attitude	diploma		parochial	student
audio-visual	disastrous	illiterate	perform	suburban
	discipline	immature	physics	successful
behavior	discrimination	incidentally	pieces	superintendent
bookkeeping	discussion	independently	plumbing	supervisor
boundaries	distraction	innocent	practically	
building	distribute	instructor	practice	technology
business	district	insurance	preference	tenure
	diverts	integration	prejudice	theories
		intelligence	premises	tried
cafeteria		irate	preparatory	truly
calendar	effect	irritated	principal	typical
Catholic	elementary		professor	
census	entrance		projector	ultimately
certain	epileptic	janitor	psychiatric	usually
channels	everything	journal		
children	excellent	judgment		vacancy
choir	exception		quiet	violent
climbing	exercise	laid	quit	vocational
commercial	experiment	languages	quite	(plus names of
community	extension	leisure		local
comparative		library	receive	businesses,
complaints	faculty	license	recess	streets, etc.)

Reprinted by permission from "When Teachers Misspell," *Improving College and University Teaching* (Spring, 1965). Corvallis, OR: Oregon State University Press.

The Last Word— National Spelling Bee Words

Here are the last words that have been spelled correctly by the winners of the National Spelling Bee since 1965. Probably most of the contestants did not know the meanings of the words. Many students would be challenged by locating meanings, derivations, and usages.

eczema	1965	hydrophyte	1974	luge	1984
ratoon	1966	incisor	1975	milieu	1985
chihuahua	1967	narcolepsy	1976	odontalgia	1986
abalone	1968	cambist	1977	staphylococci	1987
interlocutory	1969	deification	1978	elegiacal	1988
croissant	1970	maculature	1979	spoliator	1989
shalloon	1971	elucubrate	1980	fibranne	1990
macerate	1972	sarcophagus	1981	antipyretic	1991
vouchsafe	1973	psoriasis	1982	lyceum	1992
		purim	1983	kamikaze	1993

Here are 18 other words on which the championships have been won or lost since the Spelling Bee began in 1926.

abbacy	esquamulose	propitiatory
acquiesced	eudaemonic	propylaeum
asceticism	gladiolus	psychiatry
brethren	larghetto	sacrilegious
cinnabar	onerous	transept
condominium	pronunciation	uncinated

From *The Teacher's Book of Lists, Second Edition,* published by GoodYearBooks. Copyright © 1994 Sheila Madsen and Bette Gould.

CHAPTER

3

Writing

250 Things to Write

Here's the perfect solution to the common question, "But what can I write?" Students' explorations of these formats and products will lend depth to their writing abilities and interests. The end products listed require a variety of writing styles: from fiction to nonfiction, from personal to business. Any unit of study will be enriched by employing some of these products and styles in place of the standard report. Most of the writing products can be personalized to fit in with a whole language approach.

acceptance speeches
ads
advice columns
anecdotes
announcements
apologies
autobiographies
awards

ballads
banners
bedtime stories
billboards
biographies
book jackets
book reviews
books
brochures
bulletins
bumper stickers
business letters

captions
cartoons
catalogs
chants
characterizations
charts
cinquains
coded messages
columns
comedies
comic strips

condolence letters
conversations
correspondence
couplets
coupons
critiques
current events

debates
dedications
definitions
descriptions
dialogs
diaries
dictionaries
digests
directions
directories
dramas

eating out guides
editorials
encyclopedia articles
entertainment guides
envelopes
environmental checklists
epilogues
epitaphs
essays
eulogies
evaluations
exaggerations
explanations

fables
fact sheets
factual reports
fairy tales
family trees
fantasies
FAXes
fiction
flyers
folktales
fortunes

game directions
gardening tips
ghost stories
glossaries
goals
gossip
graffiti
greeting cards
grooming tips

haiku
handbooks
handouts
headlines
health guides
historical fiction
history of —
horoscopes
"how to" booklets
hypotheses

From *The Teacher's Book of Lists, Second Edition*, published by GoodYearBooks. Copyright © 1994 Sheila Madsen and Bette Gould.

ideas
impassioned pleas
inquiries
instructions
interviews
introductions
invitations
IOUs
itineraries

jargon
jingles
jokes
journals
just so stories

kiosk advertisements
knock-knock jokes
kudos

labels
lampoons
"laundry" lists
leaflets
legends
lessons
letters
letters to the editor
limericks
lists
love stories
lullabyes
lyrics

magazines
manuals
memoirs
memos
menus
messages
metaphors
movie reviews
movie scripts
mysteries
myths

news articles
news bulletins
newsletters
newspapers
New Year's resolutions
nonsense
notes
novels
numbered lists
nursery rhymes

obituaries
objectives
observations
opinions
order forms
oxymorons

pamphlets
paragraphs
plays
plots
poetry
policies
political speeches
postcards
posters
prayers
predictions
problems
procedures
prologues
promises
propaganda
proposals
pros and cons
prose
protest letters
proverbs
puns

qualifications
queries
question & answer columns
questionnaires

questions
quips
quizzes
quotations

realistic fiction
recipes
record album copy
    (liner notes)
reminders
reports
research reports
résumés
reviews
rhymes
riddles
romance stories
rules

sagas
scary stories
schedules
science fiction
scientific reports
scripts
sequels
serials
shelf carton copy (cereal
    boxes, cookie boxes, etc.)
shopping lists
short stories
signs
similes
slogans
soap operas
solutions
songs
song titles
speeches
sportscasts
stories
summaries
superstitions
surveys
synopses

From *The Teacher's Book of Lists, Second Edition,* published by GoodYearBooks.
Copyright © 1994 Sheila Madsen and Bette Gould.

tall tales
telegrams
telephone messages
thank-you notes
time lines
"to-do" lists
tongue twisters
tragedies
translations
travel guides
tributes
TV schedules
TV reviews
TV shows

ultimatums
urgent messages

valedictorian speeches
valentines
values
victory speeches
views

want ads
wanted posters
weather forecasts

weather reports
who, what, when, where,
    why & how
wills
"wish" lists
word puzzles

yarns
yearbooks
yearly calendars
yesterdays, todays,
    tomorrows

zingers

From *The Teacher's Book of Lists, Second Edition*, published by GoodYearBooks.
Copyright © 1994 Sheila Madsen and Bette Gould.

Codes and Ciphers— Secret Writing

Spacing Code

A super-simple position code is made by merely changing the position of the spaces between words.

```
DANGEROUS TO REMAIN LEAVE AT ONCE
DA NGERO USTOR EMAI NLEA VEATO NCE
```

Every Other Letter Cipher

This is a very simple cipher, in which random letters are inserted between each letter of the actual message, and then all the letters are grouped into "words" of five letters each. The cipher begins with a random letter. Meaningless letters may be added to the last "word" to complete the five-letter pattern. The message SECRET MEETING AT BLACK LAGOON would look something like this, depending on the random letters selected:

TSREF CLRNE QTXMS ELERT PIKNR GVAMT NBOLR ADCEK MLPAG GIOLO SNRTU

Double Parallel-Alphabet Cipher

Select a key word of at least seven letters that does not use the same letter twice. Following it, write the alphabet omitting any letter found within the key word. Now write the alphabet beneath this.

```
G E R M A N Y B C D F H I J K L O P Q S T U V W X Z
A B C D E F G H I J K L M N O P Q R S T U V W X Y Z
```

The message WATCH OUT, becomes VGSRB KTS using this cipher.

Alphabet Strips

Write the alphabet with an even space between each letter on a strip of paper. Now, on a longer strip, write the alphabet twice, again with an even space between each letter. A letter is agreed upon as the code name. Place the shorter strip above this letter on the longer strip. Then write the message in letters from the lower strip. Here is the set-up for a "D" code.

```
A B C D E F G H I J K L M N O P Q R S T U V W X Y Z
```
```
A B C D E F G H I J K L M N O P Q R S T U V W X Y Z A B C D E F G H I J K L ...
```

Here is a "D" code message: SODB LW VDIH

Chinese Cipher

The Chinese Cipher is a simple transposition cipher in which the letters of the message are written up and down columns, beginning in the upper right-hand corner.* MEET ME AT THE SHIP AT MIDNIGHT would first be written in columns like this:

```
N  D  E  H  M
I  I  S  T  E
G  M  H  T  E
H  T  I  A  T
T  A  P  E  M
```

The code's message would then be written: NDEHM IISTE GMHTE HTIAT TAPEM
*Meaningless letters may be added to the columns to complete the pattern.

Bacon's Cipher

Francis Bacon, the English philosopher and author, invented this cipher, which uses only two letters of the alphabet (a and b) in various combinations.

A	aaaaa	G	aabba	N	abbaa	T	baaba
B	aaaab	H	aabbb	O	abbab	UV	baabb
C	aaaba	IJ	abaaa	P	abbba	W	babaa
D	aaabb	K	abaab	Q	abbbb	X	babab
E	aabaa	L	ababa	R	baaaa	Y	babba
F	aabab	M	ababb	S	baaab	Z	babbb

Using this cipher, URGENT would read:

baabbbaaaaaabbaaabaaabbaabaaba

Tic Tac Toe Cipher

The letters of the alphabet are first arranged in a diagram.

AB	CD	EF
GH	IJ	KL
MN	OP	QR

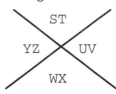

For the first letter of any pair, draw that part of the diagram. For the second letter of any pair, draw that part of the diagram, and add a dot. For example,

I = □   J = ▣   U = ⟨   T = ⌄•

The message SEND MONEY IMMEDIATELY would be written:

From *The Teacher's Book of Lists, Second Edition,* published by GoodYearBooks. Copyright © 1994 Sheila Madsen and Bette Gould.

Decode It

Decode each of the mystery titles below and write them on the lines. Use the Codes and Ciphers information sheets to help you.

When you're finished, you will be considered an expert decoder. Now you might like to send some messages to your friends in code. You may also enjoy researching other codes and finding out when and why codes are used.

Spacing Code

TH EFOU RTHFL OORTW INSAND TH EFIS HSNI TCHMY STE FY, by David A. Adler

_____

Every Other Letter Code

MTOHR ESTXU SNANR EPLNT UOCYD EYSBT FESRL DGAHY, by Jerome Beatty

_____

Double Parallel Alphabet Cipher

SBA YPAGS YPGMALKCJS IXQSAPX, by Eugene Baker

_____

Alphabet Strip in "D" Code

WKH FXUVH RI WKH EOXH ILJXULQH, by John Bellairs

_____

Chinese Cipher

TEISN XSNRO ROTEM SLHTO PCESN, by Willo Davis

_____

Bacon Cipher

abbababbaabaabaaabbbaabaaaabaaaaabbaabbaaabaa, by Gillian Cross

_____

Tic Tac Toe Cipher

⌄•⌐⌐ •⌐⌐<⌄⌐ ⌐⌐•⌐ ⌄•⌐⌐ ⌐⌐• •

By Eileen Dunlop

_____

Editor's Checklist

Many classrooms today, especially whole language-oriented ones, include editing as a part of the writing process. Students are asked to work in editing pairs, or read-around groups, or to edit with the teacher, aide, parent, or other adult. This editing is more than just looking for mechanical errors. The process encourages comments on content, character development, word usage, style, and so on. The activity not only assists a writer in improving or rethinking a story or part of a story, but also helps the editor to be more conscious of story elements, eventually strengthening both parties' writing.

The Editor's Checklist that follows is in two parts. #1 (on the left) is for younger or less advanced writers, while #2 is a bit more sophisticated for older or more mature writers. Both checklists could be used in the same classroom, depending on the range of writing skills of the students. A teacher may ask a pair of writer/editors to only pay attention to certain elements on the list. In a group, he or she may decide to focus only on content, or only on mechanics. Many teachers will want to personalize the checklists by adding some specific items.

Also useful to students when editing at the final draft stage is **Proofreader's Symbols,** p. 72.

From *The Teacher's Book of Lists, Second Edition,* published by GoodYearBooks.
Copyright © 1994 Sheila Madsen and Bette Gould.

✔ EDITOR'S CHECKLIST #1

_____
(story title)

_____
(author)

THE CONTENT

___ beginning makes you want to read on

___ length is just right

___ reader's senses are involved

___ action words are used

___ many describing words

___ interesting words used

___ interesting characters

___ clear meaning

___ well organized

___ good ending

THE MECHANICS

___ can understand spelling

___ capital letters used

___ punctuation O.K.

___ can read the writing

___ _____

___ _____

___ _____

_____
(Editor's name and date)

✔ EDITOR'S CHECKLIST #2

_____
(story title)

_____
(author)

THE CONTENT

___ exciting or inviting beginning

___ story length is appropriate

___ reader's senses are involved

___ action words are used

___ vivid descriptions

___ synonyms used

___ can identify with characters

___ clear meaning

___ well organized

___ ending is well thought out

___ tone and style are consistent

THE MECHANICS

___ sentences are well constructed

___ uses correct spelling

___ verb phrases are consistent

___ quotation marks and other punctuation used correctly

___ _____

___ _____

___ _____

_____
(Editor's name and date)

Flip-Flop Words

abba-dabba

bibble-babble
boo-hoo
boogie-woogie
bow-wow

chiller-diller
chit-chat
click-clack
clickety-clackety
clip-clop

dilly-dally
ding-a-ling
ding-dong
dribble-drabble
ducky-wucky

even-Steven

fiddle-faddle
flim-flam
flip-flop
fuddy-duddy
fuzzy-wuzzy

giggle-gaggle

hanky-panky
harum-scarum
heebie-jeebies

helter-skelter
hippety-hoppety
hocus-pocus
hoity-toity
hokey-pokey
hootchie-cootchie
hully-gully
humpty-dumpty
hurdy-gurdy
hurly-burly

itsy-bitsy

jibber-jabber
jingle-jangle

lovey-dovey

mish-mash
mumbo-jumbo

namby-pamby

okey-dokey

palsy-walsy
piggly-wiggly
piggy-wiggy
Ping-Pong
pitter-patter
plip-plop

raggle-taggle
razzle-dazzle
rinky-dinky
rowdy-dowdy
rub-dub

scribble-scrabble
see-saw
shilly-shally
splish-splash
super-duper

teeny-weeny
teensy-weensy
tick-tock
ticky-tacky
tip-top
tippety-toppety
tootsie-wootsie
trip-trap

walkie-talkie
whing-ding
wibble-wobble
wig-wag
wiggle-waggle
willy-nilly
wishy-washy

yakety-yak

zig-zag

From *The Teacher's Book of Lists, Second Edition*, published by GoodYearBooks. Copyright © 1994 Sheila Madsen and Bette Gould.

Activities: Flip-Flop Words

1. Choose several flip-flop words. Write short stories in which the flip-flop words repeat themselves, or appear in a pattern, such as in *Rikki-Tikki-Tembo* or *The Three Billy Goats Gruff.*

2. Find flip-flop words that name sounds. Use the words to represent sounds in sentences.

> "Trip-trap, trip-trap" went the boot on the bridge.
> The "click-clack" of the crickets became softer at dawn.

3. Make up story titles that include a flip-flop word and another word that is related by sound or meaning.

> The <u>Wishy-Washy</u> Laundry
> The <u>Jibber-Jabber</u> Gypsies
> The <u>Super-Duper</u> Blooper

4. Several songs have used flip-flop words—perhaps because they have a certain rhythm.

> Splish, Splash, I Was Taking a Bath
> Yakety, Yak, Don't Talk Back
> The Itsy-Bitsy Teeny-Weeny Yellow Polka Dot Bikini

Create some song titles of your own that use flip-flop words. Now write a first stanza for at least one of your song titles.

From *The Teacher's Book of Lists, Second Edition,* published by GoodYearBooks.
Copyright © 1994 Sheila Madsen and Bette Gould.

Proofreader's Symbols

A vital step in the writing process is the fine-tuning that occurs during editing. Often a student will edit with the teacher, or even alone, but perhaps the most profitable editing is done with a peer. Children will enjoy knowing some of the standard proofreading symbols to use in the editing process and, by becoming more conscious of common errors, will improve their own writing. For students who become adept with these symbols, the teacher may wish to provide others, which can be found in manuals of style and proofreaders' guides.

ℛ delete; take ~~something~~ out

⌒ close up with in the line

ℛ delete and close up

∧ insert with caret

spacemark

⌿ Start a new paragraph

no ⌿ no new paragraph

(run in) run in with previous line

(stet) let it stand; do ~~not~~ make correction indicated

∽ transpose

(sp) spell out (abbrev.)

(cap) set in capital letters

(lc) set in Lowercase letter

(lc) set in LOWERCASE letters

(ital) set in italics (like this—*italics*)

(bf) set in boldface (like this—**boldface**)

⊙ period

⋀ comma

⋁ apostrophe

⋀ colon

⋁ ⋁ quotation marks

Name _____   Date _____

Oops!

Practice your proofreading skills with the examples below. The first set of U.S. facts has already been edited. All you have to do is rewrite the sentences correctly according to the proofreader's marks. The second example needs editing. Mark the passage with proofreader's symbols. You should find at least 12 errors.

Tennessee is surrounded by eight states. So it Misouri.

_____

RI would fit into AL more than 500 times.

_____

in the spanish language, the United states is los Estados Unidos.

_____

The state nick name for Hawaii is the Aloha State.

_____

Its a fact said John the highest recorded temperature in the U.S. happened occurred in 1913. It was 134° in Death Valley CA.

_____

From *The Teacher's Book of Lists, Second Edition,* published by GoodYearBooks. Copyright © 1994 Sheila Madsen and Bette Gould.

from Rufus M., *Eleanor Estes. Harcourt, Brace, 1943.*

Rufus M.   Thats the way Rufus wrote his name on his heavy arithmetic paper and on his blue-lined speling paper. Rufus m. went on one side of the paper. His age, seven, went on the other. Rufus had not learned to write his name in School, though that is one place for leanring to write. He had not leaned to write his name at home either, tho that is an other ploce for learning to write. The pace where he had learned to write his name was the library, long ago before he ever went to schoool at all This is the way it happened.

_____

Rebus Words

Whenever a capital block letter appears in the following words, say the letter's name. When a lower case-letter appears, say the letter's sound. For example, [image] for tease and [image] for belt.

are	[image] R	belly [image] E
ate	[image] 8	belt [image] t
be	[image] B or [image]	boat [image] t
beautiful	[image] BUT ful	can [image]
beauty	[image] BUT	cartoon [image]
bee	[image] B	cookie [image] E
bees	[image] BBBB	delight D [image]
before	[image] B4	
belief	[image] B	

eerie [image] E
elbow L [image]
fancy [image] C
for [image] 4
glasses [image] or [image]
handy [image] E

From *The Teacher's Book of Lists, Second Edition*, published by GoodYearBooks. Copyright © 1994 Sheila Madsen and Bette Gould.

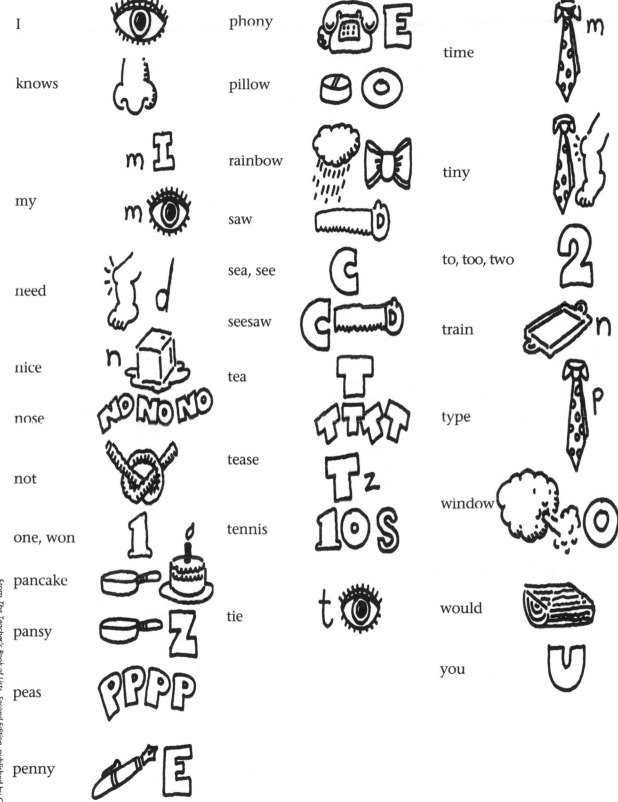

I

knows

my

need

nice

nose

not

one, won

pancake

pansy

peas

penny

phony

pillow

rainbow

saw

sea, see

seesaw

tea

tease

tennis

tie

time

tiny

to, too, two

train

type

window

would

you

 LY    LY   **MARKET**

Read the labels on the shelves. Use rebus words to write product names on the containers. Choose one item and write an advertisement on the Special Sale sign. Use as many rebus words as you can.

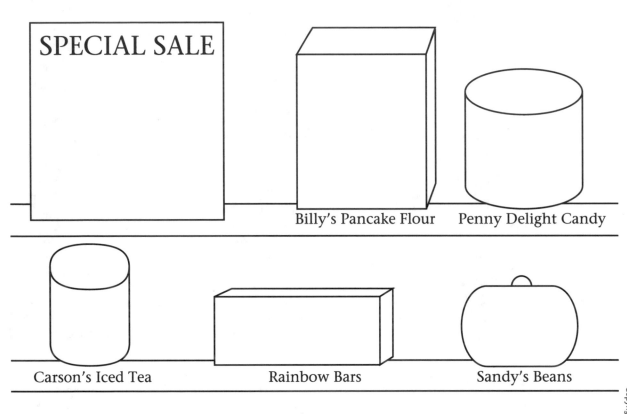

SPECIAL SALE

Billy's Pancake Flour   Penny Delight Candy

Carson's Iced Tea   Rainbow Bars   Sandy's Beans

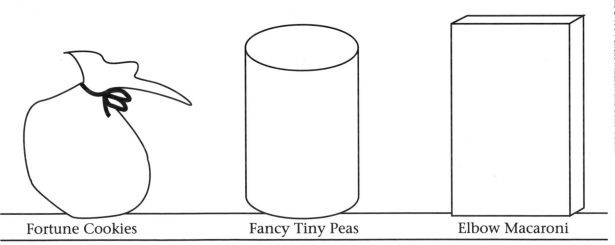

Fortune Cookies   Fancy Tiny Peas   Elbow Macaroni

Similes & Metaphors

Similes and metaphors are expressions of comparison. They differ in that similes always use the words like *or* as*, while metaphors do not. A metaphor is a comparison in which one field of expression is used to say something in another field. For example, to "land" a job uses the language of fishing to relate to job hunting. Students' ability to speak and write descriptively and expressively will be enriched by experience with these forms of imagery.*

Similes

Here are a few that are as "old as the hills."

as big as a house	as light as a feather	as quiet as a mouse
as blind as a bat	as mad as a hornet	as slow as molasses
as busy as a bee	as meek as a lamb	as straight as an arrow
as cool as a cucumber	as neat as a pin	as stubborn as a mule
as easy as pie	as pretty as a picture	as white as a sheet
as flat as a pancake	as quick as a wink	as wise as an owl
as hard as a rock		

Many similes can be found in literature, prose as well as poetry.

> O, my luve is like a red, red rose…
> —from *A Red, Red Rose*, Robert Burns

> I wandered lonely as a cloud…
> —from *Daffodils*, William Wordsworth

> My horse has a hoof like striped agate
> His fetlock is like fine eagle plume
> His legs are like quick lightning…
> —from *The War God's Horse Song*, Navajo Indian

> It is as light as a spider's web…
> —from *The Emperor's New Clothes*, Hans Christian Andersen

> Wisps of old grass stuck up here and there along the pathway like thin wet kittens.
> —from *The Hundred Dresses*, Eleanor Estes. Harcourt, Brace and Company, Inc., 1944.

> He felt like the peanut butter part of a sandwich, squeezed between Mike and Ellen.
> —from *The One in the Middle is the Green Kangaroo*, Judy Blume

Metaphors

the ball's in your court	nip it in the bud	smell a rat
couch potato	paying through the nose	squirrel away
don't make a pig of yourself	play second fiddle	take it on the chin
flood of information	raining cats and dogs	thumbnail sketch
jump the gun	rolling in dough	took the bait hook, line,
main artery of traffic	saved by the bell	and sinker
mean old buzzard	shower with praise	wolf in sheep's clothing

Some metaphors from literature:

> All the world's a stage…
> —from *As You Like It*, William Shakespeare

> The road was a ribbon of moonlight…
> —from *The Highwayman*, Alfred Noyes

> The word-coining genius, as if thought plunged into a sea of words and came up dripping.
> —from *The Common Reader* [1925], *An Elizabethan Play*, Virginia Woolf

> Little soft clouds played happily in a blue sky, skipping from time to time in front of the sun as if they had come to put it out, and then sliding away suddenly so that the next might have his turn.
> —from *Winnie-the-Pooh*, A. A. Milne, E. P. Dutton & Co., Inc., 1926 (with many subsequent reprintings)

A mixed metaphor is made up of two metaphors or a metaphor and another figure of speech. The two parts in a mixed metaphor do not "go together."

> The flood of information nipped her ambitions in the bud.

From *The Teacher's Book of Lists, Second Edition*, published by GoodYearBooks. Copyright © 1994 Sheila Madsen and Bette Gould.

Activities: Similes

1. Select a simile from the list. Write several new versions changing either part of the simile.

> as big as a mountain   as enormous as an elephant

2. Invent similes that are completed by phrases.

> as slippery as a newly polished dance floor
> as easy as turning on the tap

3. Create some comical similes to communicate the opposite meaning.

> as clear as mud (something was not clear at all)
> as heavy as a bag of marshmallows
> as pretty as Frankenstein's mother

4. Develop groups of similes.

> similes for color words: as purple as a royal robe
> similes that use animals as the basis of comparison:
>   as jumpy as a kangaroo
> similes for feeling words: as sad as the kittens who lost
>   their mittens
> similes that name famous people: as tall as Kareem
>   Abdul-jabbar
> similes that are alliterative: as slow as a sloth; as rigid
>   as a robot

5. Make up similes using the word "like." Choose two of your favorites to illustrate.

> A tree is like a chemical factory.
> The catsup oozed across the hamburger like lava trailing
>   down the side of a volcano.

From *The Teacher's Book of Lists, Second Edition,* published by GoodYearBooks.
Copyright © 1994 Sheila Madsen and Bette Gould.

Worksheet

Simile Factory worksheet, p. 81

 **Activities: Metaphors**

1. Write several mixed metaphors using a simile for one part and a metaphor for the other. Select one to use for a poem or story title.

> As Quick as a Wink I Was Saved By the Bell
> Don't Play Second Fiddle to a Couch Potato

2. Read the headlines and sub-heads from the sports section of your newspaper. Highlight or copy down some of the metaphors (and similes) you find. Here are a few examples of headlines from one day's newspaper:

> Marino Scores Knockout Over Seahawks (AP)
> Ditka Steamed After Half-Baked Victory (AP)
> Pirates Clinch National League East (AP)

Make pictures or word descriptions to illustrate what the metaphor is getting at. For example, for the first headline above, you might draw Dan Marino wearing boxing gloves, knocking out the whole Seattle Seahawks team. Display your work.
If you prefer movies to sports, try this activity with the ads for movies in the entertainment pages.

3. On a regularly scheduled basis, hold a Metaphor Marathon Day. Each student in your group or class takes a book of prose or poetry, and compete to find examples of metaphors. Whenever a metaphor is found, write it on the board or on a chart. After the "contest" is over, discuss the imagery of each metaphor and decide whether each is an effective one, or whether it seems trite. Write any effective metaphors in the class "metaphor finder" to use in your own writing and editing.

4. Get inspiration for metaphor creating by observing animals, plants, machines, and people. After a few moments of observing something, close your eyes (and don't think). After a few more moments jot down your impressions of what you saw. You can try the same thing with senses other than sight: try listening to something and jotting down your ideas; taste something slowly and carefully and write your impressions, and so on.

 From *The Teacher's Book of Lists, Second Edition*, published by GoodYearBooks. Copyright © 1994 Sheila Madsen and Bette Gould.

Simile Factory

Take the words through the Simile Factory. Complete each simile according to the directions on each machine.

as funny as cartoons

one word

as old as

as spooky as

as funny as

as loud as

as busy as

person or place

as funny as a clown

any way you wish

at least a four-word phrase

as funny as an elephant in a tree

From *The Teacher's Book of Lists, Second Edition,* published by GoodYearBooks.
Copyright © 1994 Sheila Madsen and Bette Gould.

Synonyms for Common Words

Here are some alternatives for several words overused by children in their stories. Students can look them up and discuss the subtle differences between the words, and use them to enliven the writing and editing of their stories. The list makes a good handout for students to keep in their notebooks. A class project to find other overused words and their synonyms and to chart them for display in the room would be a natural extension from experiences with this list.

run
bolt
chase
dart
flee
gallop
hurry
jog
lope
race
rush
scamper
scoot
scramble
scurry
scuttle
speed
spring
tear
trot

good
acceptable
all right
excellent
first class
great
magnificent
not bad
passable
satisfactory
so-so
super
superb
superior
well-behaved

funny
amusing
comical
hilarious
hysterical
riotous
side-splitting
silly

saw
eyed
gazed at
glimpsed
laid eyes on
noted
noticed
observed
perceived
scrutinized
sighted
spotted
stared at
understood
viewed

cry
bawl
blubber
howl
moan
sniffle
sob
wail
weep
whimper
whine

walk
amble
ambulate
lumber
meander
pace
plod
prance
ramble
saunter
shuffle
stagger
step
stride
stroll
strut
swagger
totter
trek
trudge

beautiful
attractive
comely
divine
exquisite
glamorous
good-looking
gorgeous
handsome
lovely
magnificent
striking

laugh
cackle
chortle
chuckle
crow
giggle
grin
guffaw
hoot
howl
roar
smile
snicker
titter

sad
cheerless
crestfallen
dejected
depressed
despondent
disheartened
dismal
dispirited
downcast
forlorn
joyless
melancholy
miserable
mournful
pitiable
sorrowful
sorry
unhappy
woebegone
woeful
wretched

happy
blissful
blithe
cheerful
delighted
ecstatic
elated
exultant
gay
glad
gleeful
jolly
jovial
joyful
jubilant
lighthearted
mirthful
overjoyed
sunny
thrilled
tickled

From *The Teacher's Book of Lists, Second Edition*, published by GoodYearBooks. Copyright © 1994 Sheila Madsen and Bette Gould.

Synonyms For "Said"

One of the most repetitive words used by children in their writing, said is undescriptive and dull. Once students have had some experience with the wide variety of replacements for the word said, their writing will become more colorful and descriptive. The list is especially useful for partner and group editing sessions.

More Common

added	cheered	exclaimed	nudged	roared
admitted	chuckled	explained	offered	sassed
answered	coaxed	fretted	ordered	sighed
argued	confessed	gasped	panted	smiled
asked	corrected	greeted	pleaded	smirked
babbled	cried	hinted	praised	stammered
bawled	croaked	informed	prayed	stated
bet	crowed	insisted	promised	stuttered
blurted	dared	laughed	questioned	suggested
bragged	decided	lied	quoted	tempted
bugged	declared	murmured	ranted	wailed
called	demanded	muttered	reminded	wept
cautioned	denied	named	replied	whispered
chatted	ended	nodded	requested	wondered
				yelled

Less Common

admonished	claimed	evinced	proffered	simpered
assented	conceded	indicated	projected	speculated
atoned	demurred	jeered	quibbled	sputtered
bantered	denounced	jested	quipped	squelched
bemoaned	disclosed	lamented	quizzed	stipulated
berated	drawled	leered	rebuked	stormed
broached	droned	mocked	rejoiced	theorized
cajoled	enjoined	needled	renounced	vocalized
carped	enumerated	opined	retorted	volunteered
challenged	espoused	outlined	revealed	
cited	estimated	presented	scowled	

Activities: Said

1. Categorize words from the list into groups titled *pleading, anger, laughing, crying, asking,* and *answering*.

2. Write a song title or lyric. Add a phrase to show how it might be said.

"Tie a yellow ribbon 'round the old elm tree," <u>reminded</u> Tony.

3. Make a matching game of statements and words for *said*.

4. Add adverbs or phrases to words used instead of *said* to elaborate on how something is being spoken.

<u>whispered</u> softly   <u>whispered</u> a little too loudly
breathlessly <u>gasped</u>   <u>gasped</u> in a terrified way

5. Reread/edit one of your stories. Look for places where you can substitute a better word for the word *said*. Also find places where you can add descriptive words to *said* and synonyms for *said* to make the story more interesting.

Worksheet

Cartoon Captions worksheet, p. 85

Cartoon Captions

Write a caption for each picture. For each caption choose a statement from column A and a word from column B that tells how the statement is being said. Be sure to punctuate the captions you write.

"Give me some water," gasped the flower.	_____ the chair.
_____ the menu.	_____ the soda pop.
_____ the calculator.	_____ the onion.
_____ the dictionary.	_____ the hamburger.
_____ the telephone.	_____ the refrigerator.

A
Don't forget to close the door
I guess I'll have a straw
Won't you have a seat
Have a bite
Don't cut me with that knife
Your spelling is wrong
I'll have a steak, potato, and a salad
Answer me when I ring
Also, two plus two makes four

B
cried
decided
corrected
called
tempted
ordered
reminded
invited
added

Synonyms for "Said" **85**

Writing Topics

Lists are one way to begin accumulating ideas for stories, often called "story starters." The teacher might want to simply hand out these ideas to students. But a far better approach would be to select items from both the characters and settings lists and create a chart, game, or other activity that would invite student participation. Students might also enjoy adding to either list or adding other columns such as "plots" or "problems."

Characters

a boy or girl who can't keep a secret
an orphan girl
the President
a stubborn princess
a weeping wallaby
a forgetful inventor
a brother and sister who live with their
    grandparents
a stowaway on a spaceship
a family with no TV
an environmental activist
a boy with a magic baseball cap
your own family
a team that has no teamwork
a family with nine children — eight girls
    and one boy
an amateur spy
a child whose parents are divorced
a struggling band
a foreign exchange student with his/her
    host family
you and your best friend
a person shrunk to one-tenth of his/her size
your lost pet
a family that speaks little English
your neighbors
a military person
your classmates
a poor child working to earn money for
    the family

Settings

a sports event
a school of the future
a foreign country
outer space in the future
during the Civil War
a small town
a cellar
a kitchen in a farmhouse
an apartment on the 19th story
a shopping mall
a tropical rain forest
an airplane
the year 2010 in a major city
a cemetery at midnight
a cross-country trip on Route 80
an earthquake at Disneyland
an enchanted forest
a deserted island
a museum
a national park
the 4th of July
your home
during a hurricane
your neighborhood block
a time machine
a village inhabited by talking animals
a place where people work (office,
    store, hospital)
a dream
the year your mother or father was born
an Indian village

CHAPTER

4

Communication

Comic Strips

Many ideas in comic strips are communicated without the use of words. Following are some common comic strip symbols and their usual meanings.

Symbols

confused

unprintable

gloomy or sad

thinking

sleeping

words are coming from telephone, radio, or TV

shivering from fright or cold

an idea

in love

hot or relieved

in a hurry

shiny or bright

in a daze or something has been hit

From *The Teacher's Book of Lists, Second Edition*, published by GoodYearBooks. Copyright © 1994 Sheila Madsen and Bette Gould.

Words

AAAAGII	BZZ-ZT	OOOO-OH	WHAP
AAA-CHOO	CRACK	PHZZZ	WHOMP
AARGH	EEEYAAAA	POOF	WHOOSH
AH-HAAA	GLOM	POW	WHUMP
ARRGGG	HAH	SNIP	WOK
BANG	HA-HA-HA-HA-HA	SPLAM	YEOWW
BLAM	HISS	THUD	YYYYIIII
BOM	KER-PLOP	UGH	ZAK
BONG	KLINK	UNGAAA	ZAP
BONK	KWAM	UNGARRR	
BOO	KWOMP	WHAM	

Facial Expressions

Eyebrows

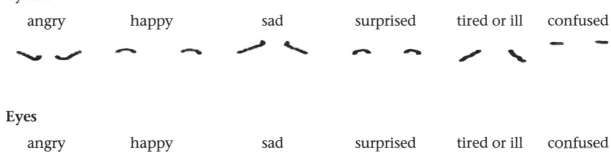

angry   happy   sad   surprised   tired or ill   confused

Eyes

angry   happy   sad   surprised   tired or ill   confused

Mouths

angry   happy   sad   surprised   tired or ill   confused

Faces

angry   happy   ill   confused

Activities: Comic Strips

1. Draw a comic strip using only symbols, facial expressions, and comic strip words to communicate the story.

2. Select several comic strip words. Describe or illustrate situations in which they would be used.

3. Cut out examples from real comic strips to match any of the symbols, facial expressions, or comic strip words on the lists. Display them on a chart or poster.

4. Cut out photographs of people or animals from newspapers and magazines. Label them with appropriate comic strip symbols or words.

5. Write an autobiography or biography of a cartoon character.

6. Keep a journal to summarize a strip day-by-day. How could the strip be written as a story? Are the events connected from day to day, or are they separate?

Worksheet

Comic Cut-up Cards worksheet, p. 93

From *The Teacher's Book of Lists, Second Edition,* published by GoodYearBooks.
Copyright © 1994 Sheila Madsen and Bette Gould.

Comic Cut-Up Cards

Choose three holidays or occasions when you might send greeting cards. Design cards by adding phrases and sentences to the comic strip bubbles. Cut out the bubbles and glue them to the cards. Draw your own if you need more. Add characters and scenery. Cut out your cards and give them to friends.

From *The Teacher's Book of Lists, Second Edition*, published by GoodYearBooks. Copyright © 1994 Sheila Madsen and Bette Gould.

Feeling Words

Exploring the vocabulary of feelings and emotions can lead to richer written and spoken expression. Students at all age levels can participate in related affective experiences once the teacher has selected appropriate words from the following list.

addled
affection
afraid
agitated
altruistic
ambivalent
anger
angst
animosity
annoyed
antagonistic
anxious
apathetic
appreciative
apprehensive
awful

badly
baffled
bashful
belligerent
bewildered
blasé
blissful
bold
bored
brave

calm
carefree
cautious
cheerful
claustrophobic
comfortable
compassion
confident
confused
contrary
cooperative
curious

defeated
defiant
dejected
delight
depressed
despondent
determined
disappointed
discouraged
disgruntled
disgust
distraught
doubt
down

ecstatic
edgy
elated
embarrassed
empathy
encouraged
energetic
enthusiastic
envious
envy
euphoric
exasperated
excited

fearful
flustered
fondness
foolish
fortunate
frantic
frenzied
friendly
frustrated
funny
furious

generous
glad
grateful
guilt

happy
hate
helpful
helpless
hopeful
hopeless
hostile
humiliated
hurt

impulsive
inadequate
indifferent
insecure
irate
irked
irrational
irritated
isolated

jealous
jittery
jolly
joyful
jubilant
jumpy

keyed-up
kind

lackadaisical
lazy
lethargic
light-headed
listless

loathing
lonely
love
loyalty
lucky

mad
merry
mirthful
mischievous
mixed up
moody
mystified

namby-pamby
needed
neglected
nervous

odd
open-minded
optimistic
outrage
overexcited
overjoyed
overwhelmed

pained
patient
peppy
perplexed
pious
pompous
preoccupied
pretty
proud
puzzled

From *The Teacher's Book of Lists, Second Edition*, published by GoodYearBooks. Copyright © 1994 Sheila Madsen and Bette Gould.

quizzical

rejected
reluctance
remorse
resentful
reverent
rotten
rueful

sad
scared
secure
shame
shy
silly
spiteful
stressed
stubborn
supportive
sympathetic

tenderness
tense
terrific
thankful
thrilled
tickled

tired
tranquil
troubled
trust

uncomfortable
undecided
uneasy
unexcited
unhappy
uninterested
unwanted
upbeat
upset

vengeful
vexed
vivacious
vulnerable

wimpy
wonderful
worthless
wrath

yucky

zealous

Activities: Feeling Words

1. Choose ten words from the list that describe feelings you have had before. Write a letter to your best friend telling him/her about the situations you were in when these feelings arose.

2. With another student develop a "Dear Feelicia" column—one strictly devoted to people's feelings. Students write in for advice on feelings issues and you write answers to them.

3. Do animals and plants have feelings? Write sentences about animals and plants and the feelings they seem to express.

> Noel, my dog, was <u>ecstatic</u> when I offered him his bone.
>
> My philodendron plant seemed <u>grateful</u> when I placed it near the window. Its leaves soon turned toward the light.

4. Develop groups of characters for a choral reading. Let each group of characters write their own dialogue, based on a common topic, such as "What I Love About Parties." Practice and then perform the choral reading for your class and other classes.

> The nervous group: Agitated Aggie, Anxious Andrew, Jumpy James
> The shy & timid group: Namby-pamby Nathan, Demure Della
> The angry group: Irate Ira, Defiant Debbie

5. Photograph each of your classmates expressing a different feeling. Remind them to use hands, arms, and legs as well as their faces to show feeling. Exhibit your photos on a bulletin board and let students label the pictures. (If you can't take photos, cut out pictures of people from magazines.)

Worksheet

Feeling Phrases worksheet, p. 97

From *The Teacher's Book of Lists, Second Edition,* published by GoodYearBooks. Copyright © 1994 Sheila Madsen and Bette Gould.

Name _____ Date _____

Feeling Phrases

Complete each feeling phrase by writing in when you have felt that way. Be as descriptive as possible.

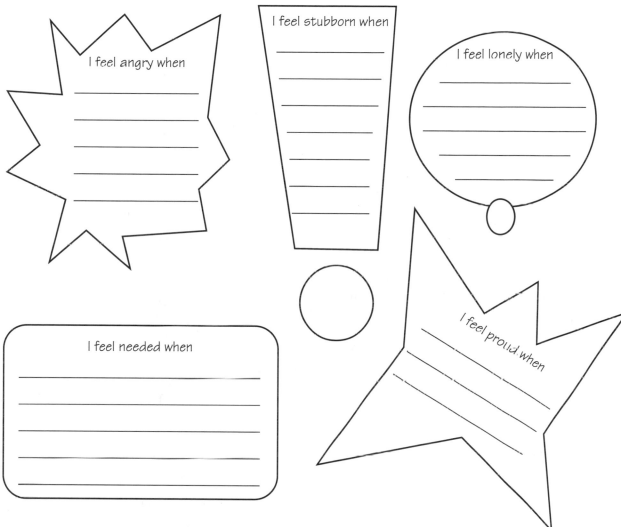

I feel angry when
_____
_____
_____
_____
_____

I feel stubborn when
_____
_____
_____
_____
_____
_____

I feel lonely when
_____
_____
_____
_____

I feel needed when
_____
_____
_____
_____
_____

I feel proud when
_____
_____
_____

Select two words from the Feelings Words list that you don't know. Look in the dictionary, or ask your teacher or another adult to find out what the word means. Write descriptions of when you have felt that way.

I feel _____ when _____
_____

I feel _____ when _____
_____

Foreign Hellos, Goodbyes, Thank Yous

Language	Hello or Good Day	Goodbye
Chinese (Mandarin dialect)	dzǎu	dzàijyàn
Danish	hallo	farvel
Farsi (Iran)	salaam	khoda hafez
French	bon jour	au revoir
German	guten tag	auf Wiedersehen
Hawaiian	aloha	aloha
Hebrew	shalom	shalom
Italian	buon giorno	addio
Japanese	kón-nichi-wa	sayonara
Korean	an nyung ha sae yo	an nyung hee ga sae yo
Polish	hallo	żegnam
Portuguese	alô	adeus
Russian	zdravstvuiyte	do svidaniya
Swahili	neno la kusalimu rafiki au mtani	kwa heri
Spanish	holá	adiós
Swedish	god dag	adjö
Tagalog (Philippines)	kumusta	paalám
Thai	sa wat dee ka	la kone na ka
Vietnamese	õng mang gi'oi khổng	hẹn gắp lạy

From *The Teacher's Book of Lists, Second Edition,* published by GoodYearBooks. Copyright © 1994 Sheila Madsen and Bette Gould.

Language	Thank You	Pronunciation
Chinese (Mandarin dialect)	shieh-shieh	shay-shay
Danish	tak	tahk
French	merci	mare-SEE
German	danke	DAWN-kah
Hawaiian	mahalo	mah-HAW-low
Hebrew	toda	toh-DAH
Italian	grazie	GRAH-tsee
Japanese	arigato	ah-ree-GAW-toh
Korean	gam sa hum nee da	come sah HOOM nee dah
Farsi Iran	moteshakeram	moh-tch-SHANK-keh-rahm
Polish	dziekuje	JEN-kuh-yeh
Portuguese	obrigado	oh-bree-GAH-doh
Russian	spasibo	spah-SEE-bah
Swahili	shukrani	shuk-RON-e
Spanish	gracias	GRA-see-us
Swedish	tack	tahk
Tagalog Phillipines	salamat	sah-lah-MAHT
Thai	kawp-kun krap/ka'	kowpkoom-krahp/khak
Vietnamese	càm 'on nhiêú	cam-on-new

Foreign Phrases

French

á la carte—meal dishes separately priced

au contraire—on the contrary

au courant—up to date

au naturel—in a natural state

au revoir—goodbye

bête noir—pet aversion

bon voyage—have a good journey

cause célebrè—situation arousing attention; noted incident

c'est la vie—that's life

cherchez la femme—a woman caused it (look for the woman)

coup de grâce—final, decisive action

coup d'état—a sudden change in government, often caused by force

crème de la crème—the very best

de rigeur—indispensable; required by fashion or custom

double entendre—double meaning

en masse—as a group

fait accompli—an accomplished and irrevocable fact or action

faux pas—a social error

hors d'ouevre—appetizer

joie de vivre—zest or enthusiasm for the pleasures of life

laissez faire—policy of noninterference

nom de plume—pen name

nouveau riche—newly or recently rich

par excellence—of highest quality

pièce de resistance—major or chief item of a series

raison d'être—reason for being

sans souci—without worry

savoir faire—sophistication: know-how

tour de force—feat of strength or brilliance

vis-à-vis—face to face; in relation to

German

Auf Wiedersehen—Goodbye

Bitte—Please

Bitte schön—Thank you

Danke schön—Thank you

Gesundheit!—used like "bless you" when someone sneezes (literally means health)

Sprechen sie …? —Do you speak …?

Verboten—Forbidden

Was ist los?—What is going on? What's up?

Wie gehts?—How are you?

Wunderbar!—Wonderful!

Wunderkind—genius (literally means wonder child)

Greek

panacea—a cure-all

hoi polloi—the general mass of people

Italian

Arrivederci—Goodbye; see you again

Avanti—Come in

Buona sera—Good evening

Ciao—Bye; goodbye

Per favore—Please

Prego—You're welcome

Scusi—Excuse me; pardon me

From *The Teacher's Book of Lists, Second Edition,* published by GoodYearBooks. Copyright © 1994 Sheila Madsen and Bette Gould.

Latin

ad hoc—for the present situation; temporary

ad infinitum—without limit

ad nauseam—to the point of disgust

alter ego—one's other self; a confidential friend

bona fide—sincere; genuine

caveat emptor—let the buyer beware

ex post facto—after the fact; retroactive

in extremis—near death

in toto—entirely

mea culpa—I'm guilty

modus operandi—method of operation

non sequitur—illogical; conclusion that does not follow from the evidence

persona non grata—an unwelcome or unacceptable person

rara avis—an unusual person or thing

status quo—the situation as is; without change

sub rosa—privately; secretly

tempus fugit—time flies

vox populi—the voice of the people

Spanish

¡Buena suerte!—Good luck!

¿Cómo está usted?—How are you?

¿Dónde está …?—Where is …?

Se habla Español aquí—Spanish spoken here.

Hasta la vista—See you again

Hasta luego—See you later

Muchas gracias—Thank you very much

No entiendo—I don't understand

Por favor—Please

¿Qué pasa?—What's happening? What's going on?

¿Quién sabe?—Who knows?

Vaya con Dios—May God be with you

Yiddish

mazel tov—good luck; congratulations

mish-mash—hodgepodge; mixture

Oy vay!—Oh, pain!; Woe is me!

From *The Teacher's Book of Lists, Second Edition,* published by GoodYearBooks. Copyright © 1994 Sheila Madsen and Bette Gould.

Foreign Words

We have adopted the following words from other languages with only some minor spelling changes. Sometimes the original spelling will appear for its interest value.

African
goober
gumbo
okra
tote
voodoo
yam
zombie

American Indian
canoe
caucus
chipmunk
hickory (pohickery)
hominy
mackinaw
moccasin
moose
opossum
papoose
pecan
persimmon
powwow
raccoon
skunk (segognw)
squash
squaw
succotash
  (msiquatash)
toboggan
tomahawk
totem
wampum
wigwam

Arabic
alcohol
algebra
azimuth
caliph
fakir

genie (jinnī)
harem
hashish
lemon (limun)
magazine
mattress
mufti
muslim
rubaiyat
sahib
sherbet
sofa
tariff
zero

Australian Aborigine
boomerang
kangaroo
kiwi
koala
wombat

Basque
jai alai

Chinese
chop suey
chow mein
gung ho
ketchup
kowtow
kumquat
tea

Dutch
brandy
Bronx
clipper
coleslaw (kool sla)
cruise

gin
Harlem
schooner
sloop
waffle (wafel)
Yonkers

East Indian (Hindi, Sanskrit)
bandana
bungalow
cashmere
cheetah
chintz
chutney
dinghy
dungarees
gunny
guru
jute
karma
loot
madras
polo
pundit
rajah
shampoo
swami
yoga

Egyptian
gum
pharaoh

Eskimo
caribou
kayak

French
amour
au gratin

avant-garde
beret
bistro
bonbon
bourbon
cadet
cadre
café
camaraderie
camouflage
carafe
cartel
champagne
chef
chiffon
cliché
clique
collage
commune
corsage
crêpe
crevasse
critique
crochet
croutons
decor
enclave
entrée
foyer
fuselage
garage
lecture
levee
litre
mademoiselle
masseur
montage
motif
naiveté
parfait
parole

partisan
pastel
penchant
portage
purée
rapport
reprise
revue
ricochet
rouge
roulette
sabotage
saboteur
sauté
savant
suite
timbre
toupee
vignette

German
blitzkrieg
cobalt
dachshund
delicatessen
dumb
edelweiss
fahrenheit
frau
fraulein
hamburger
herr
kaiser
kindergarten
leitmotiv
limburger
loafer
nickel
noodle
poodle
pretzel
pumpernickel
putsch
quartz
riesling
sauerkraut
schnapps
schnitzel
Volkswagen

waltz
wurst

Greek
aphasia
aura
circus
dialect
diaspora
dogma
eureka
genesis
nausea
paranoia
phobia
psyche
psychosis
schema

Haitian
barbecue (barbacoa)
cassava
manioc

Hebrew
amen
cinnamon
  (qinnamon)
hallelujah
jubilee
kibbutz
messiah
rabbi
shalom

Hungarian
coach
goulash
hussar
paprika

Italian
allegro
andante
balcony
balloon
bandit
baroque
bravo

broccoli
cacciatore
cadenza
cameo
cantata
fiasco
fresco
madonna
minestrone
oratorio
pasta
pianissimo
pilot
portico
prima donna
regatta
replica
salvo
sirocco
soprano
staccato
studio
trombone
vibrato
violin

Japanese
geisha
haiku
ju-jitsu
kabuki
kimono
nisei
rickshaw
samurai
soy
tempura
teriyaki
tycoon

Latin
abacus
ad hoc
alias
alibi
alma mater
alumnus
auditor
axis

bacillus
calculus
campus
cancer
dictum
etcetera
extra
forum
fungus
gratis
humus
integer
juxta
per diem
per se
pro rata
quantum
quid pro quo
ratio
recipe
regalia
rostrum
solitaire
spatula
subpoena
symposium
tabula rasa
tibia
toga
trivia
ultra

Malay
amuck
bamboo
caddy
cockatoo
gingham
gong
mango
paddy
sarong

Persian
bazaar
caravan
divan
mogul

shah
shawl

Polish
polka

Polynesian
taboo
tattoo
ukulele

Portuguese
albino
fetish
marmalade
molasses

Russian
intelligentsia
kremlin
pogrom
samovar
steppe
tundra
vodka

Scandinavian
egg
fiord
ill
saga
ski
skin
skirt
smorgasbord

South American Indian
quinine
tapioca
tapir

Spanish
adobe
amigo
banana
bolero
bonanza
bronco
burro
caballero
canyon

chili
cocoa
corral
coyote
fiesta
gaucho
gringo
hombre
junta
lariat
machete
macho
mariachi
marimba
mesa
mesquite
mustang
padre
paella
palomino
patio
plaza
poncho
pueblo
rodeo
señor

sierra
simpatico
sombrero
stampede
tamale
tomato
tortilla
vigilante

Yiddish
bagel
blintzes
chutzpah
kibitzer
kosher
mensch
nosh
schlemiel
schlepp
schmaltz

From *The Teacher's Book of Lists, Second Edition,* published by GoodYearBooks. Copyright © 1994 Sheila Madsen and Bette Gould.

Activities: Foreign Words

1. Categorize words into groups, such as foods, people, clothing, animals, furniture, objects, places, verbs, and adjectives. Do you notice a certain pattern in the types of words we've borrowed from each language?

2. Draw a word origins world map.

3. Make up a story using as many borrowed words as you can.

> Herr Schmidt's <u>broccoli</u> <u>ricocheted</u> across the <u>fiord</u> and landed in <u>Mademoiselle's</u> <u>foyer</u> on top of her <u>moccasins</u>.

4. Use the library and dictionaries to trace the origin and development of several borrowed words.

5. Make up analogies using several of the borrowed words.

> <u>Moccasin</u> is to feet as <u>beret</u> is to head; <u>garage</u> is to <u>Volkswagen</u> as <u>corral</u> is to <u>bronco</u>.

6. Look up borrowed words in a dictionary that lists word etymologies and show the word's spelling and meaning in the original language.

> magazine = makhazin (Arabic)—a storehouse
> sherbet = sharbah (Arabic)—a cool drink
> ketchup = ke-tsiap (Chinese)—a brine from pickled fish, used as sauce

Worksheet

The Borrowed Words Café worksheet, p. 106

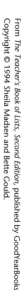

The Borrowed Words Café

Prepare an international menu for the Borrowed Words Café. Combine as many foreign words as you can to name menu items. Write a description for each dish. Fold your menu in half and design a cover.

Appetizers

_____
_____
_____
_____
_____

Entrees

_____
_____
_____
_____
_____

Soups and Salads

_____
_____
_____
_____
_____

Beverages

_____
_____
_____

Desserts

_____
_____
_____
_____
_____

Hand Alphabet

More than 5,000 signs exist in the language of the deaf. To watch two people signing is an intriguing sight for us all. Learning to communicate a few words and phrases gives students a sense of accomplishment as well as an appreciation for people with special needs, such as the deaf. Students can sign their names and simple messages by spelling them letter by letter (finger spelling). Signs for words and phrases illustrate another level of communication with the hands (signing). A beautiful book to use with this activity is Handtalk: An ABC of Finger Spelling & Sign Language, Remy Charlip, Mary Beth, and George Ancona. Four Winds Press, 1974. The elegant, yet whimsical, photographs uniquely convey each word and mirror the beauty of the language.

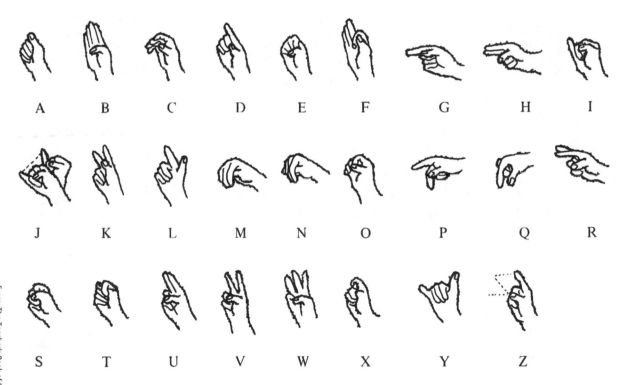

A B C D E F G H I

J K L M N O P Q R

S T U V W X Y Z

PEANUT

BUTTER

AND

JELLY

ICE CREAM

WITH

FRIENDS

KITE

I LOVE YOU

Morse Code

Samuel Morse sent the first telegraph message, "What hath God wrought." Children can transmit their own messages, spelling words, and math problems by tapping with a pencil or by using a telegraph (have your mechanical wizard make one). Another way to practice the code is by using a flashlight—a short flash represents a dot, a long flash stands for a dash. An extra pause is made at the end of each word.

A	• −	P	• − − •	5	• • • • •
B	− • • •	Q	− − • −	6	− • • • •
C	− • − •	R	• − •	7	− − • • •
D	− • •	S	• • •	8	− − − • •
E	•	T	−	9	− − − − •
F	• • − •	U	• • −	0	− − − − −
G	− − •	V	• • • −	period	• − • − • −
H	• • • •	W	• − −	comma	− − • • − −
I	• •	X	− • • −	question mark	• • − − • •
J	• − − −	Y	− • − −	colon	− − − • • •
K	− • −	Z	− − • •	semicolon	− • − • − •
L	• − • •	1	• − − − −	quotation mark	• − • • − •
M	− −	2	• • − −		
N	− •	3	• • • − −		
O	− − −	4	• • • • −		

Some brief forms often used in communications:

AR (end of message)   • − • − •   N (negative - no)   − •

EEEEEE (error)   • • • • • • •   R (message received and understood)   • − •

A (affirmative - yes)   • −   SOS (distress signal)   • • • − − − • • •

From *The Teacher's Book of Lists, Second Edition,* published by GoodYearBooks. Copyright © 1994 Sheila Madsen and Bette Gould.

Referee Signals—
Football and Basketball

Football

Offside

Illegal
Procedure

Illegal
Motion

Intentional
Grounding

Unsportsmanlike Conduct

Clipping

Dead Ball

Touchdown
or Field Goal

Personal Foul

Roughing the Kicker

Illegal Use of
Hands and Arms

Time Out

First Down

Start the Clock

Safety

Illegal Passing
or Handing Ball
Forward

Forward Pass or
Kick-Catching
Interference

Ineligible
Receiver Down
Field on Pass

Ball Illegally
Touched, Kicked,
or Batted

Incomplete Forward
Pass, Penalty
Declined,
No Play,
or No Score

From *The Teacher's Book of Lists, Second Edition,* published by GoodYearBooks.
Copyright © 1994 Sheila Madsen and Bette Gould.

Basketball

Personal Foul

Illegal Use of Hands

Pushing

Player Control Foul

Holding

Technical Foul

Traveling

Illegal Dribble

Cancel Score

Time Out

From *The Teacher's Book of Lists, Second Edition*, published by GoodYearBooks.
Copyright © 1994 Sheila Madsen and Bette Gould.

Signs & Symbols

Signs and symbols communicate information and directions in a universal pictorial language often without words. Some signs have remained unchanged over the decades; others have gone through minor changes presenting a sleeker, cleaner look. Signs reflect issues of the times. Today, for example, No Smoking and Recycle signs proliferate, while Air Raid Shelter signs are hard to find.

From *The Teacher's Book of Lists, Second Edition,* published by GoodYearBooks. Copyright © 1994 Sheila Madsen and Bette Gould.

U.S. MAIL

Activities: Signs & Symbols

1. With a group of students, build a city using blocks, boxes, or other items. Cut and glue signs from the list to cardboard and place them in appropriate locations. Draw a map, including signs, of your city.

2. Add words or rewrite the words on signs in another language.

3. *Recycle* and *Wheel Chair Access* are fairly recent signs. Design signs we may soon be seeing and signs for very futuristic situations. Display them on a bulletin board. Here are some ideas:

> No hovering by spacecraft allowed
>
> Robot recharging
>
> FAX machine available here
>
> One world, one environment
>
> No dolphin riding

4. Lay out a main street in another country. Design shop signs with words and symbols.

5. Redesign a sign or symbol in the style of an art period such as Art Nouveau, Dada, or in the style of an artist or illustrator such as Picasso, Warhol, or Sendak.

CHAPTER

5

Literature

Authors & Addresses

What better way to say, "I really liked this book!" than to write a letter to the author. Not all authors and illustrators have the time to reply to their young fans—some reply personally (really!), some send a form letter, and some send nothing at all. But how exciting when a child does receive a letter back. Listed here is a sampling of popular authors and illustrators of children's books, their addresses, and two of their book titles. A few addresses are home addresses, and since people do move, don't be disappointed if the letters are returned—they can be remailed to the author at his or her publisher's address.

To reach other authors, send letters in care of their publishers, or contact the children's reference section of the main branch of your public library. Children's librarians are an invaluable source and can often provide information and addresses of authors who live in your area. One other note: Many authors and illustrators will visit your community. Write or call the Children's Book Council, 568 Broadway, Suite 404, New York, NY 10012, telephone (212) 966-1990, for information.

Reading levels for books are indicated as follows:

        P—preschool and primary
        I —intermediate
        A—advanced

Sue Alexander
6846 McLaren
Canoga Park, CA 91307
  World Famous Muriel   I
  Witch, Goblin, and Sometimes Ghost   P

Joan Blos
1725 South University Avenue
Ann Arbor, MI 48104
  Martin's Hats   P
  Old Henry   P-I

Betsy Byars
4 Riverpoint
Clemson, SC 29631
  The Not-Just-Anybody Family   I
  Beans on the Roof   P-I

Beverly Cleary
c/o William Morrow, Inc.
105 Madison Avenue
New York, NY 10016
  Henry Huggins   I
  Ramona the Pest   I

Lucille Clifton
Coppin State College
2500 West North Avenue
Baltimore, MD 21216
  Everett Anderson's Goodbye   I
  Everett Anderson's Nine Month Long   I

Tomie dePaola, illustrator
c/o Holiday House, Inc.
18 East 53rd Street
New York, NY 10022
  Giorgio's Village   P-I
  The Art Lesson   P-I

Steven Kellogg, illustrator
Bennett's Bridge
Sandy Hook, CT 06482
  The Day Jimmy's Boa Ate the Wash   P-I
  Paul Bunyan   P-I

Joan Lexau
c/o Hastings House
10 East 40th Street
New York, NY 10016
Benjie   P
I Hate Red Rover   P

Arnold Lobel
c/o Greenwillow Books
105 Madison Avenue
New York, NY 10016
A Treeful of Pigs   P-I-A
Mouse Soup   P-I-A

Lois Lowry
34 Mt. Vernon Street
Boston, MA 02108
Number the Stars   I-A
Anastasia Krupnik   I

David Macauley, author and illustrator
27 Rhode Island Avenue
Providence, RI 02906
Underground   I-A
The Way Things Work   I-A

Patricia MacLachlan
c/o HarperCollins
10 East 53rd Street
New York, NY 10022
Arthur, for the Very First Time   I
The Facts and Fictions of Minna Pratt   I

Katherine Paterson
c/o Cromwell Junior Books
10 East 53rd Street
New York, NY 10022
Come Sing, Jimmy Jo   I
Jacob Have I Loved   A

Susan Patron
c/o Children's Services
Los Angeles Public Library
630 West Fifth Street
Los Angeles, CA 90071
Burgoo Stew   P-I
The Five Bad Boys, Billy Que, and the Dust Dobin   P-I

Marilyn Sachs
733 31st Avenue
San Francisco, CA 94121
The Bears' House   I
Fran Ellen's House   I

Maurice Sendak, author and illustrator
c/o HarperCollins
10 East 53rd Street
New York, NY 10022
The Bat-Poet   P-I
Nutshell Library   P-I

Shel Silverstein, author and illustrator
c/o HarperCollins
10 East 53rd Street
New York, NY 10022
A Light in the Attic   P-I
Where the Sidewalk Ends: Poems & Drawings
P-I

Mildred Taylor
c/o Dial Press
1 Dag Hammarskjold Plaza
245 East 47th Street
New York, NY 10017
Roll of Thunder, Hear My Cry   I
Song of the Trees   I

Judith Viorst
c/o Simon & Schuster
1230 6th Avenue
New York, NY 10020
Alexander and the Terrible, Horrible, No Good, Very Bad Day   P-I
Alexander Who Used to Be Rich Last Sunday
P-I

Cynthia Voight
The Key School
534 Carroll Drive
Annapolis, MD 21403
Homecoming   I-A
Dicey's Song   I-A

Laurence Yep
921 Populus Place
Sunnyvale, CA 94086
Dragonwings   I-A
The Rainbow People   I-A

SOME CHILDREN'S BOOK PUBLISHERS

Atheneum Publishers
966 3rd Avenue
New York, NY 10022

Carolrhoda Books
241 First Avenue North
Minneapolis, MN 55401

Clarion Books
215 Park Avenue South
New York, NY 10003

Dial Books for Young Readers
375 Hudson Street
New York, NY 10014

Little, Brown & Company
34 Beacon Street
Boston, MA 02108

Mulberry Books
1350 Avenue of the Americas
New York, NY 10019

Scholastic Books
730 Broadway
New York, NY 10003

From *The Teacher's Book of Lists, Second Edition*, published by GoodYearBooks.
Copyright © 1994 Sheila Madsen and Bette Gould.

Activities: Book Lists

Following are several lists of award-winning books and books arranged by topic. Use the lists to select read-aloud stories, as a resource for thematic units such as Change or Relationships, or in subject-oriented units such as, (in social studies) "Life During Wartime," or "City and Country Families." Copying one or more of the lists and displaying them in the classroom allows children to make their own selections of good books to read.

The lists are also useful as parent handouts to introduce them to the wide range of children's literature and to assist them in purchasing books or selecting books from the library.

Refer to other sections in this book for anthologies and book lists that provide additional categories and expansions to the lists in this section. (See **Home References**, p. 359 and **Prose and Poetry Forms**, p. 151.)

Worksheet

Reading Log worksheet, p. 142

Task Cards (teacher directions)

Reading Task Cards, p. 143–146

Prepare the task cards by duplicating on card stock or cutting and gluing to 5" x 8" index cards. Students' selection of a given card may be based on their interest or the teacher may choose a card to focus on a skill under study. Display cards in a box, on a chart ring, on a bulletin board, or on a pocket chart.

Learning centers can be developed around the idea of open-ended tasks related to any book to encourage students in an independent reading program. Make sure you also provide areas to display student products.

Caldecott Award Winners

The first Caldecott Medal, donated by Frederick G. Melcher, was awarded to the artist of the most distinguished American picture book for children published in the United States during the preceding year. The medal was named for Randolph Caldecott, a famous English illustrator of children's books.

1938   **Animals of the Bible, a Picture Book**
Illustrated by Dorothy P. Lathrop.
Text by Helen Dean Fish.
(Lippincott)

1939   **Mei Li**
Thomas Handforth (Doubleday)

1940   **Abraham Lincoln**
Ingri and Edgar D'Aulaire
(Doubleday)

1941   **They Were Strong and Good**
Robert Lawson (Viking)

1942   **Make Way for Ducklings**
Robert McCloskey (Viking)

1943   **The Little House**
Virginia Lee Burton
(Houghton Mifflin)

1944   **Many Moons**
James Thurber
Illustrated by Louis Slobodkin
(Harcourt Brace)

1945   **Prayers for a Child**
Rachel Field
Illustrated by Elizabeth Orton
Jones (Macmillan)

1946   **The Rooster Crows**
Maud and Miska Petersham
(Macmillan)

1947   **The Little Island**
Golden MacDonald
Illustrated by Leonard Weisgard
(Doubleday)

1948   **White Snow, Bright Snow**
Alvin Tresselt
Illustrated by Roger Duvoisin
(Lothrop, Lee & Shepard)

1949   **The Big Snow**
Berta and Elmer Hader
(Macmillan)

1950   **Song of the Swallows**
Leo Politi (Scribner)

1951   **The Egg Tree**
Katherine Milhous (Scribner)

1952   **Finders Keepers**
Illustrated by Nicolas Mordvinoff
(Harcourt Brace)

1953   **The Biggest Bear**
Lynd Ward (Houghton Mifflin)

1954   **Madeline's Rescue**
Ludwig Bemelmans (Viking)

1955   **Cinderella, or the Little Glass Slipper**
Illustrated and translated from
Perrault by Marcia Brown
(Scribner)

1956   **Frog Went A-Courtin'**
Retold by John Langstaff
Illustrated by Feodor Rojankovsky
(Harcourt Brace)

1957   **A Tree Is Nice**
Janice May Udry
Illustrated by Marc Simont
(Harper & Row)

1958   **Time of Wonder**
Robert McCloskey (Viking)

1959   **Chanticleer and the Fox**
Adapted from Chaucer's *The
Canterbury Tales* and illustrated
by Barbara Cooney
(T. Y. Crowell)

1960   **Nine Days to Christmas**
Marie Hall Ets and Aurora
Labastida
Illustrated by Marie Hall Ets
(Viking)

1961   **Baroushka and the Three Kings**
Ruth Robbins
Illustrated by Nicolas Sidjakov
(Parnassus)

1962	**Once Upon a Mouse** Retold and Illustrated by Marcia Brown (Scribner)	1978	**Noah's Ark** Peter Spier (Doubleday)

1962 **Once Upon a Mouse**
Retold and Illustrated by Marcia
Brown (Scribner)

1963 **The Snowy Day**
Ezra Jack Keats (Viking)

1964 **Where the Wild Things Are**
Maurice Sendak (Harper & Row)

1965 **May I Bring a Friend?**
Beatrice Schenk de Regniers
Illustrated by Beni Montresor
(Atheneum)

1966 **Always Room for One More**
Sorche Nic Leodhas
Illustrated by Nonny Hogrogian
(Holt)

1967 **Sam, Bangs & Moonshine**
Evaline Ness (Holt)

1968 **Drummer Hoff**
Adapted by Barbara Emberley
Illustrated by Ed Emberley
(Prentice-Hall)

1969 **The Fool of the World and the
Flying Ship**
Retold by Arthur Ransome
Illustrated by Uri Shulevitz (Farrar)

1970 **Sylvester and the Magic Pebble**
Wiliam Steig (Windmill Books)

1971 **A Story, a Story**
Gail E. Haley (Atheneum)

1972 **One Fine Day**
Nonny Hogrogian (Macmillan)

1973 **The Funny Little Woman**
Lafcadio Hearn, retold by Arlene
Mosel
Illustrated by Blair Lent (Dutton)

1974 **Duffy and the Devil**
Retold by Harve Zemach
Pictures by Margo Zemach (Farrar)

1975 **Arrow to the Sun**
Gerald McDermott (Viking)

1976 **Why Mosquitoes Buzz in
People's Ears**
Retold by Verna Aardema
Pictures by Leo and Diane Dillon
(Dial)

1977 **Ashanti to Zulu**
Margaret Musgrove
Pictures by Leo and Diane Dillon
(Dial)

1978 **Noah's Ark**
Peter Spier (Doubleday)

1979 **The Girl Who Loved Wild
Horses**
Paul Goble (Bradbury)

1980 **Ox-Cart Man**
Text by Donald Hall
Pictures by Barbara Cooney
(Viking)

1981 **Fables**
Arnold Lobel (Harper)

1982 **Jumanji**
Chris Van Allsburg (Houghton)

1983 **Shadow**
Blaise Cendrars
Translated and illustrated by
Marcia Brown (Scribner)

1984 **The Glorious Flight: Across the
Channel with Louis Biériot**
Alice and Martin Provensen
(Viking)

1985 **Saint George and the Dragon**
Retold by Margaret Hodges
Illustrated by Trina Schart Hyman
(Little, Brown)

1986 **The Polar Express**
Chris Van Allsburg (Houghton)

1987 **Hey, Al**
Arthur Yorinks
Illustrated by Richard Egielski
(Farrar)

1988 **Owl Moon**
Jane Yolen
Illustrated by John Schoenherr
(Philomel)

1989 **Song and Dance Man**
Karen Ackerman
Illustrated by Stephen Gammell
(Knopf)

1990 **Lon Po Po**
Ed Young (Philomel)

1991 **Black and White**
David Macaulay (Houghton)

1992 **Tuesday**
David Wiesner (Clarion Books)

Coretta Scott King Award Winners

This annual award, established in 1969, is to honor the life and words of Dr. Martin Luther King, Jr., to honor Mrs. King and her work, and to encourage artists, authors, and children to work towards the cause of peace and brotherhood. The award is presented at the American Library Association convention. Starting in 1979, an additional award has been made for illustration.

1970 **Martin Luther King, Jr.: Man of Peace**
Lillie Patterson (Garrard)

1971 **Black Troubador: Langston Hughes**
Charlemae Rollins (Rand)

1972 **Seventeen Black Artists**
Elton Clay Fax (Dodd)

1973 **I Never Had It Made**
Jackie Robinson as told to Alfred Duckett (Putnam)

1974 **Ray Charles**
Sharon Bell Mathis (Crowell)

1975 **The Legend of Africania**
Dorothy Robinson (Johnson)

1976 **Duey's Tale**
Pearl Bailey (Harcourt)

1977 **The Story of Stevie Wonder**
James Haskins (Lothrop)

1978 **African Dream**
Eloise Greenfield (Day)

1979 **Escape to Freedom: A Play About Young Frederick Douglass**
Ossie Davis (Viking)

1979 **Illustration**
Something on My Mind
Nikki Grimes, illustrated by Tom Feelings (Dial)

1980 **The Young Landlords**
Walter D. Myers (Viking)

1980 **Illustration**
Corn Rows
Camile Yarbrough, illustrated by Carole Byard (Coward)

1981 **This Life**
Sidney Poitier (Knopf)

1981 **Illustration**
Beat the Story-drum, Pum-pum
Ashley Bryan (Atheneum)

1982 **Let the Circle Be Unbroken**
Mildred D. Taylor (Dial)

1982 **Illustration**
Mother Crocodile—Maman Caiman
Birago Diop, illustrated by John Steptoe (Delacorte)

1983 **Sweet Whisper, Brother Rush**
Virginia Hamilton (Philomel)

1983 **Illustration**
Black Child
Peter Magubane (Knopf)

1984	**Everett Anderson's Goodbye** Lucille Clifton (Holt)	1988	**Illustration** **Mufaro's Beautiful Daughters** John Steptoe (Lothrop)

1984 **Everett Anderson's Goodbye**
Lucille Clifton (Holt)

1984 **Illustration**
My Mama Needs Me
Mildred Pitts Walter, illustrated by
Pat Cummings (Lothrop)

1984 **Special Citation**
**The Words of Martin Luther
King, Jr.**
selected by Coretta Scott King
(Newmarket Press)

1985 **Motown and Didi**
Walter Dean Myers (Viking Kestrel)

1985 **Illustration—no award**

1986 **The People Could Fly**
Virginia Hamilton (Knopf)

1986 **Illustration**
The Patchwork Quilt
Valerie Flournoy, illustrated by
Leo and Diane Dillon (Knopf)

1987 **Justin and the Best Biscuits in
the World**
Mildred Pitts Walter (Lothrop)

1987 **Illustration**
Half a Moon and One Whole Star
Crescent Dragonwagon, illustrated
by Jerry Pinkney (Macmillan)

1988 **The Friendship**
Mildred D. Taylor (Dial)

1988 **Illustration**
Mufaro's Beautiful Daughters
John Steptoe (Lothrop)

1989 **Fallen Angels**
Walter Dean Myers (Scholastic)

1989 **Illustration**
Mirandy and Brother Wind
Patricia C. McKissack, illustrated
by Jerry Pinkney (Knopf)

1990 **A Long Hard Journey: The Story
of the Pullman Porter**
Patricia & Fredrick McKissack
(Walker)

1990 **Illustration**
Nathaniel Talking
Eloise Greenfield, illustrated by
Jan Spivey Gilchrist (Black
Butterfly)

1991 **The Road to Memphis**
Mildred D. Taylor (Dial)

1991 **Illustration**
Aïda
Leo and Diane Dillon (HBJ)

1992 **Now Is Your Time: The African
American Struggle for
Freedom**
Walter Dean Myers (HarperCollins)

1992 **Illustration**
Tar Beach
Faith Ringgold (Crown)

From *The Teacher's Book of Lists, Second Edition,* published by GoodYearBooks.
Copyright © 1994 Sheila Madsen and Bette Gould.

Edgar Award Winners

The Edgar Allan Poe Award was established by the Mystery Writers of America in 1945. The award has numerous categories. The best juvenile mystery award was first presented in 1961. The winning author receives a ceramic bust of Poe, known as the Edgar.

1961 **The Mystery of the Haunted Pool**
Phyllis A. Whitney
Illustrated by H. Tom Hall (Holt)

1962 **The Phantom of Walkaway Hill**
Edward Fenton
Illustrated by Jo Ann Stover (Doubleday)

1963 **Cutlass Island**
Scott Corbett
Illustrated by Leonard Shortall (Atlantic-Little)

1964 **The Mystery of the Hidden Hand**
Phyllis A. Whitney
Illustrated by H. Tom Hall (Westminster)

1965 **The Mystery at Crane's Landing**
Marcella Thum (Dodd Mead)

1966 **The Mystery of 22 East**
Leon Ware (Westminster)

1967 **Sinbad and Me**
Kin Platt (Chilton)

1968 **Signpost to Terror**
Gretchen Sprague (Dodd Mead)

1969 **The House of Dies Drear**
Virginia Hamilton
Illustrated by Eros Keith (Macmillan)

1970 **Danger at Black Dyke**
Written and illustrated by Winifred Finlay (Phillips)

1971 **The Intruder**
John Rowe Townsend
Illustrated by Joseph A. Phelan (Lippincott)

1972 **Night Fall**
Joan Aiken (Holt)

1973 **Deathwatch**
Robb White (Doubleday)

1974 **The Long Black Coat**
Jay Bennett (Delacorte)

1975 **The Dangling Witness: A Mystery**
Jay Bennett (Delacorte)

1976 **Z for Zachariah**
Robert C. O'Brien (Atheneum)

1977 **Are You in the House Alone?**
Richard Peck (Viking)

1978 **A Really Weird Summer**
Eloise Jarvis McGraw (Atheneum)

1979 **Alone in Wolf Hollow**
Dana Brookins (Seabury)

1980 **Kidnapping of Christine Lattimore**
Joan Lowery Nixon (Harcourt)

1981	**The Seance** Joan Lowery Nixon (Harcourt)	1987	**The Other Side of Dark** Joan Lowery Nixon (Delacorte)
1982	**Taking Terri Mueller** Norma Fox Mazer (Avon)	1988	**Lucy Forever and Miss Rosetree,** **Shirinks** Susan Shreve (Henry Holt)
1983	**The Murder of Hound Dog** **Bates: A Novel** Robbie Branscum (Viking)	1989	**Megan's Island** Willo Davis Roberts (Atheneum)
1984	**The Callendar Papers** Cynthia Voigt (Atheneum)	1990	none
1985	**Night Cry** Phyllis Reynolds Naylor (Atheneum)	1991	**Stonewords** Pam Conrad (Harper & Row)
1986	**The Sandman's Eyes** Patricia Windsor (Delacorte)	1992	**Wanted. . .Mud Blossom** Betsy Byars (Delacorte)

Newbery Award Winners

The Newbery Medal was named after John Newbery, an 18th century bookseller. It was first given in 1921, by Frederic G. Melcher, as an incentive for better quality in children's books. The Medal is donated annually to the author of the most distinguished contribution to American literature for children published during the preceding year. Copies of award lists can be given to parents to use as a reference for selecting books for home use or purchase.

1922	**The Story of Mankind** Hendrik Willem van Loon (Liveright)	1938	**The White Stag** Kate Seredy (Viking)
1923	**The Voyages of Doctor Dolittle** Hugh Lofting (Lippincott)	1939	**Thimble Summer** Elizabeth Enright (Holt, Rinehart & Winston)
1924	**The Dark Frigate** Charles Hawes (Little Brown)	1940	**Daniel Boone** James Daugherty (Viking)
1925	**Tales from Silver Lands** Charles Finger (Doubleday)	1941	**Call It Courage** Armstrong Sperry (Macmillan)
1926	**Shen of the Sea** Arthur Bowie Chrisman (Dutton)	1942	**The Matchlock Gun** Walter D. Edmonds (Dodd, Mead)
1927	**Smoky, the Cowhorse** Will James (Scribner)	1943	**Adam of the Road** Elizabeth Janet Gray (Viking)
1928	**Gayneck, the Story of a Pigeon** Dhan Gopal Mukerji (Dutton)	1944	**Johnny Tremaine** Esther Forbes (Houghton Mifflin)
1929	**The Trumpeter of Krakow** Eric P. Kelly (Macmillan)	1945	**Rabbit Hill** Robert Lawson (Viking)
1930	**Hitty, Her First Hundred Years** Rachel Field (Macmillan)	1946	**Strawberry Girl** Louis Lenski (Lippincott)
1931	**The Cat Who Went to Heaven** Elizabeth Coatsworth (Macmillan)	1947	**Miss Hickory** Carolyn Sherwin Bailey (Viking)
1932	**Waterless Mountain** Laura Adams Armer (Longmans Green)	1948	**The Twenty-One Balloons** William Pene du Bois (Viking)
1933	**Young Fu of the Upper Yangtze** Elizabeth Lewis (Holt, Rinehart & Winston)	1949	**King of the Wind** Marguerite Henry (Rand McNally)
1934	**Invincible Louisa** Cornelia Meigs (Little, Brown)	1950	**The Door in the Wall** Marguerite de Angeli (Doubleday)
1935	**Dobry** Monica Shannon (Viking)	1951	**Amos Fortune, Free Man** Elizabeth Yates (Aladdin)
1936	**Caddie Woodlawn** Carol Brink (Macmillan)	1952	**Ginger Pye** Eleanor Estes (Harcourt Brace Jovanovich)
1937	**Roller Skates** Ruth Sawyer (Viking)	1953	**Secret of the Andes** Ann Nolan Clark (Viking)

1954	**...And Now Miguel** Joseph Krumgold (T. Y. Crowell)	1972	**Mrs. Frisby and the Rats of NIMH** Robert O'Brien (Atheneum)

1954 **...And Now Miguel**
Joseph Krumgold (T. Y. Crowell)

1955 **The Wheel on the School**
Meindert De Jong (Harper & Row)

1956 **Carry On, Mr. Bowditch**
Jean Lee Latham
(Houghton Mifflin)

1957 **Miracles on Maple Hill**
Virginia Sorensen
(Harcourt Brace Jovanovich)

1958 **Rifles for Watie**
Harold Keith (T. Y. Crowell)

1959 **The Witch of Blackbird Pond**
Elizabeth George Speare
(Houghton Mifflin)

1960 **Onion John**
Joseph Krumgold (T. Y. Crowell)

1961 **Island of the Blue Dolphins**
Scott O'Dell (Houghton Mifflin)

1962 **The Bronze Bow**
Elizabeth George Speare
(Houghton Mifflin)

1963 **A Wrinkle in Time**
Madeleine L'Engle
(Farrar, Straus & Giroux)

1964 **It's Like This Cat**
Emily Neville (Harper & Row)

1965 **Shadow of a Bull**
Maia Wojciechowska (Atheneum)

1966 **I, Juan de Pareja**
Elizabeth (Borten) de Trevino
(Farrar, Straus & Giroux)

1967 **Up a Road Slowly**
Irene Hunt (Follett)

1968 **From the Mixed-Up Files of Mrs.
Basil E. Frankweiler**
E. L. Konigsburg (Atheneum)

1969 **The High King**
Lloyd Alexander
(Holt, Rinehart & Winston)

1970 **Sounder**
William Armstrong
(Harper & Row)

1971 **The Summer of the Swans**
Betsy Byars (Viking)

1972 **Mrs. Frisby and the Rats
of NIMH**
Robert O'Brien (Atheneum)

1973 **Julie of the Wolves**
Jean Craighead George (Harper)

1974 **The Slave Dancer**
Paula Fox (Bradbury)

1975 **M. C. Higgins, the Great**
Virginia Hamilton (Macmillan)

1976 **The Grey King**
Susan Cooper (Atheneum)

1977 **Roll of Thunder, Hear My Cry**
Mildred D. Taylor (Dial Press)

1978 **Bridge to Terabithia**
Katherine Paterson (Crowell)

1979 **The Westing Game**
Ellen Raskin (Dutton)

1980 **A Gathering of Days**
Joan W. Blos (Scribner)

1981 **Jacob Have I Loved**
Katherine Paterson (Crowell)

1982 **A Visit to William Blake's Inn:
Poems for Innocent and
Experienced Travelers**
Nancy Willard (Harcourt)

1983 **Dicey's Song**
Cynthia Voight (Atheneum)

1984 **Dear Mr. Henshaw**
Beverly Cleary (Morrow)

1985 **The Hero and the Crown**
Robin McKinley (Greenwillow)

1986 **Sarah, Plain and Tall**
Patricia MacLachlan (Harper)

1987 **The Whipping Boy**
Sid Fleischman (Greenwillow)

1988 **Lincoln: A Photobiography**
Russell Freedman (Clarion)

1989 **Joyful Noise: Poems for Two
Voices**
Paul Fleischman (Harper)

1990 **Number the Stars**
Lois Lowry (Houghton)

1991 **Maniac Magee**
Jerry Spinelli (Little, Brown)

1992 **Shiloh**
Phyllis Reynolds Naylor
(Atheneum)

From *The Teacher's Book of Lists, Second Edition,* published by GoodYearBooks.
Copyright © 1994 Sheila Madsen and Bette Gould.

Topical Reading Lists

This collection of lists includes contemporary as well as classic literature categorized into current topics affecting the lives of children as well as age-old themes, such as courage, friendship, and responsibility. The classic stories, set in their historic time periods, are some of the best and are still relevant to the feelings and problems of children today.

Reading levels for books are indicated as follows:

        P—preschool and primary
        I —intermediate
        A—advanced

ADOPTION/ORPHAN

Burnish Me Bright   I-A
Julia Cunningham, illustrated by Don Freeman. Pantheon, 1970.
    A mute orphan boy is drawn out of his loneliness by a friendship with a famous mime.

The Finding   I-A
Nina Bawden. Dell, 1985.
    An 11-year-old adopted child gets an unexpected inheritance and decides to run away from home.

Maniac Magee   A
Jerry Spinelli. Little, Brown, 1990.
    Maniac, an orphan, changes people's lives in this part tall tale, part contemporary fiction story.

Me, Mop, and the Moondance Kid   A
Walter Dean Myers. Delacorte, 1988.
    "Mop" Parrish wants to be a Little League star in hopes that she will be adopted by her coaches.

Pippi Longstocking   I-A
Astrid Lindgren. Viking, 1950.
    Pippi lives alone, except for her monkey and horse.

Through Moon and Stars and Night Sky   P
Ann Warren Turner, illustrated by James Graham Hale. HarperCollins, 1990.
    Story of the arrival of an adopted Asian child.

AGING & DEATH

Annie and the Old One   P-I
Miska Miles. Little, Brown, 1971.
    Annie learns to accept her grandmother's impending death.

AGING & DEATH (cont.)

Beat the Turtle Drum   I
Constance C. Green. Viking, 1976.
　Kate's beloved younger sister dies in a freak accident and
　her world is turned upside down.

Blackberries in the Dark   I
Mavis Jukes. Knopf, 1985.
　After Grandpa dies, visiting Grandma isn't the same for
　Austin, until one unforgettable night of talk and fishing.

Child of the Owl   A
Laurence Yep. Harper Junior Books, 1977.
　A young Chinese girl living with her grandmother in
　Chinatown discovers who she really is.

A Figure of Speech   I-A
Norma Fox Mazer. Delacorte, 1973.
　Jenny tries to protect her elderly grandfather from her
　family's ridicule and abuse.

Grandma Didn't Wave Back   I-A
Rose Blue, illustrated by Ted Lewin. Watts, 1972.
　Debbie watches as her grandmother slips into senility.

Maxie   P-I
Mildred Kantrowitz. Parents Magazine Press, 1970.
　Maxie, a woman who believes no one needs her, comes to
　realize her importance to others.

My Brother Sam Is Dead   A
James L. and Christopher Collier. Scholastic, 1974.
　A son joins the rebel forces during the American
　Revolutionary War.

My Grandson Lew   P
Charlotte Zolotow. Harper, 1974.
　Lew recalls Grandpa with his mother after Grandpa's
　death.

Nadia the Willful   I
Sue Alexander. Pantheon, 1983.
　A universal story, in a Bedouin setting, of a girl losing
　her beloved brother and alleviating her grief by
　remembering.

Sadako and the Thousand Paper Cranes   I-A
Eleanor B. Coerr. Putnam, 1977.
　True story of Sadako, a Japanese girl dying of leukemia
　after Hiroshima's bombing.

AGING & DEATH (cont.)

A Taste of the Blackberries   I
Doris Buchanan Smith, illustrated by Charles Robinson.
  Crowell, 1973.
  A young boy's best friend dies from a bee sting.

The Tenth Good Thing About Barney   P
Judith Viorst, illustrated by Erik Blegvad. Atheneum, 1971.
  When Barney the cat dies, his owner tries to think about
    all the good things about Barney and to accept the
    death of his pet.

The Wall   I
Eve Bunting. Clarion, 1990.
  A boy and his father visit the Vietnam Veterans Memorial
    to find the name of the boy's grandfather.

COMING OF AGE

...And Now Miguel   I-A
Joseph Krumgold, illustrated by Jean Charlot. Crowell, 1953.
  A boy in a New Mexican sheepherding family fervently
    wishes to go to the mountains with the men and the
    herds.

Bar Mitzvah   A
Howard Greenfield. Holt, 1981.
  Nonfiction; story of the meaning of the Bar and Bat Mitzvah.

Leo the Late Bloomer   P-I
Robert Kraus. Crowell, 1971.
  Leo, a young tiger, is upset over his inability to read, write,
    talk, and so on.

Lone Bull's Horse Raid   A
Paul and Dorothy Goble. Bradbury Press, 1973.
  An Indian boy learns about becoming a man in his tribe.

Mahinhin: A Tale of the Philippines   I-A
Antonio E. Santa Elena. Downey Place, 1984.
  The experiences of a 12-year-old girl who lives near Manila
    in the 1950s.

On My Honor   A
Marion Dane Bauer. Clarion, 1986.
  A stirring story of a young boy who comes to understand
    the power of choice after his daredevil friend drowns in
    a raging river.

Peter Pan   A
James Barrie. Random House, 1983. (Original play, 1904)
  About a boy who refuses to grow up.

COURAGE/FEAR

Addie Across the Prairie   I

Laurie Lawlor. Albert Whitman, 1986.

> Addie, always known as a "fraidycat," learns about courage when her family becomes homesteaders on the Dakota plain.

The Courage of Sara Noble   I

Alice Dagliesh. Aladdin, 1986.

> The story of a pioneer child whose courage is tested when she and her father move into the Connecticut wilderness. Based on a true story.

Follow the Drinking Gourd   I

Jeanette Winter. Knopf, 1988.

> Slaves and a peg-legged sailor follow the stars and escape bondage through the Underground Railway.

A Pocket Full of Seeds   A

Marilyn Sachs. Doubleday, 1973.

> The story of Nicole, a French Jew, during five years of Nazi terror.

Sarah Bishop   A

Scott O'Dell. Houghton Mifflin, 1980.

> Historical account of the time at the start of the Revolutionary War. After her brother and father are killed, Sarah takes refuge in a cave and starts her new life.

Sleep Out   I

Carol Carrick. Clarion, 1982.

> The story of a boy spending his first night alone outdoors in the woods.

Snow Treasure   I

Marie McSwigan. Dutton, 1942.

> The true story of some brave Norwegian children who outwitted Nazi invaders.

Thunder Cake   P

Patricia Polacco. Philomel, 1990.

> A crashing thunderstorm prompts a grandmother to help her granddaughter face and overcome her fears.

Words By Heart   A

Ouida Sebestyen. Little, Brown, 1979.

> Lena, a young black girl, grows in courage after her father's violent death.

DIVORCE/REMARRIAGE

Dear Mr. Henshaw   I
Beverly Cleary, illustrated by Paul O. Zelinsky. Dell Yearling, 1983.
> Traces Leigh Botts from first grade to sixth through his letters to his favorite author; the letters and his diary reveal the changes in his relationship with his divorced parents.

Dinosaurs Divorce: A Guide for Changing Families   P-I
Marc and Laurene Krasny Brown, illustrated by Marc Brown. Little, Brown, 1986.
> Storybook with dinosaur characters deals with the traumas of divorce.

Ellen Grae   A
Vera and Bill Cleaver. Lippincott, 1967.
> Eleven-year-old Ellen, whose parents are divorced, exhibits unusual behaviors from days of silence and deep anxiety to days of telling long tall tales.

Emily and the Klunky Baby and the Next-Door Dog   P-I
Joan M. Lexau, illustrated by Martha Alexander. Dial, 1972.
> A little girl whose parents are divorced decides to run away to her daddy.

It's Not the End of the World   I-A
Judy Blume. Bradbury, 1972.
> The story of the discord and tension among three children and their parents as divorce becomes inevitable, as told by a 12-year-old.

Like Jake and Me   I-A
Mavis Jukes. Knopf, 1984.
> A fuzzy brown spider brings together Alex and his stepfather.

Me Day   P-I
Joan M. Lexau, illustrated by Robert Weaver. Dial, 1971.
> A little boy who lives with his mother is disappointed when a birthday letter from his father does not arrive.

My Dad Lives in a Downtown Hotel   I
Peggy Mann, illustrated by Richard Cuffari. Avon, 1973.
> Ten-year-old Joey deals with his parents' separation.

Sarah, Plain and Tall   I
Patricia MacLachlan. Harper, 1985.
> Two children experience apprehension and joy at the possibility of having a new mother when their father invites a mail-order bride to their prairie home.

**ETHNIC AND
CULTURAL GROUPS**

Ba-Nam   P-I
Written and illustrated by Jeanne M. Lee. Henry Holt, 1987.
Story about the special day when the Vietnamese honor their ancestors.

Baseball in April   I-A
Gary Soto. Odyssey, 1990.
Short stories that take place in Mexican-American neighborhoods in California; describes the dilemma of conflicting cultures.

Cornrows   I-A
Camile Yarbrough. Putnam, 1979.
Children have their hair braided and hear the regal history of cornrowing.

How My Parents Learned to Eat   P
Ina R. Friedman, illustrated by Allen Say. Houghton, 1984.
An American sailor and his Japanese bride learn to overcome cultural differences—one of these being table manners.

Ishi, Last of His Tribe   I
Theodora Kroeber. Houghton, 1964.
Provides insights into the culture of the Indians of what is now southern California.

Sachi: Daughter of Hawaii   I-A
Patsy Saiki. Kisaku, 1977.
Describes the life and customs of a Japanese-American girl in Hawaii.

Seven Korean Sisters   P-I
Jae Hyun Hahn. The Institute for Intercultural Studies, Los Angeles, 1980.
Story about the *sakdong chogori* worn on special days by Korean girls and women.

The Witch of Fourth Street   I-A
Myron Levoy. Harper, 1972.
A collection of short stories all set in the tenements of Lower East Side New York during the early 1900s; describes the customs of the melting pot community of Russian, Polish, Irish, Italian, German, Protestant, Catholic, and Jewish families.

FOSTER CHILD

Dorp Dead   A
Julia Cunningham, illustrated by James Spanfeller. Avon, 1974.
> Defiant boy in a foster home expresses his anger with the phrase, "Dorp Dead."

The Great Gilly Hopkins   I-A
Katherine Paterson. Avon, 1978.
> Shunted from foster home to foster home, Gilly is determined not to fit in at her latest home.

The Pinballs   I-A
Betsy Byars. Harper Trophy, 1977.
> Three unrelated children find love and friendship in a caring foster home.

FRIENDSHIP

Best Friends   P
Written and illustrated by Steven Kellogg. Dial, 1986.
> Imaginative illustrations add to the high-and-low notes of friendship, written in the voice of childhood.

Charlotte's Web   I
E. B. White. Harper, 1952.
> Charlotte, an extraordinary spider who weaves beautiful messages in her webs, and Fern, a soft-hearted farmer's child, save the life of Wilbur the pig.

Friends   P
Written and illustrated by Helme Heine. Aladdin, 1982.
> In this picture book, a rooster, a mouse, and a pig are best friends.

Frog and Toad Are Friends   P
Arnold Lobel. Harper, 1970.
> Five easy-to-read tales that recount two best friends' adventures.

The Hating Book   P
Charlotte Zolotow, illustrated by Ben Shecter. Harper Trophy, 1969.
> A classic story about being best friends.

Kitty in the Middle   I
Judy Delton. Houghton, 1979.
> Funny and thought-provoking adventures of 9-year-old Kitty and her friends while attending a parochial school in 1942.

HOMELESSNESS

The Family Under the Bridge   I
Natalie Savage Carlson, illustrated by Garth Williams.
   Scholastic, 1958.
     Three children and their mother live under a bridge in
      Paris until a hobo finds them a real home.

Fly Away Home   I-A
Eve Bunting. Clarion Books, 1991.
     A homeless boy lives with his father at an airport.

Slake's Limbo   A
Felice Holman. Dial Books, 1975.
     15-year-old Artemis, alone in the world, seeks refuge in
      the New York City subway system and learns to survive
      on his own.

LONELINESS

Behind the Attic Wall   A
Sylvia Cassedy. Harper Junior Books, 1983.
     Lonely Maggie lives with her great aunts and hears ghostly
      voices behind the wall, learning the secret to love.

Do You Want to Be My Friend?   P
Eric Carle. Harper Junior Books, 1987.
     In this picture book, a lonely mouse searches for a friend.

The Secret Garden   A
Frances H. Burnett. Lippincott, 1962.
     Mary, a lonely 10-year-old girl, discovers the mysteries of a
      locked garden; originally published in 1911.

Some of the Days of Everett Anderson   I-A
Lucille Clifton. Holt, 1970.
     Poems about a lonely boy and the things he likes to do.

ONE-PARENT FAMILY

Ida Early Comes Over the Mountain   I-A
Robert Burch. Avon, 1980.
     Love comes to a motherless family living in rural Georgia
      during the Great Depression.

My Mother, the Mail Carrier   P-I
Inez Maury. Feminist Press, 1976.
     Lupita tells about her life in a one-parent family.

Thank You, Jackie Robinson   A
Barbara Cohen. Lothrop, 1974.
     Sam gets an autographed baseball from Jackie for his adult
      friend Davy, after Davy has a heart attack.

From *The Teacher's Book of Lists, Second Edition*, published by GoodYearBooks.
Copyright © 1994 Sheila Madsen and Bette Gould.

The Friendship   A
Mildred Taylor. Dial, 1987.
> The Logan children witness and react to a cruel racist
> attack on the dignified, stubborn Mr. Tom Bee.

**A Jar of Dreams; The Best Bad Thing; and, The Happiest
Ending (Trilogy)**   I-A
Yoshiko Uchida. Atheneum, 1981.
> Rinko, a Japanese-American girl, learns to deal with racial
> prejudice in Depression-era Berkeley, California.

Maria Teresa   I-A
Mary Atkinson. Lollipop Power, 1979.
> A young Chicana faces discrimination for the first time
> after moving to a small midwestern town.

The Potlatch Family   A
Evelyn S. Lampman. Atheneum, 1976.
> A Chinook Indian girl is discriminated against.

Roll of Thunder, Hear My Cry   I-A
Mildred Taylor. Bantam, 1976.
> Black Mississippi family refuses to give in to threats by
> white neighbors; told by 9-year-old daughter
> Cassie.

Balancing Girl   I
Berniece Rabe. Dutton, 1981.
> Margaret, a child confined to a wheelchair, creatively uses
> her talent to fit with the crowd.

David in Silence   A
Veronica Robinson, illustrated by Victor Ambrus. Lippincott,
1965.
> A boy encounters various reactions to his deafness as he
> tries to participate in the everyday activities of other
> boys.

Don't Feel Sorry for Paul   I-A
Bernard Wolf. Lippincott, 1974.
> Documentary that describes in words and stark pictures
> several weeks in the life of Paul Jockiman, a child born
> without a right hand and foot, and with a deformed left
> hand and foot.

Me Too   I-A
Vera and Bill Cleaver. Lippincott, 1973.
> Lydia struggles with her frustration as she works to teach
> her retarded twin sister to speak and act normally.

**PHYSICAL AND MENTAL
HANDICAPS** (cont.)

Mine for Keeps I-A
Jean Little. Little, Brown, 1962.
> Sally's dog, "Mine for Keeps," helps her readjust to life at home after she returns from five years at a cerebral palsy center.

Stay Away from Simon! I
Carol Carrick, illustrated by Donald Carrick. Clarion, 1985.
> Lucy and her brother rethink how they feel about a mentally handicapped boy after he helps them find their way during a blizzard.

The Street of the Flower Boxes P-I
Peggy Mann, illustrated by Peter Burchard. Coward, 1966.
> Tough Puerto Rican and black youths lead a beautification campaign for their street after previous attempts to sabotage others' efforts.

The Summer of the Swans A
Betsy Byars, illustrated by Ted CoConis. Penguin, 1970.
> Sara, shy and sensitive, deals with her conflicts and love for her retarded brother.

Take Wing A
Jean Little, illustrated by Jerry Lazare. Little, Brown, 1968.
> Laurel tries to make friends with other children and protect her retarded brother.

Where the Lilies Bloom A
Vera and Bill Cleaver. Harper Trophy, 1969.
> Mary, a 14-year-old, tells about her life in Appalachia and how she tries to keep her family together after her father's death.

RESPONSIBILITY

Across Five Aprils A
Irene Hunt. Follet, 1965.
> During the Civil War, the youngest son is left to keep the farm going.

Faithful Elephants A
Yukio Tsuchiya. Houghton Mifflin, 1988.
> A zookeeper must face putting to sleep elephants who would be turned loose in a Japanese city threatened with bombing during World War II.

Juan Patricio P-I
Barbara K. Todd. Putnam, 1992.
> Juan tries to find a summer job. After many disappointments, he finds the perfect one.

RESPONSIBILITY (cont.)

Keep the Lights Burning, Abbie! I-A
Peter and Connie Roop. Carolrhoda, 1985.
> A true story about the daughter of a lighthouse keeper who keeps the lights burning while her father is away on the mainland.

A River Ran Wild A
Lynne Cherry. Gulliver Green, 1992.
> Environmentalists rescue a New England river that has been suffering devastating environmental problems.

The Superlative Horse A
Jean Merrill. William R. Scott, 1961.
> A young boy earns the right to select horses for the finest stable in China. Based on a Taoist story from c. 350 B.C.

Where the Lilies Bloom A
Vera and Bill Cleaver. Lippincott, 1969.
> Children promise to accept responsibilities to keep their family together after their father's death.

SELF-ESTEEM

Arthur's Eyes P
Marc Brown. Little, Brown, 1986.
> Arthur's friends tease him when he has to wear glasses, but he learns to wear them with pride.

Blubber I-A
Judy Blume. Dell, 1974.
> A fat fifth-grader is taunted by other students until another girl shows her sympathy and friendship.

The Flunking of Joshua T. Bates I
Susan Richards Shreve, illustrated by Diane de Groat. Scholastic, 1984.
> Joshua is supposed to repeat third grade, but is helped by a sympathetic teacher.

A Girl Called Al I-A
Constance Greene. Dell, 1969.
> Overweight Al tries to prove she doesn't care about her weight or anything else until she finds a friend.

Jelly Belly I-A
Robert Kimmel Smith, illustrated by Bob Jones. Dell Yearling, 1981.
> Fat Ned is sent off to diet camp after his friends nickname him Jelly Belly.

SELF-ESTEEM (cont.)

Oliver Button is a Sissy   P
Tomie de Paola. Voyager, 1979.
> A small boy learns that he may not be an athlete, but he can still be a winner.

Ordinary Jack: Being the First Part of the Bagthorpe Saga   A
Helen Cresswell. Macmillan, 1970.
> Jack has a burgeoning inferiority complex living in his family of madly achieving geniuses, but his uncle has a plan for Jack to become the family prophet.

The Real Me   I
Betty Miles. Avon, 1974.
> With her family's help, Barbara fights sexism in her school and on a paper route.

Shy Charles   P
Written and illustrated by Rosemary Wells. Pied Piper, 1988.
> Charles is a very shy, silent mouse, but when an emergency occurs, he takes charge.

SETTING GOALS

Dragonwings   A
Laurence Yep. Harper Junior Books, 1975.
> A Chinese boy and his father struggle to live in San Francisco in the early 1900s.

El Chino   I
Allen Say. Houghton, 1990.
> A picture book biography of how Billy Wong, a Chinese-American, became a champion matador in Spain.

The Glorious Flight: Across the Channel with Louis Blériot, July 25, 1909   I
Alice and Martin Provensen. Puffin, 1983.
> The recreation of a daredevil Frenchman's early flight across the English Channel.

The Quitting Deal   I
Tobi Tobias. Viking, 1975.
> Mother and daughter make a deal to stop their bad habits —smoking and thumbsucking, respectively.

To Space and Back   A
Sally Ride and Susan Okie. Lothrop, 1986.
> Astronaut Sally Ride gives a personalized description of a space-shuttle mission.

_____'s Reading Log

Type

A	Adventure
AB	Autobiography
B	Biography
CL	Classic
C	Contemporary
F	Fiction
FL	Folklore
HS	Historic
H	Humor
MG	Magazine Article
M	Mystery
NW	Newspaper
NF	Non-fiction
N	Novel
PB	Picture Book
PL	Play
P	Poetry
SF	Science Fiction
SS	Short Story

Rating

★	I didn't enjoy it; you can skip this one.
★★	So-so.
★★★	Good. Try it, you might like it.
★★★★	Very good. I liked it a lot.
★★★★★	Terrific book, highly recommended to all.

Title/Author/Illustrator	Start Date	Finish Date	Type	Shared? How?	Rating
El Chino, words and pictures by Allen Say	Oct. 20	Nov. 11	B	(Yes) No — made a tape	★★★★★
				Yes No	☆☆☆☆☆
				Yes No	☆☆☆☆☆
				Yes No	☆☆☆☆☆
				Yes No	☆☆☆☆☆
				Yes No	☆☆☆☆☆
				Yes No	☆☆☆☆☆
				Yes No	☆☆☆☆☆
				Yes No	☆☆☆☆☆

Any Book, Story, or Poem

SCRIPTWRITER

Write a script for a scene in a book you have read.
Follow the format below.

Brief description of setting

Names of characters and a brief description of each

Dialogue

Stage Directions (Remember you must tell your actors and actresses how to say the words, how and where to move, and what to do with any props they must handle during the scene. These directions are usually written in parentheses.)

*If you really like your script, act it out with your friends in front of the class.

Fantasy or Science Fiction Book or Story

SCI-FI EDITOR or FANTASY EDITOR

Divide a chart into three sections: Realistic, Non-Realistic, and Combination.

List events, people, and items from your story that fit into each category.

Draw conclusions, and cite the evidence for them, as to whether the book should be called Realistic, Non-Realistic, or a Combination of both.

Any Book, Story, or Poem

WINDOW DRESSER

Ask your teacher for bulletin board space. Create a store window for a book, story, or poem you have read. Include some of the following:

- a background to match the main setting
- cut-outs or models of the main characters
- quotes from the story or your own statements to invite others to read the story
- questions about the story
- a brief review with your recommendations
- real objects related to the story

Any Book, Story, or Poem

STAGE A DAY

Find several people who have read the same book as you. Describe the piece of literature to the entire class and then organize a theme day for your book, story, or poem. Encourage your fellow students to participate in the day by:

- dressing in the style of the period or setting
- bringing an item to class that is unique to the story
- reciting to the class favorite parts of the story or poem
- acting out an exciting episode
- photographing or videotaping the day's events to add to the class library
- creating posters, newspaper ads, or commercials to advertise the story

*Have a "character day" when everyone comes as their favorite story character.

From *The Teacher's Book of Lists, Second Edition*, published by GoodYearBooks.
Copyright © 1994 Sheila Madsen and Bette Gould.

Any Book, Story, or Poem

BOOKS ON TAPE

Tape a poem, short story, or your favorite part (excerpt) of a novel. Add sound effects and read with expression, accents (if appropriate), and different tones of voice depending on the character. You may want to work with a group of students to portray the various characters' voices.

You'll probably want to record and listen to yourself several times before you are satisfied.

Play the tape for your class as well as for other classes. (It might be a good read-aloud book for younger children or they may wish to follow along with their own book as they listen to the tape.)

Any Book, Story, or Poem

BOOK REVIEWER

Review a book for a magazine or newspaper.

- Write a headline (the headline doesn't have to include the title)
- Write a subhead
- Write a review in less than 100 words
- Include something about the author's other books, publisher, price, etc.
- Include an excerpt or two from the story
- Recommend the book:
  What age person would like it?
  What interests might a person have
    who would enjoy it?
  What rating would you give it?
    (You may wish to develop your
    own rating system.)

Any Book, Story, or Poem

PEN PAL

Write to a favorite author. Send him/her a sample of your writing.

Questions you might like to include in your letter:

- May I have an autograph? A photograph?
- How did you get into writing?
- What is your favorite book?
- What are you working on now?
- Would you like to visit my class sometime?
- What advice would you give to an aspiring writer?

Any Book, Story, or Poem

CHARACTER PARALLELS

Select a favorite or main character from your story.

List as many traits of the character as you can think of. Add some of your own traits to the bottom of this list.

Glue yarn or string in straight lines from each trait to the right edge of the paper (or draw straight lines). Label one end of the strings **VERY** and the other end **NOT MUCH**.

Place a stick figure for yourself and a stick figure for your character along each "trait line," to indicate where you think you both belong.

How do you two compare?

Do you think you'd get along?

From *The Teacher's Book of Lists, Second Edition,* published by GoodYearBooks. Copyright © 1994 Sheila Madsen and Bette Gould.

Greek and Roman Gods, Goddesses, and Heroes

The ancient Greeks and Romans were excellent storytellers. They made up stories of gods and their powers to explain what they saw in their world. While we do not believe in these gods anymore, we still enjoy learning these stories which have been told for thousands of years. An excellent myths book is: d'Aulaires' Book of Greek Myths, written and illustrated by Ingri and Edgar d'Aulaire (Zephyr paperback, 1962).

Greek Name	Roman Name	Role
Zeus	Jupiter ♃	King of the gods
Hera	Juno ⚹	Queen of the gods
Aphrodite	Venus ♀	Goddess of love
Ares	Mars ♂	God of war, wisdom, and crafts
Demeter	Ceres ⚳	Goddess of agriculture
Hades	Pluto ♇	God of the underworld
Hermes	Mercury ☿	Messenger of the gods
Hestia	Vesta	Goddess of hearth and home
Poseidon	Neptune ♆	God of the sea
Apollo	Apollo	God of sun, music, and medicine
Artemis	Diana	Goddess of the hunt
Asclepius	Aesculapius	God of medicine
Athena	Minerva	Goddess of wisdom
Chloris	Flora	Goddess of flowers
Dionysius	Bacchus	God of wine
Enyo	Bellona	Goddess of war
Eos	Aurora	Goddess of the dawn
Eros	Cupid	God of love
Gaea	Terra	Symbol of the earth
Hebe	Juventas	Goddess of youth and cupbearer to the gods
Hephaestus	Vulcan	God of fire and blacksmith to the gods
Hygeia	Salus	Goddess of health
Hypnos	Somnus	God of sleep
Iris		Goddess of the rainbow
	Janus	God of gates and doors and all beginnings
Morpheus		God of dreams
Nike	Victoria	Goddess of victory
Pan	Faunus	God of flocks, pastures, forests, and wildlife
Panacea		Goddess of healing
Persephone	Proserpina	Queen of the underworld
Rhea		Mother of the gods
Selene	Luna	Goddess of the moon
Thanatos	Mors	God of death
	Nox	Goddess of night

Minor Greek Divinities

nymphs—beautiful maidens who guarded things in nature
dryads—nymphs who guarded the forests
nereids—nymphs who lived in and guarded things in the sea
the Fates—three goddesses who controlled the destiny of every person
the Muses—nine goddesses of song and poetry and the arts and sciences

Heroes

Many heroes claimed gods as their ancestors, but they were largely or entirely mortal. They were born, grew old, and died. Still, they became almost as important as the gods and goddesses in mythology.

Greek Heroes and Characters

Adonis	Galatea	Orestes
Ajax	Hero and Leander	Orpheus
Amazon	Io	Pandora
Andromeda	Mentor	Penelope
Atlas	Narcissus	Pygmalion
Daedalus	Niobe	Ulysses

Trojan Heroes

Achilles—the most famous Greek warrior

Agamemnon—commander-in-chief of the Greek forces (who were fighting Troy)

Jason—led Argonauts on a quest for the Golden Fleece

Menelaus—Helen's husband (Helen was the woman the Greeks were trying to bring home)

Odysseus—a general who made a clever plan that led to Troy's defeat

Oedipus—the king of Thebes who unknowingly killed his father and married his mother

Paris—the son of the king of Troy who brought Helen, wife of the king of Sparta, back to Troy with him

Theseus—famous for killing the Minotaur (see **Literary Monsters and Creatures** list, p. 150)

From *The Teacher's Book of Lists, Second Edition*, published by GoodYearBooks. Copyright © 1994 Sheila Madsen and Bette Gould.

Activities: Greek and Roman Gods, Goddesses, and Heroes

1. Learn how to pronounce several of the gods' names. Make up a matching or lotto game of names and pronunciations for others to play.

Atlas	AT-lus
Bellerophon	Bel-LAIR-o-fon

2. Select several gods from the list whose symbols are not shown. Learn about the gods' roles or jobs and create symbols for each of them. Share the symbols you have created with others in a 3-dimensional or other interesting way.

3. Many words come from the characters of Greek and Roman myths. Do research to find some of these words and show them on word lists, pictures, or use them in modern myths you invent yourself.

Volcano comes from Vulcan, the god of fire who had a workshop underground, as does vulcanize, a method of treating rubber for tires.

January comes from Janus, the god of gates and doors and all beginnings.

The Apollo spacecraft was well named because Apollo was the sun god who drove a flaming chariot across the sky.

4. Read some legends or myths from another culture's mythology. Make a chart or other visual to compare one or more of these stories to Greek or Roman myths. Here are some books to get you started:

The Norse Myths, by Keith Crosley-Holland. Pantheon, 1980. A retelling of Norse tales that captures the humor and ferociousness of the original stories.

Jataka Tales, edited by Nancy De Roin. Houghton, 1975. Two-thousand-year-old stories of famous Indians in which clever animals outwit each other.

5. Learn to say and write the Greek alphabet. See if you can find ten examples of the Greek alphabet's use in our world.

Phi Beta Kappa = National Honor Society founded in 1776
delta = difference or change

Literary Monsters and Creatures

Students' imaginations are sure to be stimulated by a familiarity with giants, monsters, vampires, and ghosts. This list can be a good place to begin some creative writing activities, and lends itself to play writing and role playing as well. Some interesting related books for reading aloud are: Scary Stories to Tell in the Dark: Collected from American Folklore, by Alvin Schwartz; St. George and the Dragon, by Margaret Hodges; and a picture book with simple text, Eyes of the Dragon, by Margaret Leaf.

Argus—a hundred-eyed giant of Greek mythology

Centaur—Greek mythological monster, half man (from the waist up) and half horse (from the waist down)

Cerberus—a many-headed dog of Greek mythology

Chimera—a fire-breathing monster—part lion, part goat, part dragon—of Greek mythology

Cyclops—a race of one-eyed giants in Greek mythology

Dracula—a centuries-old vampire who was a corpse during the day but came to life at night; from a novel by Bram Stoker

Dragons—monsters famous in legends of many different countries

Frankenstein's monster—a manlike monster created by Dr. Frankenstein in the book of the same name by Mary Wollstonecraft Shelley

Giant—a huge, manlike monster

Gorgons—three female monsters of Greek mythology with serpents for hair

Griffin—a mythical creature, half eagle and half lion

Harpy—a dirty, winged monster with the head of a woman and the tail, legs, and talons of a bird

Hydra—Greek mythological monster; a nine-headed serpent that grew two heads for each one that was cut off

Jabberwock—the fabulous monster in the nonsense poem "Jabberwocky" in *Through the Looking Glass* by Lewis Carroll

Medusa—one of the Gorgons

Minotaur—from Greek mythology; a manlike monster with a bull's head

Pegasus—winged horse of Greek mythology

Phoenix—a legendary Egyptian bird

Roc—a very large, strong legendary bird believed to live in the area around the Indian Ocean

Sphinx—in Greek mythology, a monster with the head of a woman, body and paws of a lion, and huge birdlike wings

Titans—a group of earth giants from Greek mythology, said to have had immense size and brute strength

Unicorn—legendary beast, usually with the head and body of a horse, the hind legs of an antelope, the tail of a lion, and a single, long, sharp twisted horn in the middle of its forehead

Vampires—legendary ghosts that came out of their graves to attack the living

Werewolves—people thought to be transformed into wolves

Prose and Poetry Forms

A general review of the various types of prose and poetry, this list provides examples for each category which may be found in most school or public libraries. Students may enjoy creating their own categories to classify the books they read on their own or aloud in class. Each category has its own styles and proficient authors; children may wish to pursue one of their favorites and eventually become an "expert" on the genre.

Reading levels for books are indicated as follows:
P—preschool and primary
I —intermediate
A—advanced

PROSE

Fantasy	May touch the supernatural or offer a totally new world.
	The Phantom Tollbooth, Norton Juster, illustrated by Jules Feiffer. Random House, 1961. **A**
	A Question of Time, Dina Anastasia, illustrated by Dale Payson. Dutton, 1978. **P**
Folklore or Folk Tales	Tales from many cultures explaining the world and people's experiences that have traveled down through the ages.
	Momotaro: Peach Boy, George Suyeoka. Island Heritage, 1972. **P**
	John Henry: An American Legend, Ezra Jack Keats. Pantheon, 1965. **P-I**
	Aesop's Fables, Aesop, illustrated by Heidi Holder. Viking, 1981. **P-I-A**
Historical Fiction	Imaginative re-creation of the life and times of a past period; usually concerned with major themes which are timeless: freedom, love and hate, good vs. evil.
	The Cay, Theodore Taylor. Avon, 1977. **A**
	By Secret Railway, Enid Meadowcroft. Crowell, 1984. **I-A**
Nonfiction (factual or informative)	Books read for interest and gathering of information; the best have literary merit and present a fair and impartial point of view.
	Dinosaurs in Your Backyard, William Mannetti. Atheneum, 1982. **I**
	Lobo of the Tasaday: A Stone Age Boy Meets the Modern World, John Nance. Pantheon, 1982. **I-A**

Novels or Stories About Ethnic Issues	**All Us Come Cross the Water,** Lucille Clifton, illustrated by John Steptoe. Holt, 1973. **P**
	The Treasure of Topo-el-Bampo, Scott O'Dell, illustrated by Lynn Ward. Houghton, 1972. **I**
Picture Books With Few Words	**Color Zoo,** Lois Ehlert. HarperCollins, 1989.
	Ernest and Celestine, Gabrielle Vincent. Mulberry, 1982.
Picture Books With No Words	**Animal Alphabet**, Bert Kitchen. Pied Piper, 1984.
	The Grey Lady and the Strawberry Snatcher, Molly Bang. Scholastic, 1980.
	Paddy's Evening Out, John S. Goodall. McElderry, 1973.
Realistic Fiction of Current Times	Stories about adults, children, animals, set in modern times with realistic events; often helps the child understand him/herself and others.
	The Carp in the Bathtub, Barbara Cohen, illustrated by Joan Halpern. Lothrop, 1972. **P-I**
	The Grizzly, Annabel and Edgar Johnson, illustrated by Gilbert Riswold. Harper, 1964. **A**
	Fiona's Bee, Beverly Keller, illustrated by Diane Paterson. Coward, 1975; Dell paperback. **P**
	Maudie and Me and the Dirty Book, Betty Miles. Knopf, 1978. **I-A**
Science Fiction	May involve elements of fantasy; often includes technology, machines, robots, and computers.
	The City of Gold and Lead, John Christopher. Macmillan, 1967. **A**
	A Wrinkle in Time, Madeleine L'Engle. Farrar, 1962. **A**
POETRY	Children will enjoy hearing, repeating, saying, clapping, dancing, and even memorizing some favorite poems. We believe teachers will want students to develop an acquaintance with, and appreciation of, many types of poetic forms. Students should be encouraged to express themselves in poetry—it is quite natural for them and applies to students fluent in languages other than English.
Cinquain	An unrhymed, 5-line stanza often taught as follows:

The first line is one word and acts as the title:	Ant
Line 2 has 2 words that describe the first word:	Tiny black
Line 3 has 3 words that express action:	Scurrying darting about
Line 4 has 4 words that express feeling, emotion:	Amazing to watch closely
Line 5 has 1 word, a synonym for the first word:	Insect

From *The Teacher's Book of Lists, Second Edition,* published by GoodYearBooks. Copyright © 1994 Sheila Madsen and Bette Gould.

Actually, a cinquain is often as varied as the poet's imagination, and does not follow the pattern strictly, but does hold to the five-line length.

Concrete Poems   Poems that position words and phrases to form a picture or create a special sound effect.

SWAN AND SHADOW[1]

```
                    Dusk
                  Above the
                water hang the
                        loud
                        flies
                        Here
                        O so
                        gray
                        then
                What              A pale signal will appear
                When          Soon before its shadow fades
                Where        Here in this pool of opened eye
                In us     No Upon us As at the very edges
              of where we take shape in the dark air
                this object bares its image awakening
                  ripples of recognition that will
                  brush darkness up into light
      even after this bird this hour both drift by atop the perfect sad instant now
                  already passing out of sight
                  toward yet untroubled reflection
                this image bears its object darkening
              into memorial shades Scattered bits of
              light          No of water Or something across
              water          Breaking up No Being regathered
              soon            Yet by then a swan will have
              gone              Yes out of mind into what
                  vast
                  pale
                  hush
                  of a
                  place
                  past
          sudden dark as
            if a swan
                sang              John Hollander
```

Epic Poetry   A long narrative poem telling of the deeds of a legendary or historical figure.

Casey at the Bat, Ernest L. Thayer, illustrated by Leonard E. Fisher. Watts, 1964.   **I-A**

---

[1]"Swan and Shadow" from *Types of Shape* by John Hollander. Copyright ©1969, 1992 by John Hollander. Reprinted by permission of the author.

Free Verse No rhyme and no limiting pattern of accented syllables per line; ideas are expressed imaginatively and the language is rhythmical.

The Earth is Sore: Native Americans on Nature, adapted and illustrated by Aline Amon. Atheneum, 1981.   **I-A**

Eskimo Songs and Stories, translated by Edward Field, with illustrations by Kiakshuk and Pudlo. Delacorte Press, 1973. **I-A**

THE APPROACH OF THE STORM[1]
From the half
Of the sky
That which lives there
is coming, and makes a noise.
Chippewa Indians, North America

Haiku An unrhymed 17-syllable Japanese poem most often about some aspect of nature; written in three lines: five syllables in the first, seven in the second, and five in the third line. (Most haiku translated from Japanese will not fit the pattern exactly.) This verse pattern derived from the first three lines of the tanka and has been written since the 13th century. The best haiku paint a small, flawless picture in the reader's mind. More modern haiku often deviates from the strict syllable pattern and addresses themes other than nature.

In a Spring Garden, edited by Richard Lewis, illustrated by Ezra Jack Keats. Dial Press, 1965.   **P-I-A**

More Cricket Songs: Japanese Haiku. Translated by Harry Behn. Harcourt Brace Jovanovich, 1971. These translations hold true to the 5-7-5 pattern.   **P-I-A**

May rains![2]
Now frogs are swimming
At my door.
Sanpu 1647–1732

One person[3]
And one fly
In the big waiting room.
Issa 1763–1823

there are things sadder[4]
than you and I. some people
do not even touch.
Sonia Sanchez 1934–

With your fists ablaze[5]
with letters and colored stamps
beautiful mailman.
Paul Goodman 1875–1948

From *The Teacher's Book of Lists, Second Edition*, published by GoodYearBooks. Copyright © 1994 Sheila Madsen and Bette Gould.

---

[1]"The Approach of the Storm." Reprinted from *The Sky Clears*, by A. Grove Day, by permission of the University of Nebraska Press. Copyright ©1951 by A. Grove Day.
[2]"May rains!" by Sanpu, English translations by Kenneth Koch based on the word-for-word translations by Harold Henderson in *An Introduction to Haiku*. Reprinted by permission of the author.
[3]"One person" by Issa, English translations by Kenneth Koch based on the word-for-word translations by Harold Henderson in *An Introduction to Haiku*. Reprinted by permission of the author.
[4]"Haiku" from *Love Poems* by Sonia Sanchez. Copyright ©1973 by Sonia Sanchez. Reprinted by permission of the author.
[5]"With your fists ablaze" from *Hawkweed* by Paul Goodman, 1967. Reprinted by permission of Sally Goodman.

Limerick Humorous verse with an *aabba* rhyme scheme and a particular rhythmic pattern.

They've Discovered a Head in the Box for the Bread and Other Laughable Limericks, collected by John E. Brewton and Lorraine A. Blackburn, illustrated by Fernando Krahn. Crowell, 1978.   **I**

The Book of Pigericks: Pig Limericks, Arnold Lobel, illustrated by Arnold Lobel. Harper Trophy, 1983.   **I-A**

Complete Nonsense Book, Edward Lear. Dodd, Mead, 1943.   **P-I-A**

> There was an old man on the Border
> Who lived in the utmost disorder;
> He danced with the cat,
> and made tea in his hat,
> Which vexed all the folks on the Border.
> Edward Lear 1812–1888

Lyric Poetry Often expresses intense personal emotion in a songlike manner. This format is historically found in poems by the ancient Greeks and Romans, often sung to a harp. Also lyric poems were composed and sung by troubadours during Medieval times. Song lyrics (minus the music, at first) are a great way for children to enjoy poetry—and then later a song. It's usually done the other way around. Carole King has made a good album for this called *Really Rosie.* Many of the songs were written to go with favorite children's books such as *One Was Johnny,* by Maurice Sendak and *Eating Chicken Soup With Rice.*

Lyric Poems, selected by Coralie Howard, illustrated by Mel Fowler. Franklin Watts, 1968.   **I-A**

One of the purest lyric poets was Robert Burns:

> O my luve is like a red, red rose
>   That's newly sprung in June;
> O my luve is like the melodie
>   That's sweetly played in tune.

Modern Poetry This poetry has no precise definition, except that it arises from the imagination of the writer and therefore offers the reader a different view of the world, sometimes even of a world that is unfamiliar. Most often it follows no particular rules of rhyming, but often contains a rhythmical element. It often must be read several times to get "the feel" of the poet's style or method.

I Am the Darker Brother, edited by Arnold Adoff, illustrated by Benny Andrews. Macmillan, 1968.   A

CHOCOLATE MILK[1]
Oh God! It's great!
to have someone fix you
chocolate milk
and to appreciate their doing it!
Even as they stir it
in the kitchen
your mouth is going crazy
for the chocolate milk!
The wonderful chocolate milk!
                    Ron Padgett (1942–   )

up into the silence the green[2]
silence with a white earth in it

you will(kiss me)go

out into the morning the young
morning with a warm world in it

(kiss me)you will go

on into the sunlight the fine
sunlight and a firm day in it

you will go(kiss me

down into your memory and
a memory and memory

i)kiss me(will go)
                    e. e. cummings (1894–1962)

Narrative   The telling of an event or story in rhythmical, sometimes rhyming verse; sometimes the story may be of travels, a quest, or other experience.

Walt Whitman, fascinated with the new, vast America he lived in, wrote a poem about it that is 1,346 lines long. It has an inventive, always changing flow. (Segments, or all of this poem, would make a good companion to the social studies units of the time period.)

From *The Teacher's Book of Lists, Second Edition,* published by GoodYearBooks.
Copyright © 1994 Sheila Madsen and Bette Gould.

From SONG OF MYSELF

The bugle calls in the ballroom, the gentlemen run for their partners,
    the dancers bow to each other;
The youth lies awake in the cedar-roofed garret and harks to the
    musical rain,
The Wolverine sets traps on the creek that helps fill the Huron
. . . .
Patriarchs sit at supper with sons and grandsons and great grandsons
    around them,
In walls of adobie, in canvas tents, rest hunters and trappers after
    their day's sport.
The city sleeps and the country sleeps,
The living sleep for their time…the dead sleep for their time,
The old husband sleeps by his wife and the young husband sleeps by
    his wife;
And these one and all tend inward to me, and I tend outward to
    them,
And such as it is to be of these more or less I am.

                                                    Walt Whitman (1819–1892)

Nonsense   Rhyming and non-rhyming poems, often telling a story or
with comic characters; most children enjoy the humor of
mixed-up words.

Hurry, Hurry, Mary Dear! And Other Nonsense, N. M.
    Bodecker. Atheneum, 1976.   **I**

A Light in the Attic, Shel Silverstein. Harper Junior Books,
    1981.   **P-I-A**

The Man Who Sang the Sillies, John Ciardi, illustrated by
    Edward Gorey. Lippincott, 1961.   **P-I**

ELETELEPHONY[1]
Once there was an elephant,
Who tried to use the telephant—
No! No! I mean an elephone
Who tried to use the telephone—
(Dear me! I am not certain quite
That even now I've got it right.)

Howe'er it was, he got his trunk
Entangled in the telephunk;
The more he tried to get it free,
The louder buzzed the telephee—
(I fear I'd better drop the song
Of elephop and telephong!)
                        Laura E. Richards (1850–1943)

Poetry Collections   **Black Out Loud**, edited by Arnold Adoff. (An anthology of
    African-American writers.) Macmillan, 1970.   **A**

Early Moon, Carl Sandburg, illustrated by James Daugherty.
    Harcourt, 1930.   **I-A**

---

[1]"Eletelephony" from *Tirra Lirra: Rhymes Old and New* by Laura E. Richards. Copyright ©1930, 1932 by Laura E. Richards.
Copyright © renewed 1960 by Hamilton Richards. By permission of Little, Brown and Company.

Poetry Collections
(continued)

Wind Song, Carl Sandburg, illustrated by William A. Smith. Harcourt, 1960.   **I-A**

Sing a Song of Popcorn: Every Child's Book of Poems, selected by Beatrice Schenk de Regniers, et al. Scholastic, 1988.   **P-I-A**

Side By Side: Poems to Read Together, collected by Lee Bennett Hopkins, illustrated by Hilary Knight. Simon and Schuster, 1988.   **P**

Talking to the Sun: An Illustrated Anthology of Poems for Young People, selected and introduced by Kenneth Koch and Kate Farrell. The Metropolitan Museum of Art, New York, and Henry Holt and Company, Inc., 1985.   **I-A**

When We Were Very Young, A. A. Milne, illustrated by E. H. Shepard. Dutton, 1924.   **P**

Rhyming Verse

Poetry of two or more lines per verse which have definite rhyming patterns; traditionally, rhyming patterns are identified with the letters *a, b, c,* etc., as in the following poem, "Teacher, Teacher."

Alligator Pie, Dennis Lee, illustrated by Frank Newfield. Houghton, 1975.   **P-I**

TEACHER, TEACHER

Teacher, teacher, don't be dumb,	a
Give me back my bubble gum!	a
Teacher, teacher, I declare,	b
Tarzan lost his underwear!	b
Teacher, teacher, don't be mean,	c
Give me a dime for the coke machine!	c

traditional American (possibly a jump rope rhyme)

From ALPHABET OF GIRLS[1]
She wishes her name was different,
Like Caroline or Marie.
But they named her for Great Grandma,
Whose name turned out to be:
Xenobia.
. . . .
She is my friend—my special friend—
The one I most prefer.
She wishes her name was different,
and I agree with her—
Xenobia.

Leland B. Jacobs

From *The Teacher's Book of Lists, Second Edition,* published by GoodYearBooks. Copyright © 1994 Sheila Madsen and Bette Gould.

[1]From *Alphabet of Girls* by Leland B. Jacobs. Copyright ©1969 by Leland B. Jacobs. Reprinted by permission of Henry Holt and Company, Inc.

Scary Poems   Although not an official poetic form, this style of poetry, written to convey an eerie feeling, is immensely appealing to young people and often contains wonderful imagery and wordplay.

Nightmares: Poems to Trouble Your Sleep, Jack Prelutsky, illustrated by Arnold Lobel. Greenwillow, 1982.   **A**

See My Lovely Poison Ivy, Lilian Moore, illustrated by Diane Dawson. Atheneum, 1975.   **I**

SOME ONE[1]
Some one came knocking
At my wee, small door;
Some one came knocking,
I'm sure—sure—sure;
I listened, I opened,
I looked to left and right,
But nought there was a-stirring
In the still dark night;
Only the busy beetle
Tap-tapping in the wall,
Only from the forest
The screech-owl's call,
Only the cricket whistling
While the dewdrops fall,
So I know not who came knocking
At all, at all, at all.
                    Walter de la Mare (1873–1956)

Teacher References   **It Doesn't Have to Rhyme**, Eve Merriam. Atheneum, 1964.

There Is No Rhyme for Silver, Eve Merriam. Atheneum, 1962.

Wishes, Lies and Dreams: Teaching Children to Write Poetry, Kenneth Koch. Vintage, 1970.

Tanka   An unrhymed Japanese verse form of 5 lines or sections; lines or sections contain 5, 7, 5, 7, and 7 syllables respectively for a total of 31 syllables. (Most Tanka translated from Japanese or other languages will not fit the syllable or line pattern exactly.) The haiku form of 5, 7, and 5 syllables came from the practice of poets working on a tanka together, but in separate parts: the 5, 7, 5 portion for one poet, and the last two lines of 7 syllables each for the other poet.

A lonely pond in age-old stillness sleeps,
Apart, unstirred by sound or motion till
Suddenly into it a little frog leaps. . .!
                    Basho (1644–1694)

[1]"Some One" by Walter de la Mare. Reprinted by permission of The Literary Trustees of Walter de la Mare and The Society of Authors as their representative.

Geometric Formulas

The most rewarding experiences in geometry for elementary-age children are learning to recognize, both in drawings and in real life, and to construct the various geometric forms. Three-dimensional models are useful for learning about the solid forms. Growth of appropriate vocabulary related to each form is essential and is gained by many varied experiences with real things. For most students, memorization of formulas is not necessary or productive.

Important geometry terms: face, vertex, edge

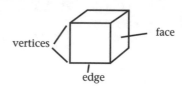

Pi is usually given as 3.14 or $^{22}/_7$ for elementary students.

To find the circumference of a

CIRCLE, multiply the diameter by pi (π).

$c = \pi d$

To find the perimeter of a

RECTANGLE, add twice the length to twice the width.

$p = 2l + 2w$

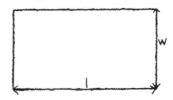

SQUARE, multiply the length of a side by 4.

$p = 4s$

TRIANGLE, add the length of the sides.

$p = a + b + c$

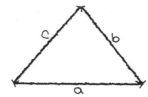

From *The Teacher's Book of Lists, Second Edition*, published by GoodYearBooks Copyright © 1994 Sheila Madsen and Bette Gould.

To find the area of a

CIRCLE, multiply the square of the radius by pi (π)

$$A = \pi r^2$$

SQUARE, square one side.

$$A = s^2 \quad \text{or} \quad A = s \times s$$

RECTANGLE, multiply the base by the height.

$$A = bh$$

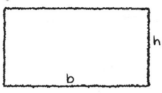

TRIANGLE, multiply the base by the height and divide by 2.

$$A = \frac{1}{2}bh \text{ or } \frac{bh}{2}$$

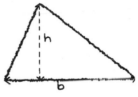

PARALLELOGRAM, multiply the base by the height.

$$A = bh$$

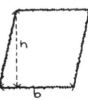

TRAPEZOID, multiply the sum of the lengths of the parallel sides by the height and divide by 2.

$$A = h \times \frac{b_1 + b_2}{2}$$

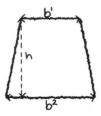

CYLINDER (lateral area or outside curved surface), multiply the diameter by the height times pi (π).

$$A = \pi dh$$

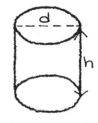

To find the total area of a

CUBE, square the length of one edge and multiply by 6.

$A = 6e^2$

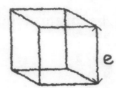

RECTANGLE, add twice the product of the length and width, twice the product of the length and height, and twice the product of the width and height.

$A = 2lw + 2lh + 2wh$ or $A = 2(lw + lh + wh)$

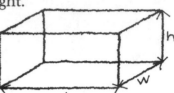

CYLINDER, add the lateral area to the area of the two bases.

$A = \pi dh + 2\pi r^2$

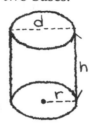

To find the volume of a

CUBE, cube the length of one side.

$V = s^3$

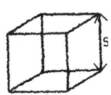

RECTANGULAR SOLID, multiply the length by the width times the height.

$V = lwh$

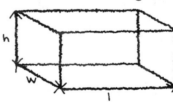

CYLINDER, multiply the square of the radius by the height times pi (π)

$V = \pi r^2 h$

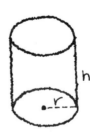

PYRAMID, multiply the area of the base by ⅓ times the height.

$V = \frac{1}{3}bh$

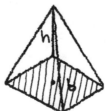

From *The Teacher's Book of Lists, Second Edition*, published by GoodYearBooks
Copyright © 1994 Sheila Madsen and Bette Gould.

Activities: Geometric Formulas

1. Using straws, paper strips, sticks (popsicle sticks), and tape, make a geometric shape. For example: you can make a hexahedron (a polyhedron with 6 faces) by taping together 12 straws. Label vertices (there are 8), edges (12), and faces (6).

2. Use a ruler to construct (draw) several simple geometric shapes on graph paper. Count the units (little squares) in each shape and write the shape's area. (Estimate whole units made up of parts of a triangle or other shapes not composed of right angles.)

3. Select 3 geometric forms. Design a simple picture with them, either by drawing or cutting and pasting. Now find and label, somewhere on the picture:
- the total perimeter (including circumferences)
- the total area

4. Select several containers—cylinders, boxes, pyramids. Estimate which has the largest volume. Now fill each, in turn, with marbles (they must be the same size marbles!) and graph your results.

5. Work with a friend to develop a set of nested containers. For example, start with an oatmeal carton, put in a large juice can, put inside that a tall fruit can, and so on. Once you have as many "nested" containers as possible in your set, measure each one's radius and height. Display your nested set and a chart of your measurements.

A challenge: Can you figure out the total volume of your nested set?

Graphs and Surveys— 99 Things To Do

Surveying and graphing activities provide an active way for children to gather numerical information and display it in such a way that the findings are quickly and easily understood. Compare reading a graph with reading a paragraph telling the same information. After finishing a graph, it is important that a student or group discuss the findings and draw conclusions that seem to be apparent. Class graphing projects are especially useful in the primary grades—often utilizing one-to-one matching, as in a birthdays graph. The ½" and 1" grids that follow the list are useful for a variety of graphing activities. Large sheets of 1" graph paper are available in school supply stores.

Questions to ask for surveying and graphing

"How many . . . ?"

. . . people in your family
. . . rooms in your house
. . . light bulbs in your house
. . . cars in your family
. . . plants in your house
. . . televisions in your house
. . . electrical appliances in your house
. . . doors in your house
. . . windows in your house
. . . teeth do you have
. . . buttons do you have on
. . . pockets on what you're wearing
. . . relatives do you have
. . . letters in your name
. . . left- and right-handed people in your class

"At what time . . . ?"

. . . do you eat dinner
. . . do you get up
. . . do you go to bed
. . . do you leave for school
. . . do you get home from school
. . . is your favorite TV show on
. . . were you born

"How much time in a day or week do you spend . . . ?"

. . . watching television
. . . doing homework
. . . playing
. . . reading
. . . in a car or on a bus
. . . eating
. . . doing chores
. . . alone
. . . in activities such as Boy Scouts, Girl Scouts, piano lessons, etc.

"Who's your favorite . . . ?"

. . . movie star
. . . TV star
. . . recording group
. . . book character
. . . sportsperson
. . . singer
. . . celebrity

From *The Teacher's Book of Lists, Second Edition,* published by GoodYearBooks
Copyright © 1994 Sheila Madsen and Bette Gould.

"What's your favorite . . . ?"

. . . ice cream flavor	. . . holiday	. . . book
. . . color	. . . film	. . . animal
. . . TV program	. . . radio station	. . . building
. . . kind of car	. . . food	. . . toy
. . . game or sport	. . . song	. . . musical instrument
. . . pet	. . . number	. . . pizza topping
. . . weather	. . . brand of jeans	

"How many times in a day or week . . . ?"

. . . do you use the telephone
. . . do you drink water
. . . does the telephone ring
. . . do you open your refrigerator

"How old do you think our teacher is?"

"What do you want to be when you grow up?"

"In which month were you born?"

"Where do you shop for groceries?"

"How much is your weekly allowance?"

"What is the first number of your telephone number?"

"What is the last number of your telephone number?"

"How many times can you jump on one foot?"

"How many sit-ups (jumping jacks, push-ups, etc.) can you do?"

"How long can you talk (filibuster)?"

"How many times can you jump rope without missing?"

"How many times can you say 'toyboat' clearly and quickly?"

From *The Teacher's Book of Lists, Second Edition,* published by GoodYearBooks.
Copyright © 1994 Sheila Madsen and Bette Gould.

The following ideas for graphing require observation or measurement of other people and things.

Within a given population or area, graph the color of:

eyes
hair
shoes
articles of clothing

cars
flowers
books

Measure and graph people's:

heights
weights

length of arms, legs, or feet
circumference of heads

The following graphs generally can be done without interaction with other people.

Do weekly graphs of:

where people are eating lunch
students present or absent in class

the highest temperature for each day
the lowest temperature for each day

Do graphs at home of:

the kinds of silverware in a drawer
the kinds of dishes on a shelf
articles of clothing in a drawer or closet

types of TV commercials seen in an evening
(cars, foods, cleaning products, etc.)

. . . And Other Things to Count and Graph

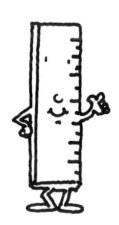

Choose a paragraph. Count and graph the number of times each letter of the alphabet appears in the paragraph.

Count and graph the number and kinds of P.E. equipment in your school.

Count and graph the number and kinds of supplies in your classroom (scissors, pencils, rulers, etc.).

Measure and graph the areas of all the rooms in your school.

Count and graph the number of times common names, such as Smith, Jones, Brown, White, Taylor, Johnson, Nelson, and Martin, appear in your telephone directory.

Count and graph the number of people in your class who have used each type of transportation: bus, airplane, taxi, ferry, train, horse, etc.

From *The Teacher's Book of Lists, Second Edition,* published by GoodYearBooks Copyright © 1994 Sheila Madsen and Bette Gould.

Title: _____

Names

_____ _____ _____ _____

Bar Graph

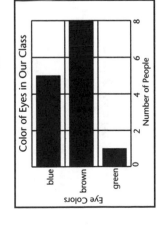

Color of Eyes in Our Class

Eye Colors: blue, brown, green

Number of People: 0 2 4 6 8

1. Make up your own survey topic or use one of these:
   - How many times can you jump on one foot?
   - How many of each color are in a bag of M & M®s?

2. Title your graph.

3. Write the name of each person you survey, or write the things you are going to count. Label the vertical axis.

4. Decide on a scale for the numbers you are comparing and label the horizontal axis.

5. Color each bar to match the results of your survey.

From *The Teacher's Book of Lists, Second Edition,* published by GoodYearBooks.
Copyright © 1994 Sheila Madsen and Bette Gould.

Graphs and Surveys **169**

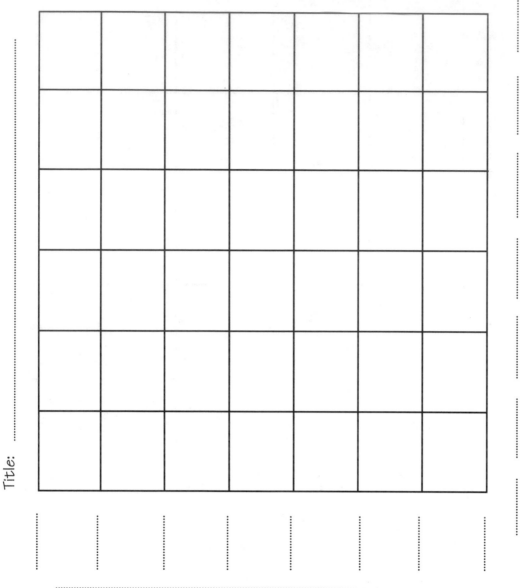

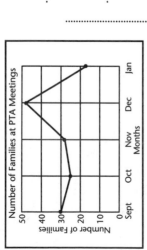

Line Graph

1. Make up your own survey topic or use one of these:
   • Record temperatures for a specific time of day during a week.
   • List the price of a product (gas, stock, 1st class stamp) over a 7-unit period: week, month, year, decade.

2. Title your graph.

3. Decide on a scale for the numbers you are comparing and label the vertical axis.

4. Label the horizontal axis with your time divisions.

5. Plot the results of your survey on the graph by marking a dot on each vertical line and then connecting the dots.

Name

Date

Title:

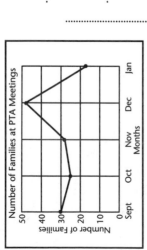

Number of Families at PTA Meetings

50
40
30
20
10
0

Number of Families

Sept   Oct   Nov   Dec   Jan
       Months

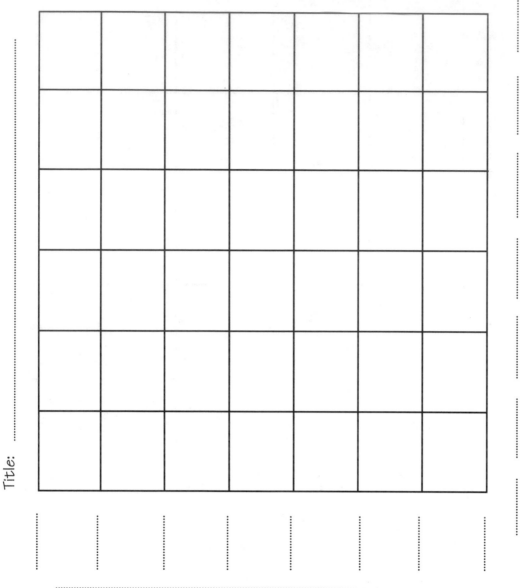

From *The Teacher's Book of Lists, Second Edition*, published by GoodYearBooks.
Copyright © 1994 Sheila Madsen and Bette Gould.

Pictograph

Title: ....

[ ] = ... (amount)

Ice Creams Eaten Last Week

🍦 =2

Jennifer	🍦	🍦	🍦	🍦
John	🍦	🍦	🍦	
Julie	🍦			

1. Make up your own survey topic or use one of these:
   - How many buttons do you have on today?
   - How many pets do you have?
   - How many light bulbs in your house?

2. Draw the picture you are going to use on your graph. Show the amount your picture stands for:

   [ ] = _____ (amount)

3. Write the name of each person you survey and draw pictures in the squares to match their answers.

Title: ....

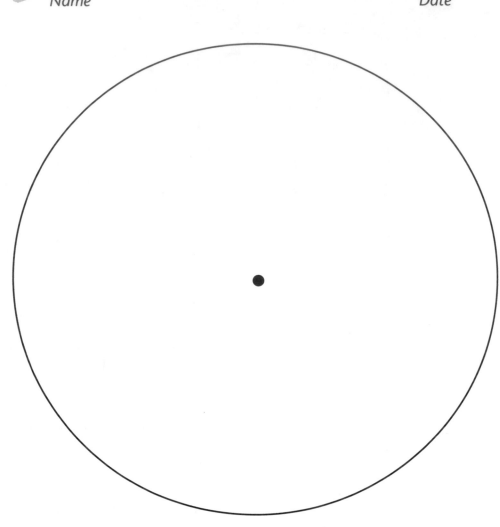

Pie Graph

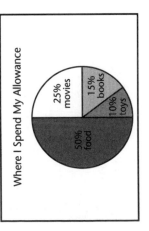

Where I Spend My Allowance

- 25% movies
- 15% books
- 10% toys
- 50% food

1. Make up your own survey topic or use one of these:
   - How much time do you spend on each activity in a day?
   - Survey 20 people to find out their favorite pizza toppings.

2. Title your graph.

3. Compute the percentages and divide the pie into sections that approximate the percentages.

4. Label each section. Include the percentages.

5. Color or create a pattern for each section.

1-inch grid

½-inch grid

Math Signs and Symbols

+	addition sign, plus, positive	$\llcorner$	right angle
−	subtraction sign, minus, negative	$\not<$	angle
±	plus or minus	**r**	radius
×	multiplication sign, multiplied by, times	**d**	diameter
÷	division sign, divided by	π	Pi, the ratio of the circumference to the diameter of a circle, approximately 3.1416
=	equals, is equal to	≅	congruent, is congruent to
≠	is not equal to	→	ray
<	less than	⊥	perpendicular, is perpendicular to
>	greater than	‖	parallel, is parallel to
$	dollar sign	@	at
¢	cent(s)	#	number or pound
£	pound sign used for monetary units (such as the Israeli and British pound)	%	percent
		°	degree(s)
::	as, equals	∞	infinity
∴	therefore	:	is to, the ratio of
∵	since, because	√	square root
△	triangle	{ }	indicates a set
□	square	Ø	empty set
▭	rectangle	2³	indicates the number ($2 \times 2 \times 2$)

Measurement Abbreviations

Metric Abbreviations

nanometer—nm
millimeter—mm
centimeter—cm
decimeter—dm
meter—m
dekameter—dam
hectometer—hm
kilometer—km

milliliter—ml
centiliter—cl
deciliter—dl
liter—l
dekaliter—dal
hectoliter—hl
kiloliter—kl

milligram—mg
centigram—cg

decigram—dg
gram—g
dekagram—dag
hectogram—hg
kilogram—kg
mectric ton—t

square millimeter—mm^2
square centimeter—cm^2
square meter—m^2
area—a
hectare—ha
square kilometer—km^2

cubic millimeter—mm^3
cubic centimeter—cm^3
cubic decimeter—dm^3
cubic meter—m^3

Other Measurement Abbreviations

inch—in, "
foot—ft, '
yard—yd
rod—rd
furlong—fur
mile—mi

gill—gi
pint—pt
quart—qt
gallon—gal

peck—pk
bushel—bu

chain—ch

cup—c
teaspoon—t, tsp
tablespoon—T, tbsp

grain—gr
pennyweight—dwt
ounce troy—oz t
pound troy—lb t

dram—dr
ounce—oz
pound—lb, #

hundredweight—cwt
ton—t

second—sec, "
minute—min, '
hour—hr
day—da
week—wk
month—mo
year—yr

barrel—bbl
cord—cd
fathom—fm

From *The Teacher's Book of Lists, Second Edition*, published by GoodYearBooks
Copyright © 1994 Sheila Madsen and Bette Gould.

Measures and Weights

Length

10 millimeters	= 1 centimeter	
10 centimeters	= 1 decimeter	= 100 mm
10 decimeters	= 1 meter	= 1000 mm
10 meters	= 1 dekameter	
10 dekameters	= 1 hectometer	= 100 m
10 hectometers	= 1 kilometer	= 1000 m

Liquid

10 milliliters	= 1 centiliter	
10 centiliters	= 1 deciliter	= 100 ml
10 deciliters	= 1 liter	= 1000 ml
10 liters	= 1 dekaliter	
10 dekaliters	= 1 hectoliter	= 100 liters
10 hectoliters	= 1 kiloliter	= 1000 liters

Liquid

8 drams	= 1 ounce	
4 gills	= 1 pint	= 16 ounces
2 pints	= 1 quart	= 8 gills
4 quarts	= 1 gallon	= 8 pints = 32 gills
31½ gallons	= 1 barrel	= 126 quarts
2 barrels	= 1 hogshead	= 63 gallons
		= 252 quarts

Dry

2 pints	= 1 quart	
8 quarts	= 1 peck	= 16 pints
4 pecks	= 1 bushel	= 32 quarts
		= 64 pints
105 quarts	= 1 barrel	

Volume

1,728 cubic inches	= 1 cubic foot
27 cubic feet	= 1 cubic yard
144 cubic inches	= 1 board foot
128 cubic feet	= 1 cord

Angular and Circular Measure

60 seconds	= 1 minute
60 minutes	= 1 degree
90 degrees	= 1 quadrant
180 degrees	= 1 straight angle
360 degrees	= 1 circle = 4 quadrants

Length

12 inches	= 1 foot	
3 feet	= 1 yard	
5½ yards	= 1 rod, pole, or perch (16½ ft)	
40 rods	= 1 furlong	= 220 yards
		= 660 feet
8 furlongs	= 1 statute mile	= 1,760 yards
		= 5,280 ft.
3 miles	= 1 league	= 5,280 yds.
		= 15,840 ft.

Area

144 square inches	= 1 square foot	
9 square feet	= 1 square yard	
	= 1,296 sq. in.	
30¼ square yards	= 1 sq. rod	
	= 272¼ sq. ft.	
960 square rods	= 1 acre	
	= 4,840 sq. yds.	
	= 43,560 sq. ft.	
1 square mile	= 640 acres	
6 miles square	= 1 township	
	= 36 sections	
	= 36 square miles	

From *The Teacher's Book of Lists, Second Edition*, published by GoodYearBooks. Copyright © 1994 Sheila Madsen and Bette Gould.

Weight—Avoirdupois

$27\frac{11}{32}$ grains	= 1 dram
16 drams	= 1 ounce = 437.5 grains
16 ounces	= 1 pound = 256 drams
	= 7,000 grains
100 pounds	= 1 hundredweight
20 hundredweights	=1 ton
	= 2,000 pounds
20 long hundredweights	= 1 long ton
	= 2,240 pounds

Weight—Troy

24 grains	= 1 pennyweight
20 pennyweights	= 1 ounce troy = 480 grains
12 ounces troy	= 1 pound troy
	= 240 pennyweights
	= 5,760 grains

Volume

1000 cubic millimeters	=1 cubic centimeter
1000 cubic centimeters	=1 cubic decimeter
	=1,000,000 mm³
1000 cubic decimeters	=1 cubic meter
	=1 stere
	=1,000,000 cm³
	=1,000,000,000 mm³

Area

100 square millimeters	= 1 square centimeter
100 square centimeters	= 1 square decimeter
100 square decimeters	= 1 square meter
	= 10,000 cm²
	= 1,000,000 mm²
100 square meters	= 1 are
10 ares	= 1 hectare
	= 10,000 mm²
100 hectares	= 1 square kilometer
	= 1,000,000 mm²

Weight

10 milligrams	= 1 centigram
10 centigrams	= 1 decigram
	= 100 mg
10 decigrams	= 1 gram
	= 1,000 mg
10 grams	= 1 dekagram
10 dekagrams	= 1 hectogram
	= 100 grams
10 hectograms	= 1 kilogram
	= 1,000 grams
100 kilograms	= 1 quintal
10 quintals	= 1 metric ton
	= 1,000 kilograms

From *The Teacher's Book of Lists, Second Edition,* published by GoodYearBooks
Copyright © 1994 Sheila Madsen and Bette Gould.

Number Facts

Although the facts in this list are interesting in themselves, there are many math problems that you or your students might develop based on a set of the following facts. The symbol or letter following each fact suggests some types of problems or activities which might be developed.

M = measurement
N = reading and writing large or small numerals and number words
G = graphing; comparisons
$ = money problems
T = time (conversions, e.g. hours to minutes, minutes to seconds, etc.)
° = temperature (conversions, reading thermometers, etc.)
R = ratios
% = percentage problems
C = conversion problems

U.S. NUMBER FACTS

	M	N	G	$	T	°	R	%	C
The Sears Tower in Chicago, one of the tallest buildings in the world, is 110 stories and 1,454 feet tall.	✓								✓
The World Trade Center in New York is 110 stories and 1,350 feet tall.	✓								✓
Records set in the United States for highest and lowest temperatures: 134°F—Death Valley, California −80°F—Prospect Creek Camp, Endicott Mountains, Alaska						✓			
The highest annual U.S. rainfall recorded was 460" in Waialeale, Kauai, Hawaii.	✓								✓
The state of Alaska has about 3,040,000 hectares (7,600,000 acres) of uninhabited land. That makes it one of the least settled areas of the world.	✓	✓							
The U.S. is now the second largest country, outranked only by the People's Republic of China. The area of the U.S. is 3,615,122 sq. miles (5,784,195 sq. km).	✓	✓							
The Mississippi-Missouri River is about 5,936 km (3,710 miles) long, making it the third longest river in the world.	✓								
Lake Superior, one of the Great Lakes, is 50,720 sq. km (31,700 sq. miles) in area. It is the second largest lake in the world.	✓								
Ellis Island was the entry point to the U.S. for 20,000,000 immigrants between 1892 and 1943. It is now part of the Statue of Liberty National Monument.		✓							

From *The Teacher's Book of Lists, Second Edition,* published by GoodYearBooks.
Copyright © 1994 Sheila Madsen and Bette Gould.

	M	N	G	$	T	°	R	%	C
U.S. NUMBER FACTS (continued) The walls of the Grand Canyon in Arizona, from bottom to top, supply a record of a geological period spanning more than 1,000,000,000 years.		✓							
SOCIAL NUMBER FACTS The world's population was more than 5 billion in 1991. It increases by about 270,000 a day, or about 200 babies each minute. If this rate continues, by the year 2000, the world's population will be more than 6 billion.*		✓							
About 1.1 million people will be diagnosed with cancer and approximately 514,000 will die of this disease—about one person every 63 seconds.*		✓			✓				
In 1989 one person died on average every 23 minutes in an alcohol-related car crash.*		✓			✓		✓	✓	
On the average, in the U.S.: • every 2.5 minutes a person is injured by a gun • every day a child is killed by a gun • every year 30,000 people are murdered, shot by a gun • every year 1,500 people die as a result of gun accident		✓	✓		✓				
In 1988, almost one out of every five people in the U.S. was a "minority." By the year 2000 the ratio will be closer to 1 in 3.*		✓					✓	✓	
The Freedom House, a human rights group, said that their 1989 survey showed that for the first time in their 18-year survey project more countries are free than not free. Out of 5,200,000,000 people in the world, 2 billion live in freedom, 1,200,000,000 live in partly free areas, and 2 billion are not free.*		✓					✓	✓	
By 2010, older citizens will make up 13.9% of the population, or 35,000,000—by 2030 they will make up 21% or 64.3 million.*		✓					✓	✓	

*Facts from *What Can I Do to Make a Difference?*, Richard Zimmerman. Penguin Group, 1992.

From *The Teacher's Book of Lists, Second Edition*, published by GoodYearBooks
Copyright © 1994 Sheila Madsen and Bette Gould.

From *The Teacher's Book of Lists, Second Edition*, published by GoodYearBooks.
Copyright © 1994 Sheila Madsen and Bette Gould.

SOCIAL NUMBER FACTS (continued)

	M	N	G	$	T	°	R	%	C
In 1990 there were approximately 35,000,000 personal and household crimes, including almost 6,000,000 violent crimes.*		✓					✓	✓	
Since 1962, approximately 140,000 Literacy Volunteers of America have tutored more than 1.75 million students in 350 programs in 38 states.*		✓							

ANIMAL NUMBER FACTS

	M	N	G	$	T	°	R	%	C
The Jurassic period was 180–135 million years ago. This was the Age of Reptiles and included the 10-ton stegosaurus.		✓			✓				
We are in the Quarternary period now. This period began 3,000,000 years ago. Human beings (homo erectus) appeared about 500,000 years ago.		✓			✓				
Mammals became dominant 50 million years ago as flowering plants had overtaken other forms of vegetation.		✓							
Insects are the largest group of animals on earth, with over 700,000 species known.		✓							
There are over 6,000 new species discovered each year.		✓							
In 1984 there were an estimated 42,000,000 cats in the United States.		✓							

WEATHER NUMBER FACTS

	M	N	G	$	T	°	R	%	C
The sunniest place in the world is the Sahara Desert, in Africa. It gets 4,300 hours of sun a year.		✓			✓				✓
The greatest snowfall was recorded on Mt. Rainier, in the U.S. in 1971. The snowfall was 31,203mm.		✓			✓				✓
The largest hailstone that has been recorded weighed 750g (in Coffeyville, Kansas, U.S.)	✓								✓

*Facts from *What Can I Do to Make a Difference?*, Richard Zimmerman. Penguin Group, 1992.

WEATHER NUMBER FACTS (continued)

	M	N	G	$	T	°	R	%	C
George V Coast, in Antarctica, is the windiest place in the world, with gales of 320 kph.	✓								✓
One of the worst smog disasters was the death of 2,850 people in London, England in 1952.		✓							
One of the worst weather disasters on record was the drought and famine in Bengal, India in 1943–1944. One and one-half million people died.		✓							
About 6½ million years ago, many scientists believe that a meteor struck the earth causing a dust cloud that changed the weather and therefore the vegetation, leading to the extinction of the dinosaurs.		✓							
About every 3 seconds, in South America a part of the tropical rain forest the size of a football field is cut down.	✓				✓				
One type of weather satellite, called a geo-stationary satellite, stays in a fixed place 22,000 miles above the Equator.	✓								✓
On May 26, 1917, a tornado traveled 293 miles across Texas, holding the speed of about 88–120 mph for 7 hours and 20 minutes.	✓				✓				
All of the energy from one hurricane could provide enough electricity to equal the energy needed to power 1,095 cars around the world 36,000 times each.	✓	✓	✓						

MONEY FACTS

	M	N	G	$	T	°	R	%	C
Nearly 2,000 Spanish galleons sunk near the coasts of Florida and the Bahamas in the 16th century. Many carried large amounts of gold, of which only a small percentage has been found. This makes this area the world's largest untapped store of treasure.		✓							
Coins and paper money are worth varying amounts at different times due to the international money market. On December 17, 1992, for example, $1.00 was equal to about 5 francs (France); 1½ deutschmarks (Germany); 123 yen (Japan); and, a little more than £0.5 (Britain). (See foreign exchange rates in your newspaper's business section)				✓					✓

From *The Teacher's Book of Lists, Second Edition*, published by GoodYearBooks
Copyright © 1994 Sheila Madsen and Bette Gould.

MONEY FACTS (continued)

	M	N	G	$	T	°	R	%	C
The largest mint (it's in the U.S.) can make 22,000,000 coins per day using almost 100 machines. The mint covers 11 sq. acres. If it operated at full production for one day, it could produce a pile of coins 5 times higher than Mt. Everest.		✓	✓				✓	✓	✓
Romania issued a 10-bani note in 1917 that was 73 times smaller than a Chinese note printed in the 1300s. The Chinese one-kwan note was 9 x 13 inches.			✓						
The Beatles, the most successful music group of all time, have sold over one billion tapes and records.		✓							
Gold is the most malleable (able to be pounded out flat) metal. One ounce of pure gold can be beaten into a fine wire that would stretch 55 miles.	✓	✓	✓						

PLANT FACTS

	M	N	G	$	T	°	R	%	C
Two famous types of trees are: the giant redwood (Sequoia washingtoniana), which may grow to a height of 350 ft. (106m), and the bristlecone pine (Pinus arisstata), probably the oldest living thing on earth, some of which are believed to have been alive for 3,000 years.		✓	✓		✓				
Saffron, from the crocus flower, is the most expensive spice in the world. It takes more than 200,000 stamens to make about 1 pound of saffron.		✓							✓
One kind of bamboo is the world's fastest growing plant. It can shoot up 90cm in a day and may reach a height of 30m.	✓	✓							✓
The Dutch grow and sell about 3,000 million flowers per year. This works out to about 80,000 flowers per square kilometer in the country.		✓	✓						✓
Wild genseng roots from China and Korea sell for about £10,000 for 1 ounce.				✓					✓
A field used to produce soy beans produces 13 times more protein than the same field used to produce cattle for meat.		✓					✓		

From *The Teacher's Book of Lists, Second Edition*, published by GoodYearBooks.
Copyright © 1994 Sheila Madsen and Bette Gould.

Roman Numerals

Quick! What does MCMXCVIII stand for? It's easy to see why we use Arabic numerals. However, Roman numerals continue to be used on clocks and sundials, copyright dates for films and books, book chapter numbers and front matter pages, musical chords, act and scene numbers in plays, and we couldn't get along without them when making an outline.

Answer: 1998

I	one		XXIV	twenty-four
II	two		XXIX	twenty-nine
III	three		XXX	thirty
IV	four		XL	forty
V	five		L	fifty
VI	six		LX	sixty
VII	seven		LXX	seventy
VIII	eight		LXXX	eighty
IX	nine		XC	ninety
X	ten		C	one hundred
XIV	fourteen		CD	four hundred
XV	fifteen		D	five hundred
IX	nineteen		CM	nine hundred
XX	twenty		M	one thousand

See if you can solve these and write the answers in Roman numerals.

1. VIII – II
2. L + L
3. CD + DC*
4. LX – XX
5. CMXCIX + I*
6. CMXCIX – CMXCVIII*
7. MCMXCII + CDLXIV*

*A Roman numeral preceding a larger Roman numeral assumes a negative sign. For example, IV can be read as V–I or 5–1 which equals 4.

1. VI, 6
2. C, 100
3. M, 1000
4. XL, 40
5. M, 1000
6. I, 1
7. MMCDLVI, 2456

From *The Teacher's Book of Lists, Second Edition,* published by GoodYearBooks
Copyright © 1994 Sheila Madsen and Bette Gould.

What's Your Number—Life Spans

Mammals

The potential highest maximum age (if a person is always healthy and accident free) for human beings is 115 years. The average life expectancy (for a baby born in 1989) is 71.3 years.

Here are the potential maximums and average life spans of some other mammals.*

Maximum		Average
77	Indian elephant	24 (in captivity)
62	horse	30
57	African elephant	40
50	donkey	40
49	hippopotamus	40
45	Indian rhinoceros	39
39	chimpanzee	15
36	gorilla	26 (in captivity)
31	grizzly bear	25
16	wolf	9
27	cat	15
34	dog	15

"The lifetimes of all mammals are scaled to their 'biological pace'." (Stephen Jay Gould)

Other Life Spans

100-watt light bulb—750 hours
sun—about 5,000,000,000 years
car muffler—2.5 years
water-based paint (unopened can)—7 years
oil-based paint (unopened can)—50 years

Legendary & Historical Life Spans

King Karke of Sumeria—28,800 years (as legend has it)
Biblical: Methuselah—969 years; Noah—950 years
Neanderthal (50,000 years ago)—28 years
humans during the Golden Age of Greece (c.500 B.C..)—38 years
humans during the Dark Ages—30 years
humans during the Renaissance—38 years
humans at the end of the 1600s—51 years
Scientists predict that by the year 2020 in Western countries the average life span will be 110 years

*Information cited in this life span section is from *Panati's Extraordinary Endings of Practically Everything and Everybody,* Charles Panati. Harper & Row, 1989.

CHAPTER

7

Science

Animal Groups—Names for Herds, Schools, and Flocks

*Children have a natural curiosity about animals and how they live, what they look like and so on. Many children will be delighted to learn some of these group names, the familiar as well as the less well known. Simple matching activities, lotto games, and card games made up of the words may interest some students. Others may be stimulated to find out more about some of the animals and could make use of one or more of the **Independent Study** worksheets, p. 368–371. A creative exercise would be to use pictures of various animals, discuss their traits, and make up "new" group names, such as a "dawdle of porcupines," or to draw pictures to illustrate some of the more picturesque names, such as "a parliament of owls" or "a crash of rhinoceroses."*

Animal	Group Name	Animal	Group Name
ants	colony	kangaroos	troop, mob
apes	shrewdness, company	kittens	kindle
badgers	cete	larks	exaltation
bears	sloth	leopards	leap
beavers	colony	lions	pride
bees	swarm	locusts	plague
buffalo	gang	magpies	tidings
cats	clowder	mallards	sord
chickens	flock	monkeys	troop
chicks	clutch	mules	barren
cows	herd	nightingales	watch
crows	murder	owls	parliament
dogs	pack	oxen	yoke
ducks	brace, flock	peacocks	muster
eagles	convocation	pheasants	nide
elephants	herd	pigs	drove, litter, sounder
elks	gang		
fish	school	quails	bevy
foxes	skulk	rabbits	colony
geese	flock, gaggle (usually when grouped together on water)	rhinoceroses	crash
		seals	pod
goats	flock	sheep	drove, flock
grouse	pack	starlings	murmuration
hawks	cast	turkeys	rafter
hogs	drift	whales	gam, pod
hogs (wild)	sounder	wolves	pack, rout
horses	herd	woodpeckers	descent
insects	swarm (moving or in flight)		

From *The Teacher's Book of Lists, Second Edition,* published by GoodYearBooks. Copyright © 1994 Sheila Madsen and Bette Gould.

Animal Offspring— Names for Animal Babies

This list makes it possible to capitalize on the natural interest and caring children have for babies, especially of other species. The class might be introduced to these words after hearing The Ugly Duckling *by Hans Christian Andersen or learning about animal young firsthand from classroom animals such as mice, fish, or guinea pigs. Younger students may wish to learn the differences between an adult animal and its young; older students may be intrigued by the derivations of the names for both the animal and its offspring. In many cases, not only do the offspring have different names, but often the adult male and adult female have different names. Use the* **Independent Study** *worksheets, p. 368–371, as students demonstrate a desire to find out more.*

Animal	Offspring	Animal	Offspring
bear	cub	horse	foal (when first born)
beaver	kit		filly (female)
cat	kitten		colt (male)
chicken	chick	kangaroo	joey
cow	calf	lion	cub
deer	fawn	otter	whelp
dog	pup, puppy	oyster	spat
duck	duckling	pig	piglet, farrow, shoat
eagle	eaglet	pigeon	squab
eel	elver	rabbit	bunny
elephant	calf	rhinoceros	calf
fish	fry	salmon	smolt
fox	cub, kit	seal	pup
frog	tadpole	sheep	lamb
giraffe	calf	swan	cygnet
goat	kid	tiger	cub
goose	gosling	turkey	poult
grouse	cheeper	whale	calf
hawk	eyas	wolf	cub, whelp

Animalogists

*Although this list only includes scientists who study animals, many other "ologies" might be explored. Start a class list of plant scientists with a mycologist, an expert on fungi; begin an earth science booklet with a seismologist (studies earthquakes) and a geologist, a scientist of the earth's crust. Interested students may wish to explore tasks associated with the field, educational backgrounds, salaries, and job opportunities. Others may want to find scientists to interview, or to research the latest findings in the field. Use the **Independent Study** worksheets, p. 368–371, for students who wish to find out more.*

arachneologist—zoologist who studies spiders

biologist—scientist who studies living organisms

biosociologist—ecologist who studies environments of groups of living things, such as schools of fish

cetologist—zoologist who studies whales

conchologist—zoologist who studies mollusks or shells

ecologist—biologist who studies the relationship between organisms and their environment

embryologist—biologist who studies the formation and development of living things prior to birth

entomologist—zoologist who specializes in the study of insects

ethologist—biologist who studies animals in their natural habitat

helminthologist—zoologist who studies worms

herpetologist—zoologist who studies reptiles and amphibians

ichthyologist—zoologist who specializes in the study of fishes

limnologist—biologist who studies the biological, chemical, geographical, and physical features of lakes and ponds (fresh waters)

malacologist—zoologist who studies mollusks

mammalogist—zoologist who specializes in the study of mammals

morphologist—biologist who examines animal form and structure

myrmecologist—entomologist who specializes in the study of ants

oologist—ornithologist who specializes in the study of bird eggs

ornithologist—zoologist who specializes in the study of birds

physiologist—biologist who studies the normal functions of living things

taxonomist—scientist who names and classifies animals

zoographer—ecologist who studies the distribution of animals in the various regions of the world

zoologist—scientist who studies animals and their classification

From *The Teacher's Book of Lists, Second Edition,* published by GoodYearBooks. Copyright © 1994 Sheila Madsen and Bette Gould.

Animal People

*The following list of biologists represents some of the many areas and types of study in the general field of biology. Students may be directed to any of the **Independent Study** worksheets, p. 368–371, to explore one or more of these people further. Many of the early people were considered naturalists; they did not have formal education in biology, but trained themselves by exploring, observing, and recording what they found. Therefore, there is some overlap between disciplines. For example, John Muir might best be considered a botanist, since trees were so important to him, but in fact, he championed the conservation of whole areas, including their animal and plant forms.*

Louis Agassiz (1807–1873)
: U.S. naturalist; famed for work on living and fossil forms of fish

Roy Chapman Andrews (1884–1960)
: American naturalist who made many expeditions; in Mongolia he discovered the first known fossil dinosaur eggs

John James Audubon (1785–1851)
: famous American naturalist and artist; one of the first to study and paint U.S. birds

Spencer F. Baird (1823–1887)
: naturalist and vertebrate zoologist

(Charles) William Beebe (1877–1962)
: American naturalist and explorer; made record descents into the ocean in a bathysphere with Otis Barton

Rachel Carson (1907–1964)
: American marine biologist and science writer

Frank Chapman (1864–1945)
: American ornithologist; one of the first to study birds with the camera

Baron Cuvier (1769–1832)
: French naturalist; first to compare the structure of animal bodies with that of man

Charles Darwin (1809–1882)
: British naturalist; developed theory of evolution based on natural selection that revolutionized the biological sciences

Raymond L. Ditmars (1876–1942)
: American naturalist; an authority on reptiles, he pioneered in developing snake-bite serums

Jean-Henri Fabre (1823–1915)
: French entomologist; pioneered research into insect instinct and behavior

William T. Hornaday (1854–1937)
: American zoologist; worked to protect and increase the herds of bison in the U.S.

William Henry Hudson (1841–1922)
: English author and naturalist; wrote articles and books on nature, particularly bird life

Sir Julian Huxley (1887–1975)
: noted British biologist

Thomas Huxley (1825–1895)
: famous zoologist, lecturer, and writer

Carolus Linnaeus (1707–1778)	developed a scientific classification system of animals and plants
Clinton Hart Merriam (1855–1942)	American physician and zoologist; helped found the National Geographic Society in 1888
John Muir (1838–1914)	American naturalist, explorer, and writer; a spokesman for forest conservation whose efforts influenced Congress to establish both Yosemite and Sequoia National Parks
Jan Swammerdam (1637–1680)	Dutch anatomist and zoologist; pioneered in the anatomy of insects; his work formed the basis of entomology
Nikolaas Tinbergen (1907–1988)	Dutch-born zoologist; studied how behavior of animals adapts to the environment
Jane Goodall Van Lawick (1934–)	English zoologist; became famous for behavior studies of chimpanzees
Alexander Wilson (1766–1813)	one of the founders of American ornithology

Activities: Animal People

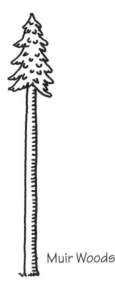

Muir Woods

1. With several friends set up a "Panel of Experts" with each of you representing one of the biologists from the list. Each panel member's job is to state the case for "their biologist" obtaining a grant of $1,000,000 for further research in their respective area of study.

2. Connect one of the biologists to the events taking place in the U.S. or the world at the time he or she was active. Create an Influences Chart to show how the biologist was influenced by events of the time, and how the biologist had an influence on events of his or her time.

3. Research one of the biologists to discover if any evidence of his or her work still exists. For example, in California, Yosemite and Sequoia National Parks are still in existence, and, near San Francisco, a small redwood forest has been named Muir Woods in honor of John Muir.

4. Write each biologist's name and dates on separate strips of paper. Place each of the biologists on a world map according to one or more locations in which they worked. Which biologists overlapped in time or location? Which ones worked in many places? In only one place?

5. For younger students: Listen to a story about one of the people (e.g. *On the Frontier with Mr. Audubon,* by Barbara Brenner, Putnam, 1977) and select one or more of these activities:

   - Paint a scene to match what the biologist studied. Several such pictures could begin a biologists gallery.
   - Write 10 facts about the biologist on a chart. Add appropriate drawings. Share your chart with others.
   - Make an award plaque or trophy for the biologist listing his or her contributions.
   - Hold a group discussion on the motivations and accomplishments of the biologist.

Rachel Carson

From *The Teacher's Book of Lists*, Second Edition, published by GoodYearBooks. Copyright © 1994 Sheila Madsen and Bette Gould.

Awards to Animals

Selecting an animal to study can be more fun if you know some interesting animal facts. Here are some animals who have earned awards for outstanding achievement. These awards can be displayed in an awards gallery from which children choose an animal to study.

Maxi Awards

blue whale—largest and heaviest mammal

African elephant—largest land animal

giraffe—tallest animal

Kodiak bear—largest land carnivore

Siberian tiger—largest member of the cat family

springbok—largest herd

gorilla—largest primate

mandrill—largest member of the monkey family

Irish wolfhound—tallest breed of dog

ostrich—largest bird, with the largest eye of any land animal

giant squid—has the largest eye of any living or extinct land or sea animal

wandering albatross—bird with the largest wing span

bald eagle—builds the largest nests

crocodile—largest reptile

Komodo monitor—largest lizard

anaconda—longest and heaviest of all snakes

Chinese giant salamander—largest amphibian

Goliath frog—largest frog

marine toad—largest toad

whale shark—largest fish

white shark—largest carnivorous fish

nephila spider—has the largest spider web

Goliath beetle—heaviest insect

stick-insect—longest insect

giant birdwing—largest butterfly*

Mini Awards

pygmy shrew—smallest mammal

sea otter—smallest totally marine mammal

bee hummingbird—smallest bird

gecko—smallest reptile*

thread snake—shortest snake*

dwarf pygmy goby—shortest fish*

common housefly—shortest-lived insect*

dwarf blue butterfly—smallest butterfly*

Tortoise and Hare Awards

pronghorn antelope—fastest land animal over a sustained distance

cheetah—fastest land animal over a short distance

three-toed sloth—slowest moving land mammal

spine-tailed swift—fastest flying bird

black mamba—fastest moving land snake*

dragonfly—fastest flying insect

marlin—fastest fish over a sustained distance

sea horse—slowest moving marine fish

*Most probable.

From *The Teacher's Book of Lists, Second Edition,* published by GoodYearBooks. Copyright © 1994 Sheila Madsen and Bette Gould.

Senior Citizens Award

killer whale—longest-lived mammal (except humans)

Asiatic elephant—longest-lived land mammal (except humans)

queen termite—longest-lived insect

Bad Guy Awards

king cobra—longest venomous snake

diamondback rattler—heaviest venomous snake

Kokoi arrow poison frog—most poisonous animal ever recorded

stonefish—most venomous sting

Japanese puffer fish—most poisonous fish if eaten

piranha—most ferocious fish

black widow—most venomous spider

blue-ringed octopus—most dangerous octopus

Maternity Award

Asiatic elephant—longest mammal gestation period

The Now Hear This Award

bat—most highly developed sense of hearing (among mammals)

Broad Jump Award

red kangaroo—longest recorded leap

Bon Voyage Award

Arctic tern—longest migration of flying birds

Whiz Kids Award

chimpanzee—most intelligent primate (except humans)

baboon—most intelligent member of the monkey family

The Big Sleep Award

edible dormouse—mammal longest in hibernation

Thick Skin Award

whale shark—the thickest skin of any animal

Loud Mouth Award

male cicada—loudest insect

Architect's Award

termites—master builders of the animal world

From *The Teacher's Book of Lists, Second Edition*, published by GoodYearBooks. Copyright © 1994 Sheila Madsen and Bette Gould.

From *The Guinness Book of Animal Facts and Feats* by Gerald L. Wood. Guinness Superlatives Ltd., Great Britain, 1972.

THE _____ AWARD

IS PRESENTED TO _____
(animal's name)

FOR _____
(animal's outstanding characteristic)

Description of Animal: _____

Habitat: _____

Interesting Facts: _____

Draw a picture of
the animal in its
natural habitat
here.

DATE:

AWARDED BY

From *The Teacher's Book of Lists, Second Edition*, published by GoodYearBooks.
Copyright © 1994 Sheila Madsen and Bette Gould.

Beastly Questions

Work with a friend, group, or the entire class to answer these 35 animal stumpers. Your teacher will tell you whether to write your answers or learn answers to share orally with everyone else. By the way, there are more than a billion different kinds of animals on earth, so you could make up a list of a lot more stumper questions for others to answer. Good luck!

1. Why could the ziczac be called "the crocodile's best friend"?
2. Where would you find some pinnipeds?
3. Which animal would get the Most Unusual Animal Award? Why?
4. Why do some animals estivate?
5. Why are some people called "dodos"?
6. What do the aardvark and the anteater have in common?
7. What is the bear's "Keep-Out" sign?
8. In the old days, why did women who wore corsets need whales?
9. How can crickets help you tell the temperature?
10. How does the platypus break all the rules of nature?
11. Why can't ants be called "litterbugs"?
12. How does the cave fish manage without any eyes?
13. How would you prepare for a hermit crab houseguest?
14. What five features makes the camel well adapted for desert travel?
15. What do the cows, horses, and dogs of the ocean look like?
16. How do you feed a giraffe?
17. What are some special jobs dogs are trained to do?
18. What are an *Odobenus rosmarus* and a *Thalarctos maritimus*?
19. What would you find in a Tiergarten?
20. What is a pangolin?
21. How is a jerboa like a kangaroo?
22. Which animals ruminate?
23. Why do birds sing?
24. How does a raccoon carry its babies?
25. How does a flying squirrel fly?
26. Why don't spiders get caught in their own webs?
27. What does the S.P.C.A. do for animals?
28. How does a bat "see with its ears"?
29. What's odd about the way sloths live?
30. How are some toads' trills (or croaks) amplified or made louder?
31. Where does a snake's tail begin?
32. What does a lepidopterist collect?
33. What happens when insects stridulate?
34. Why can a fly walk on the ceiling?
35. How are an octopus and a squid like a jet?

From *The Teacher's Book of Lists, Second Edition,* published by GoodYearBooks. Copyright © 1994 Sheila Madsen and Bette Gould.

This list will provide practice in the use of reference materials, and lends itself to cooperative learning situations. It could be a starting point for a science unit, such as on animal adaptations, and would be a good place for students to get ideas for independent study.

Computer ASCII Code

ASCII (ASK-ee), the American Standard Code for Information Interchange, is binary code (a system based on 1s and 0s only) for letters, numbers, and symbols you find on a computer keyboard. The computer reads and translates each of the values into its keyboard equivalent.

A	1000001	K	1001011	U	1010101
B	1000010	L	1001100	V	1010110
C	1000011	M	1001101	W	1010111
D	1000100	N	1001110	X	1011000
E	1000101	O	1001111	Y	1011001
F	1000110	P	1010000	Z	1011010
G	1000111	Q	1010001	.	0101110
H	1001000	R	1010010	?	0111111
I	1001001	S	1010011	!	0100001
J	1001010	T	1010100	space	0100000

Name

Date

ASCII ME!

Use the ASCII code list to decode the message below. A black circle stands for 1 and an open circle means 0. The first letter has been decoded for you.

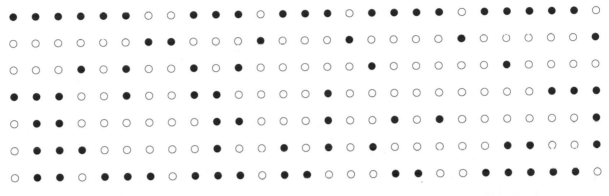

H _____

Now write messages of your own in ASCII. Give them to friends to solve.

From *The Teacher's Book of Lists, Second Edition*, published by GoodYearBooks
Copyright © 1994 Sheila Madsen and Bette Gould.

Computer Flow Chart

Computer programmers use flow charts to see how a program "flows." A flow chart is a diagram of a program that shows the instructions in the correct sequence. The example uses only three symbols; complex flow charts use many symbols. Also, because a computer only does what it is explicitly told to do, this simple example is missing a number of steps—for the program to really work you would have to include additional instructions such as how many steps to take, what degree turn to make, and details for arm and hand movements. As a group activity, see how many other missing instructions your children can come up with. Students of all ages enjoy designing a simple flow chart and it's a painless way of developing logical thinking skills.

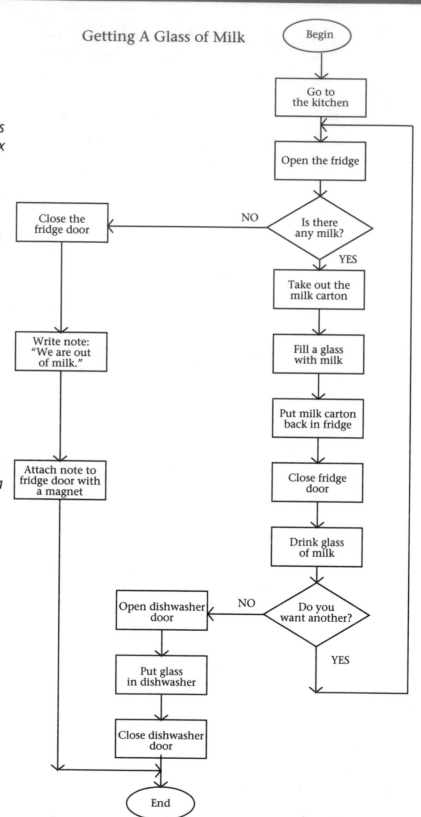

Getting A Glass of Milk

From *The Teacher's Book of Lists, Second Edition,* published by GoodYearBooks.
Copyright © 1994 Sheila Madsen and Bette Gould.

Name _____ Date _____

Design a Computer Flow Chart

You are designing a computer flow chart for your robot to perform a simple job that you take for granted. Here are a few suggestions:

- making a telephone call
- getting mail from the mail box
- making a sundae
- taking out the trash
- setting the table

1. Decide on the job.

2. Make a list of the steps required to complete the job. Remember, the robot will do only what you tell it to do, so you might have to revise your list several times.

3. List each instruction on a ▭

4. When you come to a decision point, write it on a ◇

5. Write beginnings and ends on a ⬭

6. Cut out the shapes, glue them to a large piece of paper, and add arrows to show how to follow the flow chart. If you need extra symbols (good for you!), ask for another copy of this worksheet or draw your own.

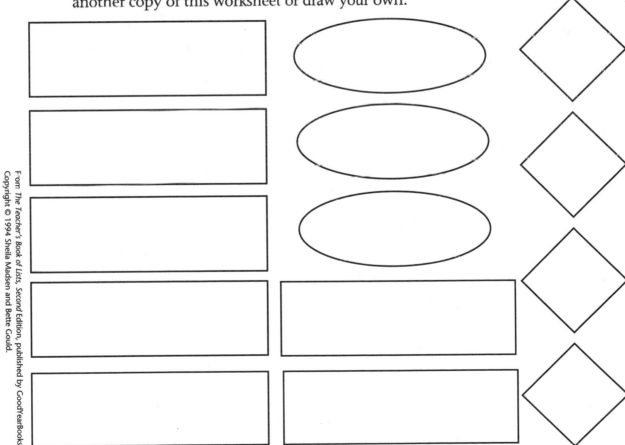

Computer Milestones

We take for granted the computer and the myriad of devices that utilize the technologies developed by the electronics industry. The advent of the transistor and the silicon chip revolutionized the design of products we use today—we expect faster, cheaper, and smaller. A look at the history of the computer and the individuals who envisioned machines that would provide greater productivity presents a new perspective on progress and the growth of technology.

13th century **Abacus**
The abacus was developed in the Orient more than 5,000 years ago and is still used today in parts of the Middle and Far East. It is made up of beads that move up and down on strings or rods. Each bead stands for a number. By moving the beads, you can add, subtract, multiply, and divide. A skilled abacus user could do computations faster than someone using one of the early electronic calculators.

1617 **Napier's Bones**
John Napier was a Scots mathematician and the inventor of logarithms. He developed a method of multiplying and dividing using rods. Because the rods were often made of ivory or a bone-like material, they were called Napier's bones.

1641 **Arithmetic Machine**
The French scientist-philosopher Blaise Pascal built the first successful adding machine. The Pascaline used a series of wheels that interlocked with gears and could add and subtract up to eight columns of numbers. A programming language is named after Pascal.

1671–1694 **Stepped Reckoner**
Gottfried Leibnitz, a German mathematician, improved Pascal's invention. His Leibnitz calculator could multiply, divide, and find the square root of numbers as well as add and subtract.

1801 **Jacquard Loom**
A loom for weaving cloth was invented by Joseph Marie Jacquard of France. Jacquard's loom used a series of punched cards that fed the pieces of thread automatically into the loom to create a pattern in the cloth.

1834–1854 **Analytical Engine**
Sir Charles Babbage was an English mathematician who worked for nearly forty years on the Analytical Engine, which was designed to do more than computations. The machine was programmed using Jacquard's punched cards, had memory and logic units, and could transfer information within the machine. Although the Analytical Engine was never built, Babbage is often thought of as the "father of the modern computer" because many of his designs and theories are used in modern computers.

1859   **Boolean Logic**
George Boole was an English mathematician and logician who developed symbolic logic. In Boolean logic any problem can be solved through a series of yes or no, true or false choices. Boolean logic is very important to the modern computer, which operates with only two choices.

1890   **Tabulating Machine**
Herman Hollerith was a U.S. statistician who worked for the Census Bureau. Every 10 years a census count of the population is taken. The 1880 census, which Hollerith worked on, took 8 years to complete. Hollerith designed a machine that used punched cards like Jacquard's, each hole representing information about a person—age, sex, marital status. The machine was used for the 1890 census, which took only two and one-half years to complete. Hollerith went on to form a company which we know today as IBM.

1939-1944   **Mark I**
Howard Aiken of Harvard University and engineers at IBM worked for five years to build a completely automatic calculator. It was an electromechanical machine about 50 feet long and 8 feet high. The Mark I was built primarily for use in the war because new weapons required complex calculations for aiming artillery and setting bomb sites. The Mark I used punched cards to input information and output was either on punched cards or an electric typewriter.

1943-1946   **ENIAC Computer**
J. Presper Eckert and John Mauchly of the University of Pennsylvania invented the Eniac (Electronic Numerical Integrator and Calculator). The ENIAC was built for the army and did the same kinds of calculations as the Mark I. It was also a very big machine—about 100 feet long and ten feet high. However, the ENIAC was completely electronic and much faster than the Mark I because it used vacuum tubes as switches instead of mechanical switches. Today's desktop computers can do everything the ENIAC did and faster.

1947   **EDVAC**
John von Neumann, an American mathematician, developed the idea of storing the computer program in the machine's memory. Other computers used programs, but none stored them in their memories. Von Neumann and others wrote a report that detailed the design of the ENIAC and expanded it. The design of a computer described in this report, with a few changes, is the basis of all modern computers. The EDVAC (Electronic Discrete Variable Automatic Computer) was built at the University of Pennsylvania. It was the first machine with a program stored inside.

1948   **Transistor**
Invented at Bell Laboratories by John Bardeen, Walter Brattain, and William Shockley.

1951   **UNIVAC**
The UNIVAC was the first computer to be mass-produced.

1958   **Integrated Circuit**
Called an IC or silicon chip, the integrated circuit contained all components of a circuit—transistors, resistors, and capacitors—within a single semiconductor wafer. This allowed computers to be smaller, faster, and use less power.

1962   **First electronic desk calculator**

1964   **First word processor**

1969   **First microprocessor**

1969   **First microcomputer**

1970   **Electronic desk calculators**

1971   **Video recorders**

1972   **Early video games**

1977   **Videodisks, voice recognition**

1985   **Portable computers**

1987   **Laptop computers**

1990s   **Notebook computers**

Multimedia (computer using video animation and stereo sound)

Virtual reality (simulation of an environment or situation that is so realistic your senses tell you that you are there)

From *The Teacher's Book of Lists, Second Edition,* published by GoodYearBooks. Copyright © 1994 Sheila Madsen and Bette Gould.

Computer Terms

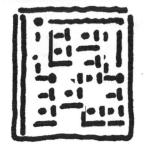

Children can run circles around adults when it comes to using a computer. Unlike many adults, they have no fear of the technology and experiment freely knowing that they cannot break the equipment. They also quickly pick up the jargon of computers and speak naturally in "megs" and bytes. So this beginners' list of computer terms is for you, if you're a computer novice, or for parents who are in the same boat.

access   To be able to see and change what is in a document or file. When you tell a computer to show you a file, you are accessing the file.

alphanumeric   Letters and numbers.

application   Means the same thing as program or the software package you use to write, draw, or layout a document. MacPaint, WriteNow, and Claris Works are applications.

ASCII   Acronym for American Standard Code for Information Interchange. A set of numbers assigned to represent letters, numbers, punctuation, and symbols. In ASCII, the letter S = 1010011.

backup   A copy of information (programs, data you have entered) that you can use if the original gets damaged or lost. Keeping a current backup is very important.

baud rate   The speed at which electronic data travels through a line. A computer might send information over telephone lines at 300 baud, which is very slow, or at 19,200 baud, which is very fast.

binary   A number system that uses only two digits—zero and one.

bit   A short form of binary digit. A bit is the smallest piece of information a computer can use—one digit in a binary number, either a one or a zero.

bit map   A mosaic of bits that make up a graphic or font.

board   Short for printed-circuit board.

buffer   A "holding place" in memory where information is temporarily stored.

bulletin board   Similar to a bulletin board you see in stores and in school. You can advertise things for sale, place a want ad, leave messages, or list meeting times. With an electronic bulletin board, you need a modem, and because a computer stores lots of information, you can also exchange games, programs, and documents.

bug   An error or problem in a computer program that causes it to function improperly.

byte   Usually means a group of eight bits. One byte represents the code for one letter of the alphabet. For example, "F" = 01000110.

chip   An integrated circuit on a "chip" of silicon. Chips are usually mounted on a carrier that has many metal pins, which are used to mount the chip to a printed-circuit board.

circuit   A path that electricity follows. In your home, the electrical circuit is yards of wiring; on a circuit board, inches; and on a chip, microscopic.

compatible   When programs or peripherals work with a computer, they are compatible. For example, MacDraw is compatible with a Macintosh, but not with an IBM.

CPU   Acronym for Central Processing Unit. The brain of a computer that controls all operations. A CPU is usually a self-contained unit that contains a disk drive, memory, and processing boards.

crash   A "crash" occurs when a program stops running or the computer "freezes up."

CRT   Acronym for Cathode Ray Tube. Many people call their monitor or screen a CRT. In fact, the CRT is only part of the monitor. It includes the screen where information is displayed.

cursor   A small shape on the screen that tells you where information will be entered. The cursor can be a blinking box or line, or sometimes an arrow.

data   Information you enter in the computer. Data can be words, numbers, or pictures (graphics).

disk   Stores software programs and documents you save.

disk drive   Disk drives store data on many types of disks: floppy, hard, and optical. Disk drives come in many shapes and sizes.

display   The information you see on a monitor screen. Display is also often used as another word for monitor. *What kind of display are you using?*

document   When you use a program to write, draw, or compute, you are creating a document. When you save the document, you create a file. File and document are often used interchangeably.

file   A place on a disk where you store information. When you save a document, you give it a name and it becomes a file just like when you label and put a file in a file drawer.

floppy disk   A removable magnetic disk that stores information and programs. Disks are made of flexible plastic and contained in cardboard or a stiff plastic container.

font   A set of letters, numbers, symbols, and punctuation that have the same look or style.

gigabyte (Gbyte)   1,000,000,000 bytes. Many storage devices have over a gigabyte capacity.

GIGO   Acronym for Garbage In, Garbage Out. It is a short way of saying that if you enter incorrect information into the computer, you will receive incorrect information from the computer.

graphic   A picture. Diagrams, photographs, and illustrations are graphics.

hard disk   A metal disk that is permanently sealed in a container that is built into a computer or as a separate unit. They store large amounts of information and run much faster than a floppy drive. Sometimes people call a hard disk a hard drive.

hardware   The electrical or mechanical parts of a computer system. Monitors, keyboards, and printed-circuit boards are hardware. Peripherals such as scanners and printers are also hardware.

input   Information that goes into a computer from an external source such as a keyboard, mouse, or modem.

integrated circuit   A complete electronic circuit contained in one place. Also called chips or ICs.

interface   The connection between two pieces of computer equipment. An interface can be a circuit board, a program, or both.

From *The Teacher's Book of Lists, Second Edition,* published by GoodYearBooks. Copyright © 1994 Sheila Madsen and Bette Gould.

kilobyte (K)   1024 bytes. You usually hear people talking about Kbytes or Ks.

megabyte (Mb)   A unit of measurement equal to 1024 kilobytes. Usually used to measure memory and often referred to as "megs." *I've got a 40-meg disk drive.*

memory   The part of the computer processor that stores data. There are two types of memory: RAM and ROM.

microprocessor   A complete computer on a chip. Microprocessors are in everyday items, such as cars, microwave ovens, and pocket calculators.

modem   Short for modulator/demodulator. A device that connects a computer to a telephone line. Think of a modem as a telephone for your computer. When your computer calls another computer with its own modem, they can "talk" to each other by exchanging files.

monitor   A TV-like device for displaying information.

mouse   A small hand-held input device that moves a pointer on the screen.

operating system   A software program that controls the computer hardware and applications programs.

optical disk   A metal disk from which data is read using a beam of light.

output   Information sent out from the computer. What you see on the screen and hardcopy from printers are output.

peripheral   Any hardware device such as a printer, joystick, or scanner that is used with a computer and under the computer's control.

pixel   Short for picture element. Everything you see on the screen is made up of pixels.

printer   A peripheral device that prints output on paper or film in black and white or in color. Dot-matrix printers are the simplest kind of printer using a pattern of dots to print. Laser printers can print alphanumerics and graphics, but at a much higher speed and quality. There are also color printers that can print up to 16 million colors.

program   A set of instructions, written in a computer language, that tells the computer how to complete a task.

programmers   People who write programs are programmers. Their job is called programming. Lady Ada Lovelace was the first programmer.

RAM   Acronym for Random Access Memory. When you input information into the computer, it goes into RAM. However, when you turn off the computer or if you have a crash, everything in RAM is erased. People always want more RAM because the more you have, the faster programs run.

ROM   Acronym for Read-Only Memory. ROM is like a book of instructions that is stored permanently inside a chip. Unlike RAM, you cannot change what is in ROM and the information is not erased when you turn off the computer.

save   To store information by transferring it from RAM to a floppy disk or your hard drive. You should save frequently to avoid losing information in case of a crash or a power failure.

silicon   An element that is found in sand. Computer chips are made of silicon.

software   Programs that run on hardware. Operating systems that make the computer run and programs are software.

system   All the pieces of software and hardware, including peripherals, make up a system or computer system.

Dinosaurs

Dinosaurs is one subject that has something for everyone from the youngest kindergartner to the mature sixth-grade learner. The subject lends itself to thematic units such as Change, Systems and Interactions, and Structures. Younger children will enjoy stepping off the length of various dinosaurs on the playground and marking with chalk or paint. Older students can become avid followers in the news media of the latest developments of scientific discovery and research in this area. Two books to get you started: Dinosaurs in Your Backyard, William Mannetti (Atheneum, 1982), and Dinosaurs of North America, Helen Roney Sattler (Lothrop, 1981).

ALLOSAURUS—(AL-uh-SAW-ruhs)
- meat eater
- more than thirty feet long
- moved on two large hind legs, used powerful tail for support in walking or standing

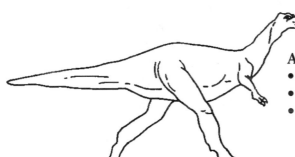

ANATOSAURUS—(uh-NAT-uh-SAW-ruhs)
- plant eater
- about forty feet long
- walked on two legs; had as many as 2,000 teeth

ANKYLOSAURUS—(ANG-kih-loh-SAW-ruhs)
- plant eater
- about ten feet long
- body was covered with overlapping bony plates with a row of spikes along each side; clublike tail tipped with a heavy mass of bone

APATOSAURUS (Brontosaurus)—(uh-PAT-oh-SAW-ruhs)
- plant eater
- over seventy feet in length, weighed nearly thirty tons
- spoon-shaped and pencil-shaped teeth
- probably traveled in herds

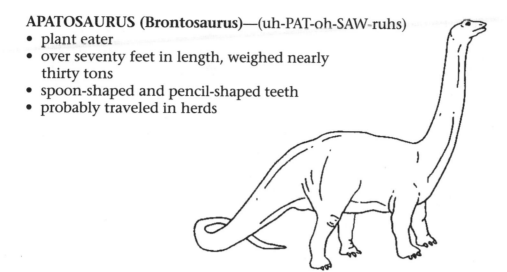

BRACHIOSAURUS—(BRAK-ee-oh-SAW-ruhs)
- plant eater
- seventy feet long, weighed eighty-four short tons

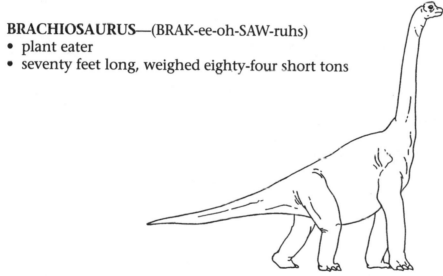

DIPLODOCUS—(dih-ploh-DAH-kuhs)
- swamp dwelling plant eater
- almost ninety feet long
- long whiplike tail; nostrils on top of head

ICHTHYOSAURUS—(ICK-thee-oh-SAW-ruhs)

- sea creature; meat eater
- adults were sometimes forty feet long
- body shape similar to sharks; mouth filled with teeth needed for catching and holding fish

MEGALOSAURUS—(MEG-uh-loh-SAW-ruhs)

- meat eater
- stood almost twelve feet high
- walked on hind legs; large head with sharp teeth; small front legs

PTERANODON—(tuh-RAN-uh-dahn)

- meat eater; ate fish and small flying things
- wingspread of nearly thirty feet; small stumpy body that probably weighed no more than twenty-five or thirty pounds
- largest of the flying reptiles (pterodactyl or pterosaurus); had no teeth or tail; long skull with a protruding bony crest

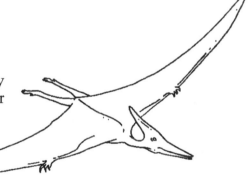

SEISMOSAURUS—(SIZE-moh-SAW-ruhs)

- plant eater
- 140 feet long
- largest animal to ever live on earth

From *The Teacher's Book of Lists, Second Edition*, published by GoodYearBooks.
Copyright © 1994 Sheila Madsen and Bette Gould.

STEGOSAURUS—(STEG-uh-SAW-ruhs)
- about 30 feet long
- plant eater
- triangular bony plates protected its neck, back, and tail; brain about the size of a walnut

TRACHODON—(TRACH-uh-DON)
- plant eater
- thirty to forty feet long
- duck-billed; walked on hind legs

TRICERATOPS—(try-SERR-uh-tahps)
- plant eater
- twenty-five feet long
- bony armor covered head; three horns protruded from head

From *The Teacher's Book of Lists, Second Edition*, published by GoodYearBooks. Copyright © 1994 Sheila Madsen and Bette Gould.

TYRANNOSAURUS REX—(teh-RAN-uh-SAW-ruhs REX)
- largest meat eater
- measured fifty feet from nose to tail, stood about twenty feet high
- had six-inch razor-sharp teeth

Activities: Dinosaurs

1. Make a graph of the lengths of the dinosaurs.

CARNIVORES	HERBIVORES
Pteranodon	Apatosaurus

2. Categorize the dinosaurs into two groups: carnivores and herbivores.

3. Convert the lengths of the dinosaurs into meters.

4. Use the length of a car, bed, or other large thing as a unit of measure. Convert the lengths of the dinosaurs into this unit. For example, ankylosaurus = about one car

    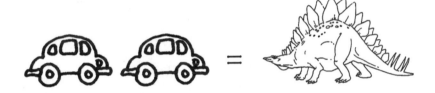

5. Choose a dinosaur and a familiar melody. Make up lyrics to fit the melody, using the information on the dinosaur list. Here's a song about a trachodon to be sung to the melody of *Three Blind Mice.*

    Trachodon, Trachodon,
    Duck-billed mouth, duck-billed mouth,
    He walked about on his two hind legs,
    His length was thirty to forty feet,
    Did you ever see such a sight in your life as Trachodon.

From *The Teacher's Book of Lists, Second Edition,* published by GoodYearBooks. Copyright © 1994 Sheila Madsen and Bette Gould.

Human Body Systems

Did you know that your body is 70% water? Or that your brain sends messages at about 240 miles per hour? Or that your heart beats about 100,000 times per day? There are about 50 trillion cells in the adult body and 26 billion cells in the newborn baby's, organized into tissues and organs that make up the body systems. Your students' natural interest in themselves (they all have a body to learn about), the easy tie-in with math, measurement, experimentation, and themes such as Systems and Interactions, make this a favorite area of study.

SKELETAL SYSTEM	Supports the body and protects the organs and tissues; bones house the bone marrow which makes red blood cells.
Major Parts	206 bones, from the skull at the top to the phalanges at the end of the toes cartilage, an elastic-like material found between bones that acts as padding
Amazing Parts	femur—the longest bone stirrup (stapes)—found in the ear, it's the body's smallest bone skull—protects the brain mandible (jawbone)—the only bone in the skull that moves
Interesting Info	The backbone is made up of 24 smaller bones called vertebrae. Each minute, millions of your red blood cells die. They are constantly being replaced by millions of healthy new cells manufactured in the bone marrow. The hardest bone of the body is the petrous bone. It is on the floor of the skull and houses the brain.
Research Questions	HOW'S YOUR FUNNY BONE? • What makes your funny bone "zing" when you hit it a certain way? • What are your joints? How do they work? • Why do some anthropologists say that human beings' most wonderful physical adaptations are their hands and feet? • Bones, both animal and human, have been used for many purposes by people in long-ago times (and up to the present). Chart or demonstrate some of these uses. • Imagine your body without any bones. Describe what life would be like.
MUSCULAR SYSTEM	Muscles pull on the bones to make them move and surround most of the soft organs of the body.

MUSCULAR SYSTEM (cont.) **Major Parts**	more than 650 muscles
	tendons—cords that attach muscles to muscles, and muscles to bones
	ligaments—reach from one bone to another to hold them together, as in your joints
Amazing Parts	diaphragm—Don't breathe without it!
	biceps and triceps—Make a muscle!
	gluteus maximus—Sit on it!
Interesting Info	It takes 14 muscles to smile.
	The cardiac (heart) muscle is different from both voluntary and involuntary muscles. It has qualities of both and is a special set of involuntary muscles that must keep your heart beating regularly all by itself.
	Every movable bone in your body has muscles attached to move it.
Research Questions	FLEX YOUR MUSCLES

- Figure out all the muscles needed to make your body run.
- Which muscles overlap each other? twine around each other? are squeezed between other muscles and bones?
- Plan an exercise program that pays attention to each of the muscle groups of the body.
- What are muscles made of? What are the different shapes and thicknesses of muscles? Why such a variety?
- What does it mean to say that muscles work in opposition to other muscles? Name several sets of opposing muscles.

NERVOUS SYSTEM	The nerves and spinal cord carry messages to and from the brain. The brain interprets these messages and sends out messages to parts of the body. The brain is also the storehouse of memory and the "mind."
Major Parts	brain
	spinal cord
	nerves
Amazing Parts	brain—the master controller and interpreter
	medulla oblongata—regulates such things as breathing, digestion of food, circulation of blood
	cerebrum—a part of the brain with many centers, such as for memory, speech, the senses, motor (motion) impulses, thinking, reasoning
Interesting Info	There are about 10,000,000 neurons (nerve cells) in your brain.
	When full size, your brain will weigh about two and a half to three pounds. Two larger brains belong to the elephant (about 8 pounds) and the male whale (about five pounds). But, in comparison to body size, the human brain is much larger than that of either the elephant or the whale.
	Many types of paralysis occur each year due to spinal cord injury, some related to sports. The type of paralysis is related to where, along its length, the spinal cord is injured.

NERVOUS SYSTEM (cont.)
Research Questions

TEST YOUR NERVES
- How have scientists mapped the brain? What is still left to be discovered about the brain?
- How do alcohol and other drugs affect the brain and other parts of the nervous system?
- Breathing is controlled by the automatic part of the nervous system. To experience this, try holding your breath. How long before your nervous system gets you to start breathing again?
- Compare computers to the human brain and nervous system. What compares to the software and hardware parts such as the hard disk, memory boards, mouse, etc.
- How does the mind relate to or compare with the brain?
- How do the sizes of brains compare to brain power (smart vs. average people, etc.)?

RESPIRATORY SYSTEM

Allows oxygen to enter the body, be picked up by the blood and carried to all the body cells, and allows carbon dioxide and other wastes to leave the body.

Major Parts

nose	epiglottis
trachea (windpipe)	bronchial tubes
larynx	alveoli (tiny air sacs)

Amazing Parts

lungs—the largest parts of the respiratory system
alveoli—the smallest parts of the respiratory system
larynx—the voice box

Interesting Info

	elephant	human	cat	mouse
• heartbeats per minute	35	70–80	120	600
• breaths per minute	10	12	26	163

(source: *Health and Growth, Book Five,* Julius B. Richmond, et al. Scott, Foresman and Company, 1974.)

Research Questions

BREATH IS THE STUFF OF LIFE
- Why is it better to breathe in through the nose, rather than the mouth, at least most of the time?
- How are the capillaries of the circulatory system related to the alveoli of the respiratory system?
- What happens to the lungs when someone smokes?
- What occupational or environmental hazards affect the respiratory system?

CIRCULATORY SYSTEM

Pumps blood throughout the body and through the lungs where oxygen and carbon dioxide (and other wastes) are exchanged.

Major Parts

heart	arteries
aorta	capillaries
veins	blood

Amazing Parts

heart—largest part of the circulatory system
capillary—smallest part of the circulatory system
aorta—largest artery

CIRCULATORY SYSTEM (cont.)
Interesting Info

If all of your blood vessels were linked up end to end, they would measure about 60,000 miles long.

In children about 10 years old, the heart beats about 90 times a minute. A baby's heart beats about 140 times per minute; an adult's about 70 to 80 times per minute.

Everyone has a blood type that must be matched if receiving a transfusion or donating blood. Here are the percentages of the different human blood types:

O = 45%	B = 10%
A = 41%	AB = 4%

85% of people have a positive Rh factor (an important blood marker); the Rh factor accompanies all the blood types, so that your blood might be identified as O positive, or B negative

Research Questions

CAN YOU HEAR YOUR HEART BEAT?
- Explain what the doctor is listening for when he uses a stethoscope to listen to your heart.
- What do the parts (auricles, ventricles, valves) of the heart do?
- How did William Harvey and Marcello Malpighi contribute to our knowledge of the circulatory system?
- Design a test or experiment to find out what happens to people's heartbeats when they are tired, sad, excited, worried, angry, have just run a race, etc.
- What are the different parts of the blood, and what is each part's function?

DIGESTIVE SYSTEM

Prepares food so that our cells can use it by absorbing food into the body; also eliminates any solid material that cannot be absorbed.

Major Parts

mouth	salivary glands
esophagus	teeth
stomach	pancreas
small intestine	liver
large intestine	gall bladder
anus	

Amazing Parts

esophagus (Can you say and spell it?)

salivary glands—digestion begins in the mouth with the production of enzymes from these glands (with a little help from your teeth)

villi—the tiny fingerlike parts that line the walls of the small intestine

Interesting Info

The small intestines are about 20 feet long.

Watery dissolved food passes through the capillaries in the walls of the villi to get into the blood; each villi is about the size of a comma on this page.

The usual time required for digestion (the time food is eaten until the undigested portions are passed from the body) is anywhere from 10 to 20 hours.

From *The Teacher's Book of Lists, Second Edition*, published by GoodYearBooks. Copyright © 1994 Sheila Madsen and Bette Gould.

DIGESTIVE SYSTEM (cont.) Research Questions

CAN YOU DIGEST THIS?

- Describe Réne de Réaumur's (c.1750) experiment with his bird, a pet kite. What did William Beaumont's work do to add to the knowledge of digestion?
- Describe all of the actions of the stomach from the time food enters it until the time it moves into the small intestine.
- What could happen if the pancreas or the liver or the gall bladder were not working properly?
- What role do teeth play in digestion?
- How does the digestive system handle alcohol?
- Develop a nutritional food plan for someone your age and with your food likes and dislikes.

URINARY SYSTEM

Rids the body of liquid wastes.

Major Parts

kidneys	bladder
ureters	urethra

Amazing Parts

kidneys—the two main organs of the urinary system; contain thousands of little filtering tubes to remove wastes from the blood

bladder—the muscular sac that distends (swells) as it is filled with urine; usually emptied when a volume of about 10 ounces is reached (in adults)

Interesting Info

About 400 gallons of blood pass through your kidneys to be cleansed each day.

From three to six glasses of waste water are passed off by our bodies as urine each day.

Research Questions

AT YOUR DISPOSAL?

- What happens to a person's body if the kidneys are not working properly? What are some common kidney diseases?
- What are artificial kidneys? How commonly are they used? What might happen if a person only lost one kidney, due to illness or accident?
- What health habits are most important to your kidneys and bladder? What are kidney stones?

REPRODUCTIVE SYSTEM

Produces the cells and environment needed to reproduce another human being.

Major Parts

ovaries	vagina
testes	penis
uterus	vas deferens
fallopian tubes	prostate gland

REPRODUCTIVE SYSTEM (cont.)

Amazing Parts

ovary—in the adult female, an ovary is about the size of an almond shell

fallopian tubes (one for each ovary)—the tubes the ovum moves through on its way from the ovary to the uterus; fertilization by a sperm may occur here

epididymis—a soft part covering a portion of each testes; it is actually a convoluted tube, about 18–20 feet long

Interesting Info

The egg is the largest human cell (but only about $\frac{1}{125}$ in. in diameter).

Females are born with all the ova (eggs) they will ever have.

Males produce sperm in the billions throughout life, from puberty on. (A single sperm is about $\frac{1}{500}$ in. in length.)

Research Questions

"REPRODUCIBLE" QUESTIONS

• Describe the various stages of the developing fetus—from a fertilized cell up to the time of birth.

• How do chromosomes, genes, and DNA influence what you are like? How are you alike/different from others? Why?

• Compare human reproduction with that of non-mammals, such as birds, insects, jellyfish. Compare with plant reproduction.

• How do the hormones produced by the ovaries in females and the testes in males influence body features?

ENDOCRINE GLANDS

Sometimes considered a system, but parts are often included separately in other systems. Regulates body functions by producing a variety of hormones.

Major Parts

islets of Langerhans (located in the pancreas)

pituitary gland   thymus

thyroid   adrenals

parathyroids

Amazing Parts

thymus—in young people, its main function is in the development of the body's immune system

adrenal glands—sit on top of the kidneys; produce sex hormones and hormones concerned with metabolic functions; also produce adrenaline

Interesting Info

The pancreas (islets of Langerhans) produces insulin, a hormone that directs the body in the processing of sugars and fats. Improper functioning leads to diabetes.

The pituitary produces growth hormone.

Other kinds of glands are oil glands, salivary glands, and sweat glands.

From *The Teacher's Book of Lists, Second Edition,* published by GoodYearBooks. Copyright © 1994 Sheila Madsen and Bette Gould.

ENDOCRINE GLANDS (cont.)
Research Questions

HOW ARE YOUR HORMONES TODAY?
- Find out, for each of the glands, what happens when too much or too little hormones are produced.
- How does the pituitary regulate your growth? Why aren't all 10- or 11-year-olds the same height?
- Which glands come into play when you are frightened or in danger? What do they do?
- What are the causes and the treatments for diabetes? What health problems are associated with diabetes?

SENSE ORGANS

Collect sensations and send as nerve impulses to the brain which interprets the information; not classified as a system, but often are studied as a group.

Major Parts

eyes
ears
nose
taste buds (on the tongue; a few in other parts of the mouth)
some nerve endings in the skin (they respond to cold, heat, pain, texture, etc.)

Amazing Parts

retina—thin filmy structure that lines the back of the eye; covered with special cells (the rods and cones) that respond to light
hammer, anvil, stirrup—three tiny bones in the middle ear that convey vibrations from the outer ear to the inner ear
papillae—tiny bumps on the tongue that contain the taste buds

Interesting Info

An estimated 10 square feet of skin is on the body of an average 10- or 11-year old.
We blink our eyes about 20,000 times a day.
There are about 9,000 taste buds in the papillae on your tongue.

Research Questions

HOW ARE YOUR RECEPTORS?
- What are the causes of blindness? What does it mean to be color blind? Why does this happen?
- What are the various nerve endings in the epidermis and dermis?
- What does chemistry have to do with your sense of taste and smell?
- Why is the cochlea said to be the most important part of the ear? What does liquid have to do with hearing? How is hearing related to physics?
- How do the rods and cones of the eye's retina work?

Insects and Spiders— Some Picturesque Names

There are many more fascinating creatures with picturesque names in the insect/arachnid world. One name may just capture a student's imagination, leading to some independent study or even a lifelong interest. A good book on spiders is Spider Magic, *by Dorothy Hinshaw Patent (Holiday, 1982). It contains amazing black-and-white photographs of spiders. Fictional tales include* The Cricket Winter, *Felice Holman (Scribner's, 1967) and* The Cricket in Times Square, *by George Selden (Farrar Strauss Giroux, 1981), the adventures of a cricket who lives in a newsstand in Times Square and rescues the owner of the stand from financial ruin. There are other groups of the natural world that have picturesque names, such as plants (Venus flytrap, lipstick plant, donkey tail) and fish (turkey fish, nurse shark, parrot fish), which the class may want to learn about.*

ant lion
assassin bug

back swimmer
bald-faced hornet
bedbug
beefly
big green darner dragonfly
black widow spider
blister beetle
buffalo tree hopper
burying beetle

cabbage butterfly
carpenter ant
carpenter bee
carpet beetle
confused flower beetle
corn earworm

daddy longlegs (harvestman)
deathwatch beetle
dog-faced butterfly

earwig
engraver beetle

firefly

garden springtail
Goliath beetle
greenbottle fly
gypsy moth

harlequin bug

June bug

lacewing
lady beetle (lady bug)
lightning bug
longhorn beetle

mayfly
monarch butterfly

paper wasp
praying mantis
punkies, no-see-ums (fly)

red admiral butterfly
robber fly

scorpion fly
silverfish

snowy tree cricket
soldier beetle
squashbug
squint-eye spider
sphinx moth
striped cucumber beetle
swallowtail butterfly

tarnished plant bug
tiger moth
tortoise beetle
trapdoor spider
triangle spider
turret spider
two-striped grasshopper

wanderer butterfly
water boatman
water penny beetle
water strider
whirligig beetle
wolf spider

yellow jacket
yellow woolybear (moth)

zebra spider

From *The Teacher's Book of Lists, Second Edition,* published by GoodYearBooks.
Copyright © 1994 Sheila Madsen and Bette Gould.

Activities: Insects and Spiders

1. Draw several of the insects and spiders as you think they would look, according to their names. Then compare your drawings with pictures of how the insects and spiders really look.

2. Categorize the insects and spiders into helpful and harmful groups.

HELPFUL	HARMFUL
Trapdoor Spider	Cabbage Butterfly

3. Categorize the insects and spiders by their names, into groups such as colors, foods, animals, and jobs.

Worksheet

Casting Call worksheet, p. 222

Casting Call

1. Color in the Current Cast. Here are their descriptions:

   Cara, the cabbage butterfly—owns the garden; hates flies

   Big daddy longlegs—the garden guard; Cara's friend

   Harvey, the harlequin beetle—makes insect jokes; happy disposition

2. Name, draw, and color each new character needed to complete the cast:

   —————— —an evil bug, up to no good

   —————— —a colorful beauty; kinda snooty

   —————— —two-striped grasshopper

3. Now, color in the background. Tell or act out a short play featuring these characters (and others if you need them).

Needed to Complete Cast

Current Cast

Inventions & Inventors

Thomas Edison is said to be the greatest of all the inventors in history. Among his many inventions and developments (he received 1,093 patents) are the electric light, a mimeograph machine, a motion-picture camera and projector, and the phonograph. The following inventions were selected because they are familiar products known by most children. Other inventions and inventors can be found in the following lists: **Computer Milestones**, p. 202; **Eponyms**, p. 14; and **U.S. Space Missions**, p. 235. Many modern inventions, especially high-tech devices such as video games, CDs, and VCRs were company or group inventions. A challenging project would be for students to compare the individual vs. the group inventive process.

airplane, the first successful—Orville and Wilbur Wright   1903

aspirin—Dresser   1889

automobile—Gottlieb Daimler and Karl Benz   1885

bakelite—one of the first plastics—L. H. Baekeland   1907

balloons that carry people in the air—Montgolfier   1783

ballpoint pen—patented by Ladislao J. and George Biro   1938

bicycle, modern type—James Starley   1884

bifocal lens—Benjamin Franklin   1780

carpet sweeper—Bissell   1876

cellophane—J. E. Brandenberger   1912

clock, pendulum type—Christian Huygens   1657

cotton gin—Catherine Greene and Eli Whitney   1793. Eli Whitney is always given credit for the invention of the cotton gin, but the idea actually came from Mrs. Greene, who, as a woman, was not allowed to apply for a patent.

dynamite—Alfred Nobel   1866

elevator, power type—Elisha Otis   1852

food preservation, by canning—Appert   1810

food preservation, by freezing—Clarence Birdseye   1920s

helicopter—Igor Sikorsky   1939

hydroplane—Glenn Curtiss   1911

kodak, roll-film hand camera—Eastman and Walker   1888

laser—Theodore N. Maiman   1960

lawn mower—A. M. Hills   1868

light bulb—Thomas Edison   1879

lightning rod—Benjamin Franklin   1752

locomotive, first successful steam—George Stephenson   1829

mason jar—J. Mason   1858

matches, friction—John Walker   1827

microphone—Emil Berliner   1877

microscope, compound—Zacharias Janssen 1590

nylon—E. I. du Pont de Nemours & Co. 1937

oleomargarine—H. Mege-Mouries   1869

pen, first successful fountain—L. E. Waterman   1884

penicillin—Alexander Fleming   1929

phonograph—Thomas Edison   1877

piano—Bartollomeo Cristofori   1709

Polaroid Land camera—Edwin H. Land   1947

polio vaccines—Jonas Salk (1953) and Albert Sabin (1955)

printing from movable type—Johann Gutenberg   1450

rabies vaccine—Louis Pasteur   1885

radar—A. Hoyt Taylor and Leo C. Young 1922

razor, electric—Schick   1931

razor, safety—Gillette   1895

refrigerating machine—John Gorie   1851

revolver—Samuel Colt   1835

rocket (liquid fuel)—Robert Goddard   1926

sewing machine—Elias Howe   1846

sextant—John Hadley   1731

telegraph—Samuel Morse   1837

telephone—Alexander Graham Bell   1876

television—J. L. Baird 1925; independently by C. F. Jenkins   1925

thermometer—Galileo   1593

thermometer, mercury—Gabriel Fahrenheit 1714

typewriter, first practicable—C. L. Sholes 1865

vacuum bottle—James Dewar   1893

Velcro®—George de Mestral   mid 1950s

vulcanization of rubber, a process that made rubber useful by giving it elasticity, hardness, and strength—Charles Goodyear 1844

xerography (dry photographic copying)—Chester Carlson   1937

x-ray—Wilhelm Roentgen   1895

zipper—Judson   1891

Medical Breakthroughs

*Many children will recognize some of these events and discoveries. The stories of struggle and discovery are rewarding and inspiring, and lead to some familiarity with and understanding of the scientific spirit and method. See **Independent Study** worksheets, p. 368–371, for activities to use with any of these breakthroughs.*

c.2700 B.C.	The Chinese emperor, Shen Nung, developed the principles of acupuncture and herbal treatments.
c.400 B.C.	Hippocrates, a Greek medical practioner known as The Father of Medicine, wrote the Hippocratic Oath, which sets ethical medical standards still followed by physicians today.
c.180	Galen wrote a summary of the medical knowledge of ancient times. He introduced the significance of studying anatomy. His views influenced medical thought for more than 1,500 years.
1590	The compound microscope was developed by Zacharias Janssen of Holland.
1628	William Harvey's book on how blood circulates is considered the most important single volume in the history of physiology. He also made important discoveries on the development of the embryo.
1674–76	Anton von Leeuwenhoek, a pioneer in microscopy, observed bacteria and protozoa calling them "very little animalcules."
1760	Benjamin Franklin developed bifocal lens.
1797	Edward Jenner inoculated a child with a viral vaccine as a protection from smallpox.
1839	Schwinn and Schleidens developed their cellular theory.
1842	Crawford Long introduced the first use of anesthetics (ether) on humans.
1850s–1880s	Louis Pasteur proposed that fermentation was caused by microorganisms or "germs." He proved that bacteria spread diseases and developed the theory and practice of vaccination. He also popularized the sterilization of medical equipment.
1854	Florence Nightingale founded modern nursing when she took 38 nurses with her to Scutari to work in the British army hospitals during the Crimean War.
1866–1869	Gregor Mendel developed his laws which became the foundation for the study of genetics.
1867	A method for antiseptic surgery was developed by Friedrich Meischer of Germany.
1882	Robert Koch further developed the germ theory of disease proposed by Pasteur.

1883	The first vaccination against rabies took place.
1890	The antitoxin for diptheria was developed by Emil von Behring of Germany.
1895	Wilhelm Roentgen accidentally discovered x-rays.
1896	Scipione Riva-Rocci devised the sphygmomanometer, still used throughout the world, to use in measuring blood pressure with only a stethoscope and inflatable cuff.
1900	The ABO blood group system was discovered by Karl Lansteiner.
1900	The role of the mosquito (Aedes aegypti) as the carrier of yellow fever was demonstrated, enabling the disease to be controlled.
1903	Willem Einthoven built the first electrocardiograph, and won a Nobel Prize for it in 1924.
1904	Sigmund Freud of Austria developed psychoanalysis for treating people with emotional and mental problems.
1906	Paul Ehrlich of Frankfurt discovered a compound which seemed to attack only unhealthy tissue, thus establishing the idea and name for chemotherapy.
1906	August von Wasserman developed the test for syphilis.
1911	Rous discovered the first cancer-causing virus.
1920	Thomas Hunt Morgan, through experiments with the fruit fly *Drosophila*, established the relationship between genes and chromosomes and the theory of heredity.
1921	Banting and Best isolated insulin as a pancreatic extract, leading to a revolutionary advance in the way diabetes is treated.
1922	Alexander Fleming discovered lysozome, an enzyme, which prepared the way for antibiotics.
1928	Alexander Fleming discovered penicillin, later developed as a therapeutic drug by Florey and Chain.
1929	Hans Berger built the first electroencephalograph after studying the alpha rhythms of the brain for several years.
1937	Alton Ochsner and Michael DeBakey suggested that a cause of lung cancer is cigarette smoking.
1944	Avery, MacLeod, and McCarty proved that DNA is the blueprint of heredity determining how an organism develops.
1952	Jonas Salk, an American, developed the first polio vaccine.
1953	Crick and Watson discovered the double-helix structure of DNA. They received the Nobel Prize in medicine.
1953	John Merrill of the U.S. first performed kidney transplants; since then tens of thousands of these operations have been performed.

1955	Albert Sabin developed the oral polio vaccine, made from live viruses.
1955	Gregory Pincus and colleagues reported successful results in developing an oral contraceptive, leading to the era of "the pill."
1961	Bell Laboratories scientists announced the first continuously operating laser, a tool that came to have many surgical uses.
1965	Soft contact lenses were invented.
1966	The production of synthesized insulin (the first hormone to be made artificially) was demonstrated independently by Katsoyannis of the U.S. and by scientists in the People's Republic of China.
1967	Christiaan Barnard of Cape Town University performed the first human heart transplants.
1969	Denton Cooley performed the first surgery on a human to implant an artificial heart.
1972–1973	The CAT (computerized axial tomographic) scanner was invented by Godfrey Hounsfield, at the British firm EMI. The CAT gives a three-dimensional view of the body or body part.
1973	Stanley H. Cohen and Herbert W. Brown cut a chunk out of one bacteria's plasmid and inserted it into an opening in a gene from a different bacteria; they succeeded in creating the first "chimera" using genetic engineering techniques.
1978	The first "test-tube" baby (conceived outside the human body) was born.
1981	Acquired immune deficiency syndrome (AIDS) was identified for the first time.
1981	University of California at San Francisco surgeons performed the first successful operation on a fetus (in utero).
1984	The first viruses believed to cause AIDS were isolated by American and French scientists.
1991	A new generation of precision instruments such as the femtosecond laser, optical tweezers, and atomic force microscopes, aided by computers were developed. These allow scientists into a previously unseen microworld, assisting exploration of everything from individual atoms to individual proteins inside a red blood cell.

Planet Table

The Planet Table can be the basis for many math activities. Older children can convert years to days, days to hours, hours to seconds, miles to kilometers, compute sums for each column, and make up problems for other children to solve. You may wish to round off some of the numbers to make them easier for children to work with.

Planet	Average Distance From Sun (Miles)	Diameter (Miles)	Period of Revolution	Period of Rotation	Satellites/ Moons	Atmosphere (main components)	Probable Temperature in °F	To Find Your Weight, Multiply Your Weight By:
Mercury	35,960,000	3,100	88 days	59 days	0	virtually none	+600	0.27
Venus	67,200,000	7,700	225 days	243 days Retrograde	0	carbon dioxide	+100	0.85
Earth	92,900,000	7,918	365¼ days	23 hours 56 minutes	1	nitrogen, oxygen	+50	1.00
Mars	141,500,000	4,200	687 days	24 hours 37 minutes	2	carbon dioxide	+0	0.38
Jupiter	483,400,000	89,000	11.86 years	9 hours 55 minutes	16	hydrogen, helium	−150	2.64
Saturn	886,200,000	71,500	29.5 years	10 hours 14 minutes	21	hydrogen, helium	−250	1.17
Uranus	1,783,000,000	30,000	84 years	17.2 hours Retrograde	15	helium, hydrogen, methane	−350	0.92
Neptune	2,790,000,000	27,700	164.75 years	18 hours 30 min. (?)	2	hydrogen, helium, methane	−400	1.12
Pluto	3,670,000,000	3,664	248.5 years	6 days 9 hours 18 min Retrograde	1	none detected	?	?

From *The Teacher's Book of Lists, Second Edition*, published by GoodYearBooks.
Copyright © 1994 Sheila Madsen and Bette Gould.

Activities: Planet Table

1. Calculate what your weight would be on each planet.

2. Rewrite any or all of the columns in number words rather than numerals.

3. Compute the differences between any two planets for each of the features shown on the table. Write statements to show your findings.

4. Design a travel brochure or poster for one of the planets. Use your imagination. It's okay to be unscientific.

Plants

The study of plants lends itself to many hands-on experiences; planting seeds, learning about what parts of plants we eat (see **Plants We Eat**, p. 234), studying plant parts and tissues with hand lenses and microscopes, creating dyes and crafts with plant parts, and testing plant foods for sugar and starch. Your class could pursue this area for many weeks. Organizing a study of the plant world around themes such as Structure and Function, Systems and Relationships, or Heredity and Change Over Time (Evolution of Groups), leads to a more comprehensive understanding of living things than studying a few types of plants at a time. Another way to plan is to integrate the study of plants with the study of other areas to develop units such as Reproduction in Living Things, Organization of Living Things, Colonial America's Dependence on Plants, etc. At the end of this list are some plant books—perusal of library shelves and bookstores will turn up many others.

Plants, like other living things, must fulfill certain needs to stay alive. These are moving, growing, responding to stimuli, reproducing, using food and gases, such as oxygen or carbon dioxide, and getting rid of wastes.

MOST FREQUENTLY USED WAY TO ORGANIZE THE PLANT WORLD
The two broad group of plants (each is called a phylum) are vascular and nonvascular.

VASCULAR PLANTS—3 MAIN CLASSES	NONVASCULAR PLANTS
Have veins or tubes that carry water to all parts of the plant; have true leaves, stems, roots	No veins to carry water; have leaf-like, stem-like, root-like parts
Ferns	**Mosses**
Ferns are perennials; leaves are fronds; do not flower; reproduce by spores formed on their fronds; vary in height from inches to 50 ft. or more; are found in all parts of the world.	Mosses grow in damp places (they require water to complete their life cycle); often in woods, on shady parts of trees, close to the ground; anchored by root-like rhizoids; found worldwide; often the first plants to establish in bare soils.
maidenhair fern bird's nest fern holly fern staghorn fern coffee fern Boston fern licorice fern sensitive fern sword fern squirrel's foot fern	sphagnums (a group of mosses native to bogs) willow moss

From *The Teacher's Book of Lists, Second Edition,* published by GoodYearBooks.
Copyright © 1994 Sheila Madsen and Bette Gould.

MOST FREQUENTLY USED WAY TO ORGANIZE THE PLANT WORLD (continued)

VASCULAR PLANTS	NONVASCULAR PLANTS
Conifers (cone-bearing plants)	**Liverworts**
Conifers usually have narrow, needle-like leaves. All bear naked seeds in cones or conelike structures; often called evergreens, as they do not lose their "greenery," or needles, in winter.	Liverworts grow in dark, moist places (they require water to complete their life cycle); have leaf-like parts that look like livers; usually found flat on the ground, on rocks, or on trees.

ponderosa pine (all pine trees)   redwood
deodar cedar (all cedars)   larch
junipers   cypress
giant sequoia
yews (bear seeds in scarlet, cup-shaped fruits instead of cones)

Flowering Plants

Flowering plants produce true flowers.

red oak   alyssum   daffodil
cucumber   bird of paradise   rose
lilac   blueberry   gourd
crocus
bamboo (rarely bloom in gardens; many are on a 30- to 60-year blooming cycle)

Less Important Groups of Vascular Plants

club mosses and horsetails (primitive plants)
fungi and bacteria (simple-celled plants)

From *The Teacher's Book of Lists, Second Edition*, published by GoodYearBooks.
Copyright © 1994 Sheila Madsen and Bette Gould.

SOME OTHER WAYS TO ORGANIZE THE PLANT WORLD

NONFLOWERING PLANTS

Reproduce without the means of seeds; do not have true flowers.

"Primitive" plants such as mosses and ferns.

Also includes horsetails, liverworts, and gymnosperms, a plant group that includes conifers.

ANNUALS

Plants that complete their life cycle in one year or less.

nasturtium	marigold
cucumber	sweet pea
larkspur	calendula

DECIDUOUS

Plants that shed all of their leaves at one time (often in winter).

apricot tree	mulberry tree	magnolia
crape myrtle	lantana*	

*Some plants can belong to more than one category of plants

SCIENTIFIC PLANT CLASSIFICATION

The hierarchy is: kingdom, phylum, subphylum, class, subclass, order, family, genus, species

While somewhat complex for student learning, it can be remembered that the species is a group of individuals which are so similar as to be more or less identical and which can be interbred.

FLOWERING PLANTS

Have true flowers; have seeds that develop inside an ovary, which later develops into a fruit.

PERENNIALS

Plants that survive for several years or more

dandelion	rose	fuschia
hibiscus	pansy (viola)	

EVERGREEN (CONIFERS)

Plants that never lose all their leaves at one time

lantana*	mint	hibiscus

*Some plants can belong to more than one category of plants.

SCIENTIFIC PLANT CLASSIFICATION

Example of hierarchical plant classification:
Common Field Rose (rosa arvensis)
kingdom: eucaryota
phylum: spermatophyta
subphylum: magnoliophytina
class: magnoliopsida
subclass: rosidae
order: rosales
family: rosaceae
genus: rosa
species: arvensis

From *The Teacher's Book of Lists, Second Edition,* published by GoodYearBooks.
Copyright © 1994 Sheila Madsen and Bette Gould.

Plant Subtopics	Questions/activities to explore
animals and plants	What connections are there between the plant and animal world?
climbing plants	What are some means by which they climb? Why are so many climbers found in jungles and forests? What forces in the environment influence climbing?
collecting	Being careful not to injure any plant, make a collection of one of these: leaves, cones, seeds, flowers, stems, fruits, stamens, etc.
herbs	What are the various herbs used in cooking and what part of the plant is used?
leaves	How have botanists categorized the large variety of leaf shapes?
meat eaters	How does a meat-eating plant catch and digest its prey? How does eating meat help the plant survive?
medicines/cosmetics/ poisons/clothing	Other than food, what uses have people found for plants? List specific plants and how they are used.
monocotyledons and dicotyledons	What are the likenesses and differences of these two classes of plants?
parasitic plants	How do they live? What is the world's heaviest flower?
plant people	Who were some famous plant collectors and what did they accomplish? Which collectors had plants named after them?
reproduction	What are the various ways plants reproduce? How does each way seem ideally suited to the plants' environments?

PLANT BOOKS

Grocery Store Botany, Joan Elma Rahn. Atheneum, 1974. An exploration of the parts of plants we eat. Includes simple tests and experiments, line drawings/diagrams. Written at an intermediate level, but would be useful as a read-aloud resource for younger children.

Growing A Green Thumb, Home Gardening For Children, Lorraine Surcouf. Barron's Educational Series, Inc., 1975. Many indoor and outdoor planting projects; toads, birds, insects, earthworms in the garden; things to make with plants. Uses mostly metric measurements.

Plant, by David Burnie. Eyewitness Books, Alfred A. Knopf, 1989. Focuses on flowering plants. Beautifully illustrated, mainly with photographs; some art reproductions and many cultural pictures and bits of information.

The Plant World, *The World Book Encyclopedia of Science*, World Book, Inc., 1985. A complete look at the world of botany, from the categories of plants to plant adaptations, economic uses of plants, and the exploitation and threatened extinction of plants. This book is well illustrated with many photographs and diagrams. For advanced readers.

Sunset Western Garden Guide, the editors of *Sunset Magazine* and Sunset Books. Lane Magazine & Book Company, 1989. Although written for the western states, the guide includes plants found in most other parts of the country. Includes a glossary, alphabetic listing and description of many plants, and gardening tips, of course. Look for guides written for your geographic area.

Plants We Eat

We eat parts—roots, stems, leaves, seeds, fruits, and flowers—of many plants, but you'd be surprised about which part we eat of many plants. The juicy strawberry is not really the fruit, it is a red stem. The fruit are the small yellow flecks that sometimes get stuck between your teeth. Use the following list with your class to find out more about edible plants—experiment, taste, grow a garden, and visit a supermarket to find items to add to the list.

Under the Ground
beets
carrots
cassava (tapioca)
ginger
licorice
onions
parsnips
potatoes
radishes
rutabagas
sassafras (bark of the root used for root beer)
sweet potatoes
turnips

Vines
beans
grapes
kiwi
peas

Bushes
alderberries
blackberries
blueberries
loganberries
raspberries

Trees
apricot
avocado
cherry
date
fig
grapefruit
kumquat
lemon
lime
loquat
olive
orange
peach
persimmon
plum
pomegranate

Above the Ground
asparagus
bay
broccoli
brussels sprouts
cantaloupe
cauliflower
celery
chicory
cilantro
collards
corn
cucumber
eggplant
endive
honeydew
kale
kohlrabi
lettuce
marjoram
oregano
parsley
peppermint
peppers
pumpkin
rhubarb
rosemary
spearmint
spinach
strawberry
swiss chard
tea
thyme
tomato
watercress
watermelon
zucchini

From *The Teacher's Book of Lists, Second Edition,* published by GoodYearBooks. Copyright © 1994 Sheila Madsen and Bette Gould.

U.S. Space Missions—Fly Me to the Moon

From *The Teacher's Book of Lists, Second Edition*, published by GoodYearBooks. Copyright © 1994 Sheila Madsen and Bette Gould.

Date	Mission & Spacecraft	Crew	Duration hr:min:sec orbits/miles	Description
May 5, 1961	Mercury-Redstone 3	Shepard	00:15:22	First American in space; a suborbital flight.
Feb. 20, 1962	Mercury-Atlas 6	Glenn	04:55:23	First American in orbit; a three-orbit flight.
June 3–7, 1965	Gemini-Titan IV	McDivitt, White	97:56:11	White becomes the first American to walk in space (for 20 minutes).
March 16, 1966	Gemini-Titan VIII	Armstrong, Scott	10:41:26	First docking of one space vehicle with another.
June 3–6, 1966	Gemini-Titan IX-A	Stafford, Cernan	72:21:00	Cernan carried out 2 hours 7 minutes of extra-vehicular activity.
Sept. 12–15, 1966	Gemini-Titan XI	Conrad, Gordon	71:17:08	Gemini set a record altitude of 739.2 miles.
Nov. 11–15, 1966	Gemini-XII	Lovell, Aldrin	94:34:31	Final Gemini flight; Aldrin set a record total of 5 hours 30 minutes of extravehicular activity.
Oct. 11–22, 1968	Apollo-Saturn 7	Schirra, Eisele, Cunningham	260:09:03	First manned flight of Apollo spacecraft.
Dec. 21–27, 1968	Apollo-Saturn 8	Borman, Lovell, Anders	147:00:42	First flight to the moon; views of lunar surface televised to earth.
March 3–13, 1969	Apollo-Saturn 9	McDivitt, Scott, Schweickart	241:00:54	First manned flight of lunar module.
July 16–24, 1969	Apollo-Saturn 11	Armstrong, Collins, Aldrin	195:18:35	First lunar landing (in the Sea of Tranquility); lunar stay time 21:36:21; took lunar surface samples of 48.5 pounds.
July 26–Aug. 7, 1971	Apollo-Saturn 15	Scott, Worden, Irwin	295:11:53	Fourth lunar landing; first use of lunar roving vehicle.
Dec. 7–19, 1972	Apollo-Saturn 17	Cernan, Evans, Schmitt	301:51:59	Last Apollo flight to moon.
May 25–June 22, 1973	Skylab 2	Conrad, Kerwin, Weitz	672:49:49 (28 days)	First U.S. manned orbiting space station mission.

Date	Mission & Spacecraft	Crew	Duration hr:min:sec orbits/miles	Description
Nov. 16, 1973–Feb. 8, 1974	Skylab 4	Carr, Gibson, Pogue	2017:16:30 (84 days)	Final Skylab manned visit; longest flight of men in space; made observations of Comet Kohoutek; set record for a space walk—7 hours, 1 minute.
July 15–24, 1975	Apollo-Soyuz Test Project	U.S.: Stafford, Brand, Slayton Russia: Leonov, Kubasov	Americans: (9 days) Soviets: (5 days)	First docking (on July 17) between U.S. and Russian spacecraft; cosmonauts and astronauts visited each other's spacecraft; ships remained linked for 44 hours.
				In 1972 the Space Shuttle was approved as a national program. By the time of its 10th anniversary, the Shuttle had carried 204 people into space and more than half a million kilograms of payload into orbit.
April 12–14, 1981	STS-1 Columbia	Young, Crippen	54:20:53 36 orbits 933,757 mil. miles	STS-1 through STS-4 were all test flights to evaluate the Shuttle's engineering design. All were in Columbia.
Nov. 11, 1982	STS-5 Columbia	Brand, Overmyer, Allen, Lenoir	122:14:27 81 orbits 1.8 mil. miles	The first operational flight of the space shuttle program. Two satellites were launched.
June 18–24, 1983	STS-7 Challenger	Crippen, Hauck, Ride, Fabian, Thagard	197:23:37 133 orbits 3.48 mil. miles	This flight had a record 5 people on board, including Sally K. Ride, the first American woman in space.
Aug. 30–Sept. 5, 1983	STS-8 Challenger	Truly, Bluford, Brandenstein, D. Gardner, W. Thornton	146:23:59 98 orbits 2.22 mil. miles	First shuttle night launch and landing. Bluford became the first African-American in space.
Nov. 28–Dec. 8, 1983	STS-9 Columbia	Young, Shaw, Parker, Garriott PS: Lichtenberg, Merbold	247:47:24 148 orbits 3.33 mil. miles	A multidisciplinary science mission. Two payload specialists (PS) were included. Merbold, a German physicist, became 1st non-U.S. citizen to fly on an American spacecraft.

Date	Mission & Spacecraft	Crew	Duration hr:min:sec orbits/miles	Description
Feb. 3–11, 1984	41-B Challenger	Brand, Gibson, McCandless, Stewart, McNair	191:15:55 127 orbits 2.87 mil. miles	Flight number designations change. "4" indicates the originally scheduled year of the launch—1984. The second digit is the launch site (1 for Florida, 2 for California). The B indicates that this was the second launch of the fiscal year.
Aug. 30–Sept. 5, 1984	41-D Discovery	Hartsfield, Coats, Resnik, Hawley, Mullane PS: Walker	144:56:04 97 orbits 2.21 mil. miles	First Discovery flight. First time to deploy three communications satellites. Walker, from McDonnell Douglas, was the first commercially sponsored payload specialist.
Oct. 5–13, 1984	41-G Challenger	Crippen, McBride, Sullivan, Ride, Leestma PS: Garneau, Scully-Power	197:23:37 133 orbits 3.4 mil. miles	Sullivan was the first American woman to walk in space. Garneau was the first Canadian in space.
Apr. 12–19, 1985	51-D Discovery	Bobko, Williams, Hoffman, Griggs, Seldon PS: Walker, Garn	167:54 108 orbits 2.5 mil. miles	Attempt to activite Syncom IV-3, a communications satellite, using an improvised "flyswatter" attached to the Remote Manipulator System (RMS) arm, fails. Senator Jake Garn is the first member of Congress to fly in space.
April 29–May 6, 1985	51-B Challenger	Overmyer, Gregory, Lind, Thagard, Thornton. PS: van den Berg, Wang	168:08:47 110 orbits 2.9 mil. miles	Second Spacelab mission. 15 experiments were performed in such areas as crystal growth, astronomy, life sciences. Aboard were 2 monkeys and 24 rats.
Oct. 3–7, 1985	51-J Atlantis	Bobko, Grabe, Hilmers, Stewart, Pailes	97:14:38 (other info not available)	First flight of Atlantis. This mission (and all others) for the Department of Defense.

From *The Teacher's Book of Lists, Second Edition*, published by GoodYearBooks. Copyright © 1994 Sheila Madsen and Bette Gould.

Date	Mission & Spacecraft	Crew	Duration hr:min:sec orbits/miles	Description
Jan. 28, 1986	51-L Challenger	Scobee, Smith, Onizuka, Resnik, McNair. PS: Jarvis, McAuliffe	00:01:13	The Challenger and entire crew, including Jarvis, a Hughes employee, and Christa McAuliffe, the designated "Teacher in Space," were lost 73 seconds into the flight when the vehicle exploded. A leak in one of the Solid Rocket Boosters was to blame. The Shuttle program was delayed nearly 3 years while safety measures were added.
May 4–8, 1989	STS-30 Atlantis	Walker, Grabe Thagard, Cleave, Lee	96:57:35	The Shuttle program's first launch of a planetary spacecraft. The Magellan Venus Radar Mapper arrived at Venus in Aug. 1990, to begin its 8-month mapping mission.
Oct. 18–23, 1989	STS-34 Atlantis	Williams, McCulley, Lucid, Baker, Chang-Diaz	119:41:00	Galileo, the Jupiter probe, was released from the cargo bay and then headed towards Venus, its first "stop" on the way to Jupiter.
April 24–29, 1990	STS-31 Discovery	Shriver, Bolden, Hawley, McCandless, Sullivan	121:16:06	Launch of the Hubble Space Telescope, the first large optical telescope ever to be placed above the Earth's atmosphere. Discovery flew the highest Shuttle orbit to date—531.08 kilometers.
April 5–11, 1991	STS-37 Atlantis	Nagel, Cameron, Apt, Godwin, Ross	143:32:44	Launch and deployment of the Gamma Ray Observatory (GRO), the second of NASA's great observatories. The GRO was the heaviest satellite ever launched from the Shuttle.
June 5–14, 1991	STS-40	O'Connor, Gutierrez, Bagian, Jernigan, Seddon. PS: F. Drew Gaffney, Millie Hughes-Fulford	218:14:20	The Spacelab Life Sciences mission was the first entirely dedicated to researching the effects of microgravity on the human body. Also onboard: 29 rats and 2400 jellyfish.

At the time of writing this book:
The Atlantis blasted off, March 25, 1992, for an eight-day mission to study the chemistry and physics of the upper atmosphere. These atmospheric studies could influence major policy decisions for protecting the global environment. This is the 46th Shuttle flight.
Onboard: 7 astronauts, 12 instruments

From *The Teacher's Book of Lists, Second Edition*, published by GoodYearBooks.
Copyright © 1994 Sheila Madsen and Bette Gould.

Two excellent sources for information on activities in space:

NASA
Lyndon B. Johnson Space Center
Houston, Texas 77058

An excellent source of printed material. Ask for NASA Fact Sheets, Information Summaries, Educational Briefs, etc.

JPL Teacher Education Center
4800 Oak Grove Avenue
MS CS530
Pasadena, CA 91109

Call 818/354-4321 and ask to be connected to Public Relations. They have a variety of recorded information available, such as updates on missions in progress, ham radio frequencies to listen in on mission communications, etc. There are also materials, posters, and often, videotapes available to teachers.

There are many fascinating books available on the topic of space travel. The following are just a sampling that have been found to be appealing to students.

Voyager: An Adventure to the Edge of the Solar System, by Sally Ride and Tom O'Shaughnessy. Crown, 1992. The extraordinary adventure of the Voyager spacecraft as related by astronaut Sally Ride.

How Do You Go to the Bathroom in Space?, by William R. Pogue. Tom Doherty Associates, 1985. Pogue, an astronaut, answers most-asked questions about being in space.

Space Camp: The Great Adventure for NASA Hopefuls, by Anne Baird. Morrow, 1991. Relates what it takes to become an astronaut, as told firsthand by astronauts and other experts.

The Magic School Bus Lost in the Solar System, by Joanna Cole. Scholastic, 1990. One night, as Mrs. Frizzle and her class are coming home from the planetarium, the school bus heads out into space.

Space Spinners, by Suse MacDonald. Penguin/Dial. Two spiders cooperate to make the first spider web in space.

From *The Teacher's Book of Lists, Second Edition*, published by GoodYearBooks.
Copyright © 1994 Sheila Madsen and Bette Gould.

Worksheet

U.S. Space Missions Debriefing Questions, p. 240. Answers to the debriefing questions are found on the *U.S. Space Missions* list; therefore duplicated copies of the list will need to be made available to students.

Name _____ _Date_ _____

U.S. Space Missions Debriefing Questions

1. Who was the first American to walk in space?

   _____

2. Which was the first flight to the Moon?

   _____

3. What was the site of the first lunar landing?

   _____

4. When did the first manned orbiting space station mission begin?

   _____

5. During which mission did the first manned flight of the lunar module occur?

   _____

6. Who were the astronauts who set a Gemini altitude record?

   _____

7. Of the notable space missions listed, which was the longest Gemini flight: How much longer was it than the shortest Gemini flight?

   _____

8. How much time did Scott spend in space according to the list?

   _____

9. What notable space event occurred on July 17, 1975?

   _____

10. What piece of equipment was used for the first time on the Apollo-Saturn 15 mission?

    _____

11. What were the two notable missions Armstrong was on?

    _____

12. Including the walks in space, what was the total time of extravehicular activity reported?

    _____

13. What types of experiments took place on flights in 1985?

    _____

14. How many days did the Space Lab Life Sciences mission last?

    _____

15. Which flight would you have wanted to go on? Give details in your answer. Answer this question on the back of this page.

    _____

From _The Teacher's Book of Lists, Second Edition,_ published by GoodYearBooks. Copyright © 1994 Sheila Madsen and Bette Gould.

Space Talk—Space Terms Used in Air-To-Ground Communication

Booster, bugs, foxtrot, footprints, and the Brooklyn Clothesline will become familiar words as children develop play and radio dialogues and reenactments of extraterrestrial travel based on the following Space Talk vocabulary. Children will want to make props, such as instrument panels and spacecraft models, incorporating items from the list.

ABORT—to cut short a mission or launch due to problems

ALL BALLS—flight crew slang for all zeroes

ALPHA—alphabet designation for the letter A

AMBIENT—the environmental condition, such as temperature, air pressure

APOGEE—the highest point in an orbit around earth

AUDIO SYSTEM—voice portion of communication system

BACKUP—item or system kept on hand to replace one that fails: astronaut or crew used to replace the prime crew in the event of illness

BARBER POLES—small gauges on control panels that are striped diagonally in black and white

BECO—booster engine cut-off

BLACKOUT—a fadeout of radio communication between a spacecraft and the ground during reentry

BLOCKHOUSE—Launch Control Center at Pad 39, Cape Kennedy

BOOSTER—launch vehicle

BRAVO—alphabet designation for the letter B

BREAKING UP—a garbling of voice transmission

BROOKLYN CLOTHESLINE—a loop of rope on pulleys used to transport film during extravehicular activities (EVAs)

BUG—an unidentified problem

BURN—the firing of engines

BUTTON UP—to completely close or seal any unit or vehicle such as the spacecraft

CHARLIE—alphabet designation for the letter C

CSM—COMMAND AND SERVICE MODULE—three-man spacecraft used in Apollo; same type of vehicle used to transport crews and equipment to and from Skylab

COMMAND MODULE—the crew portion of the CSM (see above definition)

COPY—synonym for read (understand, as during a voice transmission)

COUNTDOWN—step-by-step preparation for launch

DAMPING—restraining; slowing down or stopping

DEBRIEFING—questioning of crewmen after a mission to obtain useful information

DEBUG—remove problems or malfunctions from a system

DELTA—alphabet designation for the letter D

DEORBIT—coming out of an earth orbit into splashdown trajectory

DOWN IN THE MUD—slang for very low volume in radio reception

DOWNTIME—time during which a system is not in condition or functioning

DRAG—resistance of the air to a body in motion

ECHO—alphabet designation for the letter E

EGRESS—to exit the spacecraft

EVA—extravehicular activity

FIVE BY FIVE—a term denoting radio reception is loud and clear

FOOTPRINT—the area of possible landing points for a vehicle at reentry

FOXTROT—alphabet designation for the letter F

GLITCH—a problem of any nature, especially during countdown

GOLF—alphabet designation for the letter G

HANDOVER—to pass spacecraft communication from one tracking station to another

HOLD—a delay in the launch countdown

HOTEL—alphabet designation for the letter H

INDIA—alphabet designation for the letter I

INGRESS—to enter the spacecraft

JETTISON—to discard into space

JULIET—alphabet designation for the letter J

KILO—alphabet designation for the letter K

LAUNCH VEHICLE—the booster as opposed to the spacecraft

LAUNCH WINDOW—the limited frame of time during which launch can be accomplished

LIMA—alphabet designation for the letter L

MIKE—alphabet designation for the letter M

MURPHY'S LAW—a so-called "scientific" law that states "What can go wrong will go wrong"

NO GO—indicates something is functioning improperly; not ready to proceed

NO JOY—slang meaning an expected event has not happened or a looked-for object has not been located

NOVEMBER—alphabet designation for the letter N

OPEN ENDED MISSION—a flight of no specific duration: continues as long as equipment functions properly.

OSCAR—alphabet designation for the letter O

PAPA—alphabet designation for the letter P

PASS—the passage of a spacecraft over a tracking station or target area

PIGTAIL—a short, coiled wire or bundle of wires

POLL THE ROOM—take a consensus of flight controllers before making a go or no go decision

POO—Program Zero-Zero—clearing the spacecraft computer

POT—potable, drinkable

PUSH-TO-TALK—microphone switch which is pressed when a crewman wishes to transmit his voice

Q-BALL—device in nose cone of launch escape system which provides information

QUEBEC—alphabet designation for the letter Q

READ—understand, as during a voice transmission

REAL TIME—indicates the reporting of events at the nearly instantaneous time they occur

REV—revolution

ROGER—okay; will do

ROMEO—alphabet designation for the letter R

R & R—rest and recreation

SCRUB—to cancel or postpone a flight

SHOT—slang for launch or flight

SIERRA—alphabet designation for the letter S

SKIN TRACKING—tracking by radar bounced off the outside of the vehicle

SOM—start of message

SPLASHDOWN—impact of the spacecraft in the ocean during landing

TANGO—alphabet designation for the letter T

THRUST—push; force developed by a rocket engine

TOK—thrust O.K.

UNIFORM—alphabet designation for the letter U

VICTOR—alphabet designation for the letter V

WARMER—flight control slang for "better"

WHISKEY—alphabet designation for the letter W

X-RAY—alphabet designation for the letter X

WILCO—pilot slang for "will comply"

YANKEE—alphabet designation for the letter Y

ZIPS—all zeroes

ZULU—alphabet designation for the letter Z

CHAPTER

8

The Environment

Endangered and Extinct Animals—Going, Going, Gone

The endangered species on this list were obtained from the volumes of the Red Data Book *compiled by the IUCN (International Union for the Conservation of Nature) and the U.S. Fish and Wildlife Service. Animals were selected to illustrate the various reasons for the decline of wildlife and the many kinds of species affected.*

GOING—classified as rare or vulnerable and likely to move into the endangered category in the near future if the reasons for their decline continue

African elephant—hunted for ivory tusks; although this species currently has a large population (625,000), it is predicted that if hunting does not cease, the African elephant will be extinct in 50 years

Ceylon elephant—found in eastern and southeastern Ceylon; killed by farmers whose lands are destroyed by migrating herds

Chimpanzee—found in equatorial forests of Africa; captured for use in biomedical sciences as subjects for experiments, as pets, and for the animal trade; hunted for food and sport

Chinchilla—found in Andes mountains of Chile and Bolivia; hunted and killed for its fur

Shortnose sturgeon—a small fish inhabiting Atlantic seaboard rivers; pollution of waters is a major factor as well as overfishing

GOING, GOING—in danger of extinction; survival is not likely if the reasons for their decline continue

African gorilla—habitat destruction; killed as a food source; and babies sold

American crocodile—found in Florida, Central America, parts of Mexico; killed for skins and sport; destruction of habitat; sometimes killed as a nuisance in docks

Arabian oryx—found in Oman; declining because of uncontrolled hunting by organized hunting parties using cars and planes to overtake the animal

Aye-aye—forest-dwelling lemur of Madagascar; losing habitat through forest clearance; killed by Malagasy people for superstitious reasons

Beautiful parakeet—found in Australia; main cause of extinction is excessive hunting and trapping for the aviculturist

Blue whale—the largest animals that have ever lived (as long as 1000 ft. and 120 tons in weight); overhunting by whalers

California condor—extremely rare, facing extinction; in fall 1992, six young, raised in captivity, were released into the wild to join the single condor known still to exist in its natural habitat

From *The Teacher's Book of Lists, Second Edition,* published by GoodYearBooks. Copyright © 1994 Sheila Madsen and Bette Gould.

GOING, GOING (continued)

Cheetah—ranges from Africa to India; lack of genetic variability (population contains only a few closely related cats); hunting; changes in environment

Cicek—a fish of Lake Egridir, Turkey; preyed upon by the pike-perch introduced in the lake in 1953; may already be extinct

Giant panda—found in China's western mountains; restricted diet of bamboo shoots

Javan rhinoceros—found in Indonesia; victims of overhunting for so-called medicinal products derived from their horns and blood

Orangutan—an ape inhabiting Borneo and Sumatra; destruction of forest habitat; captured for use by pet dealers, zoos, and research laboratories

Round Island boa—found in Round Island (northwest of Mauritius); goats and rabbits introduced to the island destroyed the ecological balance by eating the grasses, leading to a reduction in the number of insects; consequently, insect-eating lizards used by the boa as food diminished

San Francisco garter snake—found in California; destruction of habitat due to housing development projects, control of waterflow, and removal of vegetation

South American river turtle (or arrau)—found in tropical South America; hunted for: eggs, which are considered a delicacy, oil, meat, and the pet trade

Whooping crane—North America's tallest bird; victim of overhunting; loss of habitat due to drainage and fill of marshes

GONE—extinct

Arabian ostrich—found in Saudi Arabia; hunted for sport in automobiles and airplanes

California grizzly bear—last known grizzly killed in 1920; grizzlies disappeared mainly due to hunting and encroachment by humans on their land

Catabasis acuminatus—a fish of the Rio Tieté, Brazil; pollution of headwaters of river by sewage from the city of São Paulo

Dodo—flightless bird lived on the island of Mauritius in the Indian Ocean; meat eaten by Dutch who came to the island in 1598; eggs devoured by dogs, pigs, and rats that came off the ships

Flightless moa—13 ft.-tall bird of New Zealand; disappeared in 1670 due to the Maoris' hunting and use of the bird for food

Great auk—found in Northern Europe and North America; killed for eggs, flesh, and feathered skin

Passenger pigeon—found in eastern North America; trapped and shot for food and sport

Quagga—distant relative of the zebra; white Dutch Boers fed it as cheap meat to their black slaves

Activities: Endangered and Extinct Animals

1. On a world map, locate the country or countries where the endangered species are presently found. Make symbols to represent the animals' present status and place your symbols on the map.

2. Write fables or "Just So" stories to explain why an animal is endangered or extinct. Use factual information or make up your own. Here are some examples of titles:

> Bye-bye, Aye-aye
> The Passing of the Passenger Pigeon
> How the Chinchilla Lost Its Coat
> The Ciçek and the Pike-Perch

3. Make a list of *other endangered and extinct things.* Endangered things might include buildings or historic sites in your city, the circus, hula hoops, and the door-to-door milkman. Your extinct list might include 23¢ a gallon for gas, the 5¢ cigar, Indian-head pennies, and the Pony Express.

Worksheet

Save-An-Animal Campaign worksheet, p. 249.

From *The Teacher's Book of Lists, Second Edition,* published by GoodYearBooks.
Copyright © 1994 Sheila Madsen and Bette Gould.

Name _____   Date _____

Save-An-Animal Campaign

Choose an endangered animal. Complete the Facts Notepad. Design your campaign materials to inform (use factual information) and to motivate others (use designs, color, and illustrations) to help you save the animal. Cut your campaign items out and display them.

Facts Notepad

Endangered animal: _____

_____

Location and description of native habitat: _____

_____

_____

Reason for endangerment: _____

_____

_____

_____

How animal can be saved:

1. _____

2. _____

3. _____

4. _____

5. _____

Campaign slogan: _____

_____

_____

Campaign Materials

BUTTON

BANNER OR
BUMPER STICKER

FLYER, POSTER, OR POSTCARD

Environmental Addresses

There are hundreds of organizations, big and small, for profit and non-profit, whose goals are to educate the public and to assist in saving the environment. The organizations on the following list provide an incentive for writing—they'll send free information and ways to get involved that children will be able to understand.

GENERAL

Environmental Protection Agency (EPA)
401 M Street, SW
Washington, DC 20460
(800) 424-9346

Write for a list of their publications: informative books, pamphlets, posters, comic books, and workbooks and curriculum guides (many at no charge) for a variety of environmental issues.

Friends of the Earth
218 D Street, SE
Washington, DC 20003
(202) 544-2600

Greenpeace USA
1436 U Street, NW
Washington, DC 20009
(800) 333-7717

Natural Resources Defense Council (NRDC)
40 W. 20th Street
New York, NY 10011
(212) 727-2700

AIR

National Clean Air Coalition
801 Pennsylvania Avenue, SE, 3rd floor
Washington, DC 20003
(202) 624-9393

Natural Resources Defense Council (NRDC)
40 W. 20th Street
New York, NY 10011

Send for *Saving the Ozone Layer: A Citizen Action Guide.*

Worldwatch Institute
1776 Massachusetts Avenue, NW
Washington, DC 20036
(202) 452-1999

Send for pamphlet, *The Bicycle: Vehicle for a Small Planet.*

FORESTS

Children of the Green Earth
P.O. Box 95219
Seattle, WA 98145

Promotes and organizes tree planting projects for children. Write for free pamphlets.

Rainforest Action Network
301 Broadway, Suite A
San Francisco, CA 94133
(415) 398-4404

Free information about the rainforests and what you can do to help.

WILDLIFE

The Cousteau Society
930 W. 21st St.
Norfolk, VA 23517
(804) 627-1144

National Wildlife Federation
1400 16th St., NW
Washington, DC 20036
(202) 797-6800

The Nature Conservancy
1815 N. Lynn St.
Arlington, VA 22209
(703) 841-5300

World Wildlife Fund
1250 24th St., NW
Washington, DC 20037

Center for Marine Conservation
1725 DeSales St., NW
Washington, DC 20036
(202) 429-5609

Free pamphlet, *Buyer Beware,* tells you how to recognize products made from endangered species.

From *The Teacher's Book of Lists, Second Edition,* published by GoodYearBooks. Copyright © 1994 Sheila Madsen and Bette Gould.

CHEMICALS (toxins)

Rachel Carson Council
8940 Jones Mill Road
Chevy Chase, MD 20815
(301) 652-1877

Mothers and Others for the Environment
A project of the NRDC, initially co-founded by many members of the entertainment industry. Students can write to the organization or write directly to a "celebrity."

> **Cher, co-founder**
> 9200 Sunset Blvd. #1001
> Los Angeles, CA 90069
>
> **Goldie Hawn, co-founder**
> c/o Hollywood Pictures
> 500 S. Buena Vista Ave.
> Burbank, CA 91505
>
> **Bette Midler**
> P.O. Box 46703
> Los Angeles, CA 90046
>
> **Meryl Streep**
> P.O. Box 105
> Taconic, CT 06079
>
> **Robin Williams**
> 9830 Wilshire Blvd.
> Beverly Hills, CA 90212

National Coalition Against the Misuse of Pesticides
530 7th St., SE
Washington, DC 20006
(202) 543-5450

ENERGY

Alliance to Save Energy
1925 K St., NW, Suite 206
Washington, DC 20006
(202) 857-0666

Free publications list on energy conservation.

Careirs
P.O. Box 8900
Silver Springs, MD 20907
(800) 523-2929

Another excellent source for information on energy is your local electric utility company.

WATER

Clean Water Action
1320 18th St., NW
Washington, DC 20036
(202) 457-1286

Texas Water Development Board
P.O. Box 13231, Capitol Station
Austin, TX 78711

Free xeriscape (plantings requiring low water maintenance) brochures.

Water Pollution Control Federation
601 Whythe St.
Alexandria, VA 22314-1994

Free household hazardous waste chart.

RECYCLING AND HAZARDOUS WASTE

Aluminum Association
900 19th St., NW
Washington, DC 20006

Free information on how to recycle and set up fundraising events.

Berkeley Ecology Center
2530 San Pablo Ave.
Berkeley, CA 94702

Free fact sheet about composting. Send SASE.

Environmental Defense Fund
257 Park Avenue South
New York, NY 10010
(800) 225-5333

Booklet *How to Recycle*.

Glass Packaging Institute
1801 K St., NW
Washington, DC 20006
(202) 887-4850

Free pamphlets on glass recycling.

Paper Recycling Committee
260 Madison Avenue
New York, NY 10016

Free pamphlets on how to recycle paper.

Environmental Checklist

*Your family can help save the earth by doing lots of things—
every little bit counts. How many of these simple actions are
routine in your household today? Mark them with an X. Circle
the ones you decide to adopt.*

Reduce Waste, Recycle

❑ Sell, donate, or pass on used clothes, appliances, and toys instead of throwing them out.

❑ Repair and maintain items.

❑ Don't accept an extra paper or plastic bag in stores.

❑ Find other uses for packaging and containers.

❑ Write on both sides of paper.

❑ Use recycled paper products whenever possible and economically feasible.

❑ Avoid buying over-packaged goods.

❑ Recycle newspapers, paper, glass, and aluminum.

❑ Don't purchase styrofoam products or products packaged in Styrofoam.

❑ Look for the recycle symbol when shopping.

❑ Recycle organic kitchen and yard waste by composting.

Save Water

❑ Install low-flow faucet aerators in kitchen and bathroom faucets.

❑ Keep showers short; turn off water when soaping.

❑ When showering, fill a bucket with the cold water that comes out before it gets warm. Use the water to flush the toilet or to water plants.

❑ Don't keep the tap running while brushing teeth, shaving, and doing the dishes.

❑ Water plants and lawns early in the morning or in the evening.

❑ Use a broom instead of a hose to clean driveways and steps.

❑ Use a bucket and sponge or a hose with a shut-off nozzle when washing the car.

Save Energy

❑ Clean or replace air conditioning filters once a month.

❑ Clean the condenser coils on the back or bottom of the refrigerator at least once a year.

❑ Keep the door gasket on your refrigerator clean to make sure the seal isn't being broken by dried-on food.

From *The Teacher's Book of Lists, Second Edition,* published by GoodYearBooks.
Copyright © 1994 Sheila Madsen and Bette Gould.

Save Energy
(continued)

- ❏ Switch off lights and heaters in rooms not being used.
- ❏ Adjust the heating themostat down to save energy; wear an extra sweater rather than turn up the heat.
- ❏ Use energy-efficient appliances.
- ❏ Use lower wattage bulbs and energy-efficient fluorescent bulbs.
- ❏ Turn off TVs that no one is watching.

Save the Ozone Layer

- ❏ Carpool.
- ❏ Use public transportation, bike, or use your legs and walk instead of driving.
- ❏ Plant trees in your yard and neighborhood.

Protect the Water Table

- ❏ Try to reduce the amount of hazardous products you use. Use or make safer substitutes whenever possible.
- ❏ Dispose of hazardous waste products properly. Whenever possible, recycle used motor oil, car batteries, and paint.
- ❏ Never put toxic or hazardous materials into a storm drain—this poisons the oceans.

Protect Wildlife

- ❏ Snip each circle of six-pack rings with a scissors before you throw them away.
- ❏ At the beach, take six-pack rings home, cut them, and then throw them away.
- ❏ Don't purchase items made of scarce or prohibited materials, such as ebony or dark hardwoods found in rain forests.
- ❏ Don't buy items made from tortoise shells, coral, reptile skins, cat pelts, or other endangered species.
- ❏ Set out a bird feeder.
- ❏ Use natural deterrents instead of chemicals to get rid of garden pests whenever possible.
- ❏ Don't buy helium-filled balloons as they might end up in our waterways and oceans. Also, there is a finite supply of helium—it is not manufactured.

Work for the Environment

- ❏ Educate others and keep the family educated.
- ❏ Write letters. Encourage local, state, and federal officials to pass environment-saving legislation.
- ❏ Cooperate with and participate in environmental programs. Join an action group.
- ❏ If there is no recycling center in your area, write to the local government and ask for one.

From *The Teacher's Book of Lists, Second Edition,* published by GoodYearBooks. Copyright © 1994 Sheila Madsen and Bette Gould.

Environmental Facts and Fix-Its

Read the facts about waste in the first column. Write the things you and your family can do to cut down waste in the Fix-Its column. Compare your notes with a friend's notes. Make a Facts and Fix-Its worksheet for another environmental problem. Have your classmates complete it.

FACTS	FIX-ITS
The average American family produces about 100 pounds of trash every week.	_____ _____ _____ _____
Each year one person wastes: • 5 pounds aluminum cans • 80 pounds glass bottles and jars • 2 trees • 72 pounds tin cans • 88 pounds plastic	_____ _____ _____ _____ _____
It takes one 15- to 20-year-old tree to make enough paper for only 700 grocery bags.	_____ _____
We throw away 24 million tons of leaves and grass every year.	_____ _____
We throw away 2.5 million plastic bottles *every hour.*	_____ _____ _____

From *The Teacher's Book of Lists, Second Edition,* published by GoodYearBooks. Copyright © 1994 Sheila Madsen and Bette Gould.

Environmental Recipes

Concern for the environment has led many families back to old-fashioned chemical-free cleaning and pest control methods. Here are just a few that are not only safe, but economical as well. Two references that contain many other "recipes" are: Heloise, Hints for a Healthy Planet, *Perigree* Books, *and* Making the Switch: Alternatives to Using Toxic Chemicals in the Home, *send $6 to Publication Dept., Local Government Commission, 909 12th St., Suite 205, Sacramento, CA 95814.*

BUG OFF

Soap Spray

2 tbsp. liquid soap   1 gal. water

spray bottle

Mix liquid soap in water. Pour into sprayer. Mist leaves of plants to kill white-flies, spider mites, mealybugs, cinch bugs, and aphids. Label properly.

BUG OFF

Flea Trap

Place a shallow aluminum pan of soapy water on the floor next to a lamp with the bulb one or two feet above the pan. Leave the lamp on overnight with no other lights on in the room. Fleas are attracted to light, and will jump toward the heat, then fall into the pan where the soapy water finish-es them off.

BUG OFF

Vegetable Spray

1 garlic bulb   1 small onion

1 tbsp. cayenne pepper   1 tbsp. liquid soap

1 qt. boiling water

Chop garlic and onion into small pieces. Mix with cayenne pepper and water. Let mixture stand for one hour, then add soap. Effective for one week as an all-purpose insect spray. Label properly.

BUG OFF

Aphid Trap

Paint a 10" x 10" piece of wood with bright yellow paint. When it is thoroughly dry, coat it with petroleum jelly. Place the wood on a stake next to the infested plants.

Ant Repellant

Find the ants' place of entry, squeeze the juice of a lemon in the area, and leave the peel. Ants also will back off from lines of talcum powder, damp coffee grounds, bone meal, charcoal dust, and cayenne pepper.

Air Freshener

Set out vingear in a shallow bowl.

Furniture Polish

1 tsp. lemon juice

1 pt. mineral or vegetable oil

Mix together. Apply to soft cloth and wipe furniture. Label properly.

Glass Cleaner

1 tbsp. vinegar or lemon juice

1 qt. water   spray bottle

newspapers

white tissue paper (from gifts, cleaners, etc.)

Mix vinegar or lemon juice and water. Pour into bottle. Spray on and wipe dry with newspapers. Shine with tissue paper. Label properly.

Scouring Powder

Sprinkle baking soda on a damp sponge or cloth and scrub.

Use to clean appliances, counters, chrome fixtures, showers, tubs, toilets and cooked-on grease and oils on cookware.

Fabric Fresheners

dry cornstarch

dash of cinnamon

Freshen (and remove minor soil) from carpets and upholstery by sprinkling with cornstarch and a touch of cinnamon. Then vacuum it up.

Activities: Environmental Recipes

1. Bring in a recycled spray bottle. Make up solutions as holiday gifts. Design labels that include ingredients and directions for use.

2. Develop a Consumer Handbook by comparing the ingredients and price of a commercial product with a homemade alternative. Rate each commercial product as SAFE or TOXIC.

3. Experiment with and develop ways to conserve cleaning materials and equipment. Estimate and measure how much material can be saved with any method designed. For example, if you cut a paper towel roll in half (without cutting through the cardboard roller) and hang it on a holder, you'll have two small rolls side by side. These smaller towels are large enough for many uses.

4. Design individual or group charts and fill with facts about household and yard pests. Complete charts by suggesting an environmental recipe or method for combatting each pest.

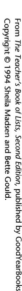
From *The Teacher's Book of Lists, Second Edition,* published by GoodYearBooks.
Copyright © 1994 Sheila Madsen and Bette Gould.

Worksheet

*Using the **Environmental Recipes** worksheet, p. 258, students make a set of cards to take home and use.*

Environmental Recipe Cards

Find an environmentally safe method or mixture for each recipe card. Write the recipe and directions on the cards and add a drawing. Cut out the cards and share them with your family and friends.

_____'s **Cleaner**
(your name)

_____'s **Bug Off**
(your name)

From *The Teacher's Book of Lists, Second Edition,* published by GoodYearBooks. Copyright © 1994 Sheila Madsen and Bette Gould.

Recycle It!

Many things we throw away can be recycled by putting them to other uses. An old car tire can be remade into a swing, a planter, and bumpers for the sides of a boat. Think about things you or your family throw away—panty hose, an empty plastic bottle, egg cartons.

Choose an item that could be put to another use. Make step-by-step instructions with pictures and words that show how to make your new product.

1.

Original Item

2.

3.

4.

5.

6.

New Product

CHAPTER

9

Social Studies

Ancient Civilizations—
Senior Citizens

Ancient Egyptian	c.3100–30 B.C.
Assyrian	c.1100–600 B.C.
Aztec	1300s–1519 A.D.
Babylonian	c.2000–1100 B.C.
Etruscan	800–500 B.C. (height of power)
Harappa (Indus Valley)	2500–1500 B.C.
Hittites	2000–1000 B.C.
Incan	1450–1532 A.D. (height of power)
Khmer civilization (Cambodia)	800–1200 A.D. (height of power)
Mayan	200–900 A.D. (height of power)
Minoan	1700–1400? B.C. (height of power)
Mycenaean	1400–1100 B.C. (height of power on mainland Greece)
Sumerian	c.3200–2000 B.C.

Research Activities

1. Where was the civilization located?
2. What geographical features favored the development of the civilization?
3. How were the remains discovered or excavated?
4. What is known about the buildings?
5. What are some of the unanswered questions about the civilization?
6. What are some of the artifacts and works of art that remain? What do they tell about the people?
7. How was the civilization ruled?
8. What were some of the religious practices of the civilization?
9. What are some unique contributions or developments of the civilization?
10. What were the causes of the decline of the civilization?
11. What was the economy of the civilization based on?
12. Did the civilization have slaves? Where were they from? How were they treated?
13. List the civilizations in chronological order.

From *The Teacher's Book of Lists, Second Edition*, published by GoodYearBooks. Copyright © 1994 Sheila Madsen and Bette Gould.

Ancient Wonders of the World

Compiled by the ancient Greeks, the following list is the most often accepted list of the Seven Wonders. Studying any one of these wonders should stimulate interest in the ancient civilization that produced it. Children may enjoy researching to find out the wonders of the modern world.

The Great Pyramid of Egypt	Built for the king Khufu, it is the only pyramid still reasonably intact today.
The Hanging Gardens of Babylon	Still remaining are ruins of crumbled walls near Baghdad, Iraq.
The Statue of Zeus at Olympia, Greece	Smashed by rulers of later times, it was finished off by an earthquake.
The Temple of Artemis (Diana) at Ephesus (Turkey)	Destroyed by invaders.
The Mausoleum of Halicarnassus (Turkey)	Destroyed by earthquake.
The Colossus of Rhodes (in the Aegean Sea)	First felled by an earthquake followed by 900 years of looting; pieces were sold as scrap.
The Lighthouse of Alexandria (Egypt)	Partly torn down by treasure seekers; the rest was felled by earthquake.

Some ancient wonders that didn't make this list but are sometimes shown on others:

The Sphinx in Egypt	
Stonehenge in England	Unknown to the Greeks who compiled the list.
The Great Wall of China	Unknown to the Greeks who compiled the list.
The Colosseum in Rome	Completed after list was compiled.
The Parthenon at Athens	

From *The Teacher's Book of Lists, Second Edition,* published by GoodYearBooks. Copyright © 1994 Sheila Madsen and Bette Gould.

Careers—Butcher, Baker, Candlestick Maker

There are many more careers and jobs than the ones found on this list—we wanted to illustrate how many unusual and varied ones there are. Children may enjoy looking through the want ads in the local paper to find out more about a job that interests them and to learn about other jobs available. A survey of parents' and neighbors' jobs, plus a quick graph to summarize findings (see graph worksheets, p. 169–174), will help to personalize this subject area. Some students will enjoy selecting an industry, such as the recording industry, and finding out about all of the jobs and roles related to that industry.

A   accountant, acrobat, actor, aircraft worker, airline worker, archeologist, architect, artist, assembler, astrologer, athlete, attorney, auctioneer, auto mechanic

B   babysitter, baker, banker, bank teller, bartender, beautician, beekeeper, biologist, bookkeeper, brick mason, broadcaster, bus driver, butcher, buyer

C   cake decorator, calligrapher, carpenter, cashier, chauffeur, chef, chemist, choreographer, clerk, computer game designer, computer programmer, computer repair technician, construction worker, contractor, controller, cook, counselor, customer service representative

D   dancer, data processor, dental hygienist, dentist, dermatologist, designer, dietician, disc jockey, draftsperson, drummer

E   ecologist, economist, editor, electrician, engineer, engraver, entertainer, environmental scientist, estimator, exercise instructor, exporter

F   factory worker, farmer, file clerk, filmmaker, firefighter, fisherman, flight attendant, florist, fortune teller, fundraiser

G   gardener, genealogist, general office worker, geologist, ghost writer, golfer, graphic artist, grocer, groundskeeper, guard

H   hair stylist, handyman, horse trainer, hospital administrator, hotel manager, human resources administrator, hypnotist

I   ice skater, illustrator, importer, innkeeper, inspector, instructor, insurance agent, interior decorator, interpreter, inventor, inventory control clerk, investigator

J   janitor, jeweler, judge

K   karate instructor, keypunch operator, kindergarten teacher, kinesiologist

L   laboratory technician, landscaper, legal secretary, librarian, linguist, lithographer, loan officer, locksmith

M   machinist, mail carrier, maintenance supervisor, manager, manicurist, manufacturer, market researcher, masseur or masseuse, mathematician, mechanic, medical assistant, medical transcriber, metallurgist, meteorologist, milliner, model, musician

N   news reporter, newswriter, numismatist, nurse, nurseryman

O   occupational therapist, oil worker, opera singer, ophthalmologist, optometrist, order clerk, organist

P   painter, paralegal, PBX operator, pediatrician, personnel worker, pharmacist, photographer, physical therapist, physician, piano tuner, picture framer, pilot, plasterer, plumber, police officer, printer, psychologist, purchasing agent

Q   quality control manager, quilt maker

R   radiologist, railroad worker, rancher, realtor, receptionist, recreation director, refinisher, repair person, research technician, restaurateur, retail salesperson, roofer

S   salesperson, scuba diver, seamstress, secretary, security officer, service man or woman (Army, Navy, etc.), shipping clerk, sign painter, social worker, speech therapist, stenographer, stockbroker, surveyor

T   tailor, tattooer, taxidermist, taxi driver, teacher, telemarketer, telephone operator, therapist, tool and die maker, tour leader, translator, travel agent, truck driver, typesetter, typist

U   umpire, union organizer, undertaker, underwriter, upholsterer, urban planner

V   valet, veterinarian, video technician

W   waiter or waitress, warehouse person, waste management specialist, watchmaker, water superintendent, winemaker, word processor, writer

X   Xerox operator, x-ray technician, xmas tree grower

Y   yoga instructor, yogurt maker

Z   zoogeographer, zoologist

Activities: Careers

1. Write verbs to describe what each worker does.

2. Use the workers listed in one category for the characters in a story. Some examples of titles might be: "The Butler Did It," using the workers in the B list, and "The Plumber's Helpers," using the workers in the P list as characters.

3. List the workers within general categories, such as Office, Entertainment, Industry, or Workers Who Come to Your Home.

4. Choose some of the following "planned communities" and list all the workers who might live there: Beauty Burg, Fix-it Ville, Healthy Hamlet, Food Farm, Sports Spa, Number Town.

5. Use the list and another source, such as the newspaper want ads, to find all the different kinds of mechanics, computer workers, engineers, doctors, designers, artists, inspectors, managers, reporters, clerks, supervisors, technicians, writers, and so on.

6. On your own, or with several friends, set up a display titled Tools of the Trade. Display actual tools, or pictures and drawings of tools used in several of the careers from the list.

7. Many surnames (last names) originally came from people's work. For example, the name Smith comes from the work of the blacksmith, or smith. Select several names you believe are last names (carpenter? painter? tailor?) and check a telephone book to see if you are correct. Make a chart of the career names you find in the phone book as people's last names. Do research on your last name to find out what it originally meant or was related to.

8. Create fancy names to make some of the careers sound more exciting or desirable.

stylist de bouffant for hairdresser

excellence expert for quality control manager

Worksheet

Business Card Design Service worksheet, p. 267.
Job Application worksheet, p. 268.

From *The Teacher's Book of Lists, Second Edition,* published by GoodYearBooks. Copyright © 1994 Sheila Madsen and Bette Gould.

Name

Date

Business Card Design Service

Use what you know about various careers and jobs to design business cards. Some are started for you to finish. The others you may create as you wish. Remember that people give out business cards to interest people in using their services or talents so they should be informative and appealing in design.

You may also enjoy making some of the blank cards for yourself to give out. Maybe you are a good artist, or an excellent speaker and you'd like to let others know.

Sally Sanderhand

11122 South St.
Pasadena, CA 90000   818/555-5555

John's Plastering
We're the Best in the West

**GOT A TREE THAT NEEDS
A HAND?**

Job Application

Choose a job. Pretend you are an adult applying for that job. Fill in the application as if you were applying for the position. Interview and write to people, read the newspaper classifieds and books about the job, to get facts needed to complete the application.

Your name: _____ Date: _____

Job you are applying for: _____

Write a brief description of job responsibilities: _____

_____

_____

_____

List skills you have that qualify you for this job:

_____

_____

List personal qualities you have that will help you do this job:

_____

_____

Education:

❏ High school   ❏ Trade or technical school   ❏ Junior college   ❏ Bachelor's degree

❏ Master's degree   ❏ PhD   ❏ Other _____

Salary per year that you will accept:

❏ $10,000–$20,000   ❏ $20,000–$30,000   ❏ $30,000–$40,000

❏ $40,000–$50,000   ❏ $50,000–$60,000   ❏ Other _____

Previous work experience: _____

_____

In your opinion what are the pros and cons of this job?

Pros	Cons
_____	_____
_____	_____
_____	_____

Ethnic Holidays—People Celebrate

January 15	Martin Luther King, Jr. Day	African-American	Commemorates the civil rights leader's birthday; now a national holiday.
January or February	Sul Nul (New Year)	Korean	New Year's Day. Children wear new clothes. Traditional foods are served.
Jan. 20–Feb. 20 (date varies)	Tet Nguyen-Den	Vietnamese	Vietnamese New Year; lasts three days.
Jan. 21–Feb. 19 (date varies)	Chinese New Year's	Chinese	Lasts several days, ending with festivities that include a parade featuring the Golden Dragon, gongs, drums, and firecrackers.
March 3	Hina Matsuri (Girl's Day)	Japanese	Festival honoring girls and their dolls. Traditional dolls are displayed in the home.
March 17	St. Patrick's Day	Irish	Feast day of St. Patrick, patron saint of Ireland. Celebrated with parades, balls, dinners.
March 21	Noruz (New Year)	Iranian	First day of spring according to the ancient Persian solar calendar.
March–April (date varies)	Pesach (Passover)	Jewish	Feast of unleavened bread. Commemorates the deliverance of the Jews from Egypt; observed for eight days.
April–May (date varies	Baiskhi (New Year)	Indian	Women and girls wear colorful saris. Day features feasts and exchange of gifts.
May 5	Ahrenee Nal (Children' Day)	Korean	Celebration honoring children. Children receive gifts and a special dinner.
May 5	Cinco de Mayo	Mexican	Celebrates, with a fiesta, the defeat of the French at the Battle of Puebla in 1867.

From *The Teacher's Book of Lists, Second Edition,* published by GoodYearBooks.
Copyright © 1994 Sheila Madsen and Bette Gould.

Date	Holiday	Culture	Description
May 5	Tango No Sekku (Boy's Day)	Japanese	Festival honoring boys. Carp kites symbolizing strength and determination are flown from rooftops.
June 24	Swedish Midsummer Festival	Swedish	Celebrated with dancing and the raising of the maypole.
July 29	Olsok Eve Festival (frequently called Norway Day in U.S.)	Norwegian	Commemorates the death of St. Olaf, the martyr king Olav Haraldsson, who brought Christianity to Norway.
August	Inter-Tribal Indian Ceremonial	Native American	Over 20 tribes gather in Gallup, New Mexico; events include parades, sports, and ceremonial dances.
September (date varies)	American Indian Day	Native American	Honors Native Americans.
September 28	Cabrillo Day	Portuguese	Six-day California festival honoring Juan Rodriguez Cabrillo, Portuguese navigator who discovered California on Sept. 28, 1542.
September (date varies)	Rosh Hashanah	Jewish	Jewish New Year
October 9	Leif Ericson Day	Norwegian & Icelandic	Commemorates the landing of Norsemen in Vinland, New England about 1000 A.D.
October 11	Pulaski Memorial Day	Polish	Commemorates the death of General Casimir Pulaski, hero of the American Revolution.
October 12 (observed on 2nd Monday of October)	Columbus Day	Italian	Commemorates the sighting of San Salvador on October 12, 1492, by Christopher Columbus.
December 15–January 1	Kwanzaa	African-American	Based on the traditional African harvest celebrations; focus is to teach African history and culture through song, dance, food, games, and stories.

From *The Teacher's Book of Lists, Second Edition*, published by GoodYearBooks. Copyright © 1994 Sheila Madsen and Bette Gould.

Explorers and Discoverers

This list makes a good starting place for a theme-based unit related to people's need to expand their boundaries for whatever purpose: space, riches, power; or the theme might be people's need to explore the unknown. It can also be a resource for children to keep in their notebooks as they study European or American history. Some excellent related books may be presented such as: Columbus, *by Ingri and Edgar D'Aulaire and* Marco Polo, *by Gian P. Ceserani. See the* **Independent Study** *worksheets, p. 368–371.*

c.1000	Leif Ericson	Thought to be the first European to reach North American mainland
1271–1295	Marco Polo	Merchant from Venice who wrote a famous account of his Asian travels and his life at the court of Kublai Khan
1487–1488	Bartolomeu Dias	First European to sail around the Cape of Good Hope in Africa
1492–1504	Christopher Columbus	Made voyages to West Indies and Caribbean Islands
1497–1498	John Cabot	Made voyages across the Atlantic to the Canadian coast for England
1498	Vasco de Gama	First European to reach India by sea (sailed around Africa)
1497–1503	Amerigo Vespucci	Made voyages to West Indies and South America
1513	Vasco Nuñez de Balboa	Crossed Isthmus of Panama; sighted Pacific Ocean
1513	Juan Ponce de León	Explored Florida
1519–1521	Hernán Cortés	Explored and conquered the wealthy Aztec empire in Mexico
1519–1521	Ferdinand Magellan	Led first voyage around the world; proved the world is round
1524	Giovanni da Verrazano	Explored Atlantic coast of the Americas while searching for a Northwest Passage
1531–1535	Francisco Pizarro	Explored and conquered Peru
1535	Jacques Cartier	Discovered and sailed up St. Lawrence River
1539–1542	Hernando de Soto	Explored Southeastern U.S.; reached Mississippi River

1540–1542	Francisco V. de Coronado	Explored Southwestern U.S., as far as central Kansas
1541	Francisco de Orellana	Explored Amazon River
1577–1580	Sir Francis Drake	First Englishman to sail around the world; explored California coast
1603–1616	Samuel de Champlain	Explored eastern coast of North America and St. Lawrence River
1609–1611	Henry Hudson	Explored Hudson Bay and River area
1642–1644	Abel Tasman	Dutch sailor who discovered Tasmania, New Zealand, Tonga, and Fiji
1673	Louis Joliet and Jacques Marquette	Explored northern Mississippi River basin
1727–1741	Vitus Bering	Danish sailor in the Russian navy who explored the Bering Strait; discovered Alaska
1768–1779	James Cook	Made extensive explorative voyages in the South Pacific
1789–1793	Sir Alexander Mackenzie	Explored western Canada
1804–1806	William Clark and Meriwether Lewis	Led expedition across the Rocky Mountains to the Pacific Ocean and back
1842–1846	John Charles Frémont	Explored extensively in western U.S.
1849–1873	David Livingstone	Greatest European explorer of Africa
1853–1855	Matthew Maury	American hydrographer; charted ocean depths, currents, and life of the Atlantic; pioneered science of oceanography
1853–1858	Sir Richard Burton	Explored Arabia and East Africa
1874–1889	Sir Henry Stanley	Proved the source of the Nile; explored Congo River
1895	Fridtjof Nansen	Norwegian who crossed Greenland for the first time; sent his ship, the *Fram,* to within 4° of the North Pole
1909	Robert Peary	Led first expedition to reach the North Pole
1911	Roald Amundsen	First to reach the South Pole
1926–1929	Richard E. Byrd	Flew over both the North and South Poles; led five expeditions into the Antarctic
1953	Edmund Hillary, Tenzing Norkay	First men to reach the summit of Mt. Everest, the world's highest mountain; Hillary was a New Zealand explorer and mountaineer; Norkay was a Sherpa from Nepal
1957–1958	Sir Vivian Fuchs	Led first expeditions across Antarctica

Task Cards

Explorers 1

1. Learn about the exploration of space and what has been discovered, both by people and by machines.

   • Who are the famous explorers and discoverers?

   • How much have some of these expeditions cost?

   • Was the money well spent? Why or why not?

2. Make a model to compare the discoveries of an unmanned expedition (such as the Magellan spacecraft) with a manned expedition (such as the voyage of Magellan).

Explorers 2

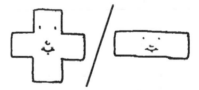

1. Design a Positive/Negative chart by dividing a chart into two columns. Label one column Positive and the other Negative.

2. Select two or three explorers to research for the purpose of learning about their positive and negative effects on the land or area they explored/discovered. Be sure to find out about the effects on any people, too.

3. Briefly list the effects in the appropriate column.*

4. Try to make a generalization based on what you find out. You may then want to read about one or two more explorers to see if your generalization applies to these other explorers.

*You may want to write positive effects in one color and negative effects in another color.

From *The Teacher's Book of Lists, Second Edition,* published by GoodYearBooks.
Copyright © 1994 Sheila Madsen and Bette Gould.

Explorers 3

1. Use a paper bag to represent a knapsack.

2. Choose an explorer and write his name on the knapsack.

3. Think about what he might have taken on the trip. List or draw the equipment on pieces of paper and put into the knapsack.

4. Now do research (reading and looking at pictures) to find out the equipment the explorer actually took. Add anything you did not originally guess, and remove anything you were wrong about.

5. Which equipment would you most like to use?

Explorers 4

1. Fold a 12" x 18" piece of paper in thirds or fourths to make a Travel Brochure.

2. Imagine you are an advertising specialist for one of the explorer's journeys. What would you illustrate and tell to make the trip seem enticing?

3. Design and create a Travel Brochure to interest others in going on the expedition.

4. Share your brochure with others.*

*Several brochures may be displayed on a travel kiosk cut from a large cardboard box.

From *The Teacher's Book of Lists, Second Edition,* published by GoodYearBooks. Copyright © 1994 Sheila Madsen and Bette Gould.

Map Symbols

Many symbols exist for the same type of landform or site shown on maps. The ones listed below are some of the common ones. Students may enjoy displaying map symbols found on a variety of maps and inventing some of their own.

Symbol	Name	Symbol	Name
✪ ★	state capital	(flag)	golf course
●	city or town	(outline)	lake
(flag building)	school	(shaded outline)	dry lake
⌂ + ▣	church	(grass tufts)	swamp
✚	hospital	(loop)	dam
—	road	(bars)	canal
═	highway	+ ⋀	mountain peak
✈	airport	(dots)	desert
▦	railroad	△	point of interest
⊓	bridge	♠	state parks and recreation areas
⋂	tunnel	⋏	campground
⌇	river	⋏ ✕	picnic areas
⌇	waterfall	(skier)	winter sports
		(crossed)	battle sites

From *The Teacher's Book of Lists, Second Edition,* published by GoodYearBooks.
Copyright © 1994 Sheila Madsen and Bette Gould.

Mapmakers

Draw symbols on the map and make up a name for each. In the Map Index, list each place name and the letter and number that shows its location.

	A	B	C	D	E	F	G	H
1								
2								
3								
4								
5								
6						⛺ Tall Pines Campground		
7								

MAP INDEX

Tall Pines Campground F6

From *The Teacher's Book of Lists, Second Edition*, published by GoodYearBooks.
Copyright © 1994 Sheila Madsen and Bette Gould.

Olympic Games

The first recorded Olympic Games in ancient Greece occurred in 776 B.C. at Olympia, Greece. The first modern Olympics in 1896 had nine nations represented. Today, more than one hundred nations send athletes to compete. An interesting look at the ancient games can be found in Olympic Games in Ancient Greece, *Shirley Glubok and Alfred Tamarin, Harper & Row/HarperCollins, 1976.*

Summer Games		Winter Games
Athens, Greece	1896	
Paris, France	1900	
St. Louis, Missouri, U.S.	1904	
Athens, Greece (unofficial)	1906	
London, England	1908	
Stockholm, Sweden	1912	
Antwerp, Belgium	1920	
Paris, France	1924	Chamonix, France
Amsterdam, Netherlands	1928	St. Moritz, Switzerland
Los Angeles, California, U.S.	1932	Lake Placid, New York, U.S.
Berlin, Germany	1936	Garmisch-Partenkirchen, Germany
No games held due to World War II	1940, 1944	No games held due to World War II
London, England	1948	St. Moritz, Switzerland
Helsinki, Finland	1952	Oslo, Norway
Melbourne, Australia	1956	Cortina d'Ampezzo, Italy
Rome, Italy	1960	Squaw Valley, California, U.S.
Tokyo, Japan	1964	Innsbruck, Austria
Mexico City, Mexico	1968	Grenoble, France
Munich, Germany	1972	Sapporo, Japan
Montreal, Canada	1976	Innsbruck, Austria
Moscow, U.S.S.R. (U.S. boycotted)	1980	Lake Placid, New York, U.S.
Los Angeles, California, U.S. (U.S.S.R. boycotted)	1984	Sarajevo, Yugoslavia
Seoul, Korea	1988	Calgary, Canada
Barcelona, Spain	1992	Albertville, France
Scheduled for Atlanta, Georgia, U.S.	1994	Scheduled for Lillehammer, Norway

Teams of Major Sports

Many activities can be developed from this list and the team address lists that follow. Children can locate teams on maps, see U.S. Map, p. 311, research a team's history, compile and track stats during a season, and categorize by names. Writing letters to any of the teams to request information, literature, posters, and other memorabilia will provide students with a welcome reward: an answer in the mail within a short time.

Baseball

Atlanta Braves
Baltimore Orioles
Boston Red Sox
California Angels
Chicago Cubs
Chicago White Sox
Cincinnati Reds
Cleveland Indians
Colorado Rockies
Detroit Tigers
Florida Marlins
Houston Astros
Kansas City Royals
Los Angeles Dodgers
Milwaukee Brewers
Minnesota Twins
Montreal Expos
New York Mets
New York Yankees
Oakland A's (Athletics)
Philadelphia Phillies
Pittsburgh Pirates
St. Louis Cardinals
San Diego Padres
San Francisco Giants
Seattle Mariners
Texas Rangers
Toronto Blue Jays

Basketball

Atlanta Hawks
Boston Celtics
Charlotte Hornets
Chicago Bulls
Cleveland Cavaliers
Denver Nuggets
Detroit Pistons
Golden State Warriors
Houston Rockets
Indiana Pacers
Los Angeles Clippers
Los Angeles Lakers
Miami Heat
Milwaukee Bucks
Minnesota Timberwolves
New Jersey Nets
New York Knicks
   (Knickerbockers)
Orlando Magic
Philadelphia 76ers
Phoenix Suns
Portland Trailblazers
Sacramento Kings
San Antonio Spurs
Seattle SuperSonics
Utah Jazz
Washington Bullets

Football

Atlanta Falcons
Buffalo Bills
Chicago Bears
Cincinnati Bengals
Cleveland Browns
Dallas Cowboys
Denver Broncos
Detroit Lions
Green Bay Packers
Houston Oilers
Indianapolis Colts
Kansas City Chiefs
Los Angeles Raiders
Los Angeles Rams
Miami Dolphins
Minnesota Vikings
New England Patriots
New Orleans Saints
New York Giants
New York Jets
Philadelphia Eagles
Phoenix Cardinals
Pittsburgh Steelers
San Diego Chargers
San Francisco 49ers
Seattle Seahawks
Tampa Bay Buccaneers
Washington Redskins

Hockey

Boston Bruins
Buffalo Sabres
Calgary Flames
Chicago Black Hawks
Detroit Red Wings
Edmonton Oilers
Hartford Whalers
Los Angeles Kings
Minnesota North Stars
Montreal Canadiens
New York Islanders
New York Rangers
Philadelphia Flyers
Pittsburgh Penguins
Quebec Nordiques
St. Louis Blues
San Jose Sharks
Tampa Bay Lightning
Toronto Maple Leafs
Vancouver Canucks
Washington Capitals

Baseball

American League
212-339-7600
350 Park Avenue
New York, NY 10022

Baltimore Orioles
410-685-9800
333 W. Camden Street
Baltimore, MD 21201

Boston Red Sox
617-267-9440
Fenway Park
Boston, MA 02215

California Angels
714-937-7200
P.O. Box 2000
Anaheim, CA 92803

Chicago White Sox
312-924-1000
333 West 35th Street
Chicago, IL 60616

Cleveland Indians
216-861-1200
Cleveland Stadium
Cleveland, OH 44114

Detroit Tigers
313-962-4000
2121 Trumbull Avenue
Detroit, MI 48216

Kansas City Royals
816-921-2200
P.O. Box 419969
Kansas City, MO 64141

Milwaukee Brewers
414-933-4114
County Stadium
Milwaukee, WI 53214

Minnesota Twins
612-375-1366
501 Chicago Avenue South
Minneapolis, MN 55415

New York Yankees
212-293-4300
Yankee Stadium
Bronx, NY 10451

Oakland Athletics
510-638-4900
Oakland Coliseum
Oakland, CA 94621

Seattle Mariners
206-628-3555
P.O. Box 4100
Seattle, WA 98104

Texas Rangers
817-273-5222
P.O. Box 90111
Arlington, TX 76004

Toronto Blue Jays
416-341-1000
The Skydome
300 Bremner Boulevard, #3200
Toronto, Ontario M5V 3B3

National League
212-339-7700
350 Park Avenue
New York, NY 10022

From *The Teacher's Book of Lists, Second Edition,* published by GoodYearBooks. Copyright © 1994 Sheila Madsen and Bette Gould.

Baseball (continued)

Atlanta Braves
404-522-7630
P.O. Box 4064
Atlanta, GA 30302

Chicago Cubs
312-404-2827
1060 West Addison Street
Chicago, IL 60613

Cincinnati Reds
513-421-4510
100 Riverfront Stadium
Cincinnati, OH 45202

Colorado Rockies
303-292-0200
1700 Broadway
Suite 2100
Denver, CO 80290

Florida Marlins
305-779-7070
100 NE 3rd Avenue, 3rd Floor
Ft. Lauderdale, FL 33301

Houston Astros
713-799-9500
P.O. Box 288
Houston, TX 77001

Los Angeles Dodgers
213-224-1500
1000 Elysian Park Avenue
Los Angeles, CA 90012

Montreal Expos
514-253-3434
P.O. Box 500, Station M
Montreal, Quebec H1V 3P2

New York Mets
718-507-6387
Shea Stadium
Flushing, NY 11368

Philadelphia Phillies
215-463-6000
P.O. Box 7575
Philadelphia, PA 19101

Pittsburgh Pirates
412-323-5000
Three Rivers Stadium
Pittsburgh, PA 15212

St. Louis Cardinals
314-421-3060
250 Stadium Plaza
St. Louis, MO 63102

San Diego Padres
619-283-7294
P.O. Box 2000
San Diego, CA 92112

San Francisco Giants
415-468-3700
Candlestick Park
San Francisco, CA 94124

Basketball

Atlanta Hawks
One CNN Center
Suite 405 South
Atlanta, GA 30303

Boston Celtics
151 Merrimac Street, 5th floor
Boston, MA 02114

Charlotte Hornets
1 Hive Drive
Charlotte, NC 28217

Chicago Bulls
One Magnificent Mile
980 North Michigan Avenue, Suite 1600
Chicago, IL 60611

Cleveland Cavaliers
The Coliseum
2923 Streetsboro Road
Richfield, OH 44286

Basketball (continued)

Dallas Mavericks
Reunion Arena
777 Sports Street
Dallas, TX 75207

Denver Nuggets
1635 Clay Street
Denver, CO 80204

Detroit Pistons
The Palace of Auburn Hills
Two Championship Drive
Auburn Hills, MI 48326

Golden State Warriors
Oakland Coliseum Arena
Oakland, CA 94621

Houston Rockets
P.O. Box 272349
Houston, TX 77277

Indiana Pacers
Market Square Arena
300 East Market Street
Indianapolis, IN 46204

Los Angeles Clippers
Los Angeles Sports Arena
3939 South Figueroa Street
Los Angeles, CA 90037

Los Angeles Lakers
Great Western Forum
P.O. Box 10
Inglewood, CA 90306

Miami Heat
Miami Arena
Miami, FL 33136

Milwaukee Bucks
1001 North Fourth Street
Milwaukee, WI 53203

Minnesota Timberwolves
600 First Avenue North
Minneapolis, MN 55403

New Jersey Nets
Brendan Byrne Arena
East Rutherford, NJ 07073

New York Knickerbockers
Madison Square Garden
Two Pennsylvania Plaza, Third Floor
New York, NY 10121

Orlando Magic
P.O. Box 76
Orlando, FL 32802

Philadelphia 76ers
Veterans Stadium
P.O. Box 25050
Philadelphia, PA 19147

Phoenix Suns
P.O. Box 515
Phoenix, AZ 85001

Portland Trail Blazers
Lloyd Building, Suite 600
700 NE Multnomah Street
Portland, OR 97232

Sacramento Kings
One Sports Parkway
Sacramento, CA 95834

San Antonio Spurs
600 East Market Street, Suite 102
San Antonio, TX 78205

Seattle Supersonics
190 Queen Avenue North
Box 900911
Seattle, WA 98109

Utah Jazz
Delta Center
301 West South Temple
Salt Lake City, UT 84101

Washington Bullets
Capital Centre
One Harry S. Truman Drive
Landover, MD 20785

Football

American Football Conference

Buffalo Bills
One Bills Drive
Orchard Park, NY 14127

Cincinnati Bengals
200 Riverfront Stadium
Cincinnati, OH 45202

Cleveland Browns
P.O. Box 679
Berea, OH 44017-0679

Denver Broncos
13655 Broncos Parkway
Englewood, CO 80112

Houston Oilers
6910 Fannin Street
Houston, TX 77030

Indianapolis Colts
7001 West 56th Street
Indianapolis, IN 46254

Kansas City Chiefs
One Arrowhead Drive
Kansas City, MO 64129

Los Angeles Raiders
332 Center Street
El Segundo, CA 90245

Miami Dolphins
Joe Robbie Stadium
2269 N.W. 199th Street
Miami, FL 33056

New England Patriots
Foxboro Stadium
Route 1
Foxboro, MA 02035

New York Jets
1000 Fulton Avenue
Hempstead, NY 11550

Pittsburgh Steelers
Three Rivers Stadium
300 Stadium Club
Pittsburgh, PA 15212

San Diego Chargers
San Diego Jack Murphy Stadium
9449 Friars Road
San Diego, CA 92108

Seattle Seahawks
11220 NE 53rd Street
Kirkland, WA 98033

National Football Conference

Atlanta Falcons
Suwanee Road at I-85
Suwanee, GA 30174

Chicago Bears
Halas Hall
250 North Washington Road
Lake Forest, IL 60045

Dallas Cowboys
Cowboys Center
One Cowboys Parkway
Irving, TX 75063-4727

Detroit Lions
1200 Featherstone Road
Pontiac, MI 48342

Green Bay Packers
1265 Lombardi Avenue
Green Bay, WI 54304

Los Angeles Rams
2327 West Lincoln Avenue
Anaheim, CA 92801

Minnesota Vikings
9520 Viking Drive
Eden Prairie, MN 55344

New Orleans Saints
6928 Saints Drive
Metairie, LA 70003

Football (continued)

New York Giants
Giants Stadium
East Rutherford, NJ 07073

Philadelphia Eagles
Veterans Stadium
Broad Street & Pattison Avenue
Philadelphia, PA 19148

Phoenix Cardinals
P.O. Box 888
Phoenix, AZ 85001-0888

San Francisco 49ers
4949 Centennial Boulevard
Santa Clara, CA 95054-1229

Tampa Bay Buccaneers
One Buccaneer Drive
Tampa, FL 33607

Washington Redskins
13832 Redskin Drive
Herndon, VA

Hockey

Boston Bruins
Boston Garden
150 Causeway Street
Boston, MA 02114

Buffalo Sabres
Memorial Auditorium
Buffalo, NY 14202

Calgary Flames
P.O. Box 1540, Station M
Calgary, Alberta T2P 3B9

Chicago Blackhawks
Chicago Stadium
1800 W. Madison Street
Chicago, IL 60612

Detroit Red Wings
Joe Louis Sports Arena
600 Civic Center Drive
Detroit, MI 48226

Edmonton Oilers
Northlands Coliseum
Edmonton, Alberta T5B 4M9

Hartford Whalers
Hartford Civic Centre Coliseum
242 Trumbull Street
Hartford, CT 06103

Los Angeles Kings
Great Western Forum
3900 W. Manchester Boulevard
P.O. Box 17013
Inglewood, CA 90306

Minnesota North Stars
Metropolitan Centre
7901 Cedar Avenue South
Bloomington, MN 55425

Montreal Canadiens
Montreal Forum
2313 St. Catherine West
Montreal, Quebec H3H 1N2

New Jersey Devils
Byrne Meadowlands Arena
P.O. Box 504
East Rutherford, NJ 07073

New York Islanders
Nassau Veterans' Memorial Coliseum
Uniondale, NY 11553

New York Rangers
Madison Square Garden
4 Pennsylvania Plaza
New York, NY 10001

Ottawa Senators
301 Moodie Drive, Suite 200
Nepean, Ontario K2H 9C4

Hockey (continued)

Philadelphia Flyers
The Spectrum
Pattison Place
Philadelphia, PA 19148

Pittsburgh Penguins
Civic Arena
Pittsburgh, PA 15219

Quebec Nordiques
Colisee de Quebec
2205 ave du Colisee
Quebec, Quebec G1L 4W7

St. Louis Blues
St. Louis Arena
5700 Oakland Avenue
St. Louis, MO 63110

San Jose Sharks
10 Almaden Boulevard, Suite 600
P.O. Box 1240
San Jose, CA 95113

Tampa Bay Lightning
501 E. Kennedy Boulevard., Suite 175
Tampa, FL 33602

Toronto Maple Leafs
Maple Leaf Gardens
60 Carlton Street
Toronto, Ontario M5B 1L1

Vancouver Canucks
Pacific Coliseum
100 N. Renfrew Street
Vancouver, British Columbia V5K 3N7

Washington Capitals
Capital Center
Landover, MD 20785

Winnipeg Jets
Winnipeg Arena
15, 1430 Maroons Road
Winnipeg, Manitoba R3G 0L5

From *The Teacher's Book of Lists, Second Edition*, published by GoodYearBooks.
Copyright © 1994 Sheila Madsen and Bette Gould.

U.S. Government Branches

Especially in a national election year, students have a natural interest in the government and how it works. At any time, a day or two of news coverage will uncover questions and confusions children may have about the national government. This list is a brief look at the three branches and their functions. There are excellent books available on the subject, such as The Supreme Court and How It Works, *by Anthony Lewis (Random House).* The President's Cabinet and How It Grew, *by Nancy Winslow Parker (HarperCollins, 1991) is excellent for younger children, while* Class President, *by Johanna Hurwitz (Scholastic, 1991) tells the story of a school election, including all the steps of organizing a campaign.*

The Executive Branch

Executive Office of the President

The President is the chief executive and chief of state. The Office of the President includes 15 councils and offices. Some of the better known ones are:

White House Office

Office of Management and Budget (OMB)

National Security Council (the CIA reports to this council)

Domestic Council

Council on Economic Policy

Council on Environmental Policy

Energy Policy Office

Council on Wage and Price Stability

Executive Departments

The heads are appointed by the President and are approved by the Senate. The head of the Justice Department is called the Attorney General. All the others are called secretaries and together form the cabinet. These departments are:

Department of State

Department of the Treasury

Department of Defense

Department of Justice

Department of the Interior

Department of Agriculture

Department of Commerce

Department of Labor

Department of Education

Department of Energy

Department of Transportation

Department of Health and Human Services

Functions of the President

enforces federal laws

appoints and removes high federal officials

commands the armed forces

conducts foreign affairs

recommends to Congress the laws he would like passed

appoints Americans to diplomatic missions in other lands and representatives to international groups

performs ceremonial duties

Independent Agencies

Each agency is headed by an administrator or director. Some are headed by several persons of equal rank. The President appoints members of the agencies with Senate approval. Some of these executive branch agencies include:

NASA (National Aeronautics and Space Administration)

banking and finance

civil service

farm credit

interstate commerce

securities and exchange

tariffs

veterans affairs

National Labor Relations Board

The Legislative Branch

The Senate

100 members, 2 from each state elected for 6-year terms

Vice President presides; the Speaker Pro Tem presides in the Vice President's absence

The House of Representatives

435 members, apportioned based on populations of states, elected for a two-year term

Speaker of the House presides

Administrative Agencies of the Legislative Branch

Architect of the Capitol

Congressional Budget Office

General Accounting Office

Government Printing Office

Library of Congress

U. S. Botanic Gardens

Functions of Congress (the Senate and House of Representatives)

makes, repeals, and amends federal laws

levies federal taxes

appropriates funds for the government

confirms or rejects presidential appointments to executive and judicial branches

participates in amending the Constitution

The Judicial Branch

The Supreme Court

This is the highest court in the land. It is made up of:

1 Chief Justice

8 Associate Justices

These justices are appointed by the President, approved by the Senate, and remain on the court until death or retirement.

Federal Courts of Appeal

Often called circuit courts, these courts hear appeals from other federal courts. There are 11 in all.

Other Federal Courts

There are about 90 federal district courts located in various cities.

Functions of the Judicial Branch

hears cases based on appeals or new ones based on federal laws

district courts may appeal a decision to an appeals court

appeals courts may appeal a decision to the Supreme Court

federal courts decide cases that involve the Constitution or federal laws

From *The Teacher's Book of Lists, Second Edition*, published by GoodYearBooks. Copyright © 1994 Sheila Madsen and Bette Gould.

U.S. History Events

*This list is an easy reference for those hard-to-remember dates and events. It is also meant to be a springboard to research or independent study. It will be useful to students interested in certain periods, such as the Civil War, certain decades, such as the '50s or 1840s, or certain developments, such as industrialization. See the **Independent Study** worksheets, p. 368–371, for additional ideas.*

± 20,000 years ago	Indians and Eskimos inhabited the Western Hemisphere.
c.900 or 1000 A.D.	It is believed that a band of Vikings explored part of the east coast of North America.
1492	The rediscovery of America. Christopher Columbus sailed from Spain to the Western Hemisphere. Europeans called him the discoverer of America.
1497	John Cabot made the first voyage to North America for England.
1513	Ponce de León of Spain explored Florida, seeking the fountain of youth.
1540-1542	Francisco Coronado of Spain explored the American southwest.
1565	Spaniards founded St. Augustine, Florida, the oldest city in what is now the U.S.
1607	Jamestown, the first permanent British settlement in North America, was established in Virginia by about 100 colonists. (*To Spoil the Sun*, by Joyce Rockwood. Holt, 1976.)
1619	Virginia established the House of Burgesses, the first representative legislature in America.
1620	Arrival of the Mayflower; Pilgrims founded Plymouth Colony, later to be known as Massachusetts.
1624	The Dutch established New Netherland, the first permanent settlement in New York colony.
1636	Harvard, the first college in the colonies, was founded.
1647	Massachusetts established the first colonial public school system.
1664	England took control of New Netherland and New Sweden (Delaware).
1672	The Boston Post Road was completed, linking Boston and New York City.
1692	The famous Witchcraft trials were held in Salem, Massachusetts; 19 people were hanged. (*The Witch of Blackbird Pond*, by Elizabeth Speare. Houghton, 1958.)
1704	*The Boston News-Letter,* the first successful colonial newspaper, began publication.

1752   Benjamin Franklin flew a kite during a storm to prove that lightning is a form of electricity.

1756   New York City and Philadelphia were linked by a stagecoach line.

c.1757   The first street lights in the colonies were installed in Philadelphia.

c.1760   The first Conestoga wagons were built.

1763   Britain defeated France in the last of the French and Indian Wars, and gained control of eastern North America.

1765   Britain passed the Stamp Act, taxing newspapers, legal documents, and other printed matter in the colonies.

1766   The first permanent commercial theater in the colonies opened in Philadelphia.

1770   British troops killed American civilians in the Boston Massacre after being taunted by colonists who were angry at the sight of British troops in their streets.

1773   Colonists staged the Boston Tea Party, dumping British tea into Boston Harbor, to show resistance to the tax on tea.

1774   The Intolerable Acts were four measures, including the closing of Boston Harbor, designed to punish Massachusetts for the Tea Party.

1774   The First Continental Congress, an intercolonial meeting in Philadelphia, drafted a resolution to assert American rights.

1775–1783   **Revolutionary War**

April 18, 1775   Paul Revere, a silversmith and engraver, rode by horseback from Boston to Lexington to warn the Massachusetts minutemen that "the British are coming." (*Paul Revere's Ride,* by Henry Wadsworth Longfellow. Dutton, 1990.)

1775   Shooting began between the Minutemen (colonists) and the British (redcoats) at Lexington and Concord, Massachusetts. The Revolutionary War had begun.

1776   Thomas Paine's *Common Sense* was published. It boosted the idea of complete independence from Britain.

July 4, 1776   Thomas Jefferson's draft of a declaration of independence was read to and passed by the second Continental Congress. It set forth a statement of the principles of human freedom and the basis for popular government. The United States of America was established.

1776 onward   Many slaves were freed, such as in Vermont (the first state to prohibit slavery, in 1777), Massachusetts, and other northeastern states. Slaves could also be freed by enlisting in the revolutionary army.

1778   Benjamin Franklin made a treaty of alliance with France, ensuring America money and some military support.

1780   Benjamin Lincoln's army, some 5,000 soldiers, surrendered to the British in Charleston, SC. This was the biggest American defeat of the war.

Oct. 18, 1781	Cornwallis surrendered his army (about 7,000 soldiers) at Yorktown. The British held only New York and Charleston. They evacuated Charleston at the end of the year.
1781	The Articles of Confederation were laws to govern a federal government, including the original 13 states.
1782	In December, the first articles of peace were signed with the British who then evacuated New York.
1783	The Peace of Paris formally ended the Revolutionary War with the signing of the Treaty of Paris. Benjamin Franklin also obtained monies from France to help sustain the new country.
1787	The Northwest Ordinance outlined a government for the Northwest, a bill of rights, and a clause prohibiting slavery.
1787	The Constitutional Convention was held between May and September to write a new Constitution. The Great Compromise spread power between three branches: the executive, legislative, and judicial. It provided for representation based on population (the House) and equal representation for each state (the Senate). The Bill of Rights, written to specifically guarantee individual rights, was added and finally the Constitution was ratified by 1788.
1789	George Washington was inaugurated in New York on April 30.
1794	The Whiskey Rebellion was a series of fights between Pennsylvania grain farmers and U.S. marshalls over a federal tax on whiskey makers. Washington's use of troops to stop it was an early test of federal power in enforcing a federal law within a state.
1796	The beginning of the two political party system; Washington's farewell address asked Americans to end party differences and to "steer clear of all foreign alliances."
1801	Thomas Jefferson became the first president to be inaugurated in Washington, DC. This was a momentous occasion for the new country: a new leader replaced another one without bloodshed, guns firing, or insurrection. Jefferson's aim was "a wise and frugal government."
1801	John Marshall became Chief Justice of the Supreme Court and remained until his death in 1835. Marshall's court, while increasing the power of the federal government, also helped ensure that government remained within the bounds of the Constitution.
1803	The Louisiana Purchase, bought for $15 million from Napoleon who was in dire need of money, added the land drained by the Missouri-Mississippi rivers and doubled the size of the U.S.
1804-1806	The Lewis and Clark expedition explored the Louisiana territory and beyond to the Pacific, covering over 3,000 miles. Sacajawea, a Shoshone woman, accompanied the group as guide and interpreter and received the Jefferson Peace Medal for her contributions.

1809   Madison's inauguration took place amidst a rising sentiment against Britain for such events as the "paper blockade" and the Chesapeake affair.

1811   The Battle of Tippecanoe was brought about by the actions of Tecumseh, an influential Sioux Indian leader. Tecumseh tried to unite all Indian tribes in defense of their homelands.

1811   Work was started on the National Road. When it was completed it linked the east and the midwest.

1812–1814   The War of 1812 was largely the result of American nationalism. During the British bombardment of Ft. McHenry, Francis Scott Key, a young poet, observed the huge U.S. flag flying over the fort, and wrote the poem that became our national anthem.

1815   In the Battle of New Orleans, Andrew Jackson beat back a major British infantry attack on January 8 (actually after the peace treaty had been signed). At the end of the day more than 2,000 redcoats lay dead, while only 7 of Jackson's men died.

1817   The Treaty of Ghent formally ended the war and included features that greatly improved relations between Britain and the U.S.

1819   The Adams-Onis Treaty (Transcontinental Treaty) was a brilliant feat of diplomacy for John Quincy Adams. Spain sold Florida to the U.S. for $5 million. A line was drawn across the west from Texas to the Pacific Ocean staking a claim for the U.S. to the Pacific Coast without spending arms or money. This started serious intentions of having a transcontinental nation.

1820   The Missouri Compromise, mediated by Speaker of the House, Henry Clay, ended a slavery dispute by establishing the line of 36° 30' north latitude. With the exception of Missouri, slavery was prohibited in states north of the line.

1821   The first public high school opened (in Boston). This was, in part, influenced by Horace Mann, who said, "In a republic, ignorance is a crime." He went on to organize Massachusetts schools into a state-wide organization, establish a state curriculum, and get the legislature to set up normal schools (special colleges to train teachers).

1823   The Monroe Doctrine stated that the U.S. would regard any European intervention in the New World as "an unfriendly act." Also, the U.S. would not allow any additional colonies to be established in either North or South America.

1825   The Erie Canal opened, providing a water route from the Atlantic Ocean to the Great Lakes, greatly saving time and money.

1828   Andrew Jackson won the presidency with ease. The tracks for the first railroad, the Baltimore & Ohio, were begun.

1830   "Tom Thumb," the nation's first commercial steam locomotive, operated in Baltimore. It was capable of running at about 10 mph.

From *The Teacher's Book of Lists, Second Edition,* published by GoodYearBooks. Copyright © 1994 Sheila Madsen and Bette Gould.

1830 The Indian Removal Act authorized exchange of certain lands in the plains for the Indians' eastern holdings. By the time Jackson left office in 1837, most eastern Indians had been resettled in the west.

1831 Nat Turner's Rebellion was the most famous of dozens of slave rebellions and conspiracies. Turner was convinced that God had directed him to free slaves. His group of recruited slaves killed about 60 whites; nearly 100 blacks were killed as well.

1832 South Carolina threatened secession over a tariff.

1834 Cyrus McCormick's patented reaper came into use, which allowed farmers to harvest grain more quickly than before.

1836 The Battle of the Alamo secured a large area of Texas territory for the Americans who had moved there. Mexican troops, led by Santa Anna, were defeated by the U.S. army. Samuel Houston became the president of the new area called The Lone Star Republic. (*Susanna of the Alamo: A True Story,* by John Jakes. HBJ, 1986.)

1837 Samuel F. B. Morse demonstrated the first successful telegraph in the United States.

1841 About this time, settlers began following the newly opened Oregon Trail, a 2,000 mile route to Oregon and the Pacific northwest.

1842–1844 Kit Carson and John C. Fremont explored vast areas of the western U.S.

1843 Dorothea Dix reported to the Massachusetts legislature on her findings of a two-year survey of every jail, prison, and poorhouse in the state. The influence of her one-woman crusade for improving the plight of the mentally ill was enormous.

1844 "Manifest Destiny" became the slogan of the day. As many Americans settled along the Pacific, more migrated westward. The Democrats picked up the term, coined by a New York newspaper, as their slogan. They wanted to expand to include Texas and Oregon and the entire northwest as far as Russian Alaska.

1846 Britain ceded the southern part of the Oregon Country to the U.S., dividing U.S. and British territory at the 54°40' parallel.

1846–1848 War with Mexico involved battles fought by troops led by Santa Anna and U.S. troops led by "Old Rough-and-Ready," Zachary Taylor. The war ended, in favor of the U.S., with the Treaty of Guadalupe Hidalgo. Mexico gave up all claims to Texas and sold the rest of the southwest, from New Mexico to California, for $15 million.

1848 Gold was discovered in California, triggering the Gold Rush.

1849 The California Gold Rush brought some 80,000 people to the territory. By the winter of 1849 California applied for statehood. This was seen as another crisis that would lead to civil war.

1850 The Compromise of 1850 was a temporary end to a national crisis which had been raging over the slavery issue.

1850   Harriet Tubman made the first of 18 trips into slave territory to lead slaves to non-slave territory and freedom.

1854   The Kansas-Nebraska Act was a bill to organize the Nebraska Territory, with an amendment that repealed the part of the Missouri Compromise that had prohibited slavery above the 36°30' line. Douglas attempted to test "popular sovereignty," or leaving the decision of slavery to the people. The turmoil led to the formation of the Republican Party and violent bloodshed in Kansas.

1856   University of Iowa admitted women, the first university to do so.

1856   The first American kindergarten opened in Watertown, Wisconsin.

1857   The Dred Scott decision, made by the Supreme Court, said that Scott had no right to sue for his freedom or anything else, as he was not a citizen, only a slave.

1860   The Pony Express began carrying mail from St. Louis, Missouri, to the far west. Due to increased railroad expansion, the Pony Express ended after less than a year.

1860   Lincoln was elected and, led by South Carolina, all the lower south, from Georgia to Texas, seceded from the U.S. (*Abe Lincoln Grows Up*, by Carl Sandburg. An adaptation of *Abraham Lincoln: The Prairie Years*. Harcourt, 1928, 1975.)

1861–1865   **Civil War**

April 12, 1861   South Carolina troops opened fire on federal troops at Ft. Sumter (in South Carolina)—the Civil War had begun.

1862   The Homestead Act passed, which offered public land to people at low prices, spurring more settlement to the west.

Jan. 1, 1863   The Emancipation Proclamation declared freedom for all slaves in Confederate territory. Although not enforceable in the south, the Proclamation gave a moral tone to the war.

July 1–3, 1863   The Battle of Gettysburg was the beginning of the end for the Confederacy. In November, Lincoln gave his Gettysburg Address to dedicate the Soldiers' National Cemetery.

January, 1865   The 13th Amendment, abolishing slavery in all American states and territories, passed Congress but only by the sheer strength of Lincoln's efforts. He earned the title, "The Great Emancipator."

April 1, 1865   Lee surrenders to Grant at Appomattox Court House. The surrender agreement was signed April 9; five days later Lincoln was assassinated. (*Across Five Aprils,* by Irene Hunt. Follett, 1965.)

1860s & '70s   An era of invention and the growth of business and production methods saw the invention of the typewriter (1867), barbed wire (1873), the telephone by Alexander Graham Bell (1867), and the phonograph (1877) and the electric light (1879) by Thomas Edison.

From *The Teacher's Book of Lists, Second Edition,* published by GoodYearBooks. Copyright © 1994 Sheila Madsen and Bette Gould.

1866	The transatlantic cable project was completed.
1867–1868	The Reconstruction Acts, passed to direct rebuilding the south, laid guidelines for new southern governments, readmission requirements, and required giving blacks the vote.
1868	The House of Representatives impeached President Andrew Johnson (the only president to be impeached), but the Senate voted (by 1 vote) against removing him from office.
1869	The first through train from California arrived in New York.
1869	Susan B. Anthony and Elizabeth Cady Stanton founded the National Woman Suffrage Association. The Territory of Wyoming became the first state to give women the vote.
1870s	The whites who regained control in the south restored segregation in the railroads, schools, and all public facilities.
1870	Old Faithful was discovered by wilderness men. It is the largest geyser on the planet.
1872	Frederick Douglass was nominated by the National Woman Suffrage Association. He was the first black vice-presidential candidate.
1876	George Custer, an American cavalry officer, led the 7th US Cavalry Regiment in an effort to herd Sioux Indians into government reservations in Montana. He foolishly misled his troops, dividing into three columns. His column was entirely wiped out. (*Chief Red Horse Tells About Custer*, Jessie B. McGaw. Lodestar Books, 1981.)
1881	Tuskegee Institute, one of the first colleges to educate freed slaves, was founded by Booker T. Washington. It supported the work of George Washington Carver.
1882	The Chinese Exclusion Act suspended immigration of Chinese for 10 years, and in 1902 the suspension was made indefinite. The act came about as a result of anti-Chinese actions in the west. (It was repealed during World War II.)
1883	The Pendleton (Civil Service) Act set up the Civil Service Commission, the first federal regulatory agency in U.S. history.
1884	In Chicago, the world's first skyscraper was started.
1885	The development of the gasoline automobile was underway.
1886	The American Federation of Labor (AFL, now the AFL-CIO) was founded and led by Samuel Gompers.
1889	Congress established the Territory of Oklahoma. In 1893, in a "land rush" at the Cherokee Outlet (Indian land), more than 50,000 persons claimed land in one day. (*My Prairie Year: Based on the Diary of Elenore Paisted,* by Brett Harvey. Holiday House, 1986.)
1890	The Battle of Wounded Knee in South Dakota was one of the last major conflicts between Plains Indians, in this case the Sioux, and U.S. army forces. This last hostile Sioux band remaining after Sitting Bull was killed, rose up, but were destroyed by army forces.

From *The Teacher's Book of Lists, Second Edition,* published by GoodYearBooks. Copyright © 1994 Sheila Madsen and Bette Gould.

1890–1917	This was a period of calls for change in the country's economic, political, and social systems. Reformers wanted to make life better for the poor and worked to make government more responsive to the people. This era became known as the Progressive Era.
1890	The Sherman Anti-Trust Act outlawed trusts and other monopolies that hindered free trade. Theodore Roosevelt, inaugurated in 1901, was the first president to really enforce this act and earned the nickname of "trust buster."
1891	In this reform-minded era, farmers and some laborers formed the People's, or Populist, Party. They wanted government to help farmers and laborers who were suffering from poverty, violent strikes, and corruption in government.
1894	The Pullman Strike by the American Railway Union, in protest of wage cuts and victimization of union leaders, was finally broken by federal troops, setting back the U.S. labor movement.
1898	Congress declared Cuba independent of Spain and gave the president power to militarily enforce their resolution, which led to war.
1898	The U.S. defeated Spain in the Spanish-American War. Cuba was freed and the U.S. "purchased" the Philippines from Spain for $20 million. Puerto Rico and Guam were ceded after the war.
1898	At the islanders' request, Hawaii was annexed as a territory.
1900	Between 1850 and 1900, the number of millionaires in the U.S. grew from about 20 to 3,000. A small group who amassed more than $100 million each included Andrew Carnegie, Marshall Field, J. P. Morgan, John D. Rockefeller, and Cornelius Vanderbilt. Meanwhile the middle class grew, while most laborers worked long hours for little pay (60-hour weeks at about 20 cents per hour), had no fringe benefits, and suffered through recessions involving high rates of unemployment, with no unemployment benefits.
early 1900s	Ransom Eli Olds and Henry Ford began making cars by mass production, which led to dropping prices and soaring sales. In 1900 about 8,000 cars were owned in the U.S.; by 1916 the number was 3,500,000.
1900	By this time, most Indians had been forced onto reservations.
1900	Baseball became the "national pastime" and motion pictures began attracting some interest.
1903	The Wright Brothers made the first successful airplane flight at Kitty Hawk, North Carolina.
1903	President Teddy Roosevelt used threat of force to obtain the right to dig the Panama Canal.
1913	The 16th Amendment passed, giving the government the power to levy an income tax. The 17th Amendment provided that U.S. Senators were to be elected by the people rather than by state legislatures.

From *The Teacher's Book of Lists, Second Edition,* published by GoodYearBooks. Copyright © 1994 Sheila Madsen and Bette Gould.

1914–1918	**World War I**
1914	World War I began in Europe; the U.S. entered the war in 1917.
1916	From 1870 to 1916 more than 25 million immigrants came to the U.S. This influx, plus natural growth, caused the population to rise from about 40 million to about 100 million.
1917–1918	The United States fought in World War I. About two million "doughboys," as American troops were called, fought in the war, and were important in bringing about the Allied victory against Germany and the Central Powers.
1920	President Woodrow Wilson suffered great disappointment when the Senate rejected U.S. participation in the League of Nations, an organization of nations that would work to maintain world peace.
1920	The 18th Amendment, prohibiting the sale of alcoholic beverages, and the 19th Amendment, giving women complete suffrage, became effective. Many law-abiding citizens ignored the law and bought liquor provided by underworld gangs. Bootlegging, the supplying of illegal liquor, helped many gangs prosper, and competition led to gang wars. The 18th amendment was repealed in 1933.
1920	For the first time, according to the Census, most Americans lived in urban areas. Many people became caught up in the Flaming Youth lifestyle which included women wearing radically new clothing styles (earning them the nickname Flappers) and men and women visiting speakeasies, night clubs which provided illegal liquor.
1920s	The beginning of the Golden Age of radio broadcasting brought news of the world and entertainment into millions of urban and rural homes.
1925	The Scopes Trial (popularly known as the monkey trial) upheld the right of a state to ban the teaching of evolution in public schools.
1925	During the 1920s, the Ku Klux Klan, which had died out in the 1870s, regained a large following. It blamed problems on "outsiders," including Jews, African-Americans, Roman Catholics, foreigners, and political radicals. At its height, the Klan claimed it had five million members.
1927	Charles A. Lindbergh made the first solo flight across the Atlantic Ocean making him a national hero. In this era of heroes, others were Jack Dempsey, Bill Tilden, Bobby Jones, and, biggest of all, Babe Ruth.
1927	The first motion picture "talkie," *The Jazz Singer,* appeared in theaters.
1929	Wild speculation and the practice of buying on the margin, in a strong if lopsided economy, led to the stock market crash which brought financial ruin to thousands of investors.

1930   In just 10 years, from 1920 to 1930, the number of cars in the U.S. almost tripled, growing from about 8 million to 23 million.

1930s   The overriding feature of this era was The Great Depression which followed the stock market crash of 1929. Much of the world was also affected by a depression, in some cases paving the way for dictators who promised reform to come into power.

1933   In 1933, the height of the depression, about 13 million Americans were without a job, and many others only worked part-time. Farm profits were so poor that 750,000 farmers lost their land. A terrible drought led to the Dust Bowl, which wiped out many other farmers. Thousands of people lost their life savings as a result of many bank failures.

1933   President Franklin D. Roosevelt began the New Deal in an effort to end the depression. The New Deal included public works projects to provide jobs, relief for farmers, and the regulation of banks. FDR's government started many agencies and developed the Social Security system. The New Deal was the beginning of a strong government role in the nation's economy.

1939–1945   **World War II**

Dec. 7, 1941   The surprise bombing of the U.S. military base at Pearl Harbor, Hawaii, by the Japanese, led to the U.S. declaring war on Japan on Dec. 8, and on Germany and Italy three days later. (War had begun in Europe on Sept. 1, 1939.)

June, 1942   The first major U.S. victories occurred in the Battle of the Coral Sea and the Battle of Midway.

June 6, 1944   D-Day, the invasion of Normandy, signaled the last phase of the war in Europe.

May, 1945   The Americans and other Allies forced the German Axis powers to surrender. Japan continued to fight on.

Aug. 6, 1945   President Harry S. Truman, who had become president upon Roosevelt's death about a month earlier, made the difficult decision to use the atomic bomb, a bomb many times more powerful than any ever known. On this date the first atomic bomb used in warfare was dropped on Hiroshima, Japan. A second one was dropped on Nagasaki on Aug. 9. Japan formally surrendered September 2.

1945   The United States became a charter member of the United Nations (UN). The UN was an organization of nations in which many Cold War disputes were to be settled. "Cold War" referred to the tensions between the U.S. and other non-Communist nations and Russia and its Communist allies. Much of the tension revolved around the U.S. and Russia having atomic weapons, giving each the power to destroy the other.

From *The Teacher's Book of Lists, Second Edition,* published by GoodYearBooks. Copyright © 1994 Sheila Madsen and Bette Gould.

1947	Truman announced the Truman Doctrine, which pledged American aid to any nations threatened by Communism.
1947	Jackie Robinson joined the Brooklyn Dodgers. He was the first African-American in major league sports.
1950s	The greatest period of economic growth in U.S. history followed World War II, mainly due to the military spending during the war, and to the upsurge in needs as returning soldiers and war workers sought housing, education, and goods of all kinds.
	A soaring birth rate, often called "The Baby Boom," which boosted the number of future consumers was a phenomenon felt for decades to come as the boomers aged.
	Television, an experimental device before the war, became a fixture in most American homes during the decade. TV watching became a main leisure activity.
	Popular enthusiasm during the decade was intent on a large number of fads—Hula-Hoops, Davy Crockett coonskin caps, 3-D movies, and competitions to stuff the largest number of college students into phone booths and Volkswagens.
1950–1953	The Korean War began on June 25, 1950, when troops from Communist North Korea, equipped by Russia, invaded South Korea. The UN sent a fighting force, as did the U.S. The war ended in a truce on July 27, 1953. In the same year, Dwight David Eisenhower became president.
1950–1954	Senator Joseph McCarthy made charges of Communist influence in the State Department and many other places in government and private life. He was eventually discredited.
1955	The Supreme Court, in the case Brown v. Board of Education of Topeka (1954), ruled that compulsory segregation in public schools was illegal.
1955	Martin Luther King, Jr. began organizing non-violent demonstrations protesting discrimination against blacks. Public protest was on the way to becoming a major tool of seeking change.
1955–1956	A major boycott of public buses began in Montgomery, Alabama, to protest the "blacks sit at the back of the bus only" policy.
1955	Los Angeles, California, suffered through its first official smog alert.
1955	The first U.S. military "advisors" were sent to Vietnam.
1956	The new rock music that had been sweeping the high schools and drive-ins for years became a national phenomenon when the 21-year-old Elvis Presley appeared on "The Ed Sullivan Show." Within four years Elvis sold $120 million worth of albums and memorabilia.
1957	Russia launched Sputnik I—the first space satellite—which caused the U.S. to put more money and activity into space research.
1959	The Soviet leader, Nikita Khrushchev, visited the U.S.

From *The Teacher's Book of Lists, Second Edition,* published by GoodYearBooks. Copyright © 1994 Sheila Madsen and Bette Gould.

1960   For the first time in the U.S., an oral contraceptive pill ("The Pill") was available for general distribution, on a doctor's prescription.

1960   A sit-in, a nonviolent form of protest against segregation of blacks and whites, began at the lunch counters of Greensboro, North Carolina.

1961   Astronaut Alan B. Shepard became the first American in space, providing a lift to the U.S. space program.

1961   The Freedom Rides began in the South in an effort to win full civil rights and fair voting practices for blacks.

1961   Kennedy commited the first American troops to aid Vietnam.

1962   Russia pulled missiles out of Cuba, ending the threat of war with the U.S. This threat had terrified Americans for six days in October.

1963   More than 200,000 civil rights demonstrators marched on Washington, D.C. in the freedom march called the March on Washington. The famous "I have a dream" speech by Martin Luther King, Jr. awed the marchers and TV viewers.

1963   Bob Dylan became a major entity in the folk-music movement, based on some 200 songs he had written which pointed out many of the deceits and inequities of the 1960s.

Nov. 22, 1963   President John F. Kennedy was killed by assassination, and Vice President Lyndon B. Johnson became president. Johnson's skill in working with Congress led to the passage of many major civil rights laws in 1964.

1964   The Beatles invaded the U.S., five weeks after appearing on "The Ed Sullivan Show," bringing rock 'n' roll to Carnegie Hall for the first time in its history.

1965   One of the first of several urban riots by blacks broke out in the Watts section of Los Angeles. Other riots occurred in Harlem, Detroit, Cleveland, Chicago, and Newark.

1965   U.S. aircraft began heavy bombardment of North Vietnam. The Marines were sent into Vietnam.

1965   Medicare was established.

1966-1967   The era of the "hippies" and "do your own thing," with its mixture of love, peace, drugs, and acid rock, was underway.

1968   First Martin Luther King, Jr. and then Robert Kennedy, were assassinated.

1968   Antiwar demonstrations brought violence to the Democratic Convention in Chicago.

July 20, 1969   At 10:56 P.M. EDT, Astronaut Neil A. Armstrong became the first person to set foot on the moon. His now famous statement was, "That's one small step for a man, one giant leap for mankind."

1969   A nationwide antiwar demonstration was held. The gulf between those who supported the Vietnam War and those who did not widened.

From *The Teacher's Book of Lists, Second Edition*, published by GoodYearBooks. Copyright © 1994 Sheila Madsen and Bette Gould.

1971	The 26th Amendment was ratified, giving the vote to 18-year-olds.
1972	President Richard M. Nixon worked to ease tensions between Russia and China, the two leading Communist powers, and the U.S. by visiting both countries and reaching agreements that led to détente.
1972	The Environmental Protection Agency banned almost all uses of DDT in the U.S.
1972	Exactly seven days after Nixon's election, the Dow Jones average closed above 1,000 for the first time in its 76-year history.
1973	Nixon recalled U.S. combat troops from Vietnam. Two years later South Vietnam and neighboring Cambodia and Laos fell to the Communists.
1973–1974	An Arab oil embargo led to high gasoline prices, lowered supply, and long lines at the gas pumps, among other things.
1974	For covering up the Watergate burglary and other illegal activities, Nixon became the first American president to resign from office, making Gerald Ford the 38th president.
1976	The U.S. celebrated its bicentennial of the year the Declaration of Independence was signed.
1977	The Department of Energy was created.
1980	President Jimmy Carter declared a U.S. boycott of the Moscow Olympics, in protest of the Soviet invasion of Afghanistan.
1980	Ronald Reagan was elected. He became the first two-term president in a generation.
1980	Mount St. Helens, a volcanic peak in Washington state, blew off 1,377 feet of its summit, releasing 500 times the power of the Hiroshima A-bomb.
1980	American commandos had to abort their mission to rescue 53 hostages in Tehran, Iran, due to equipment problems.
1981	Ronald Reagan was sworn in as the 40th president on the same day the Ayatollah released the American hostages in Tehran.
1981	Columbia, the first space shuttle, lifted off on its first mission. See **U.S. Space Missions**, p. 235.
1981	269 Americans died of a newly named disease, Acquired Immune Deficiency Syndrome, or AIDS.
1982	The Vietnam Veterans Memorial, a black granite wall inscribed with the names of 57,939 Americans killed or missing in action, was dedicated in Washington, D.C., seven years after the last American was helicoptered out of Saigon.
1982	The ERA (Equal Rights Amendment), a proposed amendment to guarantee women equal rights, was defeated by falling three states short of ratification.
1982	*E. T. The Extra-Terrestrial* became the top-grossing film in history.
1983	President Ronald Reagan showed "U.S. might" by invading and ousting the leftist rulers of the tiny Caribbean island of Grenada.

1983   Lee Iacocca, the new head man at Chrysler, led the company to its first profits in four years.

1984   The Olympics, held in Los Angeles, brought a record number of medals to U.S. athletes, as the Communist bloc countries boycotted the event.

1984   Geraldine Ferraro became the first woman vice presidential candidate of a major party—but the Democrats, with Walter Mondale running for president, lost the election to Ronald Reagan.

1986   Seven astronauts died when the Challenger spacecraft exploded shortly after takeoff, due to the rupture of a $900 gasket.

1986   The Iran-Contra affair first became public knowledge. In hopes of freeing Americans held in Lebanon, the U.S. sold arms to the Ayatollah of Iran and the profits went to buy guns for Nicaraguan contras.

1987   The tax code was supposedly simplified, but most people still struggled with the complex new IRS forms.

1987   Twenty states raised the speed limit to 65 mph, the same speed it had been some years before.

1987   Black Monday in October found the Dow Jones dropping 508 points in that single day. Paper losses totaled $500 million.

1988   Yellowstone National Park was charred by fire; drought hit 43 states; and garbage, including medical waste products, washed up onto eastern beaches.

1988   Robert Morris, a computer hacker, created and released a software virus into computer networks that brought down 6,000 computer systems. See **Computer Terminology**, p. 205–207.

1989   George Bush became America's 41st president; he declared drugs to be Public Enemy No. 1 in the U.S.

1989   The tiny Voyager 2 spacecraft ended its 12-year, four-planet exploratory mission with a Neptune flyby. It will likely be the first man-made object to ever escape the tug of the sun's gravity.

1990   Some people worried about the advent of "thought police"—those who insist there is only one politically correct (PC) way to speak about race, sex, and ideas.

1991   In January, President George Bush sent troops to the Middle East. Desert Storm, as the conflict came to be known, ended with a rout of Iraq's army in Kuwait, the country they had invaded.

1991   The U.S. offered a haven for Haitian refugees who were targets of repression (but did not accept Haitians who fled only for reasons of poverty).

1991   GM (General Motors) announced the closure of 25 plants and a layoff of 74,000 workers due to foreign competition and the recession.

1991   Freedom-loving Americans watched as 1991 ended a decade of the greatest expansion of freedom in human history with changes in Germany, Poland, South Africa, Argentina, the Philippines, and the former USSR.

Activities: U.S. History

1. Stock a Time Capsule for others to use to learn about a historical era. First, select an era, such as the Revolutionary War, or the Roaring '20s. Research the era, using both history books and books of photographs, paintings, and crafts. Now draw, write, and build items such as journals, newspaper front pages, letters, toys, tools, or kitchen implements of the time to go into the capsule. Place the items in a box or plastic carton and bury or hide it for others to find. Make a map to direct the search.

2. Write 20–30 place names from the history list on notecards. Look up each place in a Gazeteer to learn where the names came from (their derivation). Now write each derivation on the back of the matching notecard. Invent a game to play with the cards; you may want to include cards of other students as well. The cards may also be used on bulletin boards, maps, or could be stored in a class "Place-Name File" box, to be added to periodically and used as a reference tool.

3. With a friend, invent a correspondence between two people from another time in U.S. history. One of you might be a Minuteman during the pre-Revolutionary War period, and the other might be a colonist against armed rebellion. Or one of you could be a woman who wants to dress as a man so that she might fight in the Civil War, and the other letter writer might be another woman advising how to make this work. Write letters to each other regarding your experiences. (Reading letters from the period, often found in history books, is a good way to get a feel for the writing style of the time.)

4. Visit or write to your post office to learn about upcoming First Day Issues (often called First Day Covers). These are envelopes carrying a brand new postage stamp and a design or illustration. They are cancelled on the first day of issue. By sending a self-addressed envelope and the money in the amount of the stamp's value, you will receive a First Day Cover soon after the stamp is issued.

5. Select a time period from the History list, such as Colonial times from 1607 to 1760. Design a hidden word puzzle or a crossword puzzle that includes people, places, and events from the period. Make an Answer Key. Ask your teacher to make copies of your puzzle to give to other students to do.

U.S. Presidents—Hail to the Chief

In addition to making available biographies and autobiographies of presidents, it is worthwhile to search for books that have a high interest value to children. Some that we especially like are: The Buck Stops Here: The Presidents of the United States, by Alice Provensen. HarperCollins, 1980. Full-page, poster-style illustrations present the first 41 American presidents, each accompanied by a rhymed couplet and a set of facts. This book is good for primary-age children. The Look It Up President's Book, by Wyatt Blassingame. Random House, rev. ed. 1990, contains a section on each president, and gives interesting information on each man before he was president, as well as on his term of office and his later years.

President	Date of Birth	Date of Death	Date of Inauguration	Married To
George Washington	Feb. 22, 1732	Dec. 14, 1799	April 30, 1789	Martha Dandridge Washington
John Adams	Oct. 30, 1735	July 4, 1826	Mar. 4, 1797*	Abigail Smith Adams
Thomas Jefferson	Apr. 13, 1743	July 4, 1826	1801	Martha Wayles Jefferson
James Madison	Mar. 16, 1751	June 28, 1836	1809	Dolley Payne Madison
James Monroe	Apr. 28, 1758	July 4, 1831	1817	Eliza Kortright Monroe
John Quincy Adams	July 11, 1767	Feb. 23, 1848	1825	Louisa Johnson Adams
Andrew Jackson	Mar. 15, 1767	June 8, 1845	1829	Rachel Donelson Jackson
Martin Van Buren	Dec. 5, 1782	July 24, 1862	1837	Hannah Hoes Van Buren
William Henry Harrison	Feb. 9, 1773	Apr. 4, 1841	1841	Anna Symmes Harrison
John Tyler	Mar. 29, 1790	Jan. 18, 1862	1841 (April 6, after Harrison's death)	Julia Gardiner Tyler
James Knox Polk	Nov. 2, 1795	June 15, 1849	1845	Sarah Childress Polk
Zachary Taylor	Nov. 24, 1784	July 9, 1850	1849 (March 5)	Margaret Smith Taylor
Millard Fillmore	Jan. 7, 1800	Mar. 8, 1874	1850 (July 10, after Taylor's death)	Abigail Powers Fillmore
Franklin Pierce	Nov. 23, 1804	Oct. 8, 1869	1853	Jane Appleton Pierce
James Buchanan	Apr. 23, 1791	June 1, 1868	1857	(unmarried)
Abraham Lincoln	Feb. 12, 1809	Apr. 15, 1865	1861	Mary Todd Lincoln

*The following inaugurations were also on Mar. 4—through 1933, unless otherwise noted.

President	Date of Birth	Date of Death	Date of Inauguration	Married To
Andrew Johnson	Dec. 29, 1808	July 31, 1875	1865 (April 15, after Lincoln's death)	Eliza McCardle Johnson
Ulysses S. Grant	Apr. 27, 1822	July 23, 1885	1869	Julia Dent Grant
Rutherford B. Hayes	Oct. 4, 1822	Jan. 17, 1893	1877	Lucy Webb Hayes
James A. Garfield	Nov. 19, 1831	Sept. 19, 1881	1881	Lucretia Rudolph Garfield
Chester A. Arthur	Oct. 5, 1829	Nov. 18, 1886	1881 (Sept. 20, after Garfield's death)	Ellen Herndon Arthur
Grover Cleveland	Mar. 18, 1837	June 24, 1908	1885	Frances Folsom Cleveland
Benjamin Harrison	Aug. 20, 1833	Mar. 13, 1901	1889	Caroline Scott Harrison
Grover Cleveland	Mar. 18, 1837	June 24, 1908	1893	Frances Folson Cleveland
William McKinley	Jan. 29, 1843	Sept. 14, 1901	1897	Ida Saxton McKinley
Theodore Roosevelt	Oct. 27, 1858	Jan. 6, 1919	1901 (Sept. 14, after McKinley's death)	Edith Carow Roosevelt
William H. Taft	Sept. 15, 1857	Mar. 8, 1930	1909	Helen Herron Taft
Woodrow Wilson	Dec. 28, 1856	Feb. 3, 1924	1913	Edith Bolling Wilson
Warren G. Harding	Nov. 2, 1865	Aug. 2, 1923	1921	Florence Kling Harding
Calvin Coolidge	July 4, 1872	Jan. 5, 1933	1923 (Aug. 3, after Harding's death)	Grace Goodhue Coolidge
Herbert Hoover	Aug. 10, 1874	Oct. 20, 1964	1929	Lou Henry Hoover
Franklin D. Roosevelt	Jan. 30, 1882	Apr. 12, 1945	1933	Anna Eleanor Roosevelt
Harry S. Truman	May 8, 1884	Dec. 26, 1972	1945 (April 12, after Roosevelt's death)	Bess Wallace Truman
Dwight D. Eisenhower	Oct. 14, 1890	Mar. 28, 1969	Jan. 20, 1953	Mamie Doud Eisenhower
John F. Kennedy	May 29, 1917	Nov. 22, 1963	Jan. 20, 1961	Jacqueline Bouvier Kennedy
Lyndon B. Johnson	Aug. 27, 1908	Jan. 22, 1973	Nov. 22, 1963 (after Kennedy's death)	Claudia (Ladybird) Taylor Johnson
Richard M. Nixon	Jan. 9, 1913		Jan. 20, 1969	Thelma (Pat) Ryan Nixon
Gerald R. Ford	July 14, 1913		Aug. 9, 1974 (after Nixon's resignation)	Elizabeth (Betty) Bloomer Ford
Jimmy Carter	Oct. 1, 1924		Jan. 20, 1977	Rosalyn Smith Carter
Ronald Reagan	Feb. 6, 1911		Jan. 20, 1981	Nancy Davis Reagan
George Bush	June 12, 1924		Jan. 20, 1989	Barbara Pierce Bush
Bill Clinton	Aug. 19, 1946		Jan. 20, 1993	Hillary Rodham Clinton

From *The Teacher's Book of Lists, Second Edition,* published by GoodYearBooks.
Copyright © 1994 Sheila Madsen and Bette Gould.

# Activities: U.S. Presidents

1. Make a list of the president's names that is in alphabetical order.

2. Make a list of "least and most" facts, such as the president who lived the longest life, the shortest life; had the shortest term in office, the longest term; was the youngest to become president, the oldest to become president, etc.

3. Add other columns to the table, such as vice presidents, previous professions or occupations, party affiliations, and other members of the family in government.

4. Many of the presidents' wives adopted their own causes and favorite programs. For Barbara Bush, it was to promote reading and books. For Ladybird Johnson, it was to beautify America. Learn more about a first lady's project. Design and display banners or posters to illustrate the cause or program.

5. There are many places you might visit to learn about one of the presidents and first ladies. Write to one of the places and request brochures or other information to find out what you can learn.

6. Make up a "denominations game" or "denominations math" using the presidents and other officials found on our money, both paper and coin.

7. Visit a video store to locate a film made about all or part of a president's life. Watch one that interests you. Do research to find out how accurate the film seems to be. Can you find any obvious fabrications? Your class might want to make a Video Guide on the Presidents to assist others in selecting films for home or school viewing.

8. Select one president. Do research to find out about: (1) world events that occurred during his term of office; (2) important legislation passed during his term of office; and, (3) his early life. Write a brief biography of the president to share with others.

Worksheet

1600 Pennsylvania Avenue worksheet, p. 305.

From *The Teacher's Book of Lists, Second Edition,* published by GoodYearBooks. Copyright © 1994 Sheila Madsen and Bette Gould.

1600 Pennsylvania Avenue

Choose 10 United States presidents. List them alphabetically. Use the U.S. Presidents list to complete the other columns.

Names of Presidents	Age at inauguration	Age at death	Number of years in office

Using the information from your table, compute the following averages for these 10 presidents:

- The average age at inauguration is _____ .
- The average age at death is _____ .
- The average length of term in office is _____ .

U.S. States—Fifty Nifty

State/Capital	Abbrev.	State Nickname	Date Entered	Area in Sq. Miles	State Bird	State Flower and Tree
Alabama Montgomery	AL	Heart of Dixie; Cotton State	1819	51,609	Yellowhammer	Camellia Longleaf pine
Alaska Juneau	AK	The Great Land; The Last Frontier	1959	586,412	Willow ptarmigan	Forget-me-not Sitka spruce
Arizona Phoenix	AZ	Grand Canyon State	1912	113,909	Cactus wren	Saguaro cactus blossom Paloverde
Arkansas Little Rock	AR	Land of Opportunity	1836	63,104	Mockingbird	Apple blossom Shortleaf pine
California Sacramento	CA	Golden State	1850	158,693	California valley quail	Golden poppy California redwood
Colorado Denver	CO	Centennial State	1876	104,247	Lark bunting	Rocky Mt. columbine Colorado blue spruce
Connecticut Hartford	CT	Constitution State; Nutmeg State	1788	5,009	American robin	Mountain laurel White oak
Delaware Dover	DE	First State; Diamond State	1787	2,057	Blue hen chicken	Peach blossom American holly
Florida Tallahassee	FL	Sunshine State	1845	58,560	Mockingbird	Orange blossom Cabbage palmetto
Georgia Atlanta	GA	Empire State of the South; Peach State	1788	58,876	Brown thrasher	Cherokee rose Live oak
Hawaii Honolulu	HI	Aloha State	1959	6,540	Nene (Hawaiian goose)	Red hibiscus Kukui (candlenut tree)
Idaho Boise	ID	Gem State	1890	83,557	Mountain bluebird	Syringa Western white pine
Illinois Springfield	IL	Land of Lincoln; Prairie State	1818	56,400	Eastern cardinal	Meadow violet Bur oak

From *The Teacher's Book of Lists, Second Edition,* published by GoodYearBooks.
Copyright © 1994 Sheila Madsen and Bette Gould.

State/Capital	Abbrev.	State Nickname	Date Entered	Area in Sq. Miles	State Bird	State Flower and Tree
Indiana Indianapolis	IN	Hoosier State	1816	36,291	Cardinal	Peony Tulip tree
Iowa Des Moines	IA	Hawkeye State	1846	56,290	Eastern goldfinch	Wild rose Oak
Kansas Topeka	KS	Sunflower State; Jayhawker State	1861	82,264	Western meadowlark	Sunflower Cottonwood
Kentucky Frankfort	KY	Bluegrass State; Corncracker State	1792	40,395	Cardinal	Goldenrod Kentucky coffee tree
Louisiana Baton Rouge	LA	Pelican State; Creole State	1812	48,523	Eastern brown pelican	Magnolia Bald cypress
Maine Augusta	ME	Pine Tree State	1820	33,215	Chickadee	Eastern white pine cone and tassel Eastern white pine
Maryland Baltimore	MD	Old Line State; Free State	1788	10,577	Baltimore oriole	Black-eyed Susan White oak
Massachusetts Boston	MA	Bay State; Old Colony State	1788	8,257	Chickadee	Mayflower American elm
Michigan Lansing	MI	Wolverine State; Great Lake State	1837	58,216	Robin	Apple blossom Eastern white pine
Minnesota St. Paul	MN	North Star State; Gopher State	1858	84,068	Loon	Showy lady's slipper Red Norway pine
Mississippi Jackson	MS	Magnolia State	1817	47,716	Mockingbird	Magnolia blossom Southern magnolia
Missouri Jefferson City	MO	Show-Me State	1821	69,686	Bluebird	Hawthorn Flowering dogwood
Montana Helena	MT	Treasure State	1889	147,138	Western meadowlark	Bitterroot Ponderosa pine
Nebraska Lincoln	NE	Cornhusker State	1867	77,227	Western meadowlark	Goldenrod Cottonwood

From *The Teacher's Book of Lists, Second Edition,* published by GoodYearBooks.
Copyright © 1994 Sheila Madsen and Bette Gould.

State/Capital	Abbrev.	State Nickname	Date Entered	Area in Sq. Miles	State Bird	State Flower and Tree
Nevada Carson City	NV	Silver State; Sagebrush State	1864	110,540	Mountain bluebird	Sagebrush Single-leaf pinyon
New Hampshire Concord	NH	Granite State	1788	9,304	Purple finch	Purple lilac Paper birch
New Jersey Trenton	NJ	Garden State	1787	7,836	Eastern goldfinch	Purple violet Red oak
New Mexico Santa Fe	NM	Land of Enchantment; Sunshine State	1912	121,666	Roadrunner	Yucca Pinyon
New York Albany	NY	Empire State	1788	49,576	Bluebird (not official)	Rose Sugar maple
North Carolina Raleigh	NC	Tarheel State	1789	52,586	Cardinal	Dogwood Pine
North Dakota Bismarck	ND	Flickertail State; Sioux State	1889	70,665	Western meadowlark	Wild prairie rose American elm
Ohio Columbus	OH	Buckeye State	1803	41,222	Cardinal	Scarlet carnation Ohio buckeye
Oklahoma Oklahoma City	OK	Sooner State	1907	69,919	Scissor-tailed flycatcher	Mistletoe Redbud
Oregon Salem	OR	Beaver State; Sunset State	1859	96,981	Western meadowlark	Oregon grape Douglas fir
Pennsylvania Harrisburg	PA	Keystone State	1787	45,333	Ruffed grouse	Mountain laurel Eastern hemlock
Rhode Island Providence	RI	Little Rhody	1790	1,214	Rhode Island red	Violet Red maple
South Carolina Columbia	SC	Palmetto State	1788	31,055	Carolina wren	Yellow jasmine Palmetto
South Dakota Pierre	SD	Coyote State; Sunshine State	1889	77,047	Ring-necked pheasant	Pasqueflower White spruce

From *The Teacher's Book of Lists, Second Edition*, published by GoodYearBooks.
Copyright © 1994 Sheila Madsen and Bette Gould.

State/Capital	Abbrev.	State Nickname	Date Entered	Area in Sq. Miles	State Bird	State Flower and Tree
Tennessee Nashville	TN	Volunteer State	1796	42,244	Mockingbird	Iris Yellow poplar
Texas Austin	TX	Lone Star State	1845	267,339	Mockingbird	Bluebonnet Pecan
Utah Salt Lake City	UT	Beehive State	1896	84,916	Sea gull	Sego lily Blue spruce
Vermont Montpelier	VT	Green Mountain State	1791	9,609	Hermit thrush	Red clover Sugar maple
Virginia Richmond	VA	Old Dominion	1788	40,817	Cardinal	Flowering dogwood Dogwood (not official)
Washington Olympia	WA	Evergreen State	1889	68,192	Willow goldfinch	Coast rhododendron Western hemlock
West Virginia Charleston	WV	Mountain State	1863	24,181	Cardinal	Great rhododendron Sugar maple
Wisconsin Madison	WI	Badger State	1848	56,154	Robin	Violet Sugar maple
Wyoming Cheyenne	WY	Equality State	1890	97,914	Western meadowlark	Indian paintbrush Cottonwood

From *The Teacher's Book of Lists, Second Edition*, published by GoodYearBooks.
Copyright © 1994 Sheila Madsen and Bette Gould.

Activities: U.S. States—Fifty Nifty

1. Each state has a motto. Select one or more of the following state motto activities to do.

- Choose your favorite state and learn its motto. Use the state motto as the title of a patriotic speech. Write two paragraphs or more to complete the speech and, if possible, give the speech in front of the class.

- Select several state mottoes. Write 2–3 sentences about each motto to show what you think each one means.

- Develop a motto for your school, neighborhood, town, or city. Develop a way to display the motto for others to see.

2. Research the bird and flower of a state. Find out its natural habitat in the state. Draw an outline of the state and show both the bird's and the flower's areas of habitation.

3. Write to a state's tourist office. Request tourist information about the state. You may want to keep a class scrapbook of all the information gathered. You will find addresses of tourism bureaus in many magazines such as *National Geographic, Sunset,* and *Travel.*

4. Choose one state. Design a license plate for that state. Include the state bird, flower or tree, a state nickname, and a symbol or state motto.

5. States have other symbols such as fish, animal, dance, beverage, and song. Create other symbols that reflect the personality, products, or uniqueness of a state.

Activities: U.S. Map and States

*These activities are for use with the **U.S. Map** and the **U.S. States—Fifty Nifty** list. The activities can be listed on a chart, task cards, or distributed as a worksheet.*

1. Write each state's abbreviation in its outline. Then write in the state capital. Place a symbol for the capital as closely as possible to where it is located in the state.

2. Look up the states' populations. Create a different symbol for every 500,000 people. Identify each state with the symbol that most closely represents its population.

3. Research one or more of the following types of places and locate them on the U.S. map:

amusement parks   major cities   historical sites
state parks   recreation areas   major highways
observatories   trails (e.g., Chisholm Trail, Pony Express)

4. Color in the map. Find out the fewest colors it takes to color in all the states so that there is no place where two states of the same color are touching. (Touching at corners only is O.K.) Hint: See if you can do it with only 5 colors, then try it with 4, and so on.

5. Do research and add one or more of these landforms to the map: coastal islands, rivers, lakes, mountain ranges and peaks, caves, volcanoes.

6. Research some authors whose books you have recently read to find their birthplaces. Create a symbol for each author and place it on the map. Add each author's name and symbol to the map legend. Here are some authors to start with:

Laura Ingalls Wilder   Mansfield, Missouri
Jack London   Glen Ellen, California

Do the same with other famous Americans, such as:

Booker T. Washington   Tuskegee, Alabama
Kit Carson   Taos, New Mexico

7. Cut up the map and rearrange the states into categories, such as products, ethnic groups, major industries, and climates.

Worksheet

U.S. Map worksheet, p. 311.

From *The Teacher's Book of Lists, Second Edition,* published by GoodYearBooks.
Copyright © 1994 Sheila Madsen and Bette Gould.

Women

This is a list of representative women who have made contributions in a wide variety of fields. The accomplishments of the women in this list are impressive, and most of the achievements seem even more impressive as you learn about their lives and the times of their contributions. Student research will add many more women to the list. Use this list for discussions, research topics, or refer to **Independent Study** *worksheets, p. 368–371. A good general reference for older students or for the teacher is* Her Way, A Guide to Biographies of Women for Young People, *2nd ed., by Mary-Ellen Siegel, American Library Association, 1976.*

Jane Addams (1860–1935)	American social worker and humanitarian; Nobel Peace Prize winner, 1931
Louisa May Alcott (1832–1888)	American writer; author of *Little Women*
Marian Anderson (1902–1993)	American opera singer; first African-American to sing with the Metropolitan Opera Company
Susan B. Anthony (1820–1906)	Reformer and leader in the American women's suffrage movement
Elizabeth Arden (1884–1966)	Canadian-born businesswoman; founded and headed the Elizabeth Arden cosmetics empire
Pearl Bailey (1918–1990)	American jazz singer and actress, both in film and TV
Sirimavo Bandaranaike (1916–)	World's first female prime minister (of Sri Lanka)
Romana Acosta Bañuelos (1925–)	Treasurer of the U.S. (1971–1974); businesswoman; founded Pan American National Bank of East Los Angeles
Clara Barton (1821–1912)	Founded the American Red Cross; began relief work during Civil War
Simone de Beauvoir (1908–1986)	French author; leading proponent of women in politics and intellectual life
Sarah Bernhardt (1844–1923)	French actress; greatest actress of her day
Mary McLeod Bethune (1875–1955)	American educator who worked to improve educational opportunities for blacks
Nellie Bly (Elizabeth Cochrane Seaman) (1867–1922)	American journalist; famous for her attempt to beat the record of Phineas Fogg (*Around the World in Eighty Days*)
Evangeline Booth (1865–1950)	First woman to become international leader and general of the Salvation Army
Margaret Bourke-White (1906–1971)	U.S. photographer and war correspondent; covered World War II and the Korean War for Time-Life
Belle Boyd (1843–1900)	Confederate spy; caught in 1862, she was released for lack of evidence

Emily Brontë (1818–1848)	English novelist; published only one novel, *Wuthering Heights,* a masterpiece; one of three sisters who wrote novels
Elizabeth Barrett Browning (1806–1861)	Poet of Victorian England; in her day she was second in reputation only to Tennyson
Pearl S. Buck (1892–1973)	American author; most novels set in China; won the Pulitzer Prize for *The Good Earth*
St. Frances Xavier Cabrini (1850–1917)	First U.S. citizen (naturalized) to become a saint
Calamity Jane (Martha Jane Canary) (c.1852–1917)	American frontierswoman
Maria Callas (1923–1977)	Greek-American operatic soprano
Rachel Carson (1907–1964)	American marine biologist and science writer; her book *Silent Spring* first alerted the U.S. public to the dangers of environmental pollution
Mary Cassatt (1845–1926)	American impressionist painter; many of her paintings are mother-and-child studies
Carrie Chapman Catt (1859–1947)	American leader in the campaign for women's suffrage; founded what has become the League of Women Voters
Shirley Chisholm (1924–)	First black woman in U.S. Congress; campaigned for 1972 presidential nomination
Agatha Christie (1891–1976)	British writer of popular detective novels and plays
Cleopatra VII (69–30 B.C.)	Egyptian queen who greatly influenced Roman politics
Jacqueline Cochran (1912?–1980)	American businesswoman and pioneer airplane pilot; organized and headed the Women's Airforce Service Pilots (WASP) in World War II
Charlotte Corday (1768–1793)	French patriot during the French Revolution
Marie Curie (1867–1934)	Polish-born French physicist; she and her husband were early investigators of radioactivity and discovered radium
Agnes De Mille (1905–)	Pioneered combination of ballet and American folk music
Babe Didrikson (1914–1956)	Greatest U.S. woman athlete; successful in all sports including golf, boxing, swimming, shooting, fencing, tennis, track, and billiards
Dorothea Dix (1802–1887)	Led movement to build state hospitals for the mentally ill in the U.S.
Alene B. Duerk (1920–)	First woman in U.S. Navy to be promoted to admiral (in 1972)
Isadora Duncan (1878–1927)	Pioneer of modern dance in America and Europe
Amelia Earhart (1898–1937)	American aviator, writer, and lecturer; one of the first women pilots in the U.S.

From *The Teacher's Book of Lists, Second Edition,* published by GoodYearBooks. Copyright © 1994 Sheila Madsen and Bette Gould.

Mary Baker Eddy (1821–1910)	Founder of Christian Science and the *Christian Science Monitor* newspaper
George Eliot (Mary Ann Evans) (1819–1880)	English novelist who greatly influenced later writers; notable works include *Adam Bede* and *Silas Marner*
Elizabeth II (1926–)	Sixth woman to occupy the British throne; richest woman in the world
Edna Ferber (1887–1968)	U.S. author famous for her epic novels
Geraldine Ferrarro (1935–)	First woman to run for vice-president on a major party ticket
Margot Fonteyn (1919–1991)	Prima ballerina with the English Royal Ballet; ballet partner of Nureyev
Betty Friedan (1921–)	American author and one of the founders of the women's liberation movement
Indira Gandhi (1917–1984)	First woman prime minister of India
Judy Garland (1922–1969)	American singer and motion-picture actress
Whoopi Goldberg (1949–)	African-American comedian and film star; active in humanitarian causes
Emma Goldman (1869–1940)	Russian émigré to the U.S. who lectured in favor of anarchism and women's rights
Jane Goodall-Van Lawick (1934–)	English zoologist; famous for behavior studies of chimpanzees in the wild
Katherine Graham (1917–)	Influential publisher of the *Washington Post* from 1968 to 1978 and head of its parent company, which also controlled *Newsweek* magazine and several television stations
Martha Graham (1895–1991)	American pioneer of modern dance; dancer and choreographer
Angelina (1805–1879) and Sara (1792–1873) Grimké	Sisters who became abolitionists and pioneers in the U.S. women's rights movement
Alice Hamilton (1869–1970)	American physician; first woman on faculty of Harvard Medical School; did pioneer work in industrial medicine
Patricia Roberts Harris (1924–1985)	First African-American woman to serve as U.S. ambassador (to Luxembourg)
Helen Hayes (1900–1993)	American stage and screen actress
Lillian Hellman (1905–1984)	U.S. playwright and screenwriter
Carla Anderson Hills (1934–)	Secretary of Housing and Urban Development under President Ford
Billie Holiday (Eleanora Fagan) (1915–1959)	American jazz singer; the quintessential blues singer
Grace Hopper (1906–)	American mathematician, naval officer, and pioneer in computer programming; created the computer language COBOL

Julia Ward Howe (1819–1910)	American writer, lecturer, and social reformer; wrote *The Battle Hymn of the Republic*
Helen Hunt Jackson (1831–1885)	U.S. author who publicized the mistreatment of Indians and worked for their rights
Hypatia (c.370–415)	Greek mathematician, astronomer, and philosopher; professor at Alexandria teaching the views of Plato and Aristotle
Joan of Arc (c.1412–1431)	French heroine; commanded a small force to save the city of Orléans from the English
Irène Joliot-Curie (1897–1956)	Nobel Prize winner for chemistry; daughter of Marie Curie
Frida Kahlo (1910–1954)	Mexican painter; noted for highly stylized, brilliantly colored paintings; wife of Diego Rivera
Helen Keller (1880–1968)	Blind, deaf, and mute from the age of two, learned to read, write, and speak; graduated from Radcliffe College and helped thousands of handicapped people lead fuller lives
Elizabeth Kenny (Sister Kenny) (1886–1952)	Australian nurse who developed a special method of treating polio
Billie Jean King (1943–)	American tennis champion
Selma Lagerlöf (1858–1940)	Swedish novelist; first woman to receive the Nobel Prize for Literature
Dorothea Lange (1895–1965)	U.S. documentary photographer; powerful, stark pictures of the Depression, migrant workers, and rural poor greatly influenced photojournalism techniques and brought attention to the needs of her subjects
Queen Liliuokalani (Lydia) (1838–1917)	Last queen of the Hawaiian Islands
Ada Lovelace (1815–1852)	English mathematician, daughter of the poet Byron; often called the first computer programmer because of her work with Charles Babbage on the Analytical Engine
Juliette Gordon Low (1860–1927)	Founder of the Girl Scouts in America
Amy Lowell (1874–1925)	American poet and critic
Clare Booth Luce (1903–1987)	First woman to represent the U.S. in a major diplomatic post (ambassador to Italy)
Carson McCullers (1917–1967)	American southern novelist
Margaret Mead (1901–1978)	American cultural anthropologist
Golda Meir (1898-1978)	Prime minister of Israel from 1969–1974
Edna St. Vincent Millay (1892–1950)	American poet
Marilyn Monroe (1926–1962)	American film star

Maria Montessori (1870–1952)	Italian educator who revolutionized the teaching of young children; first woman to qualify as a physician in Italy
Marianne Moore (1887–1992)	American poet; winner of 1952 Pulitzer Prize
Grandma Moses (Anna Mary Robertson Moses) (1860–1961)	American primitive painter; began painting at age 76
Mother Teresa (Agnes Gonxha Bojaxhiu) (1910–)	Albanian-born nun who served the poor, sick, and dying in India; received the 1979 Nobel Peace Prize
Lucretia Mott (1793–1880)	American reformer; worked for women's rights and the abolition of slavery
Carry Amelia Moore Nation (1846–1911)	Crusaded against the use of alcoholic beverages
Martina Navratilova (1956–)	Czechoslovakian-born U.S. tennis player; eight-time Wimbledon champion
Florence Nightingale (1820–1910)	English founder of the modern nursing profession
Annie Oakley (1860–1926)	American markswoman
Sandra Day O'Connor (1930–)	First woman to serve on the U.S. Supreme Court
Georgia O'Keeffe (1887–1986)	American artist noted for abstract designs; much of her work reflects the nature of the desert
Vijaya Lakshmi Pandit (1900–)	Indian famous for work in government and the women's movement; first woman elected president of the United Nations (1950–1954)
Dorothy Parker (1893–1967)	American poet, critic, and wit
Rosa Parks (1913–)	U.S. civil rights activist; arrested for refusing to give up her bus seat to a white man, which set off a 382-day bus boycott led by Martin Luther King, Jr.
Frances Perkins (1882–1965)	First U.S. woman cabinet member, Secretary of Labor
Mary Pickford (1893–1979)	American movie actress and producer
Katherine Anne Porter (1890–1980)	American writer, famous for her short stories
Leontyne Price (1927–)	American operatic soprano
Jeannette Rankin (1880–1973)	First woman elected to the U.S. Congress (1917)
Sally K. Ride (1952–)	First American woman to travel in space
Eleanor Roosevelt (1884–1962)	Wife of Franklin Delano Roosevelt; became prominent in her own right for her humanitarian work
Nellie Tayloe Ross (1876–1977)	First woman governor (of Wyoming) in the U.S.; also was a director of the U.S. Mint
Sacajawea (c.1784–1884?)	Shoshone Indian guide and interpreter with Lewis and Clark expedition
George Sand (Amantine Dupin) (1804–1876)	French novelist; early feminist

Elizabeth Ann Seton (1774–1896)	First native-born American in the U.S. to be recognized as a saint; established first parochial school system in the U.S.
Mary Shelley (1797–1851)	English writer; best-known work is the horror story *Frankenstein*
Beverly Sills (1929–)	American opera singer; general director of the New York City Opera, 1979–1988
Shirley Smith (1927–)	Australian aborigine who has spent her life working for her fellow aborigines
Gertrude Stein (1874–1946)	American author
Gloria Steinem (1934–)	U.S. feminist and writer; founder of *Ms.* magazine
Harriet Beecher Stowe (1811–1896)	U.S. author famous for the antislavery novel *Uncle Tom's Cabin*
Maria Tallchief (1925–)	American ballerina; daughter of an Osage Indian
Helen Brooke Taussig (1898–)	American physician specializing in children's heart disease; discovered the cause of bluish tinge in skin of "blue babies"
Balentina Vladimirova Tereshkova (1937–)	Russian; the first woman to travel in space
Twyla Tharp (1942–)	U.S. dancer and choreographer; her own company reflects her innovative blending of ballroom, jazz, and tap with traditional ballet
Margaret Thatcher (1925–)	Britain's first woman prime minister
Sojourner Truth (Isabella Baumfree) (c.1797–1883)	American abolitionist; first black woman orator to speak out against slavery
Harriet Tubman (c.1820–1913)	Black American fugitive slave who helped hundreds of other slaves escape to freedom; most famous leader of the underground railroad
Madame Tussaud (1760–1850)	Swiss wax modeler; forced to make death masks of guillotined aristocrats during the French Revolution; established the London Wax Museum in 1802
Victoria (1819–1901)	Queen of England for 64 years; the Victorian age was named after her
Laura Ingalls Wilder (1867–1957)	American author of children's books
Victoria C. Woodhull (1938–1927)	First woman to run for president of the U.S. (1872 Equal Rights Party)
Wu Chao (625–705)	Chinese empress who established peace, prosperity, high cultural achievement, and improvements in government; also noted for her ruthlessness and villainy

Books About Women— A Starter List

Reading Levels:
 P—preschool and primary
 I—intermediate
 A—advanced

From *The Teacher's Book of Lists, Second Edition*, published by GoodYearBooks.
Copyright © 1994 Sheila Madsen and Bette Gould.

The Diary of a Young Girl (A)
Anne Frank (Doubleday)
The moving account of an adolescent girl who must go into hiding with two families during the Nazi occupation of Amsterdam.

Silent Storm (A)
Marion Brown and Ruth Crone (Abingdon Press)
The story of Anne Sullivan Macy and her experiences while teaching Helen Keller.

Maria Tallchief (I)
Tobi Tobias (Crowell)
The story of this famous ballet dancer, whose mother was Scotch-Irish and father was Osage.

Harriet Tubman: Conductor of the Underground Railway (A)
Ann Petry (Archway)
Through the dreams and determination of this courageous black woman, many slaves are led to freedom.

The Last Princess: The Story of Princess Ka'iulani of Hawaii (A)
Fay Stanley (Four Winds)
Beautifully illustrated (by Diane Stanley) biography of the princess and how she contested the annexation of her islands to the U.S.

Dreams Into Deeds: Nine Women Who Cared (A)
Linda Peavy and Ursula Smith (Scribner's)
A narrative history of over three hundred years of women's experiences, this collection of brief biographies includes Marian Anderson, Rachel Carson, Margaret Mead, Babe Didrikson, and many others.

Founding Mothers: Women of America in the Revolutionary Era (A)
Linda G. De Pauw (Houghton)
Various roles of women during the Revolutionary era, such as soldiers, couriers, and political activists, are told from a modern-day feminist perspective.

Women Who Changed Things (A)
Linda Peavy and Ursula Smith (Scribner's)
Although not about famous women, these fascinating biographies of accomplished women, including an astronomer, a reformer, and an educator, will interest those trying to imagine adult careers.

Swan Lake (P-I)
Margot Fonteyn, illustrated by Trina Schart Hyman (HBJ)
A captivating version of the story of true love and the battle between good and evil. Beautifully illustrated with paintings. Added notes relate the history of ballet.

Activities: Women

1. Read biographies of two women on the list. Compare influences that you think led to each woman's accomplishments. Share with the class as a play, TV news report, or panel discussion.

2. Work with a group to design an "Obstacles" bulletin board showing several mountain peaks. Select a woman for each mountain peak and show the obstacles she overcame in getting to her goal.

3. Cut out several large 1's. On each one write a woman famous for a "first" and her biographical facts including her accomplishments.

4. Read about several women on the list. Write a conversation they might have regarding a current topic, such as drugs, women in government, AIDS, etc. With several friends read or dramatize this conversation for the class.

5. Survey all of the women on the list. Classify each according to their area of expertise or accomplishment. Graph your findings. Some categories might be: Government, Entertainment, Women's Rights, Literature, and The Arts.

6. Choose a woman to study. Find out about her life and accomplishments by reading books, studying pictures, and looking at videos. Draw a puzzle on a piece of chart paper. Write the woman's name on one section. Fill the other parts by drawing pictures or writing facts about her life. Cut your puzzle into pieces, then have a classmate try to put it together.

From *The Teacher's Book of Lists, Second Edition*, published by GoodYearBooks.
Copyright © 1994 Sheila Madsen and Bette Gould.

CHAPTER

10

Art & Music

Art and Music Categories— Hues, Blues, and Fugues

Here's a list of art and music pieces grouped within some interesting categories. One way to use this list is to integrate a category with a usual topic of study. For example, Wind, Rain, Sleet, and Snow can be combined with a study of weather or the seasons. Another way is to begin with a category and expand into other subject areas and skills. For example, art and music activities that take place as a result of exposure to works in the category, Beauty in the Beast, can lead to other experiences. These experiences might include writing original stories and poems, reading animal tales, and making scientific reports and observations.

Art

SHOW BIZ

Le Cirque—Georges Seurat
Three Musicians — Pablo Picasso
Clown—Henri de Toulouse-Lautrec
Rehearsal in the Foyer of the Opera
  —Edgar Degas

COLORS

Composition in Red, Blue, and Yellow
  —Piet Mondrian
The Red Studio—Henri Matisse
Cow's Skull—Red, White, and Blue
  —Georgia O'Keeffe

ON THE ROAD

End of the Trail—James Earle Fraser
View of Toledo—El Greco (Domenicos
  Theotocopoulos)
The Scout: Friends or Enemies—Frederick
  Remington
Boulevard Montmartre, Paris—Camille
  Pissarro

Music

SHOW BIZ

"The Shrovetide Fair" from Petrouchka
  Ballet Suite—Igor Stravinsky
"Vesti La Giubba" from Pagliacci
  —Ruggiero Leoncavallo
"Clowns" from A Midsummer Night's
  Dream—Felix Mendelssohn
"Circus Music" from The Red Pony
  —Aaron Copland

COLORS

Rhapsody in Blue—George Gershwin
Mood Indigo—Duke Ellington
Le Train Bleu—Darius Milhaud
Ebony Concerto—Igor Stravinsky

ON THE ROAD

An American in Paris—George Gershwin
Grand Canyon Suite—Ferde Grofé
The Little Train of Caipira—Heitor Villa-
  Lobos
In the Steppes of Central Asia—Alexander
  Borodin

From *The Teacher's Book of Lists, Second Edition,* published by GoodYearBooks.
Copyright © 1994 Sheila Madsen and Bette Gould.

Art

ALL IN THE FAMILY

The Family—Marisol
Arrangement in Black and Grey: The Artist's Mother—James McNeill Whistler
An Old Man and His Grandson —Domenico Ghirlandaio
The Peale Family—Charles Willson Peale
Mother and Child with Bird —Suzuki Harunobu
American Gothic—Grant Wood
Family Promenade—Paul Klee

A.M. AND P.M.

The Starry Night—Vincent Van Gogh
An Impression: Sunrise—Claude Monet
Nighthawks—Edward Hopper
Day and Night—M. C. Escher

WHAT'S MY LINE?

The Gleaners—Jean François Millet
The Lacemaker—Jan Vermeer
Sugar Cane—Diego Rivera
The Anatomy Lesson—Rembrandt van Rijn
Jockeys in the Rain—Edgar Degas

H$_2$O

Hollow of the Deep-Sea Wave —Katsushika Hokusai
Water Lilies—Claude Monet
The Boating Party—Mary Cassatt
Breezing Up—Winslow Homer
Wave, Night—Georgia O'Keeffe

Music

ALL IN THE FAMILY

The Cradle Song—Johannes Brahms
"Brother Come and Dance with Me" from Hansel and Gretel—Engelbert Humperdinck
The Nursery—Modest Moussorgsky
The Bartered Bride—Bedřich Smetana
"The Bridal Procession" from Lohengrin— Richard Wagner
Prole do Bébé (Baby's Family)—Heitor Villa-Lobos
"Curious Story" from Kinderscenen —Robert Schumann

A.M. AND P.M.

Vincent (Starry, Starry Night) —Don McLean
Moonlight Sonata—Ludwig van Beethoven
Morning Mood from "Peer Gynt" —Edvard Grieg
Nights in the Gardens of Spain —Manuel de Falla
Stardust—Hoagy Carmichael

WHAT'S MY LINE?

The Barber of Seville—Gioacchino Rossini
Sorcerer's Apprentice—Paul Dukas
Spinning Song—Franz Schubert
Spinning Song, Op. 67, No. 4 —Felix Mendelssohn
H.M.S. Pinafore—Gilbert and Sullivan
Zar und Zimmermann (The Czar and the Carpenter)—Albert Lortzing

H$_2$O

La Mer—Claude Debussy
"Barcarolle" from The Tales of Hoffmann— Jacques Offenbach
Die Moldau—Bedřich Smetana
On the Beautiful Blue Danube —Johann Strauss
Water Music—George Frederick Handel

Art

THE ARTS IN ART

High Kick—Edgar Degas
The Yellow Violin—Raoul Dufy
Musical Forms—Georges Braque
The Artist in His Studio—Jan Vermeer
Claude Monet in His Floating Studio
    —Èdouard Manet

MOTHER NATURE

Flowering Trees—Piet Mondrian
Blue Landscape—Paul Cézanne
Hampstead Heath—John Constable
May Day—Andrew Wyeth
Photographs by Eliot Porter and Ansel
    Adams

DREAMS AND FANTASY

The Dream—Henri Rousseau
Sweet Dreams—Paul Gauguin
The Harlequin's Carnival—Joan Miró
Casa Milá Apartment House, Barcelona
    —Antoni Gaudí
I and the Village—Marc Chagall

NIGHTMARES

The Nightmare—John Henry Fuseli
The Persistence of Memory—Salvador Dali
House of Stairs—M. C. Escher
The Garden of Delights—Hieronymus
    Bosch
The Scream—Edvard Munch

BEAUTY IN THE BEAST

Two Bison—Lascaux cave painting
Crane—Katsushika Hokusai
Fantastic Rhinoceros—Albrecht Dürer
Tiger in the Rain—Henri Rousseau
Peaceable Kingdom—Edward Hicks
Wild Turkey—J. J. Audubon
Bird in Space—Constantin Brancusi
Lobster Trap and Fish Tail
    —Alexander Calder
Dog—Alberto Giacometti

Music

THE ARTS IN ART

Pictures from an Exhibition—Modest
    Moussorgsky
Matthias the Painter—Paul Hindemith
Walt Whitman—Dmitri Shostakovich
Seven Studies on Themes of Paul Klee
    —Gunther Schuller

MOTHER NATURE

Symphony No. 6 (The Pastoral)
    —Ludwig van Beethoven
Spring Symphony—Robert Schumann
My Country—Bedřich Smetana
"Waltz of the Flowers" from the Nutcracker
    Suite—Peter Ilyich Tchaikovsky

DREAMS AND FANTASY

Mother Goose Suite—Maurice Ravel
Hansel and Gretel—Engelbert Humperdinck
Incidental Music to A Midsummer Night's
    Dream—Felix Mendelssohn
Scheherazade—Nikolai Rimsky-Korsakov
Firebird Suite—Igor Stravinsky

NIGHTMARES

Danse Macabre—Camille Saint-Saëns
Night on Bald Mountain—Modest
    Moussorgsky
Baba Yaga—Anatol Liadov
El Amor Brujo—Manuel de Falla

BEAUTY IN THE BEAST

Papillon No. 8—Robert Schumann
Papillon—Edvard Grieg
Flight of the Bumblebee—Nikolai Rimsky-
    Korsakov
The Nightingale—Dmitri Shostakovich
Afternoon of a Faun—Claude Debussy
Peter and the Wolf—Sergei Prokofiev
Carnival of the Animals—Camille
    Saint-Saëns
Bear Dance—Béla Bártok

Art

THREE'S A CROWD

Peasant Dance—Pieter Bruegel
People Waiting—Honoré Daumier
The Night Watch—Rembrandt van Rijn
The School of Athens—Raphael
Visit of the Magi—Benozzo Gozzoli

GIVE ME YOUR TIRED, YOUR POOR...

The Third Class Carriage—Honoré Daumier
The Potato-Eaters—Vincent Van Gogh
Peasants Carrying Brushwood—Jean
    François Millet
The Liberation of the Peon—Diego Rivera
Breadline—Reginald Marsh

FUN AND GAMES

A Sunday Afternoon on the Grand Jatte
    —Georges Seurat
Swimmers—Katsushika Hokusai
Children's Games—Pieter Bruegel
Le Moulin de la Galette—Auguste Renoir
Bathers—Georges Seurat
The Card Players—Paul Cézanne
Boating—Èdouard Manet

WINING AND DINING

Campbell's Soup—Andy Warhol
The Basket of Apples—Paul Cézanne
Still Life—Diego Velázquez
Pie—Roy Lichtenstein
The Diner—George Segal
Giant Hamburger—Claes Oldenburg

Music

THREE'S A CROWD

"Pilgrim's Chorus" from Tannhäuser
    —Richard Wagner
"Hallelujah Chorus" from Messiah
    —George Frederick Handel
Symphony No. 8, in E♭ major (Symphony of
    a Thousand)—Gustav Mahler

GIVE ME YOUR TIRED, YOUR POOR...

Porgy and Bess—George Gershwin
Peasant Cantata—Johann Sebastian Bach
La Bohème—Giacomo Puccini
Poet and Peasant Overture—Franz von
    Suppé
The Threepenny Opera—Kurt Weill,
    Bertholt Brecht
The Cradle Will Rock—Marc Blitzstein
Scenes from Peasant Life—Edvard Grieg

FUN AND GAMES

Children's Games—Georges Bizet
Toy Symphony—Joseph Haydn
Till Eulenspiegel's Merry Pranks—Richard
    Strauss
Roman Carnival Overture—Louis Hector
    Berlioz
Camptown Races—Stephen Foster
Jeux (games)—Claude Debussy

WINING AND DINING

The Love for Three Oranges—Sergei
    Prokofiev
"Breakfast Waltz, Waiter's Waltz, Dinner
    Music" from Der Rosenkavalier—Richard
    Strauss
Yorkshire Feast Song—Henry Purcell
Whipped Cream (ballet)—Richard Strauss
The Long Christmas Dinner
    —Paul Hindemith

Art

A HOUSE IS NOT A HOME

Taj Mahal, India
Robie House, Chicago—Frank Lloyd Wright
Lake Shore Drive Apartment Houses
    —Mies Van der Rohe
Monticello—Thomas Jefferson
Kinkakuji (the Golden Pavilion), Kyoto

WIND, RAIN, SLEET, AND SNOW

Primavera—Sandro Botticelli
The Return of the Hunters—Pieter Bruegel
The Old Checkered House—Grandma
    Moses (Anna Mary Robertson Moses)
Waterloo Bridge (Effects of Mist)
    —Claude Monet
Landscapes of the Four Seasons
    —Tsunenobu
Threatening Weather—Rene Magritte

NUTS AND BOLTS

Computer Landscape—David Pease
Twittering Machine—Paul Klee
Brooklyn Bridge—Joseph Stella

WAR AND PEACE

Guernica—Pablo Picasso
The Executions of the 3rd of May
    —Francisco de Goya
Battle of the Amazons—Peter Paul Rubens
Recumbent Figure—Henry Moore
Peace—Jacques Lipchitz
The Kiss—Auguste Rodin
Love—Robert Indiana

Music

A HOUSE IS NOT A HOME

Skyscrapers (ballet)—John Alden Carpenter
My Old Kentucky Home—Stephen Foster
We Are Building a City (children's opera)
    —Paul Hindemith
Quiet City—Aaron Copland

WIND, RAIN, SLEET, AND SNOW

The Four Seasons—Antonio Vivaldi
Clouds, Mists—Claude Debussy
The Rite of Spring—Igor Stravinsky
"The Snow Is Dancing" from Children's
    Corner Suite—Claude Debussy
"The Storm and the Calm" from William
    Tell Overture—Gioacchino Rossini
Appalachian Spring—Aaron Copland
Summer Music for Woodwind Quartet
    —Samuel Barber
Raindrop Prelude—Frédéric Chopin

NUTS AND BOLTS

The Telephone—Gian-Carlo Menotti
Dance of Steel—Sergei Prokofiev
Catalogue of Agricultural Implements
    —Darius Milhaud
Pacific 231—Arthur Honneger

WAR AND PEACE

March Militaire—Franz Schubert
The Story of a Soldier—Igor Stravinsky
Light Cavalry Overture—von Suppe
1812 Overture—Peter Ilyich Tchaikovsky
Wellington's Victory or the Battle of
    Vittoria—Ludwig van Beethoven
Peace—Cándido Portinari
Liebestraum—Franz Liszt
Peace Train—Cat Stevens

From *The Teacher's Book of Lists, Second Edition*, published by GoodYearBooks. Copyright © 1994 Sheila Madsen and Bette Gould.

Art

THIS IS ME
SELF PORTRAITS

Leonardo da Vinci
Peter Paul Rubens
Rembrandt van Rijn
Henri Rousseau
Joan Miró
Amedeo Modigliani
Vincent Van Gogh
Francisco de Goya
Hieronymus Bosch

HIDDEN PICTURES

The Adoration of the Magi—Sandro
    Botticelli
The Maids of Honor—Diego Velazquez
The Last Judgment—Michaelangelo
At the Moulin Rouge
    —Henri de Toulouse-Lautrec
The Artist's Studio—Gustave Courbet

Music

THIS IS ME
SELF PORTRAITS

From My Life—Bedřich Smetana
From Memories of Childhood
    —Modest Moussorgsky

Art Forms

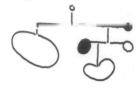

The following common art forms and media are often part of a classroom art program. The examples of works for use in children's art experiences are usually obtainable from art books, postcards, and inexpensive prints.

Sculpture

Alexander Archipenko—Woman Combing Her Hair
Umberto Boccioni—Unique Forms of Continuity in Space
Michelangelo Buonaratti—La Pietà
Alberto Giacometti—Man Pointing
Aristide Maillol—Mediterranean
Henry Moore—Reclining Figure
Rodin—The Burghers of Calais

Mosaics

Marc Chagall—Knesset, Jerusalem

Tapestries

Marc Chagall—Knesset, Jerusalem

Collage

Georges Braque—Bach
Pablo Picasso—Guitar
Kurt Schwitters—Disjointed Forces

Pastel

Mary Cassatt—Mother Feeding a Child
Jean Chardin—Self Portrait with Spectacles
Edgar Degas—The Tub
Quentin Latour—Mademoiselle Fel

Woodblock Printing

Albrecht Dürer—The Four Horsemen of the Apocalypse
Paul Gauguin—Offerings of Gratitude
Japanese and Chinese Woodblock Prints

Murals

Marc Chagall—Lincoln Art Center, New York
Jose Clemente Orozco—Catharsis, Palace of Fine Arts, Mexico City
Diego Rivera—Stairway in the National Palace, Mexico City
David Alfaro Siqueiros—Elements, National Preparatory School, Mexico City

Stained Glass

Marc Chagall—U.N. Building, New York; Hadassah Synogogue, Jerusalem

Paper Cutouts

Henri Matisse—Parakeet and Siren

Use of Line

Albrecht Dürer—All woodcuts
Jean Ingres—The Guillon-Lethière Family

Mobiles

Alexander Calder—Heads and Tails

Watercolor

John Sell Cotman—Greta Bridge
Alexander Cozens—View from Mirabella
Winslow Homer—Sloop Bermuda
John Marin—The Singer Building
Andrew Wyeth—Delphinium

Art Periods and Styles

Art experts sometimes disagree on exact dates and artists of a period or style. Approximate dates and representative works that are generally agreed upon are listed.

Gothic (c.1150–1500)
Notre-Dame Cathedral—France
Chartres Cathedral—France
Westminster Abbey—England
Milan Cathedral—Italy
Gentile da Fabriano—*The Adoration of the Magi*
Master Honoré—*Prayer Book of Phillip the Fair*

Renaissance (c.1400–1600)
Donatello—*David*
Sandro Botticelli—*The Birth of Venus*
Titian—*Bacchanal*
Leonardo da Vinci—*Mona Lisa*
Raphael—*School of Athens*
Michelangelo—*Moses*
Jan van Eyck—*The Arnolfini Wedding*
Pieter Bruegel—*Peasant Wedding*
Albrecht Dürer—*Knight, Death, and Devil*

Mannerism (c.1520–1600)
Parmigianino—*The Madonna with the Long Neck*
Tintoretto—*The Last Supper*
El Greco—*The Burial of Count Orgaz*

Baroque (c.1600–1750)
Gian Lorenzo Bernini—*Fountain of the Four Rivers*, Piazza Navona, Rome
Dominikus Zimmermann—*Die Wies*, Bavaria, Germany
Michelangelo Caravaggio—*Calling of St. Matthew*
Peter Paul Rubens—*The Garden of Love*
Diego Velazquez—*The Maids of Honor*
Frans Hals—*Yonker Ramp and His Sweetheart*
Rembrandt—*Night Watch*

Rococo (c.1720–1780)
Jean Honoré Fragonard—*The Swing*
Antoine Watteau—*Mezzetin*

Neoclassicism (c.1750–1850)
Jean Auguste Dominique Ingres—*Odalisque*
Jacques Louis David—*Napoleon Crossing the Alps*

Romanticism (c.1800–1840)
Theodore Gericault—*Mounted Officer of the Imperial Guard*
Eugène Delacroix—*Greece on the Ruins of Missolonghi*
Honoré Daumier—*The Third Class Carriage*
Joseph M. W. Turner—*The Slave Ship*

Realism (c.1848–1900)
Gustave Courbet—*The Stone Breakers*

Impressionism (c.1870–1910)
Claude Monet—*The Cathedral at Rouen*
Edgar Degas—*Woman with Chrysanthemums*
Pierre Auguste Renoir—*Lunch of the Boating Party at Bougival*
Mary Cassatt—*The Bath*
Camille Pissarro—*Afternoon at the Boulevard des Italiens*

Post Impressionism (c.1886–1905)
Georges Seurat—*La Baignade*
Vincent Van Gogh—*Sunflowers*
Paul Cézanne—*Mont Sainte Victoire*
Paul Gauguin—*La Orana Maria*

Expressionism (early 1900s)
Henri de Toulouse-Lautrec—*Dance at the Moulin Rouge*
Henri Rousseau—*The Sleeping Gypsy*

Fauvism (c.1903–1907)
Henri Matisse—*The Joy of Life*
Georges Rouault—*The Old King*
Chaim Soutine—*The Dead Fowl*

Die Brucke—"The Bridge" (c.1904–1913)
Max Beckmann—*The Dream*
Emil Nolde—*Masks and Dahlias*
Oskar Kokoschka— *Tempest*

Der Blaue Reiter—"The Blue Rider" (c.1909–1913)
Wassily Kandinsky—*Accompanied Contrast*
Paul Klee—*Fish Magic*
Franz Marc—*The Fate of Animals*

Cubism (c.1907–1914)
Juan Gris—*La Table du Café, Abstraction in Gray*
Pablo Picasso—*Ambroise Vollard*
Georges Braque—*The Musician's Table*
Fernand Léger—*The City*
Jacques Lipchitz—*Man with Mandolin*

Dadaism (c.1916–1922)
Marcel Duchamp—*To be looked at (from the other side of the glass), with one eye, close to, for almost an hour*
Hans Arp—*Collage with Squares Arranged According to the Laws of Chance*

Surrealism (c.1924–1966)
Max Ernst—*Swamp Angel*
Salvador Dali—*Mae West*
Joan Miró—*Person Throwing a Stone at a Bird*
René Magritte—*Man with Newspaper*

Abstract Expressionism (mid-1940s–present)
Jackson Pollock—*One*
William de Kooning—*Woman and Bicycle*
Franz Kline—*Painting No. 7*
Mark Rothko—*No. 10*

Pop Art (late 1950s–present)
George Segal—*Cinema*
Jasper Johns—*Three Flags*
Claes Oldenburg—*Soft Scissors*
Robert Rauschenberg—*Hot Dog*
Andy Warhol—*Coca Cola Bottles*

Op Art (mid-1960s–present)
Joseph Albers—*Fugue*
Bridget Riley—*White Disks II*
Victor Vasarely—*Vega*
Richard Anuskiewicz—*Entrance to Green*

Minimal Art (early 1960s–present)
Ellsworth Kelly—*Red Blue Green*
Frank Stella—*Empress of India*
Kenneth Noland—*Via Blues*

Art Vocabulary

armature Skeletonlike framework upon which any type of media can be hung or modeled.

Art Nouveau A decorative art movement that lasted from the 1880s to World War I. Art Nouveau is characterized by curving, twisting lines and asymmetry, as in the works of Aubrey Beardsley, Louis Comfort Tiffany, and Antoni Gaudí.

bas-relief (low relief) Sculpture carved so as to project from a flat background as on a coin.

Bauhaus School of design founded by Walter Gropius in Germany in 1919, closed by Hitler; combined all the arts, from applied arts to fine arts, with the materials and techniques of modern technology.

brayer A rubber roller used for inking printing blocks.

broken color Application of short strokes or small dabs of paint beside each other, which viewed from a distance blend together to form a new color.

calligraphy Beautiful or decorative handwriting; a design created by the arrangement of letters to form a pattern.

caricature A drawing that exaggerated the features of a person.

cartoon A full-scale drawing on paper from which a painting, especially murals, are made. Also designates humorous drawings such as comic strips, caricatures, or political satires.

chiaroscuro An Italian word meaning light and dark. Refers to the manner in which a painter handles atmospheric effects by use of values, tones, or light and dark shading.

collage A composition made by pasting scraps of various material such as newspaper, wallpaper, photographs, and fabric on a flat surface.

cloisonné (cloy-zoh-nay´) An enameling process in which cells made of metal strips or wire are filled with colored enamels and baked or fired in a kiln.

contour The line bounding a figure or object, creating an illusion of mass; outline.

crosshatch A shading made by two sets of parallel lines crossing over each other, most often used in drawing and printing.

facade Usually the front of a building.

foreshortening A method of reducing, often with distortion, parts of an object not parallel to the picture plane in order to convey depth and dimension.

fresco Italian word for fresh. The technique of painting on wet plaster with pigments mixed with water.

frottage A reproduction of a relief surface made by covering it with paper and rubbing it with pencil, pastel, crayon, etc. Also called a rubbing.

genre painting A work that depicts a scene from everyday life.

gesso (jess´-oh) A mixture of plaster and glue, or gypsum, used to prepare a surface for painting.

gouache (goo-ahsh´) An opaque water color made by adding white to a transparent watercolor.

impasto Paint applied thickly by a brush or knife.

kinetic art All art forms in which movement appears to take place or actually does take place, often induced by the effect of light. See works by Abraham Palatnik, Nicolas Schöffer, and Victor Vasarely.

lithography Printmaking process in which a design is drawn onto a polished stone or metal plate with an oily crayon or other greasy material. After moistening the entire surface, ink is applied which adheres only to the lines drawn.

monochromatic color The different values or intensities of one color.

mosaic Designs or pictures made by setting small pieces of material—glass, marble, or stones—in concrete or plaster, on surfaces such as walls or floors.

montage A composition made by fitting together pictures or parts of pictures. In motion pictures, it refers to a rapid sequence of images or pictures.

mural A large painting done directly on a wall or done separately and affixed to a wall.

negative space The space around objects or shapes.

opaque Nontransparent.

palette A thin board or tablet on which colors are placed and mixed. Also refers to the colors used by an artist or group of artists.

pastel Ground pigments compressed into a chalklike stick. Also, work done in this medium.

pointillism A painting technique in which a series of small dots of pure color are systematically placed next to each other; also referred to as Divisionism.

rhythm The recurrence or repetition of features or objects in a work of art.

shade A darker value of a color, obtained by mixing black to the hue.

symmetry A balance achieved by the arrangement of forms on both sides of an imaginary axis.

terra cotta An Italian word for cooked-earth. Reddish brown clay used for pottery, sculpture, or building material.

tesserae Small pieces of glass or stone used in making mosaics.

trompe-loeil (trohmp-loy´) French word for "deceive the eye"; a type of painting in which the objects depicted appear to be real.

vanishing point The point on the horizon toward which parallel lines appear to converge.

wash A thin, transparent film of color, usually watercolor or ink.

Color Words

Reds
carmine
cerise
cherry
coral
crimson
damask
pink
rose
ruby
salmon
scarlet
titian
vermilion

Browns
beige
bronze
chocolate
cinnamon
coffee
ecru
fawn
hazel
henna
khaki
mahogany
puce
sienna
tan
taupe
tawny
umber

Yellows
amber
buff
canary
champagne
eggshell
gold
lemon
ochre
saffron
xanthic

Purples
fuchsia
heliotrope
lavender
lilac
magenta
maroon
mauve
plum
violet

Whites
alabaster
cream
ivory
pearl

Oranges
apricot
copper
peach
rust
tangerine

Greens
chartreuse
emerald
lime
reseda

Blues
aquamarine
azure
bice
cerulean
indigo
sapphire
turquoise

Blacks
ebony
raven
sable
silver
slate

Activities: Color Words

1. Arrange the hues in each color group from light to dark by making a list, painting samples of the colors, or attaching to a sheet of paper samples from fabric, thread, magazines, clothing catalogs, paint chip samples, or nature.

2. Make lists of color words that describe colors by naming objects. These objects can either be added as adjectives or be the names of the colors themselves.

avocado green   pea green
fawn   peach
fire engine red   periwinkle blue
     salmon

3. List colors that could fit into more than one major color category.

rust—Is it brown or orange?
coral—Is it red or orange?
puce—Is it red or brown?
chartreuse—Is it yellow or green?

4. Experiment with paint to develop formulas for various hues.

1 part yellow + 2 parts orange = _____

Measure parts by a teaspoon, drops from a straw, or a medicine dropper.

5. Describe colors using words.

chartreuse—a bright greenish-yellow
reseda—a dull grayish-green
slate—dark grayish-blue

6. Use paint catalogues or color charts to find and list color names. See which of these are not in the dictionary. Tell which of these words you think may someday enter the dictionary due to common use in everyday language.

Music Makers—The Orchestra & Other Instruments

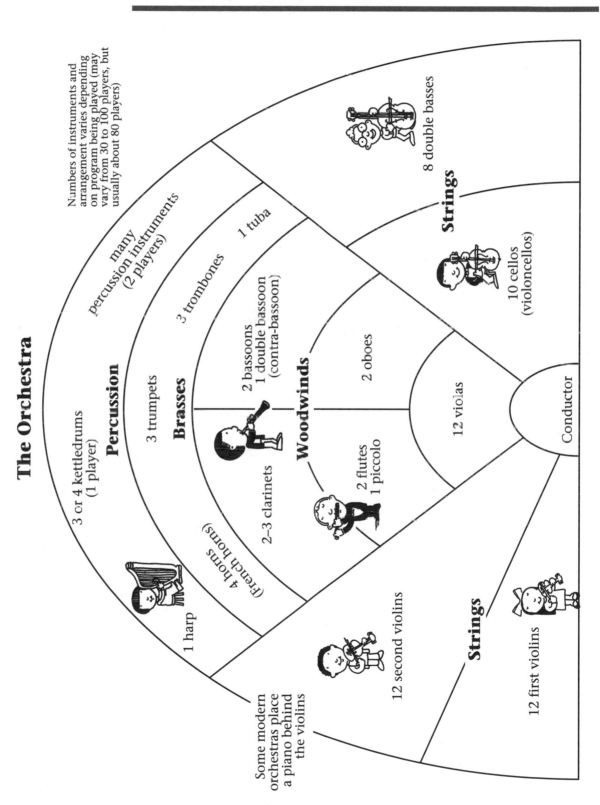

The Orchestra

Numbers of instruments and arrangement varies depending on program being played (may vary from 30 to 100 players, but usually about 80 players)

Percussion

3 or 4 kettledrums (1 player)

3 trumpets

many percussion instruments (2 players)

3 trombones

1 tuba

Brasses

2–3 clarinets

4 horns (French horns)

2 bassoons 1 double bassoon (contra-bassoon)

1 harp

Woodwinds

2 oboes

2 flutes 1 piccolo

12 violas

Conductor

Strings

8 double basses

10 cellos (violoncellos)

12 second violins

12 first violins

Strings

Some modern orchestras place a piano behind the violins

From *The Teacher's Book of Lists, Second Edition*, published by GoodYearBooks. Copyright © 1994 Sheila Madsen and Bette Gould.

Instruments sometimes used in the orchestra
(other than those identified in the Orchestra chart)

Woodwinds

bass clarinet
English horn
saxophone

Percussion

bass drum	glockenspiel
castanets	gong
chimes	marimba
claves	sandblocks
cymbals	snare drum

tambourine
triangle
woodblocks
xylophone

Some other instruments

accordion	flageolet	lur	saxhorn
bagpipe	flügelhorn	lute	serpent
balalaika	gittern	lyre	shakuhachi
banjo	glass harmonica	mandolin	shamisen
barytone	guiro	maracas	sitar
basset horn	guitar	marimba	spinet
bugle	gusle	mellophone	tablas
calliope	hardanger	monochord	tambura
celesta	harmonica	oboe do caccia	theorbo
chitarrone	harmonium	oboe d'amore	timbrel
chyn (ch'in)	harpsichord	ocarina	tom-tom
clavichord	Hawaiian guitar	oliphant	Turkish crescent
clavilux	heckelphone	ophicleide	'ud
concertina	helicon	pandora	ukulele
cornet	hornpipe	pipe	vibraharp (vibes)
crwth	hurdy-gurdy	psaltery	vielle
curtal	Irish harp	qanun	vina
dulcimer	Jew's harp	rabab	zampogna
euphonium	kantele	racket	zither
fiddle	kithara	rebec	
fife	koto	recorder	

Instruments at least 2,000 years old that are still played today

bagpipe	finger cymbals	panpipes	shofar
castanets	Jew's harp	shawn	tambourine
chyn	lyre	sheng	vina

Electronic instruments (other than usual instruments fitted with electronic devices)

chord organ	novachord
combo organ	Ondes Martenot
electronic organ (Hammond organ)	theremin

From *The Teacher's Book of Lists, Second Edition*, published by GoodYearBooks.
Copyright © 1994 Sheila Madsen and Bette Gould.

Music Vocabulary

a cappella singing without instrumental accompaniment

accent an emphasis that makes one note of a measure sound more important than others

arpeggio a series of chord tones, played in quick succession

bar *see* measure

chord tones sounded together: usually refers to three or more tones

coda a concluding section added after the main piece is finished

counterpoint combination of two or more melodies, played together, but retaining each one's identity

downbeat the first accented beat in a measure

dynamics the contrasts and progressions between the loudness and softness of the music

embellishment *see* ornament

expression the feeling or mood to be conveyed by the music; expression marks, added by the composer, give the performer detailed directions on how to play

fifth an interval of five steps between tones; fifth note of a scale

form the structure of the musical composition

glissando a "slide"; moving rapidly up or down the scale by sliding a finger along a string, on stringed instruments, or keys, on a piano

harmonics faint, flutelike sounds of string instruments produced by lightly touching a string, rather than pressing firmly

harmony the combining of tones; the study of chord combinations and progressions

homophony a single melody, with its accompanying chords and harmony

improvise to make up melodies and harmonies while singing or playing, without a preconceived plan

incidental music music added to a play or film to set a mood or add excitement

interval the difference (distance) between the pitch of two sounds

key the "home" center of a musical work; the scale or series of tones whose center (point of rest) is the key name

libretto the text of the words to be sung in an opera, oratorio, or musical play

measure (bar) a unit of time in music with a given number of beats

melody a succession of notes with a definite pattern

ornament (embellishment) decorations of the melody (grace notes, trills, etc.)

pitch sound of a musical tone, either high or low: relation of one tone to another

polyphony *see* counterpoint

rhythm the arrangement in music of accented and unaccented, long and short, sounds

scale a series of tones leading from one tone to its octave; the most common scales are major, minor, chromatic, and whole tone

staff the lines and spaces on which notes are written

syncopation a shifting of the accent (usually on the first beat of a measure) to one of the weaker beats in the measure

From *The Teacher's Book of Lists, Second Edition*, published by GoodYearBooks. Copyright © 1994 Sheila Madsen and Bette Gould.

tempo (time) the rate of speed of the music

third third note of a scale; an interval of three steps whose tones are written on adjacent lines of adjacent spaces of the staff

timbre (tone color) quality of tone; the characteristic sound of specific instruments or of the voice

time *see* tempo

tonality the quality of belonging to a definite key

tone a sound with a definite pitch

tone color *see* timbre

treble the higher range of sounds

From *The Teacher's Book of Lists, Second Edition,* published by GoodYearBooks.
Copyright © 1994 Sheila Madsen and Bette Gould.

Musical Forms

This list of musical forms is grouped according to the general period of their development or perfection. A suggested example for listening follows each form.

Middle Ages

religious chants (plainsongs)—single melodic lines sung by a group
>*Gregorian chants, Ambrosian chants*

folk music

canons (rounds) of the minstrels and troubadours
>*Summer Is Icumen In* (one of the earliest canons, 13th century)

Renaissance

madrigal—a poem set to music in two voice-parts, later developing into one-, two-, three-, and four-part cantatas
>*Now Is the Month of Maying,* Thomas Morley
>*The Swan Song,* Orlando Gibbons

motet—vocal music sung by a group, usually two-part, without orchestral accompaniment; the motet became the sacred counterpart of the madrigal
>*Motets by Palestrina and J. S. Bach*

Baroque Period: musical forms

chorale prelude—music based on a chorale melody, composed for the organ
>*Three Chorales for Organ,* César Franck (examples of chorale preludes, although not of the Baroque period)

concerto grosso—a sonata for several solo instruments (often two violins and a cello) alternating with full orchestra
>*Brandenburg Concertos,* J.S. Bach

dance suite (partita)—short, contrasting dance movements; four usual movements were the allemande, courante, saraband, and gigue
>J.S. Bach wrote six French suites, six English suites, and six partitas

fugue—a melody carried on in several overlapping voices
>*The Art of the Fugue,* J.S. Bach

passacaglia (chaconne)—slow and stately dance suite, usually in triple meter
>*Passacaglia in C Minor,* J.S. Bach

rondo—music with a theme that recurs in its original key at certain intervals; later, often used as last movements in compositions by Haydn, Mozart, Beethoven
>Last movement of *Piano Sonata in A, K. 331,* Wolfgang Amadeus Mozart

toccata—keyboard composition with elaborate and rapid passage work, such as runs and arpeggios
>*Toccata and Fugue in D Minor,* J.S. Bach
>*Toccatas,* Girolamo Frescobaldi

trio sonata—in this early development, the sonata was music of a single two- or three-part movement, usually with three voice-parts performed by four instruments
>*Golden Sonata in F,* Henry Purcell

Baroque Period: vocal forms

cantata—short version of the oratorio, usually written on secular themes
    Suddenly, Shall the Day Appear, Paul Hindemith
    Cantata No. 140—Wachet Auf, J.S. Bach

chorale—a simple hymn, enlarged and ornamented for instruments: later expanded and used in church cantatas
    A Mighty Fortress Is Our God, Martin Luther

grand opera—generally applied to early Italian operas and later works with involved, serious plots; also, today applied to operas with lavish productions
    Aïda, Giuseppe Verdi (example of grand opera, although not of the Baroque Period)

opera—a drama performed by singing, with costumes, scenery, action, and orchestral accompaniment (some later operas employed ballet groups, also)
    Carmen, Georges Bizet (example of opera, although not of the Baroque Period)

oratorio—of religious nature, usually with scriptural text; tells a story; for voices with orchestral accompaniment; usually no action, scenery, or costumes
    The Messiah, George Frederick Handel

Classical Period

concerto—sonata for solo instrument with orchestral accompaniment, usually of the following three movements: (1) sonata form, (2) movement in a slower tempo, (3) lively rondo, theme with variations, or again, a movement in sonata form
    Concerto No. 1 in B♭ Minor, Peter Ilyich Tchaikovsky

chamber music—sonata written for instrumental groupings, such as the string quartet or woodwind quintet, to be performed in a small place
    Trout Quintet, Franz Schubert

sonata—a composition for solo instrument with the following four sections: (1) the allegro, fast movement, (2) a slow movement, (3) a minuet or scherzo, sometimes omitted, (4) a finale, usually fast
    Pathétique, Ludwig van Beethoven

sonata-allegro form—a significant development of the period, used as the first movement of sonatas, symphonies, overtures, and chamber works, with the following sections: (1) statement of a theme, (2) development of theme at length, (3) restatement of original theme
    First movement from *Sonata, Op. 2, No. 1,* Beethoven

symphony—sonata for full symphony orchestra; nearly every major composer wrote at least one symphony
    Symphony No. 8 in B Minor (Unfinished), Franz Schubert

Romantic Period

art songs ("lieder")—songs with music composed to fit the text of romantic poetry (Schubert wrote over 600 lieders)
    Mullerlieder and *Gretchen Am Spinnrade,* Franz Schubert

ballet—a story told in dancing; music written for ballet is frequently used in concerts
    Giselle, Adolphe Adam

comic opera (sometimes called operetta and light opera)—lighter, less serious, usually shorter verion of the opera form; usually includes speaking roles
    The Student Prince, Sigmund Romberg

From *The Teacher's Book of Lists, Second Edition,* published by GoodYearBooks.
Copyright © 1994 Sheila Madsen and Bette Gould.

Romantic Period—(continued)

concert overture—resembles the overture to an opera but is meant to be played in a concert hall as an independent composition
Academic Festival Overture, Johannes Brahms

music-dramas—Richard Wagner's strong, cyclical operas demanding more staging, vocal stamina, and physical endurance than earlier operas
Tristan and Isolde, Richard Wagner

symphonic poem (called tone poem in the Modern Period)—a single symphonic picture, without separate movements, in which the music usually follows a story
Romeo and Juliet (symphonic poem)—Peter Ilyich Tchaikovsky
Don Quixote (tone poem)—Richard Strauss

symphonic suite (program symphony)—lighter version of the symphony, consisting of sections that are related through a chain of events or story
Scheherazade, Nikolai Rimsky-Korsakov

Some Other Forms

aleatory music—music incorporating the element of chance; not at all the pitches or rhythms are specified; performers may introduce random elements; no two performances are alike
Works by Karlheinz Stockhausen, John Cage

étude—an instrumental composition designed to help improve the player's techniques
Revolutionary Ètude, Frédéric Chopin

fantasia—a work in free form, according to the composer's desires, not following a strict scheme
Wanderer Fantasie in C, Franz Schubert

free form—may not follow any conventional succession of themes; composer then works for unity with harmonization and orchestration
Jeux (Games), Claude Debussy

march—music with a strong rhythm and regular phrases, usually in 2/4 or 4/4 time, suitable for accompanying a marching group
John Philip Sousa's marches

overture—a composition that introduces a longer work, such as an opera or oratorio
Overture on Hebrew Themes, Sergei Prokofiev

rhapsody—a free form, relatively short composition, expressing a particular mood
Rhapsody on a Theme by Paganini, Sergei Rachmaninoff

scherzo—a movement from a sonata, usually involving an element of surprise; or an independent piece of music that is serious and dramatic rather than playful
Scherzos by Frédéric Chopin, Johannes Brahms

serenade—an instrumental composition for a small group of instruments, usually consisting of several movements
A Little Night Music, Wolfgang Amadeus Mozart

theme and variations—a series of different treatments of a theme, with key changes, altered rhythm and tempo, or other elements for some of the variations
Variations on a Theme by Handel, Johannes Brahms

Musical Periods

Pre-17th Century

Madrigals and chansons of Orlando Di Lasso

Giovanni Pierluigi di Palestrina
Missa Papae Marcelli (Marcellus Mass)

Baroque Period (late 1500s to middle 1700s)

Johann Sebastian Bach—called the father of modern music
Brandenburg Concertos
Prelude and Fugue in D Major
B Minor Mass

George Frederick Handel
Fireworks Music
The Beggar's Opera

Claudio Monteverdi—a bridge between Renaissance and the Baroque
Orfeo (opera)
Hear the Murmuring Waters (from Book II of madrigals)

Henry Purcell—England's greatest composer
"Dido's Lament" from Dido and Aeneas (opera)
Golden Sonata in F

Domenico Scarlatti—remembered for harpsichord compositions; called the father of modern keyboard technique
Sonate Pastorale

"Rococo" Period (the last thirty to forty years of the Baroque period)

Karl Philipp Emanuel Bach
Solfeggietto

Antonio Vivaldi
The Seasons, Op. 8 (Le quattro stagione)

Classical Period (middle 1700s to early 1800s)

Muzio Clementi
Gradus ad Parnassum—Steps to Parnassus, 100 piano études, still used by many piano students

Joseph Haydn
Farewell Symphony
London Symphonies
Toy Symphony

Wolfgang Amadeus Mozart
Don Giovanni (opera)
The "Jupiter" Symphony (Symphony #41 in C Major)
Piano Concerto in A (K.488)

Ludwig van Beethoven—Often called the bridge between the Classical and Romantic periods; demonstrated that music could reveal the composer's character and be more than impersonal and stylized; brought the symphony to its most perfect stage of development; perhaps the most outstanding composer of western music.
Fifth Symphony, in C Minor
Pastoral (Sixth Symphony)
Ninth Symphony
Emperor Concerto (#5 in E♭ Major, Op. 73)
Pathétique sonata
Moonlight Sonata
Fidelio (Beethoven's only opera)

Romantic Period (early 1800s to late 1800s)

Hector Berlioz
Roman Carnival Overture
Symphonie Fantastique

Georges Bizet
Carmen (opera)

Johannes Brahms
First Symphony
Variations on a Theme by Haydn

From *The Teacher's Book of Lists, Second Edition,* published by GoodYearBooks. Copyright © 1994 Sheila Madsen and Bette Gould.

Romantic Period (continued)

Frédéric Chopin
Minute Waltz (Waltz in D♭, Op. 64, No. 1)
Military Polonaise (Polonaise in A, Op. 40, No. 1)
Prelude in B minor

Anton Dvořák
New World Symphony
Slavonic Dance, No. 1

Edvard Grieg
Peer Gynt Suites, Nos. 1 & 2

Franz Liszt
Hungarian Rhapsodies
Faust Symphony

Edward MacDowell
Indian Suite
Woodland Sketches

Felix Mendelssohn
Midsummer's Night Dream
Hebrides Overture (Fingal's Cave)

Modest Moussorgsky
Night on the Bare Mountain

Giacomo Puccini
La Bohème (opera)
Madame Butterfly (opera)

Nikolai Rimsky-Korsakov
Scheherazade (symphonic suite)

Gioacchino Rossini
William Tell (opera)
The Barber of Seville (opera)

Camille Saint-Saëns
The Carnival of the Animals
Cello Concerto No. 1

Franz Schubert
The Erl-King
Die Forelle (The Trout)
C Major Symphony (The Great)
Marche Militaire No. 1

Robert Schumann
Piano Concerto in A Minor
Humoresque

Bedřich Smetana
The Bartered Bride (overture)

John Phillip Sousa
Semper Fidelis
The Washington Post March

Johann Strauss (the Younger)
Die Fledermaus (opera)
Tales from the Vienna Woods

Piotr (Peter) Ilyich Tchaikovsky
Sleeping Beauty (ballet)
1812 Overture
Romeo and Juliet

Giuseppe Verdi
Aïda (opera)
La Traviata (opera)

Richard Wagner
Tannhäuser (opera)

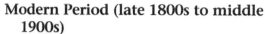

Modern Period (late 1800s to middle 1900s)

Béla Bartók
Concerto for Orchestra
Rumanian Folk Dances

Claude Debussy
The Afternoon of a Faun
Golliwog's Cakewalk

George Gershwin
Rhapsody in Blue
An American in Paris (symphonic poem)
Piano Concerto in F

Paul Hindemith
Suite 1922
When Lilacs Last in the Dooryard Bloom'd (based on a poem by Walt Whitman)

Charles Ives
Three Places in New England
The Fourth of July

Sergei Prokofiev
Classical Symphony
Peter and the Wolf

Maurice Ravel
Boléro
Pavane for a Dead Princess

Arnold Schoenberg
String Quartet, No. 3 (first movement)
A Survivor of Warsaw

Modern Period (continued)

Richard Strauss
   Der Rosenkavalier (opera)
   Also Spracht Zarathustra (Thus said Zarathustra)

Igor Stravinsky
   The Firebird (ballet)
   Ragtime for Eleven Instruments (jazz)
   The Rite of Spring (ballet)

Contemporary Period (middle 1900s to present)

Benjamin Britten
   Variations and Fugue on a Theme of Purcell (The Young Person's Guide to the Orchestra)
   Peter Grimes (opera)

John Cage
   Imaginary Landscape No. 4 (scored for 12 radios tuned at random)

Aaron Copland
   Rodeo (ballet)
   El Salón Mexico

Phillip Glass
   Einstein on the Beach

Dmitri Shostakovich
   Cello Concerto, No. 1 (written for the famous cellist Rostropovich)
   The Nose (opera)

Karl-Heinz Stockhausen—one of the pioneers of electronic music
   Zeitmasse (Measures of Time)
   Microphonie I

Heitor Villa-Lobos
   Bachiana Brazileiras, No. 5
   Chôros

Musical Tempo and Expression Marks

accelerando (accel.)—becoming quicker (opposite of ritardando)
adagio—slow and leisurely
allegro—quick and cheerful
andante—slowly; gently moving; walking tempo
brillante—bright; sparkling
cantabile—like a singing tone
dolce—sweetly
giocoso—gaily; cheerfully
grave—slow; solemn
largo—very slow; broad; stately
legato—smoothly connected (opposite of staccato)
lento—slowly; between andante and largo
maestoso — majestically
moderato—at a moderate, even pace
presto—very quickly; faster than allegro
risoluto—boldly; resolute
ritardando (ritard.)—becoming slower (opposite of accelerando)
semplice—simply
sostenuto—sustained
staccato—sharp, short notes (opposite of legato)
tranquillo—calm; peaceful
un poco (a poco)—a little
vigoroso—boldly
vivace—quick and lively; faster than allegro
vivo—animated

Some Other Marks

From *The Teacher's Book of Lists, Second Edition*, published by GoodYearBooks. Copyright © 1994 Sheila Madsen and Bette Gould.

agitato	expressivo	rigore
allargando	giusto	ritenuto
allegreto	incalzando	rotondo
allegro (molto) brioso	largamente	rubato
andantino	leggiero	sognando
animato	lento doloroso	solemne
appassionata	marcato	spirito
calando	morendo	subito
con brio	moto	tanto
energico	pesante	tempestoso

CHAPTER

11

Teacher and Family References

Awards for Students

Everybody likes recognition, so end your year with an Awards Day. Here's a list of awards that may match some of the personalities in your class. Obviously, some of the awards are stated with tongue in cheek, and need to be given and received with a sense of humor. The important thing is that everyone gets an award.

The Albert Einstein Award for outstanding achievement in science

The Always Room For One More Award to the person with the fullest desk or cubby

The Athlete Award

The Best After-School Teacher's Car Loader or Unloader

The Best Excuse-Maker Award

The Best Secretary Award

The Better-Late-Than-Never Award

The Biggest Nagger Award

The Bull in the China Shop Award

The Calligraphy Award to the person with the neatest handwriting

The Cheerleader Award to the most enthusiastic

The Cheshire Cat Award to the person with the biggest smile

The Dean of the Discos Award to the best dancer

The Do-Re-Mi Award to the best singer

The Easy-Going Award to the most agreeable

The Extra Credit Award

The Fashion Plate Award to the best dressed

The Giggler Award

The Good Health Award to the person with the best attendance

The Hermes Award to the best messenger

The "I Didn't Do It" Award to the person who is good at denying things

The "I'd Rather Do It Myself" Award to the most independent

The "I'll Do It" Award to the person who volunteers the most

The Impound Award to the person who has lost the most stuff to the teacher's desk

The Kvetch Award to the biggest complainer

The Lady Godiva Award to the person with the longest hair

The Literary Award to the person who has read the most books

The Longest Legs Award

The Lost and Found Award to the person who is always losing things

The Loudest-Spoken Award

The Most Helpful Award

The Most Improved Award

The Most Loquacious Award

The Most Serious Award

The Neatest Desk or Cubby Award

The Numero Uno Award

The Peacemaker Award

The Philanthropic Award to the most generous

The Side-By-Side Award to two people who are inseparable

The Soft-Spoken Award

The Spic and Span Award to the best cleaner-upper

The Stand-Up Comic Award to the best joke teller

The Stick With It Award to the person who stays with a task

The Thesaurus Award to the person with the biggest vocabulary

The Turtle Award to the person who gets things done slowly

The Ump Award to the best referee

The Von Gogh Award to the best artist

The Webster's Award to the best speller

The "Work Is Not Good For My Health" Award to the person who tries to avoid all assignments

Awarded to

....

....

....

Teacher

Date

Computer Software

The number of software programs for children has grown enormously. For that reason, this list does not describe specific subject- or skill-oriented programs, but does list the names of major vendors of educational software so that you can write or call for a product catalog. Also included are descriptions of popular general-purpose programs—some targeted specifically for children and others that can be used by children and adults alike. Manufacturer's suggested retail prices are noted only for the purpose of providing a point of reference. Because mail order companies offer some of the best prices—usually 20% to 30% less than retail—make sure you call one of the listed companies for a catalog.

BannerMania (ages 7–adult)
Broderbund Software, Inc.   Apple, Macintosh, DOS $59.95
Create banners, signs, posters, bumper stickers, and more. Choose from 19 fonts and 27 shapes, as well as 34 special text effects including shadows, 3D, and perspective.

Children's Writing and Publishing Center (ages 7–adult)
The Learning Company   Apple, DOS $59.95
An easy-to-use word processing and page layout program for writing reports, stories, creating newsletters, signs and more. Includes over 150 pictures that can be included in publications. Also produces daily, weekly, monthly, and yearly calendars.

HyperScreen (ages 12–17)
Scholastic Inc.   Apple, DOS $99.95
A HyperCard-like program that provides an alternative to traditional methods of collecting, organizing, and presenting information. Instead of reports children can create multimedia presentations using clip art, multiple fonts, music, and sound effects.

Kid Desk (ages 3–10)
Edmark   DOS, Macintosh $29.99
A colorful graphic interface that lets children launch their software and, here's the best part—they can't access your data! Included are their own desk accessories such as a talking clock, a calculator, and a calendar.

Kid Pix (ages 3–7)
Broderbund Software, Inc.   DOS, Macintosh, Windows $59.95
Color painting program with silly sounds and attention-grabbing special effects. The program is completely bilingual (English and Spanish), from menus to talking alphabet and numbers.

Kid Pix Companion (ages 3–12)
Broderbund Software, Inc.   Macintosh $39.95
Adds new dimension to Kid Pix. Present slide shows of pictures and sound effects and show "movies" on the Wacky TV. Includes 112 additional Rubber Stamp images and 19 new Hidden Pictures. Kid Pix is required to use Kid Pix Companion.

LOGO PLUS (ages 6–17)
Terrapin Software   Apple $119.95, Macintosh $99.95
Teaches programming to 1st-12th graders. The flexibility of this program allows young children to learn the basics while older children can move on to other challenges and dimensions in computer logic. The package includes techniques for graphics, text, music, and font capabilities.

MacDraw (ages 7–adult)
Claris Corporation   Macintosh $199.00
Popular easy-to-use drawing program. Supports 8-bit color.

Mavis Beacon Teaches Typing (ages 8–adult)
Software Toolworks   Apple, DOS, Macintosh $49.95
Lessons are customized for age, interests, and attention span. Progress is checked lesson by lesson improving typing skills with a personalized typing course.

Microsoft Works (ages 7–adult)
Microsoft Corporation   Macintosh $249.00
Easy-to-use combination of word processor, database, and spreadsheet program. In addition to student and home use, each of the basic modules are adequate for simple office needs.

The New Print Shop (ages 5–adult)
Broderbund Software, Inc.   Apple, DOS, Macintosh $69.95
An easy-to-use publishing program that simplifies the creation of greeting cards, banners, and brochures. An extensive graphics library helps you illustrate your work. Prints in color as well as black and white.

Timeliner (ages 5–adult)
Tom Snyder Productions   Apple, DOS $59.95   Macintosh (Mac TimeLiner) $69.95
Create time lines up to 99 pages long with any information you want. Print single-page or banner-length time lines. Choose your own time line format: a day, a week, a year, or many years.

Type! (ages 10–adult)
Broderbund Software, Inc.   Macintosh $29.95
Uses an interactive approach to teach keyboard skills. Constant feedback and suggestions guide you through the lively exercises and point out areas for additional practice.

WriteNow (ages 7–adult)
T/Maker Company   Macintosh $249.00
A compact word processing program that is fast and easy to learn and use. Program comes with a 1.4 million-word thesaurus and templates for Avery mailing labels.

SOFTWARE MANUFACTURERS

Activision
11440 San Vicente Boulevard
Suite 300
Los Angeles, CA 90049
310-207-4500

Broderbund Software, Inc.
P.O. Box 6125
500 Redwood Boulevard
Novato, CA 94948
800-521-6263

Claris Corporation
5201 Patrick Henry Drive
Santa Clara, CA 95052
408-727-8227

Davidson and Associates, Inc.
P.O. Box 2961
Torrance, CA
800-545-7677

Edmark Corporation
P.O. Box 3218
Redmond, WA 98073
800-426-0856

Great Wave Software
5353 Scotts Valley Drive
Scotts Valley, CA 95066
408-438-1990

The Learning Company
6493 Kaiser Drive
Fremont, CA 94555
800-852-2255

MECC
6160 Summit Drive North
Minneapolis, MN 55430
800-685-MECC

Microsoft Corporation
One Microsoft Way
Redmond, WA 98052
800-426-9400

Scholastic, Inc.
2931 E. McCarty Street
Jefferson City, MO 65101
800-541-5513

Software Toolworks
60 Leveroni Court
Novato, CA 94949
800-234-3088

Sunburst Communication
(see Wings for Learning)

Terrapin Software, Inc.
400 Riverside Street
Portland, ME 04103
207-878-8200

Timeworks, Inc.
625 Academy Drive
Northbrook, IL 60062
800-535-9497

T/Maker Company
1390 Villa Street
Mountain View, CA 94041
415-962-0195

Tom Snyder Productions
80 Coolidge Hill Road
Watertown, MA 02172
800-342-0236

Walt Disney Software Co.
P.O. Box 290
Buffalo, NY 14207
800-688-1520

Wings for Learning
P.O. Box 660002
Scotts Valley, CA 95067
800-628-8897

MAIL ORDER CATALOGS

Educational Resources
1550 Executive Drive
Elgin, IL 60123
800-624-2926
708-888-8300 Illinois

MacConnection
(see PC Connection)

MacWarehouse
1690 Oak Street
Lakewood, NJ 08701
800-255-6227

The Mac Zone
17411 NE Union Hill Road
Redmond, WA 98052
800-248-0800

PC Connection
6 Mill Street
Marlow, NH 03456
800-800-0005

Emergency Supplies

An emergency doesn't have to be a disaster—it can be as simple as a temporary power outage caused by a storm or an overtaxed utility company during a heatwave. Or it can be a major disaster that strikes without warning with devastating results. The following list has been compiled from Red Cross recommendations for home emergency supplies. Call your local Red Cross for guides to emergency preparedness and first aid. These publications are available in a variety of foreign languages.

20 Survival Items to Keep on Hand

Gather together enough supplies for at least 48 hours. Better still, a two-week supply is recommended.

1. Water—2 qts to 1 gal per person per day.
2. Portable radio with extra batteries (batteries stay fresh longer when stored in a refrigerator).
3. Flashlights with extra batteries and spare bulbs.
4. First Aid Kit including specific medicines needed by members of your household.
5. First Aid book.
6. Smoke detector properly installed.
7. Fire extinguisher—dry chemical, type ABC.
8. Adjustable wrench for turning off gas and water.
9. Escape ladder for homes with multiple floors.
10. Canned and dried foods requiring minimum heat and water. Include special diets, such as for infants and elderly.
11. Non-electric can opener.
12. Portable stove or barbeque and fuel.
13. Blankets or sleeping bag for each family member.
14. Toilet paper and plastic trash bags.
15. Household bleach.
16. Matches.
17. Food for pets.
18. Candles.
19. Money.
20. Watch or clock.

Car Mini-Emergency Kit

1. Instant food supplies—nutrition bars, dried fruit, jerky, crackers, cookies (replace every 3 to six months).
2. Fire extinguisher.
3. Blanket.
4. Bottled water.
5. Extra clothing.
6. Comfortable walking shoes.
7. Small first aid kit.
8. Flares.
9. Local maps.
10. Change for telephone.
11. Plastic bags, box of tissues, toilet paper, newspapers.
12. Flashlight with extra batteries and bulbs.
13. Candles and matches.
14. Essential medications.
15. Good book.
16. Tools—screwdriver, pliers, wire, knife.
17. Short rubber hose for siphoning.
18. Pre-moistened towelettes.

From *The Teacher's Book of Lists, Second Edition*, published by GoodYearBooks. Copyright © 1994 Sheila Madsen and Bette Gould.

Gifts That Teach and Entertain

Toys are great, but some kids' rooms look like a fully stocked toy shop with few other materials available. Writing and drawing supplies and books are important additions to a child's inventory, along with selections from the following list. Gift-givers, such as Grandpa and Aunt Lyd, will appreciate receiving a copy of this list to use as a selection guide.

GAMES

Every year a rash of new games are introduced into the marketplace, many with price tags of $30.00 and up. A few survive as classics, but most only enjoy a limited season of popularity and then disappear. The following games are survivors—generations of children and adults have enjoyed these mostly family games. This list is confined to games under $25.00—most can be purchased for $13.00 or less. The list prices were obtained from a national discount department store.

Balderdash (ages 10 to adult)
Based on an old parlor bluffing game, this packaged version promotes vocabulary building, strategy, and creative thinking.
The Games Gang, Ltd., $20.00

Battleship (ages 8 to adult)
It's subtitled as a Naval Combat Game, but there's no violence involved. The game provides hours of fun as you search for your opponent's battleships. Requires strategy, concentration, and the use of coordinates on a grid.
Milton Bradley, $11.00 Travel version, $7.69

Boggle (ages 8 to adult)
Fast-paced 3-minute word game that everyone plays at once. The game reinforces spelling skills, but its greater challenge is forcing players to visualize words in different directions.
Parker Brothers, $12.75 Travel version $7.99

Boggle, Junior (ages 3–6)
This junior edition of Boggle has several levels of play: preschoolers learn to recognize objects and letters and match letters with pictures, older children learn beginning sounds and practice spelling.
Parker Brothers, $12.00

Candyland (ages 3–6)
A first board game for children that requires no reading or counting skills. Children learn how to move toward the game's objective, the Candy Castle at the end of the path.
Milton Bradley, $6.79

Chutes and Ladders (ages 4–7)
Children learn to count from 1 to 100 as they move around the board. Chutes and ladders add the element of chance.
Milton Bradley, $5.49

Cootie (ages 3 and up)
Young children learn to count using a roll of a die to assemble a colorful bug. Little fingers learn to manipulate and attach the pieces to the correct location on the bug's body.
Milton Bradley, $4.95

Guess Who? (ages 6 and up)
A fun, simple detection game that involves only the facial characteristics of people. Promotes attention to detail, deductive thinking, and memory skills.
Milton Bradley, $17.00 Travel Version, $7.99

Jigsaw Puzzles (ages 2 to adult)
Available from 2 pieces to a monster 5,000 piece puzzle that measures 4 1/2' x 5'. Jigsaws foster manual dexterity, memory skills, and visual perception.

Monopoly (ages 8 to adult)
First introduced in the 1930s, this is the classic game of real estate buying, selling, and trading.
Parker Brothers, $11.00

Monopoly, Junior (ages 5–8)
In this junior edition, children acquire amusement concessions along the Boardwalk—the Roller Coaster, Magic Show, Cotton Candy, and Miniature Golf to name a few. Instead of charging rent, they set up ticket booths to collect money. Money, vocabulary, and situations are easily understood by youngsters who earn $2.00 allowance for passing Go, and are confined to the Restroom instead of going to Jail.
Parker Brothers, $10.00 Travel version $6.99

Pictionary (ages 12 to adult)
Even though you draw the clue, you don't have to be an artist to play this game—in fact, the best clues are often provided by the artistically disabled. This game encourages interpretation of picture clues and communication by pictures and symbols.
Pictionary, Inc., $22.99

Scattergories (ages 12 to adult)
A beautifully packaged fast-thinking categorizing game that tests your knowledge from pizza toppings to fictional characters. Includes 144 categories.
Milton Bradley, $19.95

Scattergories, Junior (ages 8–11)
This junior version of the game features 72 categories that children can relate to, such as desserts, girls names, and things at a circus.
Milton Bradley, $11.00

Scrabble, (ages 8 to adult)
A traditional favorite reinforces spelling skills, lots of communication, and use of the dictionary, especially when you have a creative speller in the family. The junior edition of this game is very different and is not worth the money.
Milton Bradley, $10.00

MAGAZINES

3-2-1 Contact (ages 8-12)
Children's Television Workshop
P.O. Box 52000, Boulder, CO 80322
10 issues per year $15.97
Specializes in science, nature, and technology. Issues are filled with informative articles, puzzles, projects, and experiments.

Clavier's Piano Explorer
200 Northfield Rd. , Northfield, IL 60093
10 issues per year $6.00
Focuses on the piano, but also includes articles about other instruments and composers as well as puzzles and quizzes. Each issue contains two easy-to-play piano pieces written by young musicians.

Cricket (ages 6–14)
Open Court Publishing Company
P.O. Box 58346, Boulder, CO 80322
12 issues per year $29.97
Literary magazine for children. Internationally known authors and artists contribute never-before-published stories, poems, articles.

Ebony Jr! (ages 6–12)
Johnson Publishing Company
820 S. Michigan Ave., Chicago, IL 60605
10 issues per year $8.00
Issues include fiction, articles on current and historical events, drafts, games, and recipes. Its purpose is to stimulate pride in and knowledge of African-American culture and history.

Kid City (ages 6–10)
Children's Television Workshop
P.O. Box 52000, Boulder, CO 80322
10 issues per year $14.97
A little trendy, but presents items about current culture that makes reading, language skills, and learning fun, especially for the reluctant reader. Educates and entertains through stories, puzzles, games, projects and special features.

Lady Bug (ages 2–7)
Open Court Publishing Company
P.O. Box 58346, Boulder, CO 80322
12 issues per year $29.97
Each issue contains games, songs, poems, and stories. Also has an activity insert with things to color, cut out, make, and draw, plus a parent's guide.

Humpty Dumpty's Magazine for Little Children (ages 4–6)
Children's Better Health Institute
P.O. Box 10681, Des Moines, IA 50381
8 issues per year $11.95
Health-oriented. Provides information on nutrition, safety, and exercise. Each issues also includes games, puzzles, and things to do and make.

National Geographic Magazine World (ages 8–13)
National Geographic Society
P.O. Box 2330, Washington, DC 10077
12 issues per year $12.95
Presents a variety of subject matter as well as games and projects. Splendid full-color photographs like its parent magazine. Subscription price includes junior membership in the National Geographic Society.

Nautica (ages 8–14)
Astro-Media Corp.
P.O. Box 92788, Milwaukee, WI 53202
12 issues per year $15.00
Nonfiction magazine devoted to the sea. Each issue includes articles on history, adventure, geography, sea life, sports, navigation science, and technology with activities, games, and puzzles.

Odyssey (ages 9–14)
Kalmbach Publishing Co.
P.O. Box 1612, Waukesha, WI 53187
12 issues per year $21.00
An astronomy and outer space magazine for children.

P3, the Earth-Based Magazine for Kids (ages 7–10)
P.O. Box 52, Montgomery, VT 05470
10 issues per year $18.00
P3 (referencing earth as the third planet from the sun) is designed to encourage environmental awareness. Each issue provides current news stories about topics such as pollution, recycling, and the rain forests. Children are also encouraged to become involved by providing suggestions.

Ranger Rick (ages 6–12)
National Wildlife Federation
1412 16th St., NW, Washington, DC 20036
12 issues per year $12.00
Each issue is designed to provide a program of activities to help children learn about wildlife and the environment. In addition to well-written articles, it includes activities, projects, and games. Subscription includes membership in the Ranger Rick Nature Club.

Sesame Street (ages 2–6)
P.O. Box 55518, Boulder, CO 80322
10 issues $15.97
From the TV show Sesame Street characters like Big Bird, Bert, and Ernie appear throughout activities in this magazine. Each issue contains read-aloud stories and activities that focus on matching, sequencing, color recognition, and early reading and counting skills. A parent's guide accompanies each issue.

Sports Illustrated for Kids (ages 8–13)
P.O. Box 83069, Birmingham, AL 35283
12 issues per year $17.95
Scaled down version of the adult magazine. Includes stories about children and professional athletes.

Zillions, Consumer Reports for Kids (ages 8–14)
P.O. Box 54861, Boulder, CO 80322
6 issues per year $13.95
Gives information on products and advice on how to spend money wisely. Young consumers participate in testing products and provide feedback on what they think about topics such as fast food and advertisements aimed at children.

From *The Teacher's Book of Lists, Second Edition,* published by GoodYearBooks. Copyright © 1994 Sheila Madsen and Bette Gould.

Home References

Books are expensive. But certain books are essential for every home library and there are ways to shop for bargains and gradually add to your family's collection. Here are suggestions for some of the basics— your particular family situation such as children's ages, interests, and hobbies will dictate other books you need. While this list deals only with reference books, don't forget that children need to have their own bookshelves of favorite books. If you are on a tight budget, consider these minimum "must" purchases: a good dictionary (somewhat more difficult than your child needs at the moment); an almanac or one-volume encyclopedia; and one anthology.

SHOPPING TIPS

- Buy paperbacks instead of hard cover books.
- Haunt used book stores on a regular basis.
- Check out the bargain tables in book stores.
- Visit garage sales and swap meets.
- Find out when your local library holds its book sales.
- Ask relatives and friends to keep you in mind when they discard a book. Also remind them that a certain book would make a good holiday or birthday gift for your child or family.

ANTHOLOGIES

Hey! Listen to This—Stories to Read Aloud
Edited by Jim Trelease
Penguin Books, 1992. $11.00
Twelve categories of stories are included, with 2–7 selections in each category. Each section is introduced as to type of story, and includes notes on authors.

The Random House Book of Poetry for Children
selected by Jack Prelutsky, illustrated by Arnold Lobel
Random House, 1983. $16.95
A wonderful collection of 572 poems and 400 illustrations. Divided into 14 thematic sections that covers every stage of growing up. Poems include old favorites by Lewis Carroll and A. A. Milne, contemporary poems of John Ciardi, Lilian Moore, and Shel Silverstein.

Children's Classics to Read Aloud
Selected by Edward Blishen
Kingfish Books, 1991. $16.95
Extracts from 20 great classics from Robert Louis Stevenson's Treasure Island *to* Charlotte's Web *by E. B. White.*

The Random House Book of Fairy Tales
Adapted by Amy Ehrlich, illustrated by Diane Goode
Random House Books, 1985. $17.00
Nineteen of the greatest fairy tales of all times.

ART & MUSIC

History of Art for Young People
Abrams. $35.00
This traditional art history book covers the development of Western art. The text is for mature independent readers, but can be enjoyed by all when read aloud. Well illustrated.

Sticks, Stones & Ice Cream Cones, The Craft Book for Children
Phyllis Fiarotta
Workman Publishing, 1991. $9.95
Spend an evening or so away from the TV and telephone with some of these ideas and projects.

Watercolor for the Artistically Undiscovered
Thatcher Hurd and John Cassidy
Klutz Press, 1992. $18.95
Ideas and stimuli for producing watercolors. Forty-eight pages of the book are actually watercolor paper with a blank area to paint on and suggestions and examples floating around the edges. A set of watercolors and brush is attached.

The Kids' World Almanac—From Rock to Bach
Elyse Sommer
Pharos Books, 1991. $14.95 hardback; $7.95 paper
Hundreds of interesting entries to appeal to children. Symbols help locate items easily. A musical calendar, with a musical fact entry for each day, is included.

The Oxford First Companion to Music
Kenneth and Valerie McLeish
Oxford University Press, $29.95
Covers diverse topics from musical terms and the physics of sound to classical music, jazz, and ethnic musical forms and instruments.

Folkways Records
Smithsonian/Folkways, distributed by Rounder Records, $9.00
Many excellent collections of authentic American music such as *Music of the Sioux and Navajo,* and *Youll Sing a Song and I'll Sing a Song,* rhythmical, rural American songs performed by Ella Jenkins.

ATLASES, MAPS, AND GLOBES

National Geographic Picture Atlas of the Universe
National Geographic Society, 1986. $21.95

National Geographic Picture Atlas of the World
National Geographic Society, 1990. $21.95

Globe
George F. Cram Co., 1992. $15.00

From *The Teacher's Book of Lists, Second Edition,* published by GoodYearBooks. Copyright © 1994 Sheila Madsen and Bette Gould.

BOOKS THAT HELP YOU SELECT BOOKS FOR CHILDREN

A Parent's Guide to Children's Reading
Nancy Larrick, The Westminster Press, 1983. $13.00
Lists of books for every age level through junior high; how to start, how to encourage love of reading at an early age.

The New Read-Aloud Handbook
Jim Trelease. Penguin Books, 1989. $9.95 paper
Advice on introducing children to books, annotated lists of books from picture books to novels; hints on discriminative TV viewing; how to read-aloud.

The New York Times Parent's Guide to the Best Books for Children
Eden Ross Lipson, Children's Book Editor of the New York Times, Times Books, 1991. $15.00 paper
Nice format, hundreds of illustrations, annotated reading lists for all ages, terrific multiple indexes: book types and topics, age appropriate.

COOKBOOKS
Cooking is one of the most pleasurable activities for families to participate in together. Cookbooks for young people are usually well illustrated, step-by-step, and easy to use. They promote an interest and facility in reading in the most natural way.

My First Cookbook
Rena Coyle, illustrated by Jerry Joyner.
Workman Publishing, 1985. $6.95

Kids' Cooking—A Very Slightly Messy Manual
Editors of Klutz Press, illustrated by Jim M'Guinness
Klutz Press, 1987. $12.95
Heavy card stock pages and spiral binding make this a sturdy kitchen book. Lavishly illustrated; all ingredients and measurements are given in both pictures and words. Includes a set of color-coded measuring spoons.

COMPUTERS
There are so many books and manuals in this category that we only mention one or two for those families or teachers just starting out with children and computers.

My First Computer Book
David Schiller and David Rosenbloom, illustrated by Tedd Arnold
Workman Publishing, 1991. $17.95
To go with Apple II and compatibles (with color recommended) this explanatory book of terms and activities comes with a floppy disk coordinated to various sections of the book. The five topics on the disk are music, paint, story, snow day, and mystery game.
There is also a version of this book for IBM PCs and compatibles.

The Ultimate Collection of Computer Facts and Fun: A Kid's Guide To Computers
Cindra Tison and Mary Jo Woodside
SAMS 1991. $12.95
Computer facts are explained clearly and simply and accompanied by illustrations that make the definitions even easier to understand. The book is also filled with games, puzzles, and activities.

DICTIONARIES
Dictionaries abound for every age child from pre-school on up. While it's important to introduce children to a dictionary at an early age, it isn't absolutely necessary to purchase a new one each time he or she advances a grade or two—schools should be providing appropriate dictionaries to use. But a good adult dictionary (even if it's outdated) in the home is a must! Browse through new and used bookstores for one that suits your needs and pocketbook.

American Heritage First Dictionary
Houghton Mifflin $11.95

Words for New Readers
Scott, Foresman $10.95

The American Heritage Children's Dictionary
Houghton Mifflin $12.95

Webster's New World Children's Dictionary
Simon & Schuster $15.95

Webster's Notebook Dictionary
(usually available in stationery stores) $2.95

The Lincoln Writing Dictionary for Children
edited by Christopher Morris
Harcourt Brace Jovanovich, 1988. $17.95
More than just a standard listing of words and meanings, this dictionary gives information to aid the user in becoming more literate. For example, there are many highlighted paragraphs discussing words related to writing, such as indenting, figurative words, and style, that go far beyond the literal meaning of the terms. Over 750 illustrations.

The American Heritage Student's Dictionary
Houghton Mifflin $12.95

Webster's Intermediate Dictionary
Merriam Webster $11.95

ENCYCLOPEDIAS AND ALMANACS
A set of enclopedias for the home is handy and useful, but very expensive—anywhere from $600 to over $1000. And in today's world of new alliances, and rapid changes in technologies, information is quickly obsolete. The purchase of a single-volume encyclopedia and yearly almanac is a worthwhile investment for up-to-date facts. Your child still needs to learn to use and value the in-depth information that a full-fledged encyclopedia provides, but that's a good reason to use your local library.

The New American Desk Encyclopedia
Signet Books, (NAL-Dutton) $12.95

The Concise Columbia Desk Encyclopedia
Columbia University Press, Avon Books $14.95

Information Please Kids' Almanac
Alice Siegel and Margo McLoone Basta
Houghton Mifflin, 1992. $6.95
An Almanac written with a definite sense of what's appealing to kids. As well as standard almanac fare, it includes items such as how many muscles it takes to smile (14) and 20 literary characters you should know, such as Encyclopedia Brown and Madeline.

The Universal Almanac
Andrews & McMeel, 1992. $12.95

The World Almanac and Book of Facts
Pharos Books $7.00

EXPEDITIONS AND EXPLORATIONS

Doing Children's Museums—A Guide to 265 Hands-On Museums
Joanne Cleaver
Williamson Publishing, 1992. $13.95
Tells what each museum offers; provides age-appropriate guidelines; lists available workshops, and mentions nearby child-appropriate destinations, such as zoos, restaurants, and parks.

Places to Go With Children in Southern California
Stephanie Kegan
Chronicle Books, 1991. $9.95
There are books for New England, Miami, Northern California, etc. Gives information about local events and attractions. Provides some unusual ideas for destinations.

FIRST AID
One of the least expensive sources for pamphlets and books on first aid is the American Red Cross. Contact your local office for a list of publications and prices.

First Aid Reference Guide, $3.50

First Aid Tips, $3.50

SCIENCE

The Amateur Naturalist
Gerald Durrell
Alfred A. Knopf, 1989. $18.95
Flora and fauna are presented in 17 environments, including a backyard, beach, and meadow. Appealing color and black-and-white illustrations make this an easy to use and fun to read reference book. Included are projects such as drying and preserving flowers and how to feed an orphan bird.

Do People Grow on Family Trees?
Genealogy for Kids and Other Beginners
Ira Wolfman, foreward by Alex Haley
Workman Publishing, 1991. $9.95
A fascinating look at immigrants and their passage through Ellis Island. Gives practical ideas for
tracing one's own heritage.

Explorabook—A Kids' Science Museum in a Book
John Cassidy
Klutz Press, Palo Alto, 1991. $17.95
Science activities based on the hands-on displays at the Exploratorium of San Francisco. Some
sections: hair dryer science, ouchless physics, magnetic light waves. The book includes several
real items such as a moiré spinner, Fresnel lens, and agar.

Eyewitness Books Series
Alfred A. Knopf, New York. $15.00 each
Beautifully illustrated (with both drawings and photographs) books of high interest to children.
There are many titles such as Fossil, *by Paul D. Taylor, 1990, and* Flying Machine, *by Andrew*
Nahum, 1990. Reading level is intermediate to advanced, but these books make excellent "read
together" books for families.

Steven Caney's Invention Book
Workman Publishing, 1985. $8.95
Describes many famous inventions and their history. The book also tells how to market your own
invention. An interesting element are the "fantasy pages" that show imaginary inventions,
including sketches and variations. One such example is the "hover hook," a hook to hang things
on that is not attached to anything such as walls, doors, etc.

The Way Things Work
David Macauley
Houghton Mifflin, 1988. $29.95
This humorously illustrated book explains the scientific principles behind a number of machines
from the can opener to the laser. A must for everyone from an at-home tinkerer to a budding
physics student.

THESAURUS
Junior Thesaurus (ages 10-14)
Scott Foresman $11.95

Roget's Thesaurus (paperback)
Berkeley Books, 1988. $4.99

Roget's International Thesaurus
HarperCollins, 1992. $16.95

Independent Study

From *The Teacher's Book of Lists, Second Edition*, published by GoodYearBooks.
Copyright © 1994 Sheila Madsen and Bette Gould.

Whether you call it research or independent study, this activity provides opportunities for children:

- *to learn on their own*
- *to use the skills they have acquired in a real-life hands-on project*
- *to challenge their inherent creativity*
- *to work together in cooperative learning groups.*

Research projects require careful planning by you as well as your students. With older students, it's easy to assume that they've mastered the necessary skills and can organize and plan their time; but, this isn't always the case. Many will need a framework to keep them on track and ideas for alternate methods to use as they develop their studies. Use the worksheets on pages 368–371 to help students:

- *plan their studies*
- *develop topics and related questions*
- *use multiple resources*
- *collect and share information.*

The chart on pages 365–367 lists four major steps in the independent study process (these are the four we use, other teachers may break up the process differently) and common problems and suggested solutions associated with each step. At the end of the list you'll find some ways to deal with the general problem of "Teacher, teacher, I need...I want...I can't..."

1
Selecting a Topic, Subtopics and Related Questions

Common Problems	Possible Solutions
Can't decide on a topic.	Provide a variety of books, pictures, films, videos, and real objects to stimulate interest in a topic. Discuss student's interests and hobbies. Pair with another student. As a last resort, give two choices—that's it!
Selected topic is too big. (*Plants*)	Use the **Topic Web** worksheet, p. 369 or other technique to narrow down topic. (*Plants We Eat*)
Selected topic is too small or lacks depth. (*Zipper*)	Use the **Topic Web** worksheet, p. 369, a technique such as brainstorming, or look up topic in encyclopedia and find related references to expand topic. (*History of Clothing Fasteners*)

Common Problems	Possible Solutions
	Possible Solutions
Common Problems	
Topic is too difficult or inappropriate for age/skill level of student.	Before you try to talk the student out of the selection, find out what he/she knows about the topic—you may be surprised.
	Make a list with the student identifying subtopics and questions.
	Allow a limited time period to find information. If no information is found, move on to another topic.
2 Using Multiple Resources	
Limited resources on topic or information available is out of date.	Help student find alternate sources of information (see **Using Multiple Resources** worksheet, p. 370).
Resources are too difficult to read/understand.	Enlist older students and parents to read and discuss to assist in interpreting information.
3 Collecting Information	
Copies too much verbatim information.	Teach note taking skills such as key words, main ideas.
Tape records too much information.	Teach simple editing using using two tape recorders.
Collects too little information.	Allow student to photocopy information; highlight or cut and paste relevant facts.
Doesn't know when to stop.	Meet with student regularly, discuss goals and set deadlines, make a time schedule with due dates (see **Research Planning** worksheet, p. 368)
Disorganized.	Limit student to only one method of collecting information. For example, notecards on a ring are easy to keep together.
4 Sharing Information	
End product sloppily prepared.	Develop a quality standards checklist.
Continually uses the same sharing method.	Encourage selection of other means from the **Independent Study Products** list, p. 372.

From *The Teacher's Book of Lists, Second Edition*, published by GoodYearBooks.

Common Problems

Creates a product not appropriate for the topic of study.

Lack of materials.

End product shows student has not really studied topic.

Possible Solutions

Decide on the end product before the student begins to work on it.

Be creative and also help the student to be imaginative. Beg, borrow, and substitute materials.

Prepare a format for the student to follow such as a chart with predefined categories to fill in.

Take a second look at the product and discuss it with the student; though lacking information it might be a step in the right direction. Encourage the student to "stretch" on the next project.

One Big General Problem

Too many students need help at the same time.

Start slowly. Introduce the steps and go through the process with only a few students. They can then become trainers or group leaders for the next group.

Start small. Prepare a list of "small" topics and questions for a short-term study so that children can become familiar with the overall process. Topics might include: A Hen's Egg, How Does A Carrot Grow? A Light Bulb, How Do Cacti Live Without Water? The Mailcarrier.

Divide children into small groups to work on a study. Appoint a leader and instruct students to first get help from their leader before asking you.

Schedule blocks of time for independent study throughout the day for various groups instead of having the whole class work on projects at the same time.

Arrange for volunteers (parents, relatives, community members) and older students to assist you at a scheduled time each day.

Research Planning

Topic: ....

Subtopics or questions (what I want to find out): ....

....

....

....

Resources I think I will use: ....

....

....

How I'm going to collect and organize information: ....

....

....

How I will share the information: ....

....

....

Topic Web

1. Write in the name of your independent study topic.

2. Write 5 subtopics of your topic.

3. Extend the web by writing related topics or questions.

Lightly color in topics and subtopics that you decide to learn about.

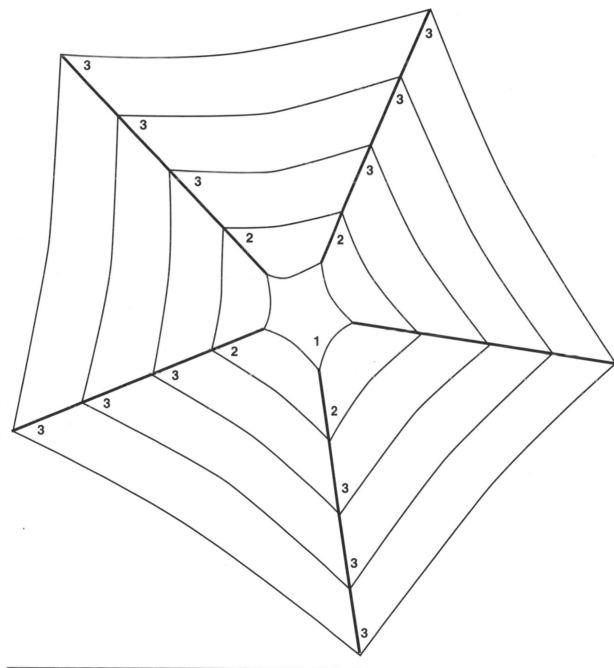

From *The Teacher's Book of Lists, Second Edition*, published by GoodYearBooks.
Copyright © 1994 Sheila Madsen and Bette Gould.

Using Multiple Resources

You probably get most of your research information from books. It's a good idea, however, to check other kinds of resources for the unique types of information they can offer. Use the following list to get ideas for different kinds of resources. Your selection will depend on the topic you are studying and the need to explore methods you have not tried before. Check the resources you plan to use.

❏ Interview someone in person or on the telephone.

❏ Conduct experiments or tests.

❏ Write letters to experts for information and to companies for brochures and pamphlets.

❏ Interpret pictures, illustrations, and diagrams.

❏ Study maps.

❏ Read books, magazines, and newspapers.

❏ Watch videos, filmstrips, and TV programs.

❏ Listen to audio tapes and records.

❏ Develop a survey form and conduct the survey.

❏ Visit museums, places of business, colleges, and government agencies.

❏ Observe people, places, and things.

From *The Teacher's Book of Lists, Second Edition,* published by GoodYearBooks.
Copyright © 1994 Sheila Madsen and Bette Gould.

Collecting and Organizing Information

There are ways to collect information other than the standard "pencil writing on notebook paper." The following list suggests other methods you can use. Some methods make it easy to organize your information later, such as collecting on note cards, Post-its™, or in a HyperCard stack. Other methods are especially useful when gathering first hand information, such as in interviews, or during scientific tests or experiments. You may even end up using several methods in one study.

❏ Collect notes on cards.

❏ Tape record information.

❏ Videotape information.

❏ Record information in a log book.

❏ Jot down notes on Post-its™.

❏ Write notes using a computer word processing program.

❏ Write notes and collect pictures in a HyperCard stack.

❏ Make quick sketches of things you observe.

❏ List facts, figures, and dates.

❏ Photocopy information, then highlight key words, phrases, and important ideas.

Independent Study Products

There are many types of products. Some go better with some studies than others. Use this list to help you select a way to share information from your independent study. As a class, you can make up a whole set of examples of these products to use as a reference.

advertisement
atlas

bar graph
billboard
board game
book
brochure
bulletin board

card game
cartoon
catalog
chart
collage
collection
coloring book
comic book
commemorative stamp
commercial
concentration game
costume
crosswood puzzle

demonstration
diagram
diary
dictionary
diorama
display
drawing

exhibit
experiment

fact book

game
graph
guide

hidden word puzzle
how-to booklet
how-to diagram
HyperCard presentation

instructions

jigsaw puzzle
journal

kit

labeled diagram
lesson
line graph
list
lotto game

magazine
manual
map
matching puzzle
materials display chart
miniatures
mobile
model
montage
multi-media presentation
mural

newsletter
newspaper article

owners manual

painting
party
photograph album
pictograph

picture chart
pie graph
play or script
poem
postcards
poster
presentation
puppet show

radio show
recipe
report

sign
slide show
song
speech
stages or steps diagram
story
story chart
study prints

tape recording
time line

radio show

travel brochure
TV quiz program
TV show
TV talk show

video

wallpaper
word chart
word jumble puzzle
wrapping paper

From *The Teacher's Book of Lists, Second Edition*, published by GoodYearBooks. Copyright © 1994 Sheila Madsen and Bette Gould.

Answer Keys

Tell-A-Phone Answering Service

Rewrite the telephone messages, using complete words in place of each abbreviation.

MESSAGE
To: Sam
Call your apartment manager as soon as possible about the package he received.

MESSAGE
To: Assistant Coach Brown
The center is ill. His double with a shooting average of 60% will replace him for the East versus South Game.

MESSAGE
To: Paul
Your encyclopedia will be sent cash on delivery in care of your attorney.

MESSAGE
To: Sally
Your assignment is to read chapter 5, pages 114-130 and do problem numbers 2-6.

MESSAGE
To: Doctor Jones
Freeway closed. Take alternate route. Best bet would be South Boulevard.

MESSAGE
To: Jane
Your account at Smith Corporation was paid on Wednesday, February 9.

6 Words

Antonym Album

Look at the pictures on this album page. Label each picture with a pair of antonyms.

up	down	big	little	closed	open
happy	sad	night (or) dark	day light	empty	full
hot	cold	fat	thin	on	off
front	back	top	bottom	girl (or) female	boy male
stand	sit	crooked	straight	clean	dirty

Antonyms **9**

Categorize the Compounds

Read the list of compounds words. Write the words on the pictures below.

bellhop
bridegroom
bridesmaid
yourself
busboy
everyone

FOOD
meatballs
pancake
popcorn
blackberry
blueberry
chestnut
strawberry
catfish
doughnut
grapefruit
mushroom
oatmeal
peanut
pineapple
swordfish

PEOPLE
fireman
fisherman
mailman
nobody
housekeep
landlady
landlord
lifeguard
roommate
salesperson
tenderfoot
undertaker
someone
spaceman
workman
chairperson
gentleman
grownup
yourself

WORDS THAT RHYME WITH SAY
birthday
doorway
driveway
ashtray
freeway
highway
faraway
getaway
someday
seaway

ANIMALS
bluebird
catfish
goldfish
starfish
butterfly
grasshopper
swordfish
wildcat
woodpecker

Compound Words **19**

A Homonym Gift List

Write in a homonym for the underlined word and the name or kind of person who might get the gift.

1. a new boat ___sail___ on _sale_ for ___Captain Hornblower___
2. a ___whole___ donut with a _hole_ for ___Homer Price___
3. a pretty ___flower___ and a bag of _flour_ for ___Betty Crocker___
4. _hoes_ and a ___hose___ for ___Mary, Mary Quite Contrary___
5. a night at the ___inn___ _in_ Washington, D.C. for ___Chelsea Clinton___
6. every _Sunday_, an ice cream ___sundae___ for ___the minister___
7. a new _red_ book that can be easily ___read___ for ___Dick and Jane___
8. a ___piece___ of music would bring _peace_ to ___Beethoven___
9. a ___pail___ of paint in a _pale_ color for ___Van Gogh___
10. _wood_ ___would___ be good for ___Paul Bunyan___
11. a fishing _reel_ made of ___real___ steel for ___a fisherman___
12. a ___tale___ about the monkey's _tail_ for ___Rudyard Kipling___
13. the _right_ kind of pen to ___write___ with for ___an editor___
14. a sweet-smelling ___scent___ to be _sent_ to ___Flower, the skunk___
15. a ___pair___ of knives to _pare_ a _pear_ for ___the cook___
16. a _scene_ from a play to be ___seen___ by ___a casting director___
17. a pink _rose_ and three ___rows___ of sunflowers for ___a gardener___
18. the bus ___fare___ to get to the county _fair_ for ___Farmer Brown___
19. ___you're___ giving a party in _your_ castle for ___the Queen of Hearts___
20. ___two___ tickets _to_ Disneyland for ___Mickey and Minnie___
(Answers for the last blanks will vary)

18 Words

Answer Keys **373**

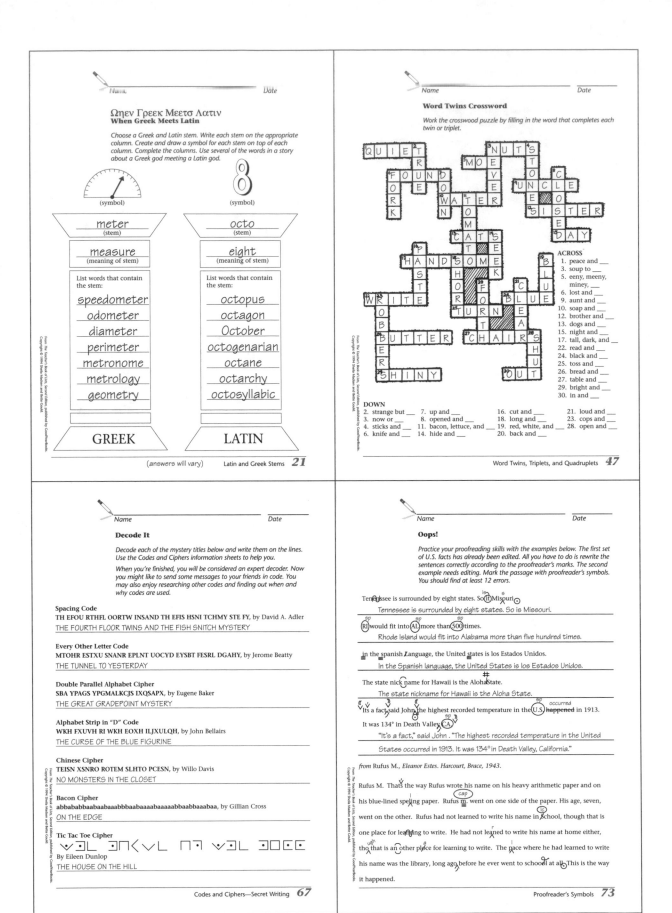

Ωηεν Γρεεκ Μεετσ Λατιν
When Greek Meets Latin

Choose a Greek and Latin stem. Write each stem on the appropriate column. Create and draw a symbol for each stem on top of each column. Complete the columns. Use several of the words in a story about a Greek god meeting a Latin god.

(symbol)   (symbol)

meter (stem)   octo (stem)

measure (meaning of stem)   eight (meaning of stem)

List words that contain the stem:

speedometer   octopus
odometer   octagon
diameter   October
perimeter   octogenarian
metronome   octane
metrology   octarchy
geometry   octosyllabic

GREEK   LATIN

(answers will vary)   Latin and Greek Stems **21**

Word Twins Crossword

Work the crosswood puzzle by filling in the word that completes each twin or triplet.

ACROSS
1. peace and ___
3. soup to ___
5. eeny, meeny, miney, ___
6. lost and ___
9. aunt and ___
10. soap and ___
12. brother and ___
13. dogs and ___
15. night and ___
17. tall, dark, and ___
22. read and ___
24. black and ___
25. toss and ___
26. bread and ___
27. table and ___
29. bright and ___
30. in and ___

DOWN
2. strange but ___
3. now or ___
4. sticks and ___
6. knife and ___
7. up and ___
8. opened and ___
11. bacon, lettuce, and ___
14. hide and ___
16. cut and ___
18. long and ___
19. red, white, and ___
20. back and ___
21. loud and ___
23. cops and ___
28. open and ___

Word Twins, Triplets, and Quadruplets **47**

Decode It

Decode each of the mystery titles below and write them on the lines. Use the Codes and Ciphers information sheets to help you.

When you're finished, you will be considered an expert decoder. Now you might like to send some messages to your friends in code. You may also enjoy researching other codes and finding out when and why codes are used.

Spacing Code
TH EFOU RTHFL OORTW INSAND TH EFIS HSNI TCHMY STE FY, by David A. Adler
THE FOURTH FLOOR TWINS AND THE FISH SNITCH MYSTERY

Every Other Letter Code
MTOHR ESTXU SNANR EPLNT UOCYD EYSBT FESRL DGAHY, by Jerome Beatty
THE TUNNEL TO YESTERDAY

Double Parallel Alphabet Cipher
SBA YPAGS YPGMALKCJS IXQSAPX, by Eugene Baker
THE GREAT GRADEPOINT MYSTERY

Alphabet Strip in "D" Code
WKH FXUVH RI WKH EOXH ILJXULQH, by John Bellairs
THE CURSE OF THE BLUE FIGURINE

Chinese Cipher
TEISN XSNRO ROTEM SLHTO PCESN, by Willo Davis
NO MONSTERS IN THE CLOSET

Bacon Cipher
abbababbaabaabaaabbaabaaaabaaaaabbaabbaaabaa, by Gillian Cross
ON THE EDGE

Tic Tac Toe Cipher
By Eileen Dunlop
THE HOUSE ON THE HILL

Codes and Ciphers—Secret Writing **67**

Oops!

Practice your proofreading skills with the examples below. The first set of U.S. facts has already been edited. All you have to do is rewrite the sentences correctly according to the proofreader's marks. The second example needs editing. Mark the passage with proofreader's symbols. You should find at least 12 errors.

Tennessee is surrounded by eight states. So it Missouri.
Tennessee is surrounded by eight states. So is Missouri.

RI would fit into AL more than 500 times.
Rhode Island would fit into Alabama more than five hundred times.

in the spanish Language, the United states is los Estados Unidos.
In the Spanish language, the United States is los Estados Unidos.

The state nick name for Hawaii is the Aloha State.
The state nickname for Hawaii is the Aloha State.

Its a fact said John the highest recorded temperature in the U.S. happened in 1913.
"It's a fact," said John. "The highest recorded temperature in the United States occurred in 1913. It was 134° in Death Valley, California."

from Rufus M., Eleanor Estes. Harcourt, Brace, 1943.

Rufus M. Thats the way Rufus wrote his name on his heavy arithmetic paper and on his blue-lined speling paper. Rufus m. went on one side of the paper. His age, seven, went on the other. Rufus had not learned to write his name in school, though that is one place for learning to write. He had not leaned to write his name at home either, tho that is an other place for learning to write. The pace where he had learned to write his name was the library, long ago before he ever went to school at all This is the way it happened.

Proofreader's Symbols **73**

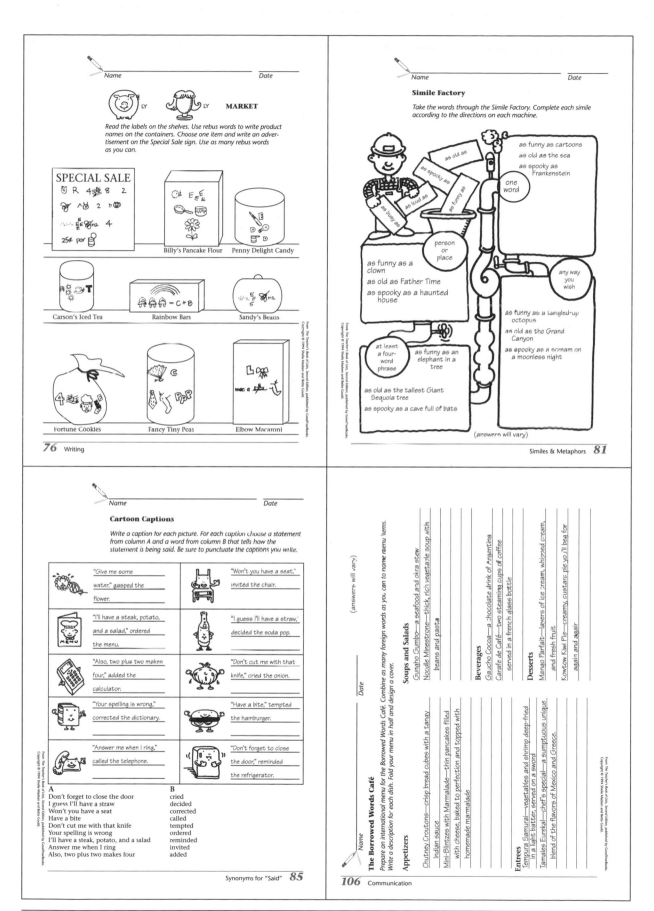

Top-left worksheet (page 76):

Name _____ Date _____

🐷 LY   👩 LY   **MARKET**

Read the labels on the shelves. Use rebus words to write product names on the containers. Choose one item and write an advertisement on the Special Sale sign. Use as many rebus words as you can.

SPECIAL SALE

Billy's Pancake Flour   Penny Delight Candy

Carson's Iced Tea   Rainbow Bars   Sandy's Beans

Fortune Cookies   Fancy Tiny Peas   Elbow Macaroni

76 Writing

Top-right worksheet (page 81):

Simile Factory

Take the words through the Simile Factory. Complete each simile according to the directions on each machine.

as old as
as spooky as
as loud as
as funny as
as busy as

one word

as funny as cartoons
as old as the sea
as spooky as Frankenstein

person or place

as funny as a clown
as old as Father Time
as spooky as a haunted house

any way you wish

as funny as a tangled-up octopus
as old as the Grand Canyon
as spooky as a scream on a moonless night

at least a four-word phrase

as funny as an elephant in a tree

as old as the tallest Giant Sequoia tree
as spooky as a cave full of bats

(answers will vary)

Similes & Metaphors 81

Bottom-left worksheet (page 85):

Name _____ Date _____

Cartoon Captions

Write a caption for each picture. For each caption choose a statement from column A and a word from column B that tells how the statement is being said. Be sure to punctuate the captions you write.

"Give me some water," gasped the flower.

"Won't you have a seat," invited the chair.

"I'll have a steak, potato, and a salad," ordered the menu.

"I guess I'll have a straw," decided the soda pop.

"Also, two plus two makes four," added the calculator.

"Don't cut me with that knife," cried the onion.

"Your spelling is wrong," corrected the dictionary.

"Have a bite," tempted the hamburger.

"Answer me when I ring," called the telephone.

"Don't forget to close the door," reminded the refrigerator.

A
Don't forget to close the door
I guess I'll have a straw
Won't you have a seat
Have a bite
Don't cut me with that knife
Your spelling is wrong
I'll have a steak, potato, and a salad
Answer me when I ring
Also, two plus two makes four

B
cried
decided
corrected
called
tempted
ordered
reminded
invited
added

Synonyms for "Said" 85

Bottom-right worksheet (page 106):

(answers will vary)

Name _____ Date _____

The Borrowed Words Café

Prepare an international menu for the Borrowed Words Café. Combine as many foreign words as you can to name menu items. Write a description for each dish. Fold your menu in half and design a cover.

Appetizers

Chutney Croutons—crisp bread cubes with a tangy Indian sauce

Mini-Blintzes with Marmalade—thin pancakes filled with cheese, baked to perfection and topped with homemade marmalade

Soups and Salads

Gungho Gumbo—a seafood and okra stew

Noodle Minestrone—thick, rich vegetable soup with beans and pasta

Beverages

Gaucho Cocoa—a chocolate drink of Argentina

Carafe de Café—two steaming cups of coffee served in a french glass bottle

Entrees

Tempura Samurai—vegetables and shrimp deep-fried in a light batter, served on a sword

Tamales Eureka!—chef's special—a sumptuous unique blend of the flavors of Mexico and Greece.

Desserts

Mango Parfait—layers of ice cream, whipped cream, and fresh fruit.

Kowtow Kiwi Pie—creamy, custard pie you'll beg for again and again

106 Communication

Answer Keys **375**

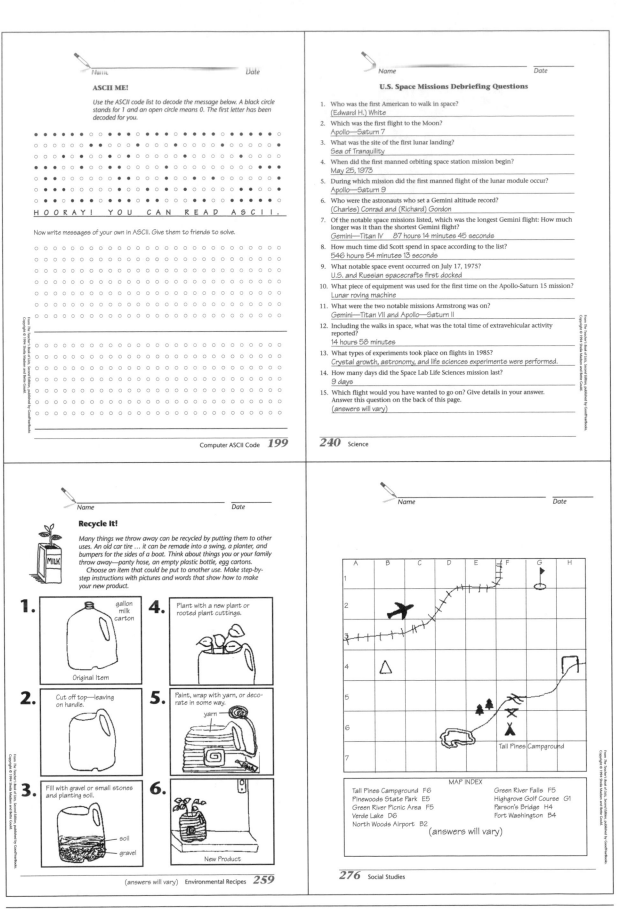

ASCII ME!

Use the ASCII code list to decode the message below. A black circle stands for 1 and an open circle means 0. The first letter has been decoded for you.

H O O R A Y !   Y O U   C A N   R E A D   A S C I I .

Now write messages of your own in ASCII. Give them to friends to solve.

Computer ASCII Code **199**

U.S. Space Missions Debriefing Questions

1. Who was the first American to walk in space?
(Edward H.) White

2. Which was the first flight to the Moon?
Apollo—Saturn 7

3. What was the site of the first lunar landing?
Sea of Tranquility

4. When did the first manned orbiting space station mission begin?
May 25, 1973

5. During which mission did the first manned flight of the lunar module occur?
Apollo—Saturn 9

6. Who were the astronauts who set a Gemini altitude record?
(Charles) Conrad and (Richard) Gordon

7. Of the notable space missions listed, which was the longest Gemini flight: How much longer was it than the shortest Gemini flight?
Gemini—Titan IV   87 hours 14 minutes 45 seconds

8. How much time did Scott spend in space according to the list?
546 hours 54 minutes 13 seconds

9. What notable space event occurred on July 17, 1975?
U.S. and Russian spacecrafts first docked

10. What piece of equipment was used for the first time on the Apollo-Saturn 15 mission?
Lunar roving machine

11. What were the two notable missions Armstrong was on?
Gemini—Titan VII and Apollo—Saturn II

12. Including the walks in space, what was the total time of extravehicular activity reported?
14 hours 58 minutes

13. What types of experiments took place on flights in 1985?
Crystal growth, astronomy, and life sciences experiments were performed.

14. How many days did the Space Lab Life Sciences mission last?
9 days

15. Which flight would you have wanted to go on? Give details in your answer. Answer this question on the back of this page.
(answers will vary)

240 Science

Recycle It!

Many things we throw away can be recycled by putting them to other uses. An old car tire ... it can be remade into a swing, a planter, and bumpers for the sides of a boat. Think about things you or your family throw away—panty hose, an empty plastic bottle, egg cartons.

Choose an item that could be put to another use. Make step-by-step instructions with pictures and words that show how to make your new product.

1. gallon milk carton / Original Item

2. Cut off top—leaving on handle.

3. Fill with gravel or small stones and planting soil. / soil / gravel

4. Plant with a new plant or rooted plant cuttings.

5. Paint, wrap with yarn, or decorate in some way. / yarn

6. New Product

(answers will vary) Environmental Recipes **259**

Tall Pines Campground

MAP INDEX

Tall Pines Campground   F6
Pinewoods State Park   E5
Green River Picnic Area   F5
Verde Lake   D6
North Woods Airport   B2

Green River Falls   F5
Highgrove Golf Course   G1
Parson's Bridge   H4
Fort Washington   B4

(answers will vary)

276 Social Studies

Name _____ Date _____

1600 Pennsylvania Avenue

Choose 10 United States presidents. List them alphabetically. Use the U.S. Presidents list to complete the other columns.

(answers will vary)

Names of Presidents	Age at inauguration	Age at death	Number of years in office
John Adams	61	90	4 years
Jimmy Carter	52	—	4 years
Bill Clinton	46	—	—
Millard Fillmore	50	74	2½ years
Andrew Jackson	62	78	8 years
John F. Kennedy	43	46	3 years
Abraham Lincoln	52	56	4 years
Franklin D. Roosevelt	51	63	12 years
Zachary Taylor	64	65	1 year
Harry S. Truman	60	88	8 years

Using the information from your table, compute the following averages for these 10 presidents:

- The average age at inauguration is ___54 years old___ .
- The average age at death is ___70 years old (Carter and Clinton not included).___
- The average length of term in office is ___5.2 years (Clinton not included).___

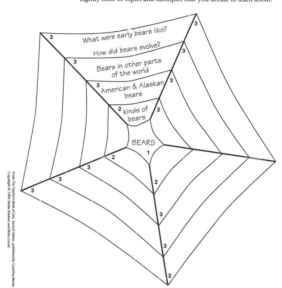

U.S. Presidents—Hail to the Chief **305**

Name _____ Date _____

Topic Web

1. Write in the name of your independent study topic.

2. Write 5 subtopics of your topic.

3. Extend the web by writing related topics or questions.

Lightly color in topics and subtopics that you decide to learn about.

What were early bears like?
How did bears evolve?
Bears in other parts of the world
American & Alaskan bears
kinds of bears
BEARS

Independent Study **369**

Beastly Questions

Work with a friend, group or the entire class to answer these 35 animal stumpers. Your teacher will tell you whether to write your answers or learn answers to share orally with everyone else. By the way, there are more than a billion different kinds of animals on earth, so you could make up a list of a lot more stumper questions for others to answer. Good luck!

1. Why could the zizcac be called "the crocodile's best friend"?

This small bird (some are called lapwings or crocodiles' friends) spends a lot of time sitting on top of crocodiles and eating parasites from the crocodile's skin. Its cry may serve as a danger warning for the crocodile. Some also hop right into the crocodile's mouth to feed on leeches found there.

2. Where would you find some pinnipeds?

The pinnipeds (fin-footed animals, including true seals, fur seals, sea lions, and walruses) live in subarctic waters and coastal waters of the Arctic Ocean. At the beginning of winter they migrate farther south to seek food in warmer waters.

3. Which animal would get the Most Unusual Animal Award? Why?

(Answers will vary.)

4. Why do some animals estivate?

Some animals estivate (enter a torpid, sleep-like state similar to hibernation, but done during the summer) to survive the heat or lack of water in their environment during summer months.

5. Why are some people called "dodos"?

Dodos were large, awkward, flightless birds. They had few defenses and once discovered by Europeans about 1598, had disappeared completely within 100 years. They were often made fun of in pictures and writings and perhaps that is why awkward, silly people are called dodos.

6. What do the aardvark and the anteater have in common?

Anteaters are several types of mammal that feed almost entirely on ants or termites. They have a long, narrow snout, lack teeth, and usually have a long tongue and huge salivary glands. An aardvark is one type of anteater that lives in Africa and eats mostly termites.

7. What is the bear's "Keep-Out" sign?

Bears will mark their area with urine or other spoor. While travelling, a grizzly bear will circle back off the trail at intervals in order to get windward of his own back tracks.

8. In the old days, why did women who wore corsets need whales?

Whalebone (the horny substance making up the plates attached to the upper jaw of certain whales—those without teeth) was cut into strips and used as stays, or stiff pieces, that help corsets and some dress bodices upright.

9. How can crickets help you tell the temperature?

Get a digital watch that indicates seconds or a watch with a second hand. Now count the number of chirps from a black cricket in 14 seconds and add 40 to get the temperature in Fahrenheit degrees. (The higher the air temperature, the faster the chirps.) Be careful not to move around while counting the chirps as too much movement may alarm the cricket and cause it to stop chirping.

10. How does the platypus break all the rules of nature?

This strange animal has the characteristics of both reptiles and mammals (and some birds). It lays eggs, but nurses its young; it has a fleshy bill resembling that of a duck; has dense fur and webbed feet; and has a broad flattened tail.

This list will provide practice in the use of reference materials, and lends itself to cooperative learning situations. It could be a starting point for a science unit, such as an animal adaptations, and would be a good place for students to get ideas for independent study.

Beastly Questions **197**

From *The Teacher's Book of Lists, Second Edition,* published by GoodYearBooks.
Copyright © 1994 Sheila Madsen and Bette Gould.

Answer Keys **377**

11. Why can't ants be called "litterbugs"?
All ant colonies have one group of ants whose only job is to tend the nest, keeping it clean of debris. Also, the food gatherers of the nest help clean our yards (and sometimes our homes) by gathering crumbs, decaying plants, and other items and taking this material to their nest.

12. How does the cave fish manage without any eyes?
Although different cave fishes have sight that varies from totally blind to perfect sight, those in the most isolated caves are blind. These types have more highly developed lateral line systems which detect vibrations or changes in water pressure. Some also have an increase in taste buds, many being located on the outer skin. In some the lateral line system is often extended on to the head in the form of tiny sense organs, which act as "touch at a distance" organs.

13. How would you prepare for a hermit crab houseguest?
You'd need some container such as an aquarium or deep, large plastic box. Cover the bottom with sandy, gravelly material and some rocks. Put water in up to a depth of about 1 to 1½ inches. Provide several sizes of snail or mollusk shells, as the crab will need new homes as it grows. Feed with small crustaceans, such as shrimp, or even bits of raw hamburger.

14. What five features makes the camel well adapted for desert travel?
Its humps are made up of fat, and during nondrinking periods (which can be up to seven days) water is manufactured in the body chiefly by the oxidation of fat which occurs to provide energy. Camels' large hooves, which are tough and well padded, are well suited to desert sand and rocks. Its nostrils which may be closed against the wind and long eyelashes help keep out blowing sand. Camels will eat almost any food, including thorny and bitter plants rejected by other animals. Their long legs and rolling gait enable them to cover long distances more easily than other beasts of burden and they are capable of carrying up to about 400 lbs. Their large body surface (long neck and legs) allows for easy loss of heat.

15. What do the cows, horses, and dogs of the ocean look like?
Manatees and dugongs (sometimes called cows of the sea) are shaped like a large seal with a blunted snout, wrinkled neck, and a rounded paddle-like tail. Sea horses seem to sit up and swim vertically with tiny fins on either sides of their bodies. Their tail curls beneath them and the heads are sharply flexed, somewhat resembling a horse's head. The dogfish (a variety of several small sharks) have thorn-like scales, rounded and tapering bodies, and two dorsal fins, each armed with a short spine. Some are spotted.

16. How do you feed a giraffe?
Feed it branches containing green leaves by tying together and hanging from other trees or trellises. Some hay or other food may be placed nearer the ground but the giraffe has more difficulty reaching it, having to spread its front legs and lean over to get at it and often having to straighten up to swallow.

17. What are some special jobs dogs are trained to do?
Some jobs of dogs are: herder (of sheep and cattle), guard dogs, seeing-eye dogs, sled dogs, police dogs, sentries, narcotics- and bomb-sniffing dogs, hunting dogs, companion-aid dogs such as for the handicapped, and entertainers (in movies, racing, trained for the circus, etc.).

18. What are an *Odobenus rosmarus* and a *Thalarctos maritimus*?
The walrus and the polar bear.

19. What would you find in a Tiergarten?
The same things you'd find in a zoo—tiergarten is the German word for zoo.

20. What is a pangolin?
The pangolin is an edentate (lacking teeth) mammal with a body covered with large overlapping horny scales. Various types reside in Asia and Africa.

21. How is a jerboa like a kangaroo?
They are both mammals. Both have large back legs for jumping, their primary means of locomotion. (The jerboa is a small rodent; the kangaroo a marsupial.)

22. Which animals ruminate?
Animals that ruminate (chew a cud) include sheep, giraffes, cattle, deer, and camels.

23. Why do birds sing?
They sing to attract a mate or to warn off another bird of the same sex. They also sing to help establish territories, and to recognize mates and neighbors. Sometimes singing or other sounds are used as alarms or to keep the flock together. The begging sounds of young birds stimulate their parents to provide food.

24. How does a raccoon carry its babies?
A mother raccoon carries her babies one at a time in her teeth, by the back skin (scruff) of the baby's neck, or by the skin along the middle of the back.

25. How does a flying squirrel fly?
It has folds of skin that connect the forelegs and hind legs. The folds, when stretched open, allow the squirrel to make long gliding leaps between tree branches. It doesn't actually fly.

26. Why don't spiders get caught in their own webs?
Only certain threads of the webs are sticky, so while the prey is unaware of where to step, the spider knows which threads are safe. A spider can add sticky drops to any threads at any time. They also may put out sticky or non-sticky threads. The orb weaver, the spider who spins the beautiful radial webs, walks only on the radial threads. Only the circular threads of the web are sticky.

27. What does the S.P.C.A. do for animals?
The Society for the Prevention of Cruelty to Animals sets standards and oversees the use of animals in research, movies, plays, or other types of activities. It may also take legal action against those who mistreat animals.

28. How does a bat "see with its ears"?
Actually most bats see well with their eyes, but navigate in the dark by echolocation. This is a method of sending out sounds whose sound waves are then reflected back to the bat from objects nearby, allowing the bat to adjust its flight depending on the closeness of the objects.

29. What's odd about the way sloths live?
They live most of their lives hanging down backwards from tree branches, feeding on leaves, shoots, and fruits.

30. How are some toads' trills (or croaks) amplified or made louder?
The throat skin under the lower jaw is made of very stretchable skin. When trilling, the sac made by this skin is inflated and provides a large vibrating surface which amplifies the sound. Some toads look like they have a big balloon under their chin when they are trilling.

31. Where does a snake's tail begin?
The tail is a continuation of the vertebrae, but has no ribs attached. In both males and females, the vent marks the end of the snake's trunk and the beginning of its tail. The vent is the opening at the end of the cloaca, a cavity that passes waste products out of the snake's body.

32. What does a lepidopterist collect?
Butterflies, moths, and skippers.

33. What happens when insects stridulate?
Some insects, such as male crickets and grasshoppers, rub together special body parts to create a shrill creaking noise. This is called stridulating.

34. Why can a fly walk on the ceiling?
Flies have legs that end in claws which help them to cling to walls and ceilings. They also have hairy pads (pulvilli) on their feet. A sticky substance on these pads enable flies to walk on slippery surfaces such as mirrors and windows.

35. How are an octopus and a squid like a jet?
Squid and octopuses swim by quickly ejecting water, or if in danger, ink, with the result of ejecting in one direction and moving in the opposite direction. A jet moves in the same way, but is ejecting combusted air and gases instead of liquid.